# Federal Regulation Of Personnel and Human Resource Management

# Federal Regulation Of Personnel and Human Resource Management

*James Ledvinka*
*University of Georgia*

**K**ent **Human Resource Management Series**
Richard W. Beatty, University of Colorado at Boulder
Series Consulting Editor

Kent Publishing Company    Boston, Massachusetts
A Division of Wadsworth, Inc.

Editor: John McHugh
Production Editor: Dale Anderson
Text Designer: DeNee Reiton Skipper
Manufacturing Coordinator: Linda Card

Kent Publishing Company
A Division of Wadsworth, Inc.

Printed in the United States of America

1   2   3   4   5   6   7   8   9—86   85   84   83   82

Library of Congress Cataloging in Publication Data

Ledvinka, James.
    Federal regulation of personnel and human resource management.
    Bibliography: p.
    Includes index.
    1. Labor laws and legislation—United States.   I. Title.

| KF3455.L42 | 344.73'01 | 81–20826 |
| ISBN 0–534–01160–8 | 347.3041 | AACR2 |

# Series Preface

Historically, the personnel/human resources (P/HR) field has received little attention academically as well as within organizations. Organizations have assumed, incorrectly, that P/HR cannot benefit them because of a dearth of technical information and skills. Colleges of business, reflecting this attitude, often hid P/HR in the teaching of management, seldom including the subject as a course requirement.

Thankfully, much of this is changing. First, the passage of Title VII of the 1964 Civil Rights Act generated interest in human resource planning, selection validation, and performance appraisal. Economic decline, the growth of Reaganomics, and the loss of competitiveness in international markets have also focused attention on the contribution that P/HR can make to organizations.

The books in this series address these issues. The first concerns federal regulation in P/HR management in EEO, job health and safety, and employee benefit plans. The second explores the costing of human resources by measuring the financial impact of behavior in organizations. The volume on performance appraisal became required because of the onus that EEO has placed on criterion measures in organizations for test validation and P/HR decision making. The fourth book, on compensation, address the critical issues of internal, external, and individual equity and how compensation systems may be effectively and efficiently administered. Clearly, fifteen years ago these books could not have been written, but with the growth of technical information in P/HR and the significance of P/HR problems within organizations, these important contributions are now possible. What is most exciting is to see the results of recent research in these important areas being disseminated to students and practitioners. This is a major objective of this series, and it gives me great pleasure to see that plan coming to life. The books in this series are designed to be adopted in university level courses in human resource management and personnel administration. Practitioners, too, will find much valuable information in these books.

For the appearance of this important series, I would like to thank Keith Nave, Wayne Barcomb, and Jack McHugh of Kent Publishing Company, and also the many reviewers who have encouraged the development of this series and provided feedback. The authors included in this series represent the best research in this growing field, and I am proud to be associated with them.

Richard W. Beatty

# Preface

In the past twenty years, federal regulation has dramatically transformed the relationship between employers and employees. The purpose of this book is to provide an understanding of the process responsible for that transformation. The book attempts to fill a void in the literature by focusing on regulations designed to solve social problems. It is those regulations—in areas such as equal employment, job safety, and retirement benefits—that have prompted most of management's concern and consternation over federal regulation.

The book is based on the premise that it is more important to understand *why* regulations are the way they are than to understand *what* the regulations say management can or cannot do. Many managers would prefer to learn the subject as a list of dos and don'ts. While such a list would be reassuringly specific, it would not help the manager adjust to regulatory changes. Responses to the constant changes in regulation are hard to list in advance. Yet managers are increasingly being asked to make those responses.

To respond competently to changing regulation, managers need a fundamental understanding of the process of regulation. In that regard, the first step is to realize that there *are* principles of federal regulation, that the process *does* have some predictability. The familiar lament that federal regulation is a chaotic nightmare indicates how desperately unaware of those principles some managers are. The view that federal regulation is chaos is destructive, because it implies that federal regulation cannot be coped with. This book, on the other hand, views regulation as understandable and, to a degree, predictable—wrongheaded, perhaps, but capable of being comprehended and adapted to.

For readers not wishing to cover the entire book, certain key chapters should be read before others. Chapter 1 should be read before any other chapter. In Part I, Chapter 2 should be read before the others, while Chapter 5 is the most advanced and thus appropriate to consider omitting first. Chapter 3 helps in understanding Chapter 4. In Part II, Chapter 8 should be read before Chapter 9. While Chapter 7 logically precedes Chapter 8 and provides a good foundation for understanding it, it is not essential to read it before Chapter 8. In Part III, Chapter 11 can be read alone for an overview of ERISA if the reader understands the basic terminology reviewed in Chapter 10.

This book has grown out of my course in federal regulation of personnel and human resource management at the University of Georgia, and it is to the students in that course over the years that I owe my first debt of gratitude. Early on, they sat patiently as I orally developed the ideas in print here. More recently, they indulged me while I inflicted the first manuscript on them as a pre-text (in both senses of the word). Their constructive comments on that manuscript contributed much to whatever clarity and coherence the final version has. Also, the late William F. Glueck was most encouraging while we were colleagues at Georgia, and the fact that Keith Nave and Wayne Barcomb at Kent Publishing were willing to commit themselves to a book in an untried subject area meant a lot. Richard J. Beatty, Paul Greenlaw, John M. Smokevitch, and Frank Thompson reviewed the manuscript and offered valuable suggestions. And without the help of my graduate assistants, Cathy Hedrick and Adrienne Pakis-Gillon, I doubt that the book would ever have materialized.

Most important has been my family, particularly the support and tolerance of my wife, Kathleen, and our children, Chris, Amy, and Michael. With remarkable grace, they weathered all the predictable temporary insanities that come to afflict writers. And I am also grateful to my mother and my late dad, Harriette and Roy, for always having encouraged me to think and to try new things.

James Ledvinka

# Contents

# 1

# Introduction:
# The Regulatory Model

A few years ago, an article appeared in *Fortune* magazine entitled "Personnel Directors Are the New Corporate Heroes."[1] That was quite a change; the personnel office had often been the dumping ground for managers whose careers were headed nowhere, and the personnel director (so the joke went) could always be spotted at the company picnic as the one carrying the watermelon. That miraculous transformation, the article made clear, was largely the result of the growth in federal regulation of personnel and human resource management during the 1970s.

No one needs to be convinced that federal regulation is a growing influence in American life. According to some estimates, government expenditures on federal regulation have increased from $745 million in 1970 to $4 billion in 1979,[2] an increase of 644 percent in less than a decade. But that is only a small fraction of the total cost of regulation. The public spends twenty times what the government spends just to comply with regulations, according to the Center for the Study of American Business at Washington University. That amounted to $65 billion in 1976.[3] While others have quarreled with those figures, no one quarrels with the conclusion that government regulation is a pervasive fact of life in the 1980s.

Much of this regulatory burden has been thrust upon the personnel department, leaving little time for carrying the watermelon to the company picnic. Washington University estimated the cost in 1976 of complying with regulations of job safety and working conditions to be about $4.5 billion.[4] Further, the federal regulation that falls in the domain of personnel management is quite visible and controversial. An example is quotas for hiring women and minorities. Regulation has brought about developments such as affirmative action recruiting, validation requirements for employment testing, more objective and time-consuming performance appraisals and salary reviews, and greater documentation of just about everything that happens to employees at work. Currently, sexual harassment is a prominent personnel concern, but it would be largely ignored if it were not for federal regulation. Another personnel concern, safety, is regulated by a law that has become a rallying point for conservatives in their battle against government regulation.

The growth of federal regulation has changed the rules for people management, primarily by giving employees specific rights in their relationship with their employer. Employee rights were not unheard of before the 1970s, but neither were they commonplace. Employees covered by a union contract have always had certain rights, and government employees have enjoyed merit system protections for most of this century. But those exceptions accounted for only a minority of the work force, and the rights they had were more modest than the rights conferred in the 1970s. For the majority of employees, management power was nearly absolute, particularly in hiring and firing. Essentially, management had the right to discipline or discharge an employee "for good cause, for no cause, or even for cause morally wrong."[5] Considered in that light, the changes brought about by federal regulation were momentous indeed.

The personnel and human resources manager is affected by those regulatory developments because they make a lot of the traditional ways of managing people illegal and place new burdens on management. Managing people is something that just about all self-respecting managers think they can do, and so the personnel manager has often had a hard time telling other managers how to do it. But now that other managers can no longer rely on common sense to meet government regulations, they are beginning to turn to the personnel director for guidance.

Unfortunately, the personnel director may not be any better equipped than other managers for interpreting government's intent. Even a good personnel manager of 1970, one who followed all the practices recommended in personnel textbooks, would by now have a track record that was mixed at best. The state of the art in those innocent days before federal involvement is hopelessly out of date now. And today's personnel and human resources manager risks being just as out of date in another ten years if he or she does not comprehend the federal regulatory system. It is not enough to master whatever regulations and court cases are current; such mastery is of no help in anticipating the changes to be made in the regulations and the new directions to be taken by the courts. One must understand the regulatory *system*—the governmental apparatus and how it operates to produce the regulations that govern the management of people at work.

It is this understanding that this book attempts to further, insofar as its modest length permits. This first chapter provides an overview of the federal regulatory process, and the last chapter covers three regulatory areas of lesser impact. The remaining chapters explore the three main areas of federal regulation of personnel and human resources management:

*Equal employment opportunity (EEO):* laws prohibiting discrimination against members of particular groups

*Employee safety and health:* laws prohibiting work hazards and requiring employer compensation for victims of those hazards

*Employee pensions and other benefits:* laws governing benefit plans and the employer's communication to employees about those plans

In focusing on those three recent regulatory themes, this book leaves some significant areas untouched. Most obviously, the regulation of union-management relations is omitted. However, that area has been important to personnel and human resources managers for so long that there are already several excellent books treating it.[6] Other areas are discussed in Chapter 12, but perhaps not as extensively as some readers might wish. However, the book is not intended to be encyclopedic, but to impart an understanding of federal regulation through an examination of its three most significant manifestations.

Several chapters begin with short case vignettes illustrating some of the legal issues discussed in the chapter. Usually, the cases describe some incident or management practice that results in a lawsuit. The implicit question in such cases is whether a court would rule in favor of the complainant or management. The chapter eventually addresses that question for each case. Accordingly, it is helpful to consider the cases first when reading the chapter; those cases capture in concrete terms some of the concepts covered more abstractly in the rest of the chapter.

## Chapter Objectives

This chapter has three main purposes:

1. To indicate how regulation today is different from earlier regulation
2. To present the *regulatory model* as a way of viewing the regulatory process
3. To use the regulatory model to organize the confusing array of laws, agencies, and the regulatory actions that those agencies take

Later chapters will examine specific areas of the regulation of personnel management in depth, using the regulatory model as a method for organizing and explaining those areas. This chapter is designed to present an overview, a general way of understanding what the federal government is up to when it regulates personnel and human resources.

## How Regulation Has Changed

Despite the fact that federal regulation seems to be a recent social issue, the federal government has been regulating business for many years. For example, the Interstate Commerce Commission (ICC), which regulates trucking and railroads, was established in 1887; the Federal Communications Commission (FCC), which regulates broadcasters, was created in 1934; the National Labor Relations Board (NLRB) was created in 1935; and the Civil Aeronautics Board (CAB), which regulates airlines, was established in 1938. Also the Food and Drug Administration (FDA) was established, under a different title, by the Food and Drug Act of 1906; and the Federal Energy Regulatory Commission (FERC), which regulates utilities, is the heir to the Federal Power Commission, which was established in 1920.[7] Yet today's critics of federal regulation focus more of their attention on a different set of federal agencies, created or empowered by laws passed in the 1960s and 1970s. Those new laws and agencies deal with social issues that are often controversial: environmental protection, consumer product safety, occupational safety and health, discrimination in employment, and the financial security of retired people. While almost all federal regulatory agencies arouse concern on the part of managers, it is these more recent agencies that seem to inflame greater passions and provoke louder cries of outrage.

## Horizontal and Vertical Regulation

One distinction between old regulation and new is that most of the older agencies regulate a specific *industry,* while most of the newer agencies regulate a specific *management function* across several industries. For instance, the Interstate Commerce Commission, an older agency, regulates interstate transportation industries such as railroads and trucking. On the other hand, the Equal Employment Opportunity Commission regulates one management function, the personnel function, across all industries.

Murray Weidenbaum has called the old regulatory agencies *vertical* and the new agencies *horizontal:* vertical agencies are primarily concerned with all management functions within a given industry, and horizontal agencies focus on one functional area across several industries.[8] Exhibit 1.1 demonstrates this distinction. Each column corresponds to an industry. At the bottom of each column is indicated the vertical agency that has responsibility for regulating management functions within that industry. Each row corresponds to a management function, and at the left of each row is the horizontal agency responsible for regulating that function across all industries; at the right is the interest group most concerned with it.

More important, the missions of the horizontal and vertical agencies differ. The older vertical agencies were created to solve problems that were specific to the industry involved, generally problems involving the market that the industry operated in. Typically, the agencies acted to increase competition and prevent monopoly. The purpose was to curb the misuse of market power and thus promote the well-being of the industry; other interests were subordinated or even ignored.[9]

On the other hand, the newer horizontal agencies were created to solve social problems, not industry problems. For instance, the Equal Employment Opportunity Commission was created to solve problems of employment discrimination. Because of their narrow concern with a particular social problem and their coverage of many industries, the newer agencies do not develop any intimate concern with the overall well-being of any company.[10] And because they focus on emotionally charged, non-

**Exhibit 1.1**   Horizontal and Vertical Regulation

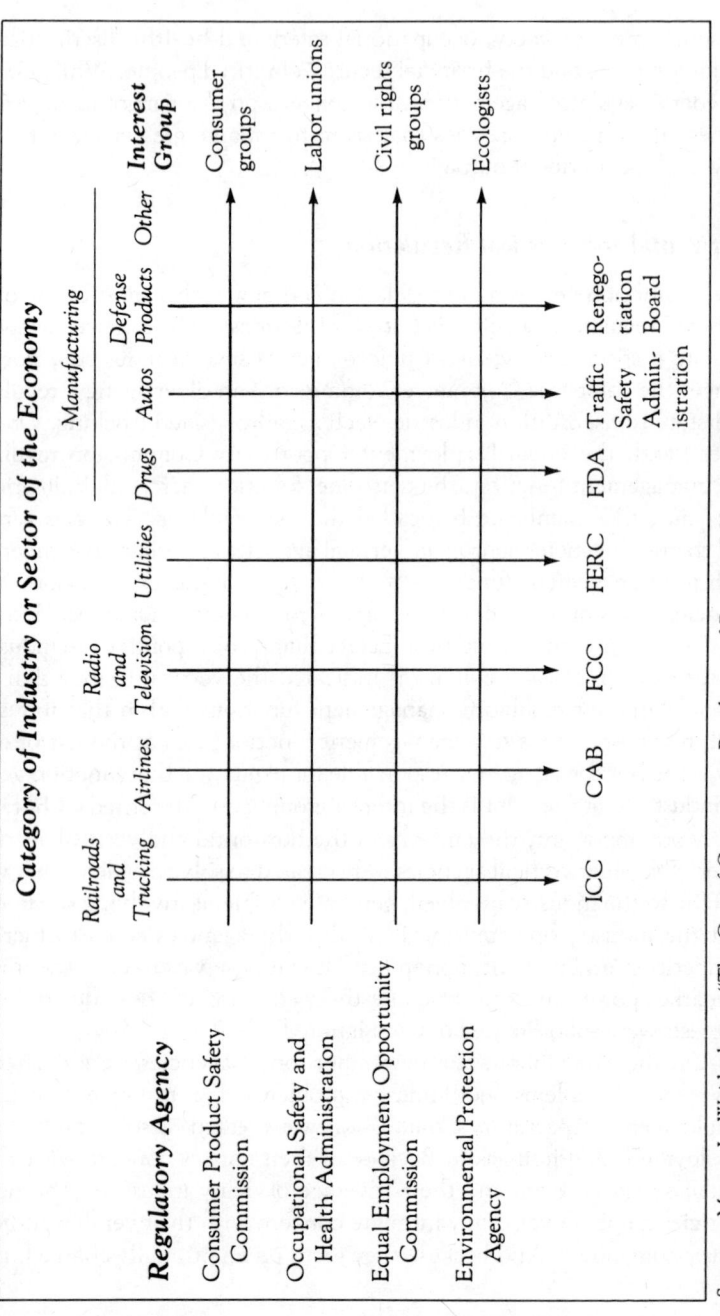

*Source:* Murray L. Weidenbaum. "The Cost of Government Regulation of Business," Hearings Before the Subcommittee on Economic Growth and Stabilization of the Joint Economic Commission, 95th Congress, 2d Session, April 11 and 13, 1978, p. 39.

financial concerns such as fairness, the value of human life, and the value of a secure retirement, they attract much public attention. [11]

George Steiner has enumerated six causes for the growth of horizontal regulation:

1. The realization in the 1960s that, although it had not totally eliminated poverty, the nation had solved the problem of providing a minimum economic standard of living to the majority of the population

2. An intensified concern over the problems of the individual in society

3. The failure of the free market to solve these problems

4. Attention to business abuses by the news media

5. A changing population: more educated, more cynical, more apt to go to government for redress from grievance, real or imaginary

6. Attempts to legislate other social policies, such as allocation of scarce resources and income redistribution [12]

## Significance of the Distinction

To the extent that the older vertical agencies have subordinated public interest to the interest of the industry, the industry is the constituency of the agency, in that the agency exists to solve industry problems. This relationship is reinforced by the prevalent tendency of industry people to leave the industry to work for the agency regulating that industry, and vice versa. This "revolving door" is a familiar feature of life in Washington.

On the other hand, the horizontal agencies are established to solve social problems. They are staffed by individuals more sympathetic to the interest of people affected by those problems and less sympathetic to the interest of industry than the staffs of vertical agencies, and they are thus more likely to be influenced by groups concerned with the social problems and less likely to be influenced by industry organizations. Thus, for example, the constituency of the equal employment agencies seems to be civil rights and women's rights groups; the constituency of the safety and health agencies is labor unions.

The importance of the intimate connection between the agency and its constituents, then, is simply that it is easier for the constituents to influence the agency. It may not be exaggerating to say that the constituents own the agencies that represent them.

### *The Resulting Problem for Employers*

One problem in this situation is that horizontal agencies often pay little attention to the mission of the organizations they regulate. Their concern with social problems makes them less likely than vertical agencies to be sensitive to broad business and economic issues such as productivity, costs to consumers, and inflation.[13]

Indeed, horizontal agencies, more than vertical, are apt to see the organizations they regulate as part of the problem. Horizontal agencies' purpose is to promote the well-being of parties other than the organization: employees, consumers, or the general public. By the very definition of the social problem that the horizontal agency is trying to solve, its mission is to institute change within the organization being regulated. In short, horizontal agencies view organizations as the targets of, rather than the beneficiaries of, their regulatory activities. Understandably, this view is often accompanied by an ideological animus against the private sector among horizontal agency staff members.[14]

Moreover, it is difficult to argue against the missions of the horizontal agencies. Safer working conditions, an end to discrimination, and the like were mandated by Congress in response to demands from the public. And there is a strong belief in some quarters that business will solve those problems only if forced to do so by government.[15] All that explains why much of the recent discontent over federal regulation concerns horizontal rather than vertical regulation.

## The Effectiveness of Management
## Responses to the Federal Presence

Just how well management has responded to horizontal regulation is open to debate. Certainly there seem to be few managers who are satisfied. Still, no matter how management's performance is judged, it seems reasonable to ask how it could be improved.

One way to improve might be to focus less on specifics. Management may be taking the wrong approach in expecting a list of precise mandates from regulatory agencies. It seems like heresy to advocate less attention to specifics, and it seems unjust for agencies to avoid giving a complete list of dos and don'ts, but defining the problem as a matter of specifics is an incomplete approach to regulation. Even if an agency can state precisely what it expects an organization to do, even if it comes up with a list of dos and don'ts, the problem of responding to regulation usually involves items that no one would think to put on a list. Management needs to ask:

> What if someone complains about something new, something that is not on the list that the agency has provided—in other words, how can management gain the understanding that allows it to form its own list of appropriate policies and procedures?

> Government changes, and regulatory activities change—how can management anticipate the direction of those changes?

> What explains the motivations of the agencies and their staff members?

> How can management influence regulatory activities? Is it reasonable to consider a proactive strategy instead of a reactive strategy?

In short, managers must seek an understanding of the regulatory system. It is not enough to know the laws and regulations if one does not understand the cause-and-effect relationships by which those laws and regulations are implemented.

## The Regulatory Model

Once the operation of the regulatory system is understood, the organization can operate with greater confidence, even in the absence of specific mandates, because it can more reliably predict what an agency's position will be on new problems. Moreover, the organization can understand the social and political forces that motivate the regulatory agency and identify the points at which the entire system, and thus the agency in question, can be influenced.

Exhibit 1.2 presents one model depicting such an understanding of the system. This regulatory model organizes the complexity of government regulation, identifying the principal actors in the drama, specifying the most important laws, sorting through the melange of alphabet-soup agencies, and making meaningful the seemingly incoherent body of agency directives, inspections, reviews, regulations, and determinations.

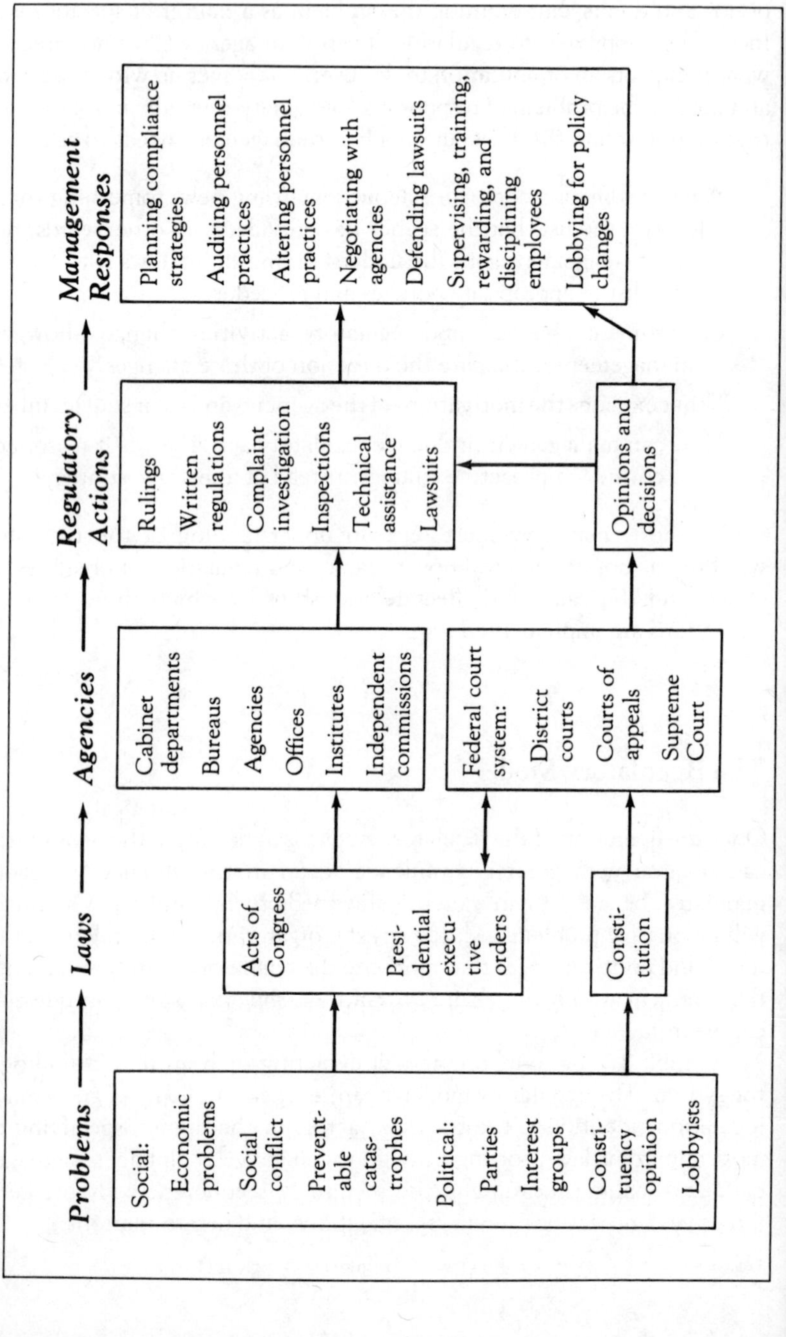

**Exhibit 1.2**  The Regulatory Model

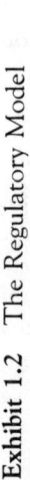

**Problems → Laws → Agencies → Regulatory Actions → Management Responses**

**Problems**

Social:
- Economic problems
- Social conflict
- Preventable catastrophes

Political:
- Parties
- Interest groups
- Constituency opinion
- Lobbyists

**Laws**

- Acts of Congress
- Presidential executive orders
- Constitution

**Agencies**

- Cabinet departments
- Bureaus
- Agencies
- Offices
- Institutes
- Independent commissions

Federal court system:
- District courts
- Courts of appeals
- Supreme Court

**Regulatory Actions**

- Rulings
- Written regulations
- Complaint investigation
- Inspections
- Technical assistance
- Lawsuits

- Opinions and decisions

**Management Responses**

- Planning compliance strategies
- Auditing personnel practices
- Altering personnel practices
- Negotiating with agencies
- Defending lawsuits
- Supervising, training, rewarding, and disciplining employees
- Lobbying for policy changes

## Elements of the Regulatory Model

The most succinct way of summarizing Exhibit 1.2 is to say that (1) regulation begins with social and political problems, which cause law makers to pass laws; (2) those laws empower agencies to take the regulatory actions that trigger management responses; and (3) the courts oversee this process by settling disputes between the parties to it. Management is most naturally concerned with the right-hand side of the regulatory model more than the left, for it must be concerned with appropriate responses. Unfortunately, management often neglects the left side; it is easy for management, in its quest for the "legal" practices, to overlook the cause-and-effect relationships of the process. Until the organization understands what leads to the regulatory action, it cannot hope to forecast directions of the agency or to speculate on what the agency might do when presented with a new situation.

When the question of cause and effect is examined, two things become clear immediately. First, the agencies are created and empowered by specific laws. Those laws define the purpose and authority of the agency, and they are the place to learn the legitimate scope of agency activities.

Second, and perhaps more important, the laws themselves were passed for certain purposes. Lawmakers enact laws to solve social and political problems. Whenever there is doubt about the interpretation of a law, that law will be interpreted so as to fulfill the purpose for which it was passed. This fact is particularly important in the consideration of equal employment law in Part I.

The focus on problems imparts an unavoidable bias to this book. The book dwells on personnel management gone awry—discriminatory hiring practices, unsafe working conditions, inadequate retirement income plans. Like newspapers, which are perennially criticized for printing only the bad news, this book neglects the good news. It is the bad management practices that motivate lawmakers to create regulations. Fair employment may well be more typical than discrimination, but fair employment practices do not lead legislators to pass equal employment laws. Similarly, safe work may be the norm and sound pension plans may be far more common than weak ones, but that does not account for the regulation that exists in those areas. It does little good for the reader to be immersed in the good news; what is essential is an awareness of the bad news, unpleasant though it may be. But the reader must realize that the bad news is not supposed to be a faithful portrayal of the state of management practice in the areas regulated.

## The Federal Court System

The courts are the interpreters of the law. They settle disputes over whether organizations have violated the law and whether agencies have behaved properly in enforcing the law. In doing so, the courts interpret the written words of the law, determining what they should mean when applied to a specific situation.

A full description of how the judicial system operates is beyond the scope of this book.[16] Worth mentioning, however, are two important principles that determine how a court will arrive at a decision:

1. *Congressional intent:* where the written words of the law do not clearly establish how a dispute should be settled, the court will be guided by the evident intent of the lawmaker. To gauge intent, the court will consult the *Congressional Record* for the history of debate, amendments, and other events leading up to the passage of the law. Generally, the court will attempt to determine what Congress was attempting to accomplish when it passed the law.

2. *Precedent:* the court will ordinarily abide by principles that were laid down in earlier cases.[17]

The courts, then, are not wholly arbitrary. Indeed, those two principles give the judicial branch less discretion than the legislative and executive branches have. While the courts often make judgments that enrage some observers, even knowledgeable ones, their actions are not anarchic but are, in a very real sense, bound by the past.

The judicial process also deserves brief mention. When a dispute is reviewed by the federal courts, it ordinarily follows a well-defined path:

1. When one of the parties to a dispute is dissatisfied with the outcome of an agency action, the usual first step is to file suit in a federal district court. A district court is a federal trial court serving a state or a section of a state. In most cases arising under the laws discussed in this book, a district judge, not a jury, will weigh the evidence and arguments, then render a decision. The decision is usually accompanied by a written opinion justifying the decision, which stands as precedent for the district.

The written opinion is generally the source of important information on the proper interpretation of the law. For most areas of federal regulation, particularly for EEO, it is as important to understand what the courts say as to understand what the words of the statute say. The court opinion clarifies ambiguities, resolves apparent conflicts between parts of laws, and indicates what the law requires in specific situations.

2. After the district court trial, if any party to the case is dissatisfied with the outcome, the usual place to appeal is a federal circuit court of appeals. Under some laws (such as the Occupational Safety and Health Act), it is possible to bypass the district court and go directly from the agency to the court of appeals. There are twelve circuit courts of appeals in the United States, with each state assigned to one circuit. The function of the court of appeals is to review the judgment and opinion of the district court. Ordinarily a panel of three or more appeals judges will sit in review. The court of appeals may affirm the district court's opinion, reverse it, or send the case back for further examination and a new trial. Or the court of appeals may combine more than one of those options in its disposition of the case.

3. The final appeals court in the federal judiciary is the United States Supreme Court. While a circuit court of appeals consents to hear all cases presented for appeal, the Supreme Court can refuse to hear cases, and in fact does refuse to hear most of the appeals that reach it. Many factors influence the Supreme Court's decision whether to hear a case on appeal; there are no firm rules. However, the Supreme Court prefers cases that allow it to (1) resolve conflicts among the lower courts, (2) advance its own interpretations of significant legal matters, (3) examine allegations that a given statute is unconstitutional, (4) define the appropriate bounds of government authority, and (5) reconcile evident conflict among statutes. The Supreme Court refuses cases that do not seem to provide an opportunity for saying something legally significant.

## The Significance of Court Involvement in Regulation

The foregoing leaves much unsaid, but it does underscore the importance of the courts in the regulatory process. Just how mistaken is the belief that agencies are the only protagonists in the regulatory drama can be shown simply by pointing out that agencies are legally bound by court rulings and that agency regulations are often written to implement or elaborate on court opinions.

The courts make it difficult to change federal regulation very drastically or quickly. Courts are not supposed to respond to political changes that take place after the law in question has been passed. Moreover, while a new president can appoint new agency heads, federal judges have lifetime tenure. That even new judges abide by the principles of congressional intent and precedent provides the regulatory system with a permanence (some would say rigidity) that is not immediately apparent to the casual observer.

## Practical Implications of the Regulatory Model

As you progress through this book, the usefulness of the regulatory model and the futility of trying to understand regulation just by reading the laws should become evident. In the meantime, the following propositions seem to arise from the regulatory model:

1. Order can emerge from the apparent chaos of government regulation; it is possible to comprehend the regulatory process.

2. The limits of agency power are found in the laws, not in the average manager's notions of what is reasonable. Thus it is essential to know the law in order to know whether the agency is operating within its legal bounds.

3. Problems generate laws, and the laws often are interpreted with a problem-solving purpose in mind. Thus it is necessary to know the context in which a law was passed in order to anticipate how the law might be interpreted.

4. The courts are the final arbiter of disputes over regulation. Thus one must read court opinions to understand the system.

5. The regulatory system has several interrelated parts, each of which is difficult for even the politically powerful to move. That is, even if change is induced in one of the parts, changes will not necessarily take place in the rest of the system. Thus we should take with a grain of salt any politician's promises to "get government off the backs of the people."

6. The regulatory system is directed by the outside forces of politics and social problems. Thus, in order to change the system, one must understand those outside forces.

To some readers, these points may seem self-evident. But to others less familiar with regulation, the regulatory model should help to demystify the process of federal regulation.

## Notes

1. Herbert E. Meyer, "Personnel Directors Are the New Corporate Heroes," *Fortune,* February 1976, pp. 84–88, 140.

2. Jay Palmer, "The Rising Risks of Regulation," *Time,* November 27, 1966, pp. 85–87.

3. Murray L. Weidenbaum, "The Cost of Government Regulation of Business," Hearings on the Cost of Government Regulation Before the Subcommittee on Economic Growth and Stabilization of the Joint Economic Committee, 95th Congress, 2d Session, April 11 and 13, 1978.

4. Ibid., p. 46.

5. *Payne* v. *Western & A. RR.,* 81 Tenn. 507, 519–20 (1884), overruled on other grounds; *Hutton* v. *Walters,* 179 S.W. 134 (1915); discussed in Lawrence B. Blades, "Employment at Will vs. Individual Freedom: On Limiting the Abusive Exercise of Employer Power," *Columbia Law Review* 67 (1967):1404–35.

6. James L. Hunt, *Employer's Guide to Labor Relations* (Washington, D.C.: Bureau of National Affairs, 1979); Arthur A. Sloane and Fred Witney, *Labor Relations* (Englewood Cliffs, N.J.: Prentice-Hall, 1981); Howard A. Myers and David P. Twomey, *Labor Law and Legislation* (Cincinnati: South-Western, 1975); and J. A. Fossum, *Labor Relations: Development, Structure, Process* (Dallas: Business Publications, Inc., 1979).

7. *U.S. Government Manual, 1980–81* (Washington, D.C.: National Archives and Records Service, General Services Administration); E. Healey, ed., *Federal Regulatory Directory, 1979–80* (Washington, D.C.: Congressional Quarterly, 1979).

8. Hearings Before the Subcommittee on Economic Growth and Stabilization of the Joint Economic Committee, 95th Congress, 2d Session, April 11 and 13, 1978, pp. 20ff; Murray L. Weidenbaum, *Business, Government, and the Public* (Englewood Cliffs, N.J.: Prentice-Hall, 1977).

9. Weidenbaum, *Business, Government, and the Public,* p. 12; John Mendeloff, *Regulating Safety: An Economic and Political Analysis of Occupational Safety and Health Policy* (Cambridge, Mass.: MIT Press, 1979), p. 5.

10. Weidenbaum, *Business, Government, and the Public,* p. 14.

11. Mendeloff, *Regulating Safety,* p. 5.

12. George Steiner, "New Patterns in Government Regulation of Business," *MSU Business Topics* 26 (Autumn 1978):53–61.

13. Weidenbaum, *Business, Government, and the Public,* p. 15.

14. Irving Kristol, "A Regulated Society," *Regulation,* 1 (1977):12–13.

15. Weidenbaum, *Business, Government, and the Public,* p. 15.

16. See Robert Corley, Robert L. Black, and O. Lee Reed, *The Legal Environment of Business* (New York: McGraw-Hill, 1981).

17. *Black's Law Dictionary,* 4th ed. (St. Paul, Minn.: West Publishing Company, 1968), p. 1340.

# I

# Equal Employment Opportunity

# 2

# Basic Principles of EEO

*Case 2.1*  The paper mill had been racially segregated since it opened, with separate facilities, separate jobs, separate promotion ladders, and even separate union locals for blacks and whites. Blacks were relegated to the lowest-level jobs. In fact, the top of the black line of progression was at roughly the same level as the bottom of the white line of progression. A system of job seniority had long governed promotions at the mill. Any job opening was given to the candidate with the most seniority in the next job below on the line of progression.

When the 1964 Civil Rights Act was passed, management had to decide what changes to make in order to bring the mill into compliance. They decided to merge the black and white lines of progression into a single promotion sequence. Since the black progression went no higher than the bottom of the white progression, it was tacked on to the bottom of the white progression in making up the new merged line. Job seniority continued to govern promotions, but vacancies were to be awarded without regard to race: if a black candidate had more seniority in the next lower job than a white candidate did, then the black candidate would be promoted into the vacancy. In all other respects, the new system operated in a color-blind manner. Several long-term black employees alleged that the new system was racially discriminatory.

***Case 2.2*** To be hired for one of the higher paying jobs at an electric utility, new employees were required to have a high school diploma and to achieve satisfactory scores on two professionally prepared aptitude tests. Several black applicants were rejected because they had neither; they filed charges of racial discrimination.

***Case 2.3*** A railroad had a rule against hiring anyone who had been convicted of a criminal offense. A black applicant for employment as a clerk was turned down because he had been convicted of the felony of refusing military induction; he filed a charge of racial discrimination against the railroad.

***Case 2.4*** An airline refused to hire a black applicant into its pilot training program because he did not have a college degree and did not meet the minimum flight time requirement that the airline established for its pilot trainees. The applicant charged the airline with racial discrimination.

***Case 2.5*** Several women in an electronics assembly and distribution facility, both outside applicants and current employees, complained that the company discriminated on the basis of sex in selecting participants in its supervisory development program. Most of the supervisors were men.

Employees were chosen for the program based on the performance appraisal given by their supervisors. Supervisors were given the following appraisal sheet:

| *Performance Characteristics* | *Appraisal* | | | | |
|---|---|---|---|---|---|
| | Outstanding | Above average | Satisfactory | Marginal | Unsatisfactory |
| 1. Knowledge of work | _____ | _____ | _____ | _____ | _____ |
| 2. Dependability | _____ | _____ | _____ | _____ | _____ |
| 3. Productivity | _____ | _____ | _____ | _____ | _____ |
| 4. Safety | _____ | _____ | _____ | _____ | _____ |
| 5. Quality of output | _____ | _____ | _____ | _____ | _____ |
| 6. Cooperation | _____ | _____ | _____ | _____ | _____ |
| 7. Relationships with others | _____ | _____ | _____ | _____ | _____ |
| 8. Initiative | _____ | _____ | _____ | _____ | _____ |

| Performance Characteristics | **Appraisal** | | | | |
| --- | --- | --- | --- | --- | --- |
| | Outstand-ing | Above average | Satisfac-tory | Marginal | Unsatis-factory |
| 9. Organizing and planning | _____ | _____ | _____ | _____ | _____ |
| 10. Judgment | _____ | _____ | _____ | _____ | _____ |

Summary: Indicate your overall appraisal of the performance of this employee in his or her present duties and responsibilities. Bear in mind the appraisal assigned on all individual factors above.

_____   _____   _____   _____   _____

Outside applicants were selected by interviews with selected supervisors. The company felt that those supervisors knew better than anybody else the requirements of the training program as well as the requirements of supervisory work at the facility. Supervisors were instructed to use their best judgment in weighing the attributes of those they interviewed against those requirements.

This book devotes more time to equal employment opportunity (EEO) than to the other areas of federal regulation for several reasons. First, EEO regulation has been in existence longer than the other two general areas of federal regulation covered in this book. It has generated more court opinions and agency initiatives, as well as a larger body of management lore regarding how to handle it. EEO has more principles of importance to personnel and human resources management than do the other two areas.

Second, no other regulatory area has so thoroughly affected personnel management as EEO. EEO has implications for almost all aspects of personnel management: hiring, recruiting, promoting, training, compensation, performance appraisal, human resource planning, discipline, and even union relations. By touching so many aspects of personnel management, EEO has largely been responsible for the increased importance of the personnel manager in the organization.

Finally, EEO can be regarded as the province of personnel and human resource management, at least to a greater degree than the other regulatory areas. Occupational safety and health expertise is shared by the personnel manager with engineering, production, and medical staff. Employee benefits expertise is shared with insurance, accounting, and financial planning staff. EEO, however, is personnel's territory.

## Chapter Objectives

The purpose of this chapter is to provide a foundation for understanding EEO and to examine the most basic interpretations of EEO that have emerged from the courts. The first part of the chapter is a straightforward description of the principal regulatory activities of EEO, the agencies that are responsible for those activities, and the laws that authorize the agencies to engage in those activities. The vehicle for that description is the regulatory model introduced in Chapter 1.

The second part of this chapter examines the history behind EEO regulations—the left-hand column of the regulatory model. In no other regulatory area of personnel and human resource management does history play a greater role than it does in the area of equal employment regulation. The events leading up to the passage of EEO laws seriously affected the social and economic life of the nation at the time, and an understanding of EEO is impossible if one is not familiar with that historical context.

Finally, the chapter answers the question, "What is illegal discrimination?" In the process of answering that question, it examines what is generally regarded as the most significant EEO statute, Title VII of the 1964 Civil Rights Act, as amended, as well as what is generally regarded as the most significant EEO court opinion, the one issued by the Supreme Court in the case of *Griggs* v. *Duke Power Company*.[1] Directly or indirectly, the *Griggs* case provides the answer to many questions concerning the interpretation of Title VII. Much of the subsequent EEO discussion in this book can be traced, at least in part, to the principles of *Griggs* set forth in this chapter. This chapter covers basic *Griggs* law and concludes with a brief discussion of how evidence is used in EEO cases.

## The Regulatory Model Applied to EEO

Exhibit 2.1 shows the major elements of EEO regulation, organized along the lines set forth in Chapter 1 for the regulatory model. It enumerates the major laws, agencies, and regulatory activities of EEO, along with the

**Exhibit 2.1   The Regulatory Model Applied to EEO**

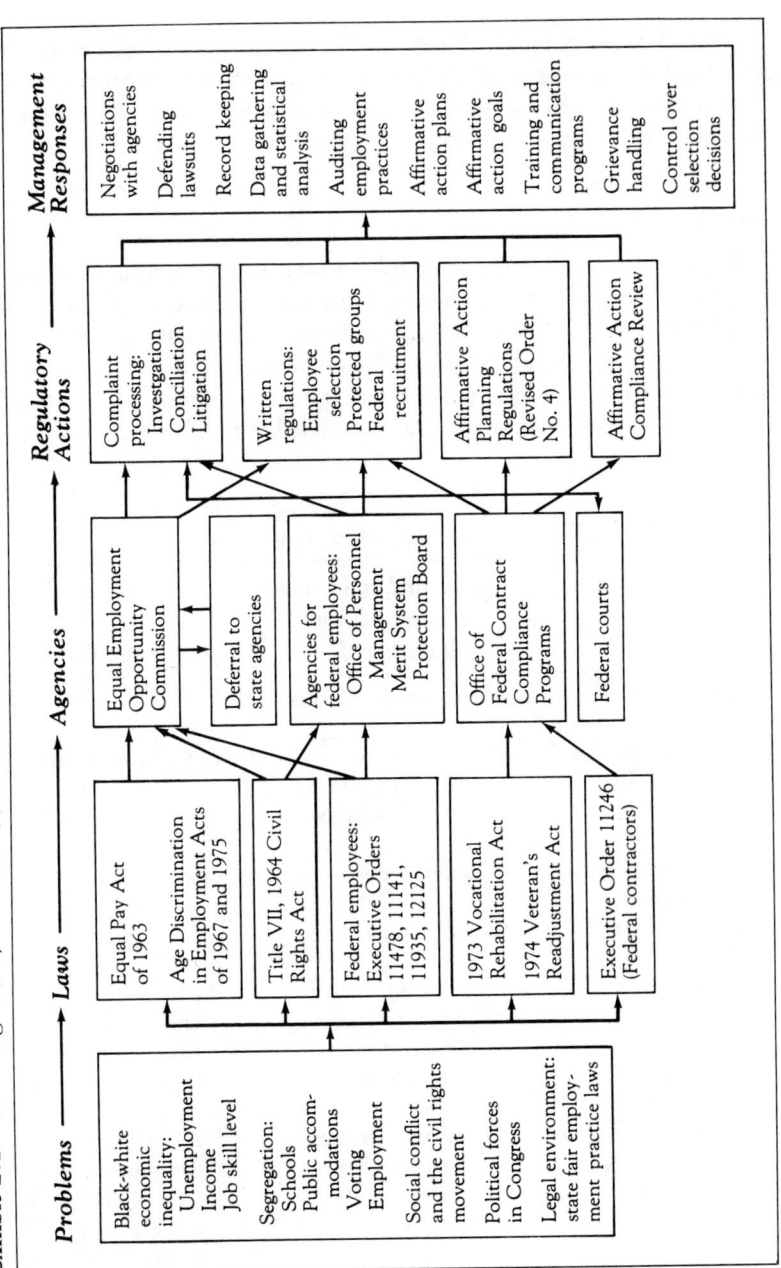

social and political problems responsible for creating the regulatory apparatus and the management activities that are undertaken in response to that apparatus. This section and the next will explain the content of Exhibit 2.1.

## The Laws

Exhibit 2.2 lists some of the principal federal laws governing discrimination in employment, along with the discrimination prohibited and the types of employers covered. It is a more comprehensive list of laws than the one in Exhibit 2.1. Even that long list is not complete, but it does cover the more significant sources of legal prohibition against discrimination. Most EEO compliance problems related to laws included in Exhibit 2.2.

**Exhibit 2.2**   Federal Antidiscrimination Laws

| Law | Type of Employment Discrimination Prohibited | Employers Covered |
| --- | --- | --- |
| U.S. Constitution, First Amendment | Religious discrimination | Federal government |
| U.S. Constitution, Fifth Amendment | Deprivation of employment rights without due process of law | Federal government |
| U.S. Constitution, Fourteenth Amendment | Deprivation of employment rights without due process of law | State and local governments |
| Civil Rights Acts of 1866 and 1870 (based on Thirteenth Amendment) | Race discrimination in hiring, placement, and continuation of employment | Private employers, unions, employment agencies |
| Civil Rights Act of 1871 (based on Fourteenth Amendment) | Deprivation of equal employment rights under cover of state law | State and local governments (private employers if conspiracy is involved) |

**Exhibit 2.2**   Federal Antidiscrimination Laws (*continued*)

| Law | Type of Employment Discrimination Prohibited | Employers Covered |
|---|---|---|
| National Labor Relations Act of 1935 | Unfair representation by unions, or interference with employee rights, that discriminates on the basis of race, color, religion, sex, or national origin | Private employers and unions |
| Equal Pay Act of 1963 | Sex differences in pay for substantially equal work | All employers and labor organizations |
| Executive Order No. 11141 (1964) | Age discrimination | Federal contractors and subcontractors |
| Title VI, 1964 Civil Rights Act | Discrimination based on race, color, or national origin | Employers receiving federal financial assistance |
| Title VII, 1964 Civil Rights Act (as amended in 1972) | Discrimination or segregation based on race, color, religion, sex, or national origin | Private employers with 15 or more employees, governments, unions, employment agencies |
| Executive Order No. 11246 (1965) | Discrimination based on race, color, religion, sex, or national origin (affirmative action required) | Federal contractors and subcontractors |
| Age Discrimination in Employment Act of 1967 (as amended in 1978) | Age discrimination against those between the ages of 40 and 70 | Private employers with 20 or more employees, unions with 25 or more members, employment agencies |
| Title I, 1968 Civil Rights Act | Interference with a person's rights due to race, religion, color, or national origin | Persons generally |

**Exhibit 2.2**    Federal Antidiscrimination Laws (*continued*)

| Law | Type of Employment Discrimination Prohibited | Employers Covered |
|---|---|---|
| Executive Order No. 11478 (1969) | Discrimination based on race, color, religion, sex, national origin, political affiliation, marital status, or physical handicap | Federal government |
| Revenue Sharing Act of 1972 (as amended in 1976) | Discrimination based on race, color, national origin, sex, age, handicap, or religion | State and local governments receiving revenue sharing funds |
| Education Amendments of 1972 | Sex discrimination | Educational institutions receiving federal financial assistance |
| Vietnam Era Veterans Readjustment Act of 1974, Executive Order No. 11701 (1973) | Discrimination against disabled veterans and Vietnam era veterans (affirmative action required) | Federal contractors, federal government |
| Rehabilitation Act of 1973; Executive Order No. 11914 | Discrimination based on physical or mental handicap (affirmative action required) | Federal contractors, federal government |
| Age Discrimination Act of 1975 | Age discrimination | Employers receiving federal financial assistance |
| Civil Service Reform Act of 1978 | Specifically incorporates Title VII, 1964 Civil Rights Act; mandates federal government "workforce reflective of the nation's diversity" | Federal government |
| Federal Employees Part-Time Career Employment Act of 1978 | Requires increased part-time career employment opportunities | Federal government |

Only two of those laws are discussed in detail in this chapter, Title VII and Executive Order No. 11246. Other laws are discussed in later chapters:

*The United States Constitution,* which protects government employees and limits government involvement in religious discrimination, is discussed in Chapter 4.

*The Equal Pay Act,* which mandates equal pay for men and women doing equal work, is discussed in Chapter 5.

*The Age Discrimination in Employment Act,* which prohibits discrimination because of age against those aged 40 to 69, is discussed in Chapter 4.

*The Vocational Rehabilitation Act of 1973,* which governs employment of the handicapped, is discussed in Chapter 4.

In the meantime, it is useful to concentrate on understanding the basic principles of Title VII. The principles of that law have broad applicability to other laws as well.

Title VII of the 1964 Civil Rights Act was passed by Congress in 1964 and first took effect in 1965, with major amendments added by Congress in 1972 and in 1979. As amended, Title VII covers almost all employers having more than fifteen employees, with the following exceptions: (1) private clubs are not covered, (2) religious organizations are allowed to discriminate because of religion, and (3) places of employment connected with an Indian reservation are not covered.[2]

Exhibit 2.3 reproduces some significant excerpts from Title VII. Most

**Exhibit 2.3**   Excerpts from Title VII

---

### Section 703

(a)   It shall be an unlawful employment practice for an employer

(1) to fail or refuse to hire or to discharge any individual, or otherwise to discriminate against any individual with respect to his compensation, terms, conditions, or privileges of employment, because of such individual's race, color, religion, sex, or national origin; or

(2) to limit, segregate, or classify his employees or applicants for employment in any way which would deprive or tend to deprive any individual of employment opportunities or otherwise adversely affect his status as an

employee, because of such individual's race, color, religion, sex, or national origin.
. . . .

(e)  Notwithstanding any other provision of this title, (1) it shall not be an unlawful employment practice for an employer to hire and employ employees . . . on the basis of his religion, sex, or national origin in those certain instances where religion, sex, or national origin is a bona fide occupational qualification reasonably necessary to the normal operation of that particular business or enterprise.
. . . .

(h)  Notwithstanding any other provision of this title, it shall not be an unlawful employment practice for an employer to apply different standards of compensation, or different terms, conditions, or privileges of employment pursuant to a bona fide seniority or merit system, or a system which measures earnings by quantity or quality of production or to employees who work in different locations, provided that such differences are not the result of an intention to discriminate because of race, color, religion, sex, or national origin, nor shall it be an unlawful employment practice for an employer to give and to act upon the results of any professionally developed ability test provided that such test, its administration or action upon the results is not designed, intended or used to discriminate because of race, color, religion, sex, or national origin.
. . . .

(j)  Nothing contained in this title shall be interpreted to require any employer . . . to grant preferential treatment to any individual or to any group because of the race, color, religion, sex, or national origin of such individual or group on account of an imbalance which may exist with respect to the total number or percentage of persons of any race, color, religion, sex, or national origin employed by any employer . . . in comparison with the total number or percentage of persons of such race, color, religion, sex, or national origin in any community, State, section, or other area, or in the available work force in any community, State, section, or other area.

## Section 704

(a)  It shall be an unlawful employment practice for an employer to discriminate against any of his employees or applicants for employment . . . because he [the employee or applicant] has opposed any practice made an unlawful employment practice by this title, or because he has made a charge, testified, assisted, or participated in any matter in an investigation, proceeding, or hearing under this title.

important is Section 703(a), particularly the list of prohibited classifications: race, color, religion, sex, and national origin. Essentially, Title VII prohibits any employment action based on any of the prohibited classifications. That even includes discrimination against white males, discussed in Chapter 6. Keeping that firmly in mind helps avoid some of the more common misunderstandings about Title VII.

Executive Order 11246 was issued by President Lyndon B. Johnson in 1965.[3] Executive orders have the force of law, even though they are issued unilaterally by the president without congressional approval and can be altered unilaterally as well. Like Title VII, Executive Order 11246 prohibits discrimination based on race, color, religion, sex, and national origin.

In most respects, the two laws are alike, but there are two principal features that make Executive Order 11246 different. One is that it governs federal contractors and subcontractors only. The executive order uses the president's procurement authority to require that a nondiscrimination clause be placed in government contracts. The clause commits the entire organization to abide by its terms. That is why many facilities are covered by it even though they carry out no contract work; if just one facility in the company has a contract, all the facilities of that company are subject to Executive Order 11246.

The second feature distinguishing Executive Order 11246 from Title VII is a provision requiring that employers "take affirmative action to ensure that applicants are employed, and that employees are treated during employment, without regard to their race, color, religion, sex, or national origin."[4] For larger employers, compliance with Executive Order 11246 requires the preparation of an "affirmative action plan," a major personnel management task described in Chapter 6. The natural question at this juncture is, What is affirmative action? The answer is subject to much debate. Chapter 6 discusses this question in depth and enumerates the major requirements for compliance with Executive Order 11246.

### The Agencies and Their Regulatory Actions

There are far more agencies than enumerated in Exhibit 2.1. But for Title VII, the principal regulatory agency is the Equal Employment Opportunity Commission (EEOC). Limited Title VII responsibilities are given to other agencies such as the U.S. Office of Personnel Management and the Merit

System Protection Board, which are involved in EEO for federal employees. But the EEOC has the major responsibility.

As Exhibit 2.1 indicates, the EEOC's principal activities are (1) processing complaints of discrimination and (2) issuing written regulations governing employment practices. *Processing complaints,* the EEOC's most prominent regulatory activity, can be divided into three phases.[5]

1. *Investigation:* when someone brings a complaint of employment discrimination, the EEOC examines the evidence that the employer violated Title VII. The EEOC may conduct the investigation itself, or, in states with their own EEO laws that meet EEOC standards, it may begin by referring the complaint to the state or local enforcement agency.[6] Agencies that are approved by the EEOC for complaint processing are called *deferral agencies.* Most areas of the country are covered by a local deferral agency. Whether carried out by the EEOC or by a deferral agency, the investigation usually involves a visit to the employer's workplace. During the visit, the people involved are interviewed and records examined. If the employer resists that intrusion, the EEOC often can legally compel the employer to produce the information that the agency seeks in its investigation. After the information is gathered, the EEOC arrives at a *determination* of whether there is *probable cause*[7] to believe that the employer has violated Title VII.

2. *Conciliation:* if the EEOC finds no probable cause, the agency ends its involvement and notifies the complainant that he or she has the right to file a private lawsuit against the employer in federal district court (see Chapter 1). However, if the EEOC does find probable cause to believe that the employer has violated Title VII, the agency attempts to settle the matter through a process called *conciliation.*[8] Conciliation is a negotiation between the complainant, the employer, and the EEOC. The objective of the EEOC during conciliation is to obtain an agreement that is tolerable to the interests of all parties, including its own interest in upholding Title VII's requirement that the employer compensate the victims of its discriminatory acts. In short, conciliation is a process of out-of-court settlement.

3. *Litigation:* if conciliation fails, the EEOC may litigate by filing suit in federal district court against the employer. In most cases, though, the EEOC drops the matter. Going to court requires an expensive commitment of legal resources. Consequently, litigation is generally reserved for important cases with favorable prospects for the agency. Unless there is a

good chance of winning, the possibility of a large cash award for the complainant, or the opportunity for the court to break new ground in legal interpretation, the EEOC generally does not go to court. Regardless, however, the complainant has the right to sue in federal court, even when the EEOC has found no probable cause to believe that the employer has violated Title VII.

This final step, litigation, is where most of the important lawmaking in EEO takes place. Nowhere is the influential role of the federal courts in shaping federal regulation more prominent than in the area of equal employment. The courts have taken the general prohibitions of Title VII and turned them into specific mandates about employment practices. Without an understanding of those mandates and the rationale behind them, employers have little hope of solving their EEO compliance problems.

The EEOC issues its written regulations under two broad grants of power in Title VII: the power to issue procedural regulations[9] and the power to provide "technical assistance"[10] to those subject to the title. Accordingly, many of the EEOC's regulations are interpretations of Title VII and the other statutes that the EEOC enforces; they tell employers what the EEOC thinks the law requires. Exhibit 2.4 lists a few of the more important EEOC regulations, some of which are discussed in later chapters. Perhaps the most significant regulation is the Uniform Guidelines on Employee Selection Procedures,[11] which govern the employer's procedure for hiring, promotion, and other staffing decisions (see Chapter 5). Another regulation, the Guidelines on Sexual Harassment,[12] has attracted considerable attention as complaints of unwanted sexual advances have become more numerous and more public (see Chapter 3).

**Exhibit 2.4**    Principal EEOC Regulations

| | |
|---|---|
| Sex discrimination | Questions and answers on employee selection guidelines |
| Questions and answers on pregnancy disability and reproductive hazards | Sexual harassment guidelines |
| Religious discrimination | Record keeping and reports |
| National origin discrimination | Affirmative action for state and local government agencies |
| Age discrimination | |
| Employee selection guidelines | EEO in the federal government |

It is easy for someone unfamiliar with federal regulation to dismiss those guidelines because they are not acts of Congress or orders of the president. However, acts of Congress are often written so broadly that the agency is given authority to provide specific guidance. Thus, when the courts are faced with a case where the applicable part of Title VII is unclear, they often turn to agency regulations. For example, in *Griggs* v. *Duke Power Co.*, discussed below, the Supreme Court had to decide what section 703(h) meant when it referred to "professionally developed ability test." The Court resolved the issue by turning to, among other things, the EEOC guidelines.[13] In doing so, the Court observed that an enforcement agency's interpretations are "entitled to great deference."[14]

For Executive Order 11246, the regulatory agency is the Office of Federal Contract Compliance Programs (OFCCP), a division of the Employment Standards Administration of the U.S. Department of Labor. Since Title VII and Executive Order 11246 are parallel in so many regards, the written regulations of the two agencies are very similar as well. In fact, the OFCCP has adopted the same Uniform Guidelines on Employee Selection Procedures that the EEOC has adopted.

Unlike the EEOC, however, the OFCCP devotes less attention to processing complaints and more attention to determining whether the employer actually does "take affirmative action." In Exhibit 2.1, this is called affirmative action compliance review, and it has two components: (1) examination of the employer's written documents and records, including its written affirmative action plan, and (2) on-site visits, including inspections and interviews with both the managerial and nonmanagerial employees. Compliance review is discussed further in Chapter 6.

### Management Responses

The right-hand column of Exhibit 2.1 lists a few of the more common management responses to EEO regulation. While most of these are discussed further in the chapters indicated, some explanation is in order here:

> *Records, data,* and *statistics* are important because they are used as evidence in EEO lawsuits; it is foolish for managers to neglect them (see Chapter 5).
>
> *Auditing* employment practices simply means examining them to see if they meet EEO standards. Some auditing criteria are discussed in Chapter 5 as well (see pages 45–48 and 101–14).

*Affirmative action*—the written plan and the goal setting—are elaborate activities closely regulated by the OFCCP (see Chapter 6).

*Training programs, communication,* and *grievance handling* include a variety of managerial methods for improving the organization's EEO posture, many of which are carried out as part of the organization's affirmative action obligations. Some of them are discussed in Chapter 6 as well (see pages 127–29).

*Selection decision control* generally involves reducing subjectivity in hiring, promotion, and pay decisions. That is discussed later in this chapter.

## Congressional Intent: The Key to Understanding the Meaning of Title VII

How stringently should Title VII be interpreted? The answer is found in the intentions that Congress had in passing the law. Evidence of what Congress intended a law to mean is important because it helps the courts resolve ambiguities in the wording of the law. To understand congressional intent in passing Title VII, it is necessary to consult two sources. One is the history of congressional deliberation over Title VII and its subsequent amendments, as recorded in the *Congressional Record.*[15] The second source, which is particularly important in understanding how Title VII is interpreted, is the history of the events of the time. The list of problems in Exhibit 2.1 reflects those two sources and is discussed here.

### Economic Inequality

Economic considerations play a major role in the development of federal legislation. The principal economic fact motivating Congress to pass Title VII was the dramatic economic inequality between blacks and whites, which had been discouragingly high ever since Congress began to keep track of such matters. The inequality was reflected in many ways. For example, at the time of congressional deliberation over Title VII, black unemployment was about twice as high as white unemployment, and the average black family income was barely half the average white family income. Blacks were three times as likely as whites to be employed in unskilled positions, while whites were three times as likely as blacks to be employed in professional or managerial jobs.[16] Blacks were also three times as likely as whites to work less than full time.[17] Those inequalities could not be attributed entirely to educational differences: the average income of black high school graduates was less than the average income of white grade school graduates.[18]

Much of this economic inequality was brought about by segregation. Before the civil rights laws of the 1960s, segregation was commonplace in schools, public transportation, public accommodations such as restaurants, and voting. Segregation was also reflected in the world of work. Frequently, blacks were relegated to segregated jobs, lines of progression, or departments, usually less desirable than those to which whites had access. This was particularly true in the tobacco, paper, trucking, and construction industries. In construction, blacks were concentrated in lower-paying trades, and some unions excluded blacks altogether, while others had a system of segregated locals.[19]

## Social Conflict

The civil rights movement of the 1960s was a response to economic inequality and racial segregation. In much of the South, integration was illegal, and when civil rights demonstrators attempted to integrate lunch counters and buses, conflict was inevitable.

Probably the most important thing about this conflict was the attention it attracted, both in the United States and abroad. In a decade marked by social conflict, civil rights conflicts were the prevailing news topic. Accounts of civil rights demonstrators being attacked with fire hoses, dogs, and cattle prods shocked people into realizing that civil rights was the most pressing social problem of the times. The civil rights struggle challenged the nation's commitment to the American dream that any individual could succeed through hard work regardless of his or her origins. The public turned to Congress for a resolution of this conflict involving such fundamental questions of value.

## Political Forces

The Civil Rights Act was controversial legislation. It had to overcome substantial opposition in Congress, particularly from southern legislators who were convinced that the law was an attack on their region. For example, one southern senator said:

> Mr. Ellender: The substitute is directed at the South—at all States which do not have [fair employment practice] laws. It is generally known that the Southern States do not have such laws, for they have never needed them.[20]

Those legislators mounted a filibuster,[21] and the bill was amended eighteen times in the House and eighty-seven times in the Senate before it finally won approval.[22]

One conservative senator who did much to shape the final legislation was Everett McKinley Dirksen from Illinois, who was concerned about the bill's possibilities for abuse of federal power.[23] Dirksen's skeptical questions about the proposed legislation were answered reassuringly by the bill's supporters, and those answers became part of the public record. Even today, when analysts attempt to fathom congressional intent, they must acknowledge and incorporate the points of view such as the following from the Clark-Case Memorandum, an interpretive statement prepared by two Title VII supporters in the Senate:

> It has been suggested that the concept of discrimination is vague. In fact it is clear and simple and has no hidden meanings. To discriminate is to make a distinction, to make a difference in treatment or favor, and those distinctions or differences in treatment or favor which are prohibited by section 704 are those which are based on any five of the forbidden criteria: race, color, religion, sex, and national origin. Any other criterion or qualification for employment is not affected by this title.
>
> There is no requirement in Title VII that an employer maintain a racial balance in his work force. On the contrary, any deliberate attempt to maintain a racial balance, whatever such a balance may be, would involve a violation of Title VII because maintaining such a balance would require an employer to hire or to refuse to hire on the basis of race.[24]

Perhaps because of such assurances, Dirksen supported the bill, and it seems unlikely that it would have passed without his support.

Those statements are taken by some observers to mean that Congress intended Title VII to be a moderate law, one that did not intrude drastically in personnel functions. However, other observers point to Congress's overriding concern with economic inequality and social conflict, noting the repeated references to black economic adversity scattered throughout the record.[25] Surely Congress did not intend to pass a law that was impotent in dealing with those problems. Some would insist that the illness of economic inequality was so severe that Congress intended the dose of medicine to be as strong as necessary to bring about a cure.[26]

### Legal Environment: State Fair Employment Practice Laws

State fair employment practice laws had been in existence for several years when Congress debated Title VII. One reason that Congress chose to duplicate those state efforts was that the state laws were generally limited in their capacity to deal with the problem of economic inequality. That they had been in existence for some years without remedying the problem was taken as evidence of their ineffectiveness. Some of the specific limitations of state fair employment practice laws were:

Twenty-two states, including all the Deep South states, did not have such laws.[27]

States had difficulty dealing with large employers with operations in several states.[28]

To prove that an employer was guilty of a violation of state law, the complainant often had to present evidence that the employer intended to discriminate.

Sometimes under state law black complainants were obliged to demonstrate that their qualifications were greater than the qualifications of the white employees that were hired.

Four states had no agency to administer their fair employment laws.[29]

Generally, the penalty for violations of those laws was limited; back pay and other forms of redress for discriminatorily rejected applicants were out of the question.[30] Three states had no enforcement whatever.[31]

For some civil rights supporters in Congress, then, the state laws seemed to serve as examples of an inadequate approach, a lesson on what to avoid in fashioning a federal law.

## What Is Illegal Discrimination?

The reason it is necessary to examine congressional intent so closely in order to understand Title VII is that Congress did not define the word *discriminate* in Title VII. Thus it is important to consider congressional statements such as the following by Senator Clifford Case of New Jersey, a supporter of the bill:

> Objection: The language of the statute is vague and unclear. It may interfere with the employers' right to select on the basis of qualifications.
>
> Answer: Discrimination is a word which has been used in State FEPC statutes for at least 20 years, and has been used in Federal statutes, such as the National Labor Relations Act and the Fair Labor Standards Act, for even a longer period. To discriminate is to make distinctions or differences in the treatment of employees, and are prohibited only if they are based on any of the five forbidden criteria (race, color, religion, sex, or national origin); any other criteria or qualification is untouched by this bill.[32]

Such statements suggest that discrimination might be defined as follows:

> *Definition 1:* discrimination is using race, color, religion, sex, or national origin as a basis for treating people unequally.
>
> *Examples:* an absolute refusal to consider blacks for a job; paying women less than men for the same work; any decision rule with a racial or sexual premise or cause.[33]

That is the common sense notion of what discrimination means; it equates nondiscrimination with color-blind decision making. If someone had asked for a precise definition, it seems clear that Congress would have offered something along those lines. But it also seems likely that there could have been substantial agreement in Congress on the following as a second type of illegal discrimination:

> *Definition 2:* discrimination is any unnecessary practice that has unequal consequences for people of different race, color, religion, sex, or national origin.
>
> *Example:* any unnecessary screening that excludes a greater proportion of women or minorities than white males, or any decision rule with racial or sexual consequences.

This definition goes much further than the common sense definition, but it has the virtue of getting closer to the problem of economic inequality that Congress was trying to solve, because it covers all unnecessary practices that contribute to economic inequality.

Congress thought that it could bring about economic equality for blacks by requiring color blindness,[34] without requiring that consequences be equal, because it believed that economic inequality could be cured by ending definition 1 discrimination.[35] But Congress was wrong.

The issue, then, is whether Congress would have wanted to do more than eliminate race-conscious employment practices if such were required to eliminate the economic inequality.

Case 2.1 illustrates why Congress was wrong in assuming that color-blind employment practices would bring about economic equality between blacks and whites. The situation in Case 2.1 was typical among employers in the South prior to the passage of the Civil Rights Act, particularly in the paper industry.[36] The company's elimination of deliberately unequal treatment of blacks and whites and the adoption of a racially neutral *job* seniority system did not bring about equality between black and white employees. By merging the previously segregated lines of progression, black job seniority was treated the same as white job seniority—a wholly color-blind approach. But none of the blacks had seniority in any job above the bottom rung of the job ladder. Senior black employees could move up to the second lowest position, but they had no seniority credit to move to the next step. Instead, they were obliged to build up seniority credit in the second job until they had enough to move into a vacancy at the third job level—where they would again have to begin from scratch building up job seniority. On the other hand, whites had been moving up through the ranks all along and thus had acquired the necessary job seniority.

In other words, even though the company's new policy eradicated the old segregated system and replaced it with a racially neutral one, it locked in veteran black employees behind the whites in the job progression because of the company's previous policy of relegating blacks to the lowest jobs. While the new policy was color-blind, it perpetuated the effects of past discrimination: not definition 1 discrimination, but definition 2 discrimination.

### The Griggs Case

Many other common employment practices were neutral but affected blacks adversely. Case 2.2 presents an example. The company used two neutral, color-blind criteria: a high school education requirement and a standardized ability test. Blacks and whites were treated the same: a black with a high school education had the same opportunity that a white with a high school education had; a black with a passing test score was regarded as favorably as a white with a passing test score. The problem was that this policy of equal treatment had unequal consequences for blacks and whites. Blacks in the state were less likely than whites to have a high school education, and blacks who took the test were less likely than whites to pass it.[37] Thus, the company was guilty of definition 2 discrimination.

However, Title VII contains an exemption for "professionally developed ability tests." Section 703(h) in Exhibit 2.3 seems to grant immunity to companies such as described in Case 2.2. Besides, the prevailing view of the law was based on definition 1, not definition 2. It seemed reasonable, even natural, to prohibit the deliberate, color-conscious action against blacks that was so characteristic of the segregation being attacked at the time by the civil rights movement. It was quite another matter, however, to make it illegal to engage in any practice, even a racially neutral one, simply because it had unequal results for blacks and whites.

Yet, to permit such practices might encourage their abuse in ways that would vitiate congressional interest in eliminating economic inequality. Indeed, many managers apparently interpreted section 703(h) as a blanket authorization of any test obtained from a professionally reputable publisher of psychological tests. They seemed to view testing as a personnel practice exempt from Title VII, and accordingly adopted tests widely, frequently with little regard for their relationship to job performance. Education was often used more as a handy screening device than as a predictor of job ability. Predictably, those practices had deleterious consequences for blacks. Compared with whites, blacks as a group tended to have less formal education than whites and tended to score lower on paper-and-pencil ability tests.[38]

The U.S. Supreme Court faced a situation similar to Case 2.2 and decided against the company. In *Griggs* v. *Duke Power Co.*, the most significant EEO case, the Court addressed the question of whether definition 2 was included in what Congress intended to prohibit:

> The objective of Congress in the enactment of Title VII is plain from the language of the statute. It was to achieve equality of employment opportunities and remove barriers that have operated in the past to favor an identifiable group of white employees over other employees. Under the Act, practices, procedures, or tests neutral on their face, and even neutral in terms of intent, cannot be maintained if they operate to "freeze" the status quo of prior discriminatory employment practices.[39]

Clearly, the company's tests and education requirements did tend to " 'freeze' the status quo":

> on the record in the present case, "whites register far better on the Company's . . . requirements" than Negroes. . . . This consequence would appear to be directly traceable to race. Basic intelligence must have the means of articulation

> to manifest itself fairly in a testing process. Because they are·Negroes, petition-
> ers have long received inferior education in segregated schools. . . .[40]

Yet, just because whites do better does *not* mean the requirements are necessarily illegal:

> Congress did not intend by Title VII, however, to guarantee a job to every
> person regardless of qualifications. In short, the Act does not command that any
> person be hired simply because he was formerly the subject of discrimination, or
> because he is a member of a minority group. Discriminatory preference for any
> group, minority or majority, is precisely and only what Congress has proscribed.
> What is required by Congress is the removal of artificial, arbitrary, and unneces-
> sary barriers to employment when the barriers operate invidiously to discrimi-
> nate on the basis of racial or other impermissible classification.[41]

Thus the main legal conclusion that the Supreme Court reached was:

> The touchstone is business necessity. If an employment practice which operates
> to exclude Negroes cannot be shown to be related to job performance, the
> practice is prohibited.[42]

Moreover, good intentions are not sufficient to excuse the employer, because "Congress directed the thrust of the Act to the *consequences* of employment practices, not simply the motivation."[43]

Judged against those standards, many commonplace employment practices such as Duke Power Company's were clearly inadequate:

> The facts of this case demonstrate the inadequacy of broad and general testing
> devices as well as the infirmity of using diplomas or degrees as fixed measures of
> capability. History is filled with examples of men and women who rendered
> highly effective performance without the conventional badges of accomplish-
> ment in terms of certificates, diplomas, or degrees. Diplomas and tests are useful
> servants, but Congress has mandated the commonsense proposition that they
> are not to become masters of reality.[44]

Nor did section 703(h) of Title VII exempt the test used by Duke Power Company. The Court took the EEOC's interpretation of "professionally developed ability test" to mean

> a test which fairly measures the knowledge or skills required by the particular
> job or class of jobs which the applicant seeks, or which fairly affords the em-
> ployer a chance to measure the applicant's ability to perform a particular job or
> class of jobs. The fact that a test was prepared by an individual or organization
> claiming expertise in test preparation does not, without more, justify its use
> within the meaning of Title VII.[45]

What Congress intended to do with section 703(h) was allow the use of *job-related* tests having adverse impact on blacks, not give blanket approval to any test put out by a publisher of professional tests.[46]

## Legal Principles Established by Griggs

The main result of *Griggs* was to make definition 2 discrimination illegal. The court's holding can be reduced to two principles:

1. Title VII prohibits practices having *unequal impact* on different race, color, sex, religion, or national origin groups.
2. Business necessity or job relatedness is a defense for using such practices.

The first holding is particularly momentous because it officially establishes definition 2 as a category of illegal discrimination. Exhibit 2.5 lists some of the phrases and legal terms used to characterize the two kinds of discrimination. In legal terminology, definition 1 is called *disparate treatment* discrimination, while definition 2 is called *disparate impact* discrimination.

Many employment practices have disparate impact. Consider for a moment the various criteria that an organization uses to screen job can-

**Exhibit 2.5**   Two Kinds of Discrimination

| *Definition 1*<br>*Disparate Treatment* | *Definition 2*<br>*Disparate Impact* |
|---|---|
| Direct discrimination | Indirect discrimination |
| Unequal treatment | Unequal consequences or results |
| Decision rules with a racial/sexual premise or cause | Decision rules with racial/sexual consequences |
| Intentional discrimination | Unintentional discrimination |
| Prejudiced actions | Neutral, color-blind discrimination |
| Individual discrimination | Discrimination against groups (statistical discrimination) |
| Different standards for the different groups | Same standards, but with different consequences for different groups |

didates. In typical situations, a substantial proportion of them tend to work to the disadvantage of some race, sex, or ethnic group. An example is shown in Case 2.3. In *Green v. Missouri Pacific Railroad,*[47] which concerned such a situation, the court noted that blacks were more likely than whites to be disqualified because of a conviction record and ruled that the practice could not be defended as a business necessity. Many other tests and screening devices have failed for the same reason; Exhibit 2.6 presents a partial list of them. These are not always illegal—only when they operate to exclude a greater proportion of one group than another and are not defensible as job related.

How can an employer demonstrate that a practice is job related or necessary to the business? Usually the answer is, with great difficulty. A few screening devices are so obviously job related that a court will always accept them: licensing requirements for nurses and teachers and apprenticeship training for skilled craft positions, for example. But other job requirements are more vulnerable and must be supported by special research into their job relatedness. The agency guidelines for such research,[48]

**Exhibit 2.6** Employee Screening Devices Rejected Because of Disparate Impact

| | |
|---|---|
| Educational requirements | Preference for applicants with honorable discharges |
| Tests | |
| Experience requirements | Preference for relatives of present employees |
| Height and weight requirements | |
| Physical agility tests | Use of walk-in or word-of-mouth recruiting |
| Excluding applicants with arrest-conviction records | |
| | Reference checks |
| Credit record requirements | Promoting from within |
| Excluding unwed parents | Promotion based on supervisory recommendations |
| Excluding applicants with less than honorable discharges | |

*Note:* These devices are not always illegal; see the discussion on pages 41 and 42.

*Source:* Bureau of National Affairs, *Fair Employment Practices Manual,* 421:401ff; B. L. Schlei and P. Grossman, *Employment Discrimination Law* (including *1979 Supplement*), Ch. 5.

discussed in Chapter 5, are so technical and obscure that most organizations turn to industrial psychologists for the necessary expertise.

Not all questions of job relatedness are so technical, however. For example, consider Case 2.4. The airline's screening requirements did have an unequal impact on blacks and whites, a fact that was established by the statistics presented. However, in *Spurlock* v. *United Airlines*, the court accepted those requirements as job related:

> It cannot seriously be contended that [the flight time] requirement is not job-related. United . . . showed through the use of statistics that applicants who have higher flight hours are more likely to succeed in the rigorous training program which United flight officers go through after they are hired. . . . The evidence also showed that because of the high cost of the training program, it is important to United that those who begin its training program eventually become flight officers. This is an example of business necessity. . . .
>
> With regard to the college degree requirement, . . . a person with a college degree, particularly one in the "hard" sciences, is more able to cope with the initial training program and the unending series of refresher courses than a person without a college degree. We think United met the burden of showing that its requirement of a college degree was sufficiently job-related to make it a lawful pre-employment standard.[49]

Among other things, this case illustrates that it may be easier to convince a court of job relatedness when the job is one in which a bad performance could be disastrous. It also shows that it is not impossible to prove job relatedness to the satisfaction of a federal court, although other courts have been more stringent than the *Spurlock* court. What the courts look for, at a minimum, is a degree of logical argument and factual evidence, not just a subjective appeal to intuition and so-called common sense.

## Implication: The Problem of Subjectivity in Performance Appraisals and Job Interviews

Weighed against those criteria, the problems of Case 2.5 are evident. The job interview and the performance appraisal system in use at the company lacked objectivity. Interviewers were given no concrete selection criteria upon which to base a hiring decision, and supervisors were not told the specific behaviors indicating the presence of the broad traits that were rated in the performance appraisals. Yet those conditions are widespread in practice.

Subjectivity such as that found in Case 2.5 encourages both direct, definition 1 discrimination and indirect, definition 2 discrimination. It encourages direct discrimination because it makes it more likely that any prejudice, conscious or unconscious, on the part of the interviewer or supervisor will manifest itself in employment decisions. Unstructured situations encourage the expression of personal motivations and prejudices; that is why tests like the Rorschach inkblot test are so widely used in psychological diagnosis. Just as the ambiguous inkblot invites the observer to project personal feelings, so does an unstructured interview or performance appraisal invite the interviewer or appraiser to do the same.

Often the problem is a conscious belief about the employability of women, blacks, or some other groups. A common example is the belief that women with preschool children sometimes cannot handle simultaneously both the demands of child care and the demands of the jobs they seek. Another is the fear that clients will abandon the company if a black account representative is hired. Whether or not such concerns are justified is irrelevant to their legal status. They are instances of disparate treatment, which is clearly illegal under Title VII, and they must be removed from the organization's decision-making process.

Subjectivity also encourages disparate impact. If specific criteria are not supplied, even unprejudiced decision makers are apt to substitute criteria that have disparate impact. Of course the organization needs to use *some* criteria, but it is legally risky to leave those criteria wholly in the hands of individual decision makers who may not realize the government's tough requirements. If the organization specifies the criteria in advance, it can assess their impact and their job relatedness.

Another problem with most subjective systems is that they are inherently impossible to defend if they have disparate impact. Consider the hopelessness of proving job relatedness in Case 2.5, where the interviewers' criteria changed from candidate to candidate and the performance-rating criteria were not tied to specific aspects of the job. Understandably, both interviews and performance appraisals have been struck down in EEO cases.[50] Performance appraisals are apparently the greater EEO problem. Feild and Holley have identified several features of performance appraisal systems that judges in EEO cases have mentioned and note that the following features seem to characterize the systems used by employers who won their cases:[51]

1. Specific written instructions were given to raters.

2. Employees were rated on observable behavior or results.
3. Appraisals were based on a written job analysis.
4. Appraisal results were reviewed with the employee.

The implications for management are clear: subjective employment practices make the organization more vulnerable by robbing it of a major line of defense. Therefore, while controls are never popular in an organization, it is advisable to provide specific, observable standards for people carrying out job interviews and performance appraisals. To make those standards job related, a good job description is the logical starting point. If the job interviewer were to evaluate those characteristics that are needed for the job, and if the performance appraiser were to appraise performance on tasks that are part of the job, then the organization could do much to reduce its vulnerability to charges of discrimination.[52]

There is an alternative: hire by the numbers. The euphemism for this hiring of a certain number of minorities and women is "avoid disparate impact." If an employment practice does not have disparate impact, then the employer is not required to show that it is job related. The conditions under which it is legal to hire by the numbers are discussed in Chapter 6.

## Evidence and Proof: An Introduction

The importance of evidence and proof in a court case is that both the complainant and the employer are expected to present evidence to prove their sides, and the party that does not carry its burden of proof is usually the party that loses the case. Thus, if management understands enough about evidence and proof to anticipate which employment practices would be vulnerable if the organization were sued, then it can change those practices. Otherwise, there is a greater risk that management will overlook those problems out of ignorance while needlessly eliminating some defensible and valuable employment practices out of a misplaced fear of adverse EEO judgments. For that reason, Chapter 5 is devoted entirely to evidence and proof. In the meantime, it is worth considering the fundamentals.

There is an important logical sequence in an EEO trial. First, the complainant must present facts and arguments suggesting that the organization violated EEO law. Next, the organization must present its own evidence that rebuts that charge. Then the complainant is given further opportunity to attack the organization's evidence. The chronology of events at the trial may not follow that sequence precisely, but the evidence can usually be sorted out that way by the judge when the trial is over.

Exhibit 2.7 presents a brief outline of the required sequence of evidence, as drawn from various EEO court cases. The left-hand column shows the sequence for disparate treatment cases. The disparate treatment column was set forth by the U.S. Supreme Court in *McDonnell-Douglas* v. *Green*,[53] a case in which a black employee was terminated for participating

**Exhibit 2.7**    Evidence and Proof in Title VII Cases

| *Burden of Proof* | *Disparate Treatment* | *Disparate Impact* |
|---|---|---|
| 1. Plaintiff's* (prima facie case) | He or she belongs to the discriminated-against group<br>He or she applied and was qualified<br>He or she was rejected<br>The position remained open to applicants with equal or fewer qualifications | Unequal impact of the practice in question<br>Does the practice have equal impact on the groups in question?<br>Are the groups in question adequately represented in the organization's workforce? |
| 2. Defendant's | A "legitimate, nondiscriminatory reason" for the rejection | Business necessity<br>Job relatedness |
| 3. Plaintiff's | Stated reason is pretext:<br>Does the employer apply that reason to all?<br>Was the prior treatment of the plaintiff fair?<br>Are the employer's general employment practices nondiscriminatory? | A less discriminatory alternative practice does exist |

* Plaintiff's initial burden may differ from case to case depending on the type of discrimination alleged.

in an illegal protest activity against the company. The upper left-hand area of Exhibit 2.7 shows the facts that the plaintiff must prove. In most cases, proving them is a straightforward matter. Once they are proven, the plaintiff is said to have established a prima facie case of discrimination, and the burden of proof shifts to the defendant. The middle area in the left column shows what the defendant must do then in order to shift the burden back. Note that all the defendant must do is state a legitimate nondiscriminatory reason for treating the employee in the way it did.[54] Essentially, that means that the employer must state an objective reason besides race or sex. Finally, in the lower left-hand area, the plaintiff is given the opportunity to show that the defendant's reason is actually a pretext for discrimination, by presenting evidence of other discriminatory treatment by the employer, either against the plaintiff personally or against the plaintiff's group in general.

For disparate impact cases, the main source of principles regarding evidence and proof is the *Griggs* case, which has been reviewed already. While evidence of the employer's motives is important in disparate treatment cases, it is generally irrelevant in cases of disparate impact such as *Griggs*. The key holding of *Griggs* regarding evidence and proof, already quoted above, is the following statement: "If an employment practice which operates to exclude Negroes cannot be shown to be related to job performance, the practice is prohibited." Thus the plaintiff can establish a prima facie case and shift the burden of proof to the defendant by showing that the practice has disparate impact, or "operates to exclude" his or her group. Many cases are decided entirely on such evidence regarding adverse impact, as discussed in Chapter 5.

However, the defendant can rebut a prima facie case by showing that the practice in question is job related or a matter of business necessity. The nature of job-relatedness evidence is also discussed in Chapter 5. Finally, as shown in the lower right-hand area of Exhibit 2.7, the plaintiff can defeat the defendant's rebuttal by showing that there is an alternative practice that will serve the employer's interest with less of an adverse impact on the plaintiff's group.[55]

The manager's role in all of this is to examine evidence before the organization is sued. A simplified strategy is:

1. Look for evidence of race, sex, and ethnic disparities in staffing by examining who was hired or promoted in comparison to who was available (see Chapter 5).

2. Identify the employment practice responsible for each disparity.
3. Determine whether the practice is job related (see Chapter 5).
4. If the practice is not job related, eliminate it.

Those four steps gloss over innumerable complexities, many of which are discussed in Chapter 5. But they do indicate the basic relevance of evidence and proof to the manager.


## Has EEO Legislation Worked?

Considering the momentous social and economic problems that led the lawmakers to pass EEO laws, it seems appropriate to ask whether those laws have succeeded in improving economic conditions for the traditional victims of discrimination. A partial answer to that question was provided in August 1978, by the United States Commission on Civil Rights, which examined changes in the economic and employment picture during the time that EEO laws were in effect.[56] The commission found that the disparities between minority and nonminority and between men and women had generally gotten *worse* for the victims of discrimination during the period. While there were a few small bright spots, the overall picture was undeniably dismal in most all respects: unemployment, occupational mobility, earnings, and prospects for economic advancement. To be sure, things may have gotten bad for white males, but they got worse for nonwhites and females; the discriminated-against groups were further behind white males after a decade or more of EEO regulation.

One cannot say that EEO laws have done no good—the picture may have been even worse without those laws. But clearly there is cause for concern. Why hasn't EEO legislation done what its creators wanted it to do? Three possible explanations come to mind.

First, some say the laws are too weak. Even though most managers feel the government has too much power already, results like the ones to date are an incentive for Congress to grant even more power to the EEO agencies to bring about improvements. Thus Title VII was strengthened, and the EEOC given more power, in 1972 and again in 1978.

Second, the EEO agencies are (or were) disorganized. Not too long ago, the EEOC had a mountainous backlog of as many as 150,000 unresolved discrimination charges. Charges took years to be investigated. During such long periods, records got lost and memories faded, making it hard for investigators to determine how justifiable the original charges were. When the agency sought to clear away some of the backlog, its employee union complained this was a speed-up and forced employees to violate the law in processing the cases too hastily. Each year, the agency tried to deal with the backlog by requesting sharp increases in its budget. Besides that problem, critics claimed that investigations were not conducted competently enough to uncover all information.

The OFCCP had its own problems. It used to delegate its compliance review authority to thirteen other agencies. Not surprisingly, contractors complained of conflicting agency regulations.[57] Moreover, the principal purpose of the thirteen agencies was something other than ensuring equal employment. For instance, the Department of Defense's EEO operation was housed in the bureau that was principally responsible for making sure that defense contracting was carried out well, that the right goods and services were delivered at the right time. Undue concern with EEO can impede contract fulfillment. Predictably, then, EEO was not an overriding concern in some delegate agencies.[58]

Fortunately, some changes have been made. In 1977, a new chairperson of the EEOC, Eleanor Holmes Norton, initiated major changes designed to speed up the processing of discrimination charges and eliminate the backlog. Then in 1978, President Carter issued an executive order reorganizing the entire EEO establishment. That order took the compliance review authority over affirmative action away from the thirteen agencies and gave it back to the OFCCP, and it gave authority over age discrimination, equal pay cases, and EEO for federal employees to the EEOC. These changes may make the EEO agencies more efficient—and they may also make them more effective in cracking down on employers.

The third explanation for the failure of EEO legislation is that the EEO agencies allegedly do not know what they are doing. In many respects, EEO is a technical area, and some critics have said that the EEO agencies' ignorance of the technicalities has led to enforcement that is ineffective or worse. For example, the agencies examine evidence in a way that leads them to dwell on the supposed sins of small employers to the neglect of large employers.[59] Spending time on small employers is certainly not the most efficient way to close the economic gap between minorities and whites. Also, the employee selection guidelines adopted by the agencies have made employers so fearful of employment tests that they turn to selection methods that are less accurate in identifying the best candidates.[60] The result is that the people selected (women and minorities included) are more likely to be failures on the job. In a related area, the agencies have inadvertently adopted some technically complex regulations (called "fairness" standards, discussed on page 112) that would have a devastating impact on *black* employment if employers were to treat those regulations seriously.[61]

If anything can be concluded from the discussion of the effectiveness of EEO regulation, it is that equality is difficult to achieve in the world of work—at least without some very basic and drastic solutions that the government has thus far failed to effect. It remains to be seen whether drastic solutions such as quotas, agency reorganizations, and more powerful new laws will succeed in achieving the ends that the lawmakers have had in mind for EEO. It is the author's belief, however, that any optimism in that matter should be tempered by the realization that, thus far, Murphy's Law has worked all too well in EEO.

## Further Information on EEO

The number of information sources on EEO is imposing, but it might be helpful to enumerate just a few of them here. Among the more comprehensive EEO textbooks is Barbara L. Schlei and Paul Grossman's *Employment Discrimination Law* (1976), along with the *1979 Supplement* to that work. Also, most EEO specialists use one of the comprehensive EEO subscription information services offered by certain legal publishers, such as the *Fair Employment Practice* series, published by the Bureau of National Affairs, and the *Employment Practices Guide,* published by Commerce Clearing House. Subscribers to those services are given loose-leaf volumes of statutes, regulations, court opinions, and interpretations of the law. New material is periodically sent to subscribers, who add it to their loose-leaf binders, discarding whatever materials are obsolete. As court cases accumulate, the publishers send bound volumes of them, so that subscribers can remove the loose-leaf issues of opinions from their binders to make room for the constant stream of new ones.

Among the periodicals that cover EEO are *Employee Relations Law Journal* and *Labor Law Journal.* In addition, hundreds of periodical law reviews offer interpretive articles on EEO as well as other areas of the law. A useful guide to the law reviews is the *Index to Legal Periodicals.* Finally, many business periodicals, particularly in the area of personnel, frequently publish articles on various aspects of EEO compliance.

# Notes

1. *Griggs* v. *Duke Power Co.*, 401 U.S. 424 (1971).

2. Civil Rights Act of 1964, Title VII, Secs. 701(a), 702, and 703(i).

3. (September 24, 1965) as amended by Executive Order 11375 (October 13, 1967) and Executive Order 12086 (October 8, 1978).

4. Executive Order 11246, Sec. 202(1).

5. James Ledvinka and Hugh J. Watson, "Processing of Discrimination Charges by EEOC," *Journal of Business Research* 3 (1976):149–56; Barbara Lindemann Schlei and Paul Grossman, *Employment Discrimination Law* (Washington, D.C.: Bureau of National Affairs, 1976), chap. 26.

6. Schlei and Grossman, *Employment Discrimination Law*.

7. Ibid.

8. Title VII, Sec. 706(b).

9. Ibid., Sec. 713.

10. Ibid., Sec. 705(g)(3).

11. 29 Code of Federal Regulations, Part 1607.

12. 29 Code of Federal Regulations, Part 1604.

13. The current guidelines are at 29 Code of Federal Regulations, Part 1607.

14. *Griggs* v. *Duke Power Co.*

15. Equal Employment Opportunity Commission, *Legislative History of Titles VII and XI of Civil Rights Act of 1964* (Washington, D.C.: Government Printing Office, 1968).

16. George Simpson and J. Milton Yinger, *Racial and Cultural Minorities,* 3rd ed. (New York: Harper & Row, 1965), pp. 268–69, 274–75.

17. Charles Silbermann, *Crisis in Black and White* (New York: Random House, 1964), p. 37.

18. St. Clair Drake, "The Social and Economic Status of the Negro in the United States," in Talcott Parsons and Kenneth B. Clark, eds., *The Negro American* (Boston: Houghton Mifflin, 1966), pp. 3–46.

19. Simpson and Yinger, *Racial and Cultural Minorities.*

20. *Legislative History of Titles VII and XI,* p. 3072.

21. Ibid., p. 3092.

22. Ibid., p. 10.

23. Ibid., p. 3009ff.

24. Ibid., p. 3042–43.

25. Ibid., p. 2148ff.

26. For example, see Alfred W. Blumrosen, "Strangers in Paradise: *Griggs* v. *Duke Power Co.* and the Concept of Employment Discrimination," *Michigan Law Review,* 71 (1972):59–111.

27. *Legislative History of Titles VII and XI,* p. 3045.

28. Ibid.

29. Ibid., p. 6.

30. George Cooper, Harriet Rabb, and Howard J. Rubin, *Fair Employment Litigation* (St. Paul, Minn.: West, 1975).

31. *Legislative History of Titles VII and XI,* p. 6.

32. Ibid., p. 3015.

33. Schlei and Grossman, *Employment Discrimination Law,* p. 1.

34. "Employment Discrimination and Title VII of the Civil Rights Act of 1964," *Harvard Law Review* 84 (March 1971):1109–1316.

35. Blumrosen, "Strangers in Paradise."

36. *Local 189, Papermakers & Paperworkers* v. *U.S.*, 416 F.2d 980 (5th Cir. 1969). Also se Quarles v. *Philip Morris, Inc.*, 279 F.Supp. 505 (E.D. Va., 1968); *Robinson* v. *Lorillard Corp.*, 44 F.2d 791, 3 FEP 653 (4th Cir.), *cert. denied*, 404 U.S. 1006 (1971).

37. *Griggs* v. *Duke Power Co.* at n. 6. Also see *Albemarle Paper Co.* v. *Moody*, 422 U.S 405, 10 FEP 1181 (1975); *Washington* v. *Davis*, 426 U.S. 229, 12 FEP 1415 (1976); *Townsend* v *Nassau County Medical Center*, 558 F.2d 117, 15 FEP 237 (2d Cir. 1977), *cert. denied*, 434 U.S 1015 (1978).

38. Ivar Berg, *Education and Jobs: The Great Training Robbery* (New York: Praeger, 1970)

39. *Griggs* v. *Duke Power Co.*, pp. 429–30.

40. Ibid., p. 42 and n. 6.

41. Ibid., pp. 430–431.

42. Ibid., p. 431.

43. Ibid., p. 432.

44. Ibid., p. 433.

45. Equal Employment Opportunity Commission, Guidelines on Employment Testir Procedures, August 24, 1966.

46. *Griggs* v. *Duke Power Co.*, pp. 435–36 and n. 12.

47. *Green* v. *Missouri Pacific R.R. Co.*, 523 F.2d 1290 (8th Cir. 1975).

48. Uniform Guidelines on Employee Selection Procedures, 29 Code of Federal Regula tions, Part 1607.

49. *Spurlock* v. *United Airlines*, 475 F.2d 216 (10th Cir. 1972), pp. 218–19. Also see *Cast* v. *Beecher*, 459, F.2d 725 4 FEP 700 (1st Cir. 1972).

50. For example, see *King* v. *New Hampshire Department of Resources and Economic Deve opment*, 562 F.2d 80 (1st Cir. 1977); *Smith* v. *Union Oil Co. of California, Inc.*, 17 FEP Cases 96 (N.D. Cal. 1977); *Rowe* v. *General Motors Corp.*, 467 F.2d 348 (5th Cir. 1972); and Chap. 6 of Schlei and Grossman, *Employment Discrimination Law*.

51. Hubert S. Feild and William H. Holley, "The Relationship of Performance Apprais System Characteristics to Verdicts in Selected Employment Discrimination Cases," unpublishe manuscript. Also see Laurence S. Kleiman and Richard L. Durham, "Performance Appraisa Promotion and the Courts: A Critical Review," *Personnel Psychology* 34 (1981):102–21.

52. Robert D. Gatewood and James Ledvinka, "Selection Interviewing and EEO: Manda for Objectivity," *The Personnel Administrator* 21, no. 4 (1976):15–18.

53. *McDonnell-Douglas* v. *Green*, 411 U.S. 972 (1973).

54. Ibid.

55. *Albemarle Paper Co.* v. *Moody*, 422 U.S. 407 (1975).

56. U.S. Commission on Civil Rights, *Social Indicators of Equality for Minorities and Wome* August 1978.

57. U.S. Commission on Civil Rights, *The Federal Civil Rights Enforcement Effort—197* vol. V, *To Eliminate Employment Discrimination*, July 1975.

58. Ibid.

59. See chap. 5 for a discussion of the agencies' four-fifths rule.

60. Hal Lancaster, "Job Tests Are Dropped by Many Companies Due to Antibias Drive *Wall Street Journal*, September 3, 1976, pp. 1, 19; James Ledvinka and Lyle F. Schoenfeldt, "Leg Developments in Employment Testing: *Albemarle* and Beyond," *Personnel Psychology* 3 (1978):1–13.

61. James Ledvinka, "The Statistical Definition of Fairness in The Federal Selectio Guidelines and Its Implications for Minority Employment," *Personnel Psychology* 32 (1979):551–6.

# 3

# Sex Discrimination

*Case 3.1*   An airline refused to hire men as flight attendants. When challenged in court by a male applicant, the airline pointed to section 703(e) of Title VII and claimed that sex was a "bona fide occupational qualification" for the position of flight attendant. As evidence, the airline offered the following:

1. *Passenger preference:* surveys showed that passengers preferred women to men as cabin attendants.

2. *Psychological needs:* a clinical psychologist testified that women, simply because they were women, could provide comfort and reassurance to passengers better than men could.

3. *Feasibility:* an industrial psychologist testified that sex was the best practicable screening device to use in determining whom to hire for the position.

*Case 3.2*   The manager was confronted with a large room packed with applicants for only a handful of openings. To screen out some of the people, he announced that all the women with pre–school-age children should go home. One of those sent home filed a charge of sex discrimination. The company responded by saying that it did not discriminate against women; in fact, many women worked at the facility in question. It was only women with young children that the company preferred not to hire, because child care responsibilities often interfered with work responsibilities.

Therefore, the company said since it did not discriminate because of sex, it had not violated Title VII.

***Case 3.3***    A major electrical equipment manufacturing concern offered its employees a disability insurance plan. The plan excluded disabilities due to pregnancy. The purpose of the exclusion was to make the insurance plan affordable. Even with the exclusion, the benefit payout per employee was higher for women than for men. Still, a group of women employees who had suffered pregnancy-related disabilities and were refused benefits filed charges of sex discrimination.

***Case 3.4***    Because women live longer than men, a city government required its women employees to contribute more than men each month to its retirement fund. The contributions were arranged so that women contributed in proportion to their expected benefits, as did men. The resulting system allowed equal monthly retirement benefits to men and women without having either sex subsidize the other. Several women employees complained that the unequal contributions constituted sex discrimination.

***Case 3.5***    Sexual advances toward female employees were standard operating procedure in a government agency. In one instance, a female employee was propositioned first by a fellow employee, and later by her own first-line supervisor, who asked her to join him at a motel and on a trip to the Bahamas. Even her second-line supervisor constantly called her into his office to request she spend the afternoon with him at his apartment and to question her about her sexual proclivities. She rejected all those advances, and she complained about them to the general manager, who supervised both her first-line supervisor and her second-line supervisor. The general manager casually dismissed her complaints, saying that "any man in his right mind would want to rape you." Then he himself proceeded to proposition her, and she turned him down. Later, she learned that she had lost a promotion for which she was eligible. At that, she filed a Title VII lawsuit against the agency. In its defense, the agency claimed that:

1.  Title VII prohibits discrimination because of biological sex only, not discrimination because of refusal to submit to sexual advances.
2.  Even so, there was no evidence that refusal to submit to sexual advances was the cause of her losing the promotion. The complainant lost the promotion because her performance ratings were too low—nobody at the agency took the sexual games seriously enough to make them a basis for personnel decisions.

Although most of the situations discussed in Chapter 2 concerned race discrimination, the principles of Chapter 2 apply to all forms of discrimi-ation; in fact, Chapter 2 is basic to all EEO regulation. Still, certain types f discrimination raise special concerns, and those concerns are addressed n this chapter and the next. Both chapters presume a thorough familiarity /ith the material of Chapter 2. Chapter 3 examines some additional points hat are essential to an understanding of sex discrimination law. Chapter covers discrimination based on age, religion, and handicap, plus some ictors that are unique to EEO regulation of state and local government mployees.

## Chapter Objectives

This chapter discusses three major themes of importance to sex discrimi-ation law:

1. The unusual congressional history underlying the inclusion of sex as one of the prohibited classifications in Title VII

2. The stubborn persistence of overt discrimination against women—blatant definition 1 discrimination (disparate treatment) that would be unthinkable today if it were directed against blacks or other minorities

3. The legal status of some prime examples of disparate treatment: sex as a job requirement; "sex-plus" discrimination (discriminating against a subset of women rather than against all women); employment practices based on generalizations about differences between the sexes; and sexual harassment

The last, sexual harassment, is currently a major management concern. It s also an area of regulation that has produced some relatively specific uidelines for management. Therefore, it is discussed in greater detail than he other three types of disparate treatment because of sex.

## Legislative History

The first question to consider about sex discrimination is how it came to e included in Title VII. As we saw in Chapter 2, civil rights activity was major force behind Title VII. But in those days civil rights did not include vomen's rights. Widespread concern over that issue was to come some years later. There was a lot more joking about women's rights then than there is now, and fewer people regarded the issue seriously. What, then motivated Congress to include sex in its list of illegal classifications?

Lest the reader jump to the conclusion that Congress was uncharacteristically ahead of its time in outlawing sex discrimination, it is important to point out that the prohibition against sex discrimination was proposed as an amendment to the civil rights bill by Representative Howard K. Smith of Virginia, a legislator who was no friend of civil rights:

> Mr. Smith of Virginia: Mr. Chairman, this amendment is offered to the fair employment practices title of this bill to include within our desire to prevent discrimination against another minority group, the women, but a very essential minority group, in the absence of which the majority group would not be here today. . . . [T]o show you how some of the ladies feel about discrimination against them, I want to read you an extract from a letter that I received the other day. This lady has a real grievance on behalf of the minority sex . . . :
>
> "I suggest that you might also favor an amendment or a bill to correct the present 'imbalance' which exists between males and females in the United States. Just why the Creator would set up such an imbalance of spinsters, shutting off the 'right' of every female to have a husband of her own, is, of course, known only to nature. But I am sure you will agree that this is a grave injustice."
>
> And I do agree, and I am reading you the letter because I want all the rest of you to agree, you of the majority.[1]

Smith insisted that he was serious about his amendment.[2] But it is important to realize that amendments to congressional bills are voted on before the main bill. If an amendment is passed, then the main bill is voted on as amended. So, perhaps civil rights opponents like Smith thought that if they could convince enough legislators to pass the amendment, then they could later convince enough legislators that the amendment made the main bill too foolish to pass as a whole.

Indeed, the amendment did attract some support from civil rights opponents, but it also was supported, as may have been expected, by women's rights advocates in Congress:

> [Mrs. Griffiths:] Mr. Chairman, I presume that if there had been any necessity to have pointed out that women were a second-class sex, the laughter would have proved it.
>
> Mr. Chairman, I rise in support of the amendment primarily because I feel as a white woman when this bill has passed this House and the Senate and has been signed by the President that white women will be last at the hiring gate.

In his great work "The American Dilemma," the Swedish sociologist pointed out 20 years ago that white women and Negroes occupied relatively the same position in American society.[3]

ut the amendment also drew opposition from supporters of civil rights. ome were in favor of women's rights but feared that the amendment ould subvert the main purpose of eradicating race discrimination:

> [Mrs. Green of Oregon:] I wish to say first to the gentleman who offered this amendment and to others who by their applause I am sure are giving strong support to it that I, for one, welcome the conversion, because I remember when we were working on the equal pay bill that, if I correctly understand the mood of the House, those gentlemen of the House who are most strong in their support of women's rights this afternoon, probably gave us the most opposition when we considered the bill which would grant equal pay for equal work just a very few months ago. I say I welcome the conversion and hope it is of long duration.
>
> . . . .
>
> After I have said all of this Mr. Chairman, I honestly cannot support the amendment. For every discrimination that has been made against a woman in this country there has been 10 times as much discrimination against the Negro of this country. . . .
>
> . . . As much as I hope the day will come when discrimination will be ended against women, I really and sincerely hope that this amendment will not be added to this bill. It will clutter up the bill and it may later very well be used to help destroy this section of the bill by some of the very people who today support it. And I hope that no other amendment will be added to this bill on sex or age or anything else, that would jeopardize our primary purpose in any way.[4]

)thers seemed to have some traditional reluctance about granting equal ights to men and women:

> Mr. Celler: You know, the French have a phrase for it when they speak of women and men. When they speak of the difference, they say "vive la différence."
>
> I think the French are right.
>
> Imagine the upheaval that would result from adoption of blanket language requiring total equality. Would male citizens be justified in insisting that women share with them the burdens of compulsory military service? What would become of traditional family relationships? What about alimony? Who would have the obligation of supporting whom? Would fathers rank equally with mothers in the right of custody to children? What would become of the

crimes of rape and statutory rape? Would the Mann Act be invalidated? Would the many State and local provisions regulating working conditions and hours of employment for women be struck down?

You know the biological differences between the sexes. In many States we have laws favorable to women. Are you going to strike those laws down? This is the entering wedge, an amendment of this sort. The list of foreseeable consequences, I will say to the committee, is unlimited.[5]

Of course, Smith's amendment passed, but it failed to sabotage the main bill. Women's rights advocates joined civil rights opponents to pass the amendment, then joined civil rights advocates to pass the entire bill, amendment and all. Thus it was a series of ironies that led Congress to outlaw sex discrimination well ahead of public concern over the problem.

## Types of Sex Discrimination

Just as concern over sex discrimination lagged behind concern over race discrimination when Title VII was being debated in Congress, so it does today. Practices and attitudes that would be unthinkable if directed toward blacks are frequently directed against women, as we shall see. In general, sex discrimination is socially acceptable in quarters where race discrimination is not. The amusement that greeted Representative Smith's amendment indicated a lack of seriousness about sex discrimination that prevails in some places to this day.

Several factors account for the persistence of sex discrimination; they go far beyond the scope of a book on federal regulation. Suffice it to say that sex differences are very much a part of the way we look at the world from birth, so it should not be surprising that we bring those ways of looking at the world into the world of work. That is not to say that race differences are not also a part of peoples' perceptual apparatus. But our perceptions of race begin at a later age than do our perceptions of sex, and clearly race differences do not order our lives in the same way that sex differences do.

In sum, then, people develop habitual ways of viewing sex differences from an early age, and those habits die hard. Thus stereotypes about women and men at work are commonplace, while race stereotypes are socially unacceptable and generally taken to be a mark of ignorance on the part of those who harbor them.

Consequently, sex discrimination in employment is generally more blatant than race discrimination. Sex discrimination is often overt; race discrimination often takes the form of neutral practices (such as tests and educational requirements) that screen out black candidates disproportionately but have no effect on women. In the terms of Exhibit 2.5, sex discrimination is more likely to involve disparate treatment, while race discrimination is more likely to involve disparate impact without disparate treatment. In recent years it has become unacceptable to single out blacks for different treatment in the world of work, but habits of thought regarding sex difference are more ingrained, so there is less reluctance at the idea of singling out women. The forms of sex discrimination below are typical instances of disparate treatment based on sex.

### Sex as a Job Requirement

Total exclusion of one sex from employment is the clearest form of sex discrimination. Yet the "bona fide occupational qualification" (BFOQ) clause of Title VII (see section 703(e) in Exhibit 2.3) suggests that Congress wanted to allow employers to engage in such discrimination whenever it is "reasonably necessary to the normal operation" of the organization. The BFOQ clause can be regarded as a loophole in Title VII. But how big is that loophole?

To answer that question, it is necessary to define BFOQ. Congressional debate over section 703(e) provides some insight regarding the situations that legislators felt would justify the exclusion of one sex:

> [Mr. Goodell:] There are so many instances where the matter of sex is a bona fide occupational qualification. For instance, I think of an elderly woman who wants a female nurse. There are many things of this nature which are bona fide occupational qualifications, and it seems to me they would be properly considered here as an exception.[6]

The legislators wanted to make it clear that Representative Smith's amendment adding sex to the list of illegal classifications in Title VII could not be interpreted as prohibiting certain well-established practices:

> [Mr. Multer:] Will this [sex discrimination] amendment permit a man to get maternity leave at the same time as his working wife gets it? When we come to hire a masseur in the gymnasium of the House or the Senate, will we be justified

in saying, when a woman applies for the job, that a "masseuse" qualifies as a "masseur"?

. . . .

[Mrs. Green of Oregon:] For example, under the amendment offered by the gentleman from Virginia [Mr. Smith], if a college wanted to hire a dean of women they would be prohibited from advertising and interviewing just women for this position, because it would be discrimination based on sex. Or if a college wanted to hired a dean of men, they would be prohibited under the language adopted from advertising or interviewing just men for this position because it also would be discrimination based on sex. Let us take another example: In a large hospital an elderly woman needs special round-the-clock nursing. Her family is seeking to find a fully qualified registered nurse. It does not make any difference to this family if the nurse is a white or a Negro or a Chinese or a Japanese if she is fully qualified. But it does make a great deal of difference to this elderly woman and her family as to whether this qualified nurse is a man or a woman.[7]

Thus sex was included in the list of allowable bona fide occupational qualifications.

To interpret section 703(e), it is important first of all to distinguish between the BFOQ exemption of 703(e) and the job-relatedness defense that was opened to management by the *Griggs* opinion. The BFOQ exemption allows management to engage in disparate *treatment* of men and women by overtly excluding one sex; the job-relatedness defense only allows disparate *impact.* Naturally, the courts expect management to offer better reasons for an outright exclusion of one group than they require for a neutral practice that happens to affect that group more adversely than another group.

Therefore, section 703(e) does not allow management automatically to indulge traditional notions of what work is appropriate for men or for women. For instance, management cannot exclude women from heavy manual labor or from hardware sales positions because those are traditionally men's positions; similarly management cannot exclude men from secretarial or cosmetic sales positions because such work is traditionally done by women. Generally, management bears a heavy burden of justification for any policy of excluding one sex or the other for any position.

Consider Case 3.1. Nowadays such a policy seems clearly illegal, but it did not seem so in 1970 when the case was tried in court (*Diaz* v. *Pan American Airways*).[8] In fact, the district court upheld the airline. It wasn't until the case was appealed that the practice was struck down.[9] The appeals court identified two possible justifications that might allow an organization to exclude one sex: First, the essence of the business requires the exclusion. The appeals court said:

> We begin with the proposition that the use of the word "necessary" in section 703(e) requires that we apply a business necessity test, not a business convenience test. That is to say, discrimination based on sex is valid only when the essence of the business operation would be undermined by not hiring members of one sex exclusively.
>
> The primary function of an airline is to transport passengers safely from one point to another. While a pleasant environment, enhanced by the obvious cosmetic effect that female stewardesses provide as well as, according to the finding of the trial court, their apparent ability to perform the non-mechanical functions of the job in a more effective manner than most men, may all be important, they are tangential to the essence of the business involved.[10]

The second possible justification for excluding one sex is that all or substantially all members of one sex are unable to perform adequately. The appeals court said:

> We do not mean to imply, of course, that Pan Am cannot take into consideration the ability of individuals to perform the non-mechanical functions of the job. What we hold is that because the non-mechanical aspects of the job of flight cabin attendant are not "reasonably necessary to the normal operation" of Pan Am's business, Pan Am cannot exclude all males simply because most males may not perform adequately.
>
> . . . We do not agree that in this case "all or substantially all men" have been shown to be inadequate.[11]

In summarizing its finding, the court said:

> Before sex discrimination can be practiced, it must not only be shown that it is impracticable to find the men that possess the abilities that most women possess, but that the abilities are necessary to the business, not merely tangential.[12]

The fact that the court stressed the importance of making judgments about people as individuals rather than as members of one of the prohibited classifications is revealing. It indicates a general judicial antipathy toward the denial of opportunities to individuals based on generalizations about the group of which they are members. All this means that the BFOQ exemption of 703(e) is very limited indeed.

## Sex-Plus Discrimination

Another type of discrimination that was openly practiced in the early days of EEO enforcement was the exclusion not of one sex entirely, but of a subset of one sex: "sex plus" some other attribute disqualified a person. Case 3.2 provides an example.[13] Intuition correctly tells us that the practice of refusing women with small children is illegal. The important thing, however, is the logic that makes it so: by imposing a prerequisite (no young children) on women that was not imposed on men, the company "classified" applicants in a way that "would deprive or tend to deprive" women of employment opportunities.[14]

Case 3.3 presents another form of sex-plus discrimination: discrimination against pregnant women. As recently as 1976, the Supreme Court ruled that such an exclusion was lawful under Title VII,[15] reasoning that the employer could lawfully choose not to cover a certain risk in its insurance plans, even if that risk happened to be experienced by women only. But the U.S. Congress overruled the court in 1978 by amending Title VII's definition of sex:

> The terms "because of sex" or "on the basis of sex" include, but are not limited to, because of or on the basis of pregnancy, childbirth or related medical conditions; and women affected by pregnancy, childbirth, or related medical conditions shall be treated the same for all employment-related purposes, including receipt of benefits under fringe benefit programs, as other persons not so affected but similar in their ability or inability to work.[16]

That simple provision has necessitated changes in certain employee benefit plans. Medical insurance for employees must cover pregnancy as fully as it covers other medical conditions, of course. And if the insurance covers spouses, then it must cover spouses' pregnancies—otherwise, married male employees would be at a disadvantage. But the insurance does not have to cover pregnancies of non-spouse dependents, for male and female *employees* are equally likely to have female non-spouse dependents, and Title VII governs employment only.[17] All things considered, the pregnancy discrimination amendments to Title VII have increased the cost of employee benefit plans. And, perversely, by increasing the insurance premiums for such benefit plans, the amendments tend to penalize employers who pursue vigorous affirmative action programs for women.[18]

The reason it is important to understand the logic that makes sex-plus discrimination illegal is that such discrimination is surprisingly prevalent even today. Although the forms it now takes are not as egregious as the example in Case 3.2, they do deprive women of employment opportunities. For example, an employer in a college town who is hiring for responsible positions with good choices for career advancement might refuse to hire wives of students, for fear that they would leave when their husbands graduated. Note that the policy is not directed against all women, just a subset of women. But also note that the policy does not exclude husbands of students, presumably because management figures that a man would be more likely to stay around after the spouse's graduation to keep a good job than would a woman. Here again, a generalization is being made about the likely behavior of women as compared with men under the same circumstances. It too is illegal.

## Generalizations Based on Sex

Generalizations are a basic part of personnel selection. When an organization hires an applicant because of that applicant's previous experience, it is implicitly making a generalization about people with that experience. When a manager considering candidates for promotion examines the job performance ratings of those candidates, he or she implicitly assumes that people with higher performance ratings in their present jobs will do better in jobs for which they are being considered—a generalization about employees with high performance ratings. Many valid generalizations guide personnel decisions, so an absolute legal prohibition of decision based on generalizations would be unthinkable.

Only certain kinds of generalizations are illegal—those based on one of the illegal classifications. Generalizations about race, color, sex, religion, and national origin are the only ones prohibited by Title VII. Probably the most common example of illegal generalizations are those based on sex, such as those in Cases 3.1 and 3.2. To use a person's sex as a basis for deciding whether to hire that person is clearly a form of unequal treatment based on sex, illegal definition 1 discrimination (see Exhibit 2.5).

What happens when the generalizations based on sex are valid? Case 3.4 presents an example that used to be commonplace. It is true that women, on the average, live longer than men. Consequently, if men and women retire at the same age and receive the same monthly retirement income, women will collect more retirement income than men will. The employer in Case 3.4 instituted its policy of requiring women employees to contribute more to the retirement fund so that the ultimate retirement payouts to men and women would be equalized.

In a sense, the organization in Case 3.4 was damned if it did and damned if it didn't. If it adopted the challenged policy, it engaged in disparate *treatment* of men and women by requiring unequal contributions from them during the time they were active employees. On the other hand, if the organization required equal contributions from men and women employees, it arguably engaged in a practice having adverse *impact* on men, in that the ultimate payment of retirement income resulted in women receiving a higher lifetime income than men received. The U.S. Supreme Court resolved Case 3.4 in a straightforward way: it affirmed that unequal *treatment* is illegal regardless of the validity of the generalization upon which it is based. The case, *Los Angeles* v. *Manhart,* is worth quoting at length:

> It is now well recognized that employment decisions cannot be predicated on mere "stereotyped" impressions about the characteristics of males or females. Myths and purely habitual assumptions about a woman's inability to perform certain kinds of work are no longer acceptable reasons for refusing to employ qualified individuals, or for paying them less. This case does not, however, involve a fictional difference between men and women. It involves a generalization that the parties accept as unquestionably true; women, as a class, do live longer than men. The Department treated its women employees differently from its men employees because the two classes are in fact different. It is equally true, however, that all individuals in the respective classes do not share the characteristic which differentiates the average class representatives. Many women do not live as long as the average man and many men outlive the average woman. The question, therefore, is whether the existence or nonexistence of "discrimination" is to be determined by comparison of class characteristics or individual characteristics. . . .
>
> The statute makes it unlawful "to discriminate against any *individual* with respect to his compensation, terms, conditions or privileges of employment, because of such *individual's* race, color, religion, sex, or national origin." . . . (emphasis added). The statute's focus on the individual is unambiguous. It precludes treatment of individuals as simply components of a racial, religious, sexual, or national class. [19]

The significance of those observations is, first, that the U.S. Supreme Court has made all the animated managerial discussion about sex differences in employment legally irrelevant. Managers cannot use even facts about sex differences as a basis for employment decision making. It is common to encounter assertions that women are less aggressive than men, more inclined to absenteeism problems, more tied to their spouses' jobs, and the like. Some managers, citing research as well as personal observation, strenuously assert that such generalizations are based on fact. But it is illegal for managers to operate on the basis of those generalizations, valid or not.

## Sexual Harassment

No other area of EEO is of greater current concern than sexual harassment, and no other area has changed as much recently. Like the other forms of sex discrimination discussed in this chapter, sexual harassment is a form of disparate treatment. Yet sexual harassment situations differ legally from the others. With sexual harassment there are often two new arguments in the employer's favor, as Case 3.5 illustrates. One argument is that the "discrimination" involved in situations such as Case 3.5 is not really based on sex, but on refusal to submit to sexual advances. Second, in sexual harassment cases there is often insufficient evidence that the employer actually did retaliate in any tangible way against those who refused to submit, so the employer can argue that the complainant's employment was not really affected by the harassment.

Those two features seem to present obstacles to complainants in sexual harassment cases. But recently it has appeared that the obstacles can be overcome. Thus it is important to specify what defines unlawful sexual harassment in the eyes of the courts. The following discussion addresses that point, then it turns to the question of what actions management should take regarding the problem of sexual harassment.

***What Is Unlawful Sexual Harassment?***   The first of the two defenses raised in Case 3.5 is predicated on the fact that the word "sex" in Title VII means gender or biological sex, which is true. Then the argument is that the discrimination in question is not "because of sex," but because of refusal to submit to the sexual advances. This would mean that sexual harassment is not a violation of Title VII, no matter how reprehensible it might be.

The courts have rejected that line of reasoning, ruling against employers in several cases. The logic is stated clearly in *Barnes* v. *Costle*:

> But for her womanhood, . . . her participation in sexual activity would never have been solicited. To say, then, that she was victimized in her employment simply because she declined the invitation is to ignore the asserted fact that she

was invited only because she was a woman subordinate to the inviter in the hierarchy of agency personnel. Put another way, she became the target of her superior's sexual desires because she was a woman, and was asked to bow to his demands as the price for holding her job. The circumstances imparting high visibility to the role of gender in the affair is that no male employee was susceptible to such an approach by appellant's supervisor. [footnotes omitted][20]

The "but for her womanhood" logic establishes sexual harassment as a form of sex discrimination.

However, the employer in Case 3.5 also argued that, since there was no provable connection between the harassment and the failure to promote, then there was no proof that harassment had any tangible effect on employment, and hence no proof of a Title VII violation. On that issue the authorities are divided. Some courts have looked for a clear connection before ruling against an employer. For example, in a case involving an employee who was obviously terminated for refusing to submit to sexual advances, the court said:

A cause of action does not arise from an isolated incident or a mere flirtation. These may be more properly characterized as an attempt to establish personal relationships than an endeavor to tie employment to sexual submission. Title VII should not be interpreted as reaching into sexual relationships which may arise during the course of employment, but which do not have a substantial effect on that employment.

. . . .

Title VII does not concern itself with sexual liaisons among men and women working for the same employer. Title VII does, however, become involved when acceptance of sexual advances is transformed into a condition of continued employment. . . .

Under the facts of this case, the frequent sexual advances by a supervisor do not form the basis of the Title VII violation that we find to exist. Significantly, termination of plaintiff's employment when the advances were rejected is what makes the conduct legally objectionable.[21]

More recently, however, other authorities have held that sexual harassment is a violation of Title VII even when there is no tangible effect on employment. For example, the EEOC guidelines say:

Harassment on the basis of sex is a violation of Sec. 703 of Title VII. Unwelcome sexual advances, requests for sexual favors, and other verbal or physical conduct of a sexual nature constitute sexual harassment when (1) submission to such conduct is made either explicitly or implicitly a term or condition of an individual's employment, (2) submission to or rejection of such conduct by an individual is used as the basis for employment decisions affecting such individual, *or* (3) such conduct has the purpose *or* effect of unreasonably interfering with an individual's work performance *or* creating an intimidating, hostile, or offensive working environment. [emphasis added][22]

How can EEOC interpret sexual harassment to be a violation of employment discrimination law even when it has no evident impact on pay, privileges, promotion, or any other concrete personnel decision? The answer lies in the words of Section 703(a) of Title VII, that it is unlawful to discriminate because of sex with respect to a person's "terms, *conditions*, or privileges of employment" (emphasis added). One court, in a sexual harassment case similar to Case 3.5, upheld the plaintiff's claim that the word "conditions" should be interpreted to:

include the psychological and emotional work environment . . . the sexually stereotyped insults and demeaning propositions to which she was indisputably subjected and which caused her anxiety and debilitation.[23]

The court reasoned that, if Title VII were interpreted to prohibit only tangible employment decisions based on sexual harassment, then:

an employer could sexually harass a female employee with impunity by carefully stopping short of firing the employee or taking any other tangible actions against her in response to her resistance, thereby creating the impression . . . that the employer did not take the ritual of harassment and resistance "seriously."[24]

To eliminate such a possibility, the court joined EEOC in interpreting the definition of unlawful sexual harassment quite broadly.

***Management Action*** Clearly, then, those recent developments have made it more important than ever for management to act to alleviate the problem of sexual harassment.[25] One court has even specified what employers can do to avoid liability for charges of sexual harassment:

. . . where the employer has no knowledge of the discrimination, liability may be avoided if the employer has a policy or history of discouraging sexual harassment of employees by supervisors and the employee has failed to present the matter to a publicized grievance board. If the employer is aware of the situation and rectifies it, the employer may not be held liable for the acts of its agent.[26]

Not all authorities let management off so easily. EEOC, for example, in its own guidelines on sexual harassment, considers an employer liable for employment discrimination due to unwanted sexual advances even if the employer has a policy and a grievance board. Their recommendations include:

> affirmatively raising the subject, expressing strong disapproval, developing appropriate sanctions, informing employees of their right to raise and how to raise the issue of harassment under Title VII, and developing methods to sensitize all concerned.[27]

Thus, sexual harassment is one EEO area in which it has been possible to develop some clear, specific program steps. First management should issue a *specific written policy* against sexual harassment. This seems like an obvious step, but it is a difficult one. Management often fears that such a policy would be an embarrassment and an insult to the supervisors whose behavior is the subject of the policy. Supervisors may also resent what they see to be an unwarranted management intrusion into personal matters. Generally, sex is still a taboo topic in business, and management may consider it indiscreet to issue any explicit policy about it. This is unfortunate, for the direction of judicial opinion is clear, and the cost of not complying with that opinion is enormous.

Second, management should establish a grievance system, a specified procedure that individuals claiming to be victims of sexual harassment can follow to present their claims, have them investigated by management, and secure compensation if the investigation indicates that the claim is justified. To be effective, a grievance system must be perceived by the complainant as an opportunity that can be used without fear of retribution.

Finally, training and control procedures are necessary to implement the policy. Courts have made it clear in sexual harassment cases that "the employer is responsible for the discriminatory acts of its agents,"[28] including supervisors who use their authority to elicit sexual favors without the knowledge of management. Training can make supervisors and other employees more aware of the legal demand that the organization eradicate sexual harassment. Control includes disciplinary steps for violations of the policy as well as regular review of personnel decisions. Not every personnel decision with the potential for sexual harassment need be reviewed, only those that seem otherwise inexplicable or those that are inadequately documented. EEO laws have made undocumented, subjective decision making riskier. That means that management should insist upon documentation and justification for personnel actions generally, not just ones that might involve sexual harassment.

Those steps are a heavy dose of preventive medicine, but one that can provide a degree of legal immunization in sexual harassment cases. Further, an organization that has raised its consciousness about problems of sexual harassment might be less likely to engage in other forms of sex discrimination as well.

## Notes

1. Equal Employment Opportunity Commission, *Legislative History of Titles VII and XI of the Civil Rights Act of 1964* (Washington, D.C.: U.S. Government Printing Office, 1968), pp. 3213–14.

2. Ibid., p. 3213.

3. Ibid., pp. 3216–17.

4. Ibid., pp. 3221–22.

5. Ibid., p. 3215.

6. Ibid., p. 3229.

7. Ibid., p. 3231.

8. *Diaz* v. *Pan American Airways,* 311 F. Supp. 559 (U.S. Dist. Ct. Fla. 1970). Also see *Dothard* v. *Rawlinson,* 433 U.S. 321 (1977); Thomas Stephen Neuberger, "Sex as a Bona-Fide Occupational Qualification Under Title VII," *Labor Law Journal* 29 (1978):425–29; and *Rosenfeld* v. *Southern Pacific Co.,* 444 F.2d 1219 3 FEP 604 (9th Cir. 1971).

9. *Diaz* v. *Pan American Airways,* 422 F.2d 385 (5th Cir. 1971); see also *Weeks* v. *Southern Bell Telephone and Telegraph Co.,* 409 F.2d 228, 1 FEP 656 (5th. Cir. 1969); and *Nashville Gas Co.* v. *Satty,* 434 U.S. 136, 16 FEP 136 (1977).

10. Ibid., p. 388.

11. Ibid.

12. Ibid., pp. 388–89.

13. *Phillips* v. *Martin Marietta,* 400 U.S. 542 (1971); see also *Sprogis* v. *United Air Lines,* 444 F.2d 1194, 3 FEP 621 (7th Cir.), *cert. denied,* 404 U.S. 991, 4 FEP 39 (1971).

14. Civil Rights Act of 1964, Title VII, Sec. 703(a)(2).

15. *General Electric Co.* v. *Gilbert,* 429 U.S. 125 (1977). But see *Cleveland Board of Education* v. *Lafleur,* 414 U.S. 632, 6 FEP 1253 (1974); and *Holthaus* v. *Compton & Sons, Inc.,* 514 F.2d 651, 10 FEP 601 (8th Cir. 1975).

16. Title VII, Sec. 701(k).

17. Equal Employment Opportunity Commission, Guidelines on Discrimination Because of Sex, 29 Code of Federal Regulations 1604. 10 (Appendix).

18. Paul S. Greenlaw and Diana Foderaro, "Some Practical Implications of the Pregnancy Act," *Personnel Journal,* 1979, 58, 677–708.

19. *City of Los Angeles, Dept. of Water & Power* v. *Manhart,* 435 U.S. 702 (1978), pp. 707–8.

20. *Barnes* v. *Costle,* 561 F.2d 983 (D.C. Cir. 1977), p. 990.

21. *Heelan* v. *Johns-Manville Corp.,* 451 F. Supp. 1382 at 1388, 1390 (U.S. Dist. Ct. Colo. 1978).

22.  EEOC, Guidelines on Sex Discrimination Because of Sex, 29 C.F.R. 1604.11(a). See also *Bundy* v. *Jackson,* _____ F.2d _____ 24 Fair Employment Practice Cases 1155 (D.C. Cir. 1981); *Dacus* v. *Southern College of Optometry,* 22 Fair Employment Practice Cases 963 (W.D. Tenn. 1979); and *Brown* v. *City of Guthrie,* 22 Fair Employment Practice Cases 1627 (W.D. Okla. 1980).

23.  *Bundy* v. *Jackson,* 1155 at 1160.

24.  Ibid., p. 1161.

25.  See Terry L. Leap and Edmund R. Gray, "Corporate Responsibility in Cases of Sexual Harassment," *Business Horizons* 23 (1980):58–65; Kathryn A. Thruston, "Sexual Harassment: An Organizational Perspective," *The Personnel Administrator,* 25, No. 12 (1980):59–64; and Michele Hoyman and Rhonda Robinson, "Interpreting the New Sexual Harassment Guidelines," *Personnel Journal,* 59 (1980):996–1000.

26.  *Heelan* v. *Johns-Manville,* p. 1389.

27.  EEOC, Guidelines on Discrimination Because of Sex, 1604.11(f).

28.  *Heelan* v. *Johns-Manville,* p. 1389.

# 4

# EEO Classifications
# Other Than Race and Sex

**Case 4.1**  A bus company refused to hire intercity drivers over forty years of age, and an applicant who was turned down because he was over forty charged the company with age discrimination. In its defense, the company argued that, for most people, physical changes that begin around age thirty-five have an adverse effect on driving skills. Because the company could not practicably determine when such changes take place in an individual applicant, it used chronological age as an indicator. Also, the company presented evidence that experience tended to offset the adverse effects of age. Its safest drivers had a particular blend of age and driving experience with the company—age between fifty and fifty-five with experience of about twenty years. Any driver hired past age forty would not be able to attain that optimal blend.

**Case 4.2**  A woman with a serious hearing impairment was denied admission to a training program to become a registered nurse. The reason behind the rejection was that, even with lip reading, she would have had difficulty performing certain duties, such as working with staff wearing surgical masks. She filed charges of discrimination against the handicapped.

**Case 4.3**  An airline's shift assignments were based on seniority, and one employee assigned to Saturday shifts did not have enough seniority to change his shift.

This employee was a member of the Worldwide Church of God, which forbids its members to work on Saturdays. At the employee's request, the airline agreed to look for someone to trade shifts with the employee voluntarily, but no one stepped forward to do so. The union refused to make the trade forcibly, for that would have violated the collective bargaining agreement. The company refused to allow the employee to work only four days a week, because the employee's job was essential to operations. Finally, the employee failed to report for work on Saturday and was fired. He filed charges of religious discrimination against the company, pointing out that the airline could have filled his position by assigning a supervisor to it or by giving another employee overtime pay to do it.

***Case 4.4***   A male high school teacher "came out of the closet" and proclaimed his homosexuality. The incident was well publicized, as the teacher appeared on television talk shows and gave interviews to reporters. Finally the public controversy was disruptive enough that the school board dismissed him. The teacher made his case public, discussing it on television repeatedly and noting that there was little factual basis for concern that homosexuals have an adverse effect on the children they teach. The school board's response was that, in any event, the teacher's notoriety since his dismissal made any reinstatement out of the question. The teacher filed suit in court, charging that the school board had violated his rights to due process and equal protection of the law by discriminating against him because of his homosexuality.

This chapter discusses the status of three prohibited classifications and then examines how EEO regulation in public employment differs from that in the private sector. The three prohibited classifications—age, handicap status, and religion—are subject to the same general considerations of Chapter 2 as the other prohibited classifications (and Chapter 2 should therefore be read before Chapter 4), but these three classifications raise some issues that Chapter 2 does not cover.

Public sector employment is also subject to the principles discussed in Chapter 2. Public employees enjoy essentially the same EEO protections that employees in private industry enjoy. However, the public sector employer is subject to an additional set of legal constraints that private industry can ignore. This chapter discusses those constraints.

## Chapter Objectives

The purpose of this chapter parallels that of Chapter 3: to supplement the basic EEO principles of Chapter 2. The chapter will identify five factors that distinguish EEO enforcement for these categories:

Different laws (statutes) affect EEO regulation of age and handicap discrimination.

The U.S. Constitution affects EEO regulation of religious discrimination and public sector employment.

A different regulatory agency affects EEO regulation of handicap discrimination.

The concept of bona fide occupational qualification affects EEO regulation of age and handicap discrimination.

The concept of reasonable accommodation affects EEO regulation of handicap and religious discrimination.

A fourth prohibited classification, national origin, is not discussed in detail because, in most respects, the principles that apply to race discrimination apply to national origin discrimination as well. It is worth noting, however, that the EEOC guidelines define national origin discrimination quite broadly, including not only discrimination because of a person's country of origin, but also discrimination because of a person's name, accent, and the like.[1] Moreover, any procedure having a disparate impact on national origin groups must be justified by proving its business necessity or job relatedness. For example, a requirement of fluency in English must be backed up by evidence that is genuinely needed on the job, if it has an adverse impact on any national origin group.[2] Nevertheless, even though discrimination against a national origin group is unlawful, discrimination against *aliens* is not in itself prohibited by Title VII.[3]

## Age Discrimination

One feature that age and sex discrimination have in common is the prevalence of overt disparate treatment. Apparently disparate treatment because of age or sex is not as socially unacceptable as is disparate treatment because of race. Another feature the two share is that the disparate treatment is rationalized by stereotypes or generalizations. Generalizations about older people govern employment decisions just as generalizations about women do. As with those based on sex, many of the generalizations based on age are demonstrably false; for instance, there is evidence to contradict the view that employees lose their faculties as they age[4] and that older employees have more safety and absenteeism problems.[5]

However, some generalizations about older people are valid, just as some generalizations about women are. Title VII makes it illegal to base employment decisions on generalizations about women, even valid generalizations such as the fact that they live longer then men (see Chapter 3). But Title VII does not govern age discrimination. Is it also illegal to base employment on valid generalizations about older employees? To answer that question it is necessary to consider first the statute that outlaws age discrimination and then some cases that have arisen under that statute. Those two considerations suggest that regulation of age discrimination is not as demanding of employers as race and sex discrimination regulation.

## The Age Discrimination in Employment Act

Exhibit 4.1 presents excerpts from the Age Discrimination in Employment Act. Note the similarities between parts of that act and parts of Title VII (Exhibit 2.3). Section 4(a) is almost identical to section 703(a) of Title

**Exhibit 4.1**    Excerpts from the Age Discrimination in Employment Act of 1967

---

### Section 4

(a)  It shall be unlawful for an employer
    (1) to fail or refuse to hire or to discharge any individual or otherwise discriminate against any individual with respect to his compensation, terms, conditions, or privileges of employment, because of such individual's age;
    (2) to limit, segregate, or classify his employees in any way which would deprive or tend to deprive any individual of employment opportunities or otherwise adversely affect his status as an employee, because of such individual's age; or
    (3) to reduce the wage rate of any employee in order to comply with this Act.
. . . .

(d)  It shall be unlawful for any employer to discriminate against any of his employees or applicants for employment . . . because such individual member, or applicant for membership, has opposed any practice made unlawful by this section, or because such individual, member, or applicant for membership has made a charge, testified, assisted, or participated in any manner in an investigation, proceeding, or litigation under this Act.

(e)  It shall be unlawful for an employer . . . to print or publish, or cause to

---

be printed or published, any notice or advertisement relating to employment by such an employer . . . indicating any preference, limitation, specification, or discrimination, based on age.

(f) It shall not be unlawful for an employer, employment agency, or labor organization

(1) to take any action otherwise prohibited . . . where age is a bona fide occupational qualification reasonably necessary to the normal operation of the particular business, or where the differentiation is based on reasonable factors other than age:

(2) to observe the terms of a bona fide seniority system or any bona fide employee benefit plan such as retirement, pension, or insurance plan, which is not a subterfuge to evade the purpose of this Act, except that no such employee benefit plan shall excuse the failure to hire any individual, and no such seniority system or employee benefit plan shall require or permit the involuntary retirement of any individual specified by section 12(a) of this Act because of the age of such individual.

### Section 12

(a) The prohibitions in this Act shall be limited to individuals who are at least 40 years of age but less than 70 years of age.

VII; sections 4(d) and 4(e) are equivalent to section 704 of Title VII; and the BFOQ part of section 4(f)(1) is worded the same as section 703 (e) of Title VII. This suggests that many of the EEO principles governing age are similar to those governing the illegal classifications of Title VII.

However, there are some important features of the Age Discrimination in Employment Act that are not shared with Title VII:

1. Only one group is protected; thus, reverse discrimination is not prohibited. Section 12(a) states that people aged forty through sixty-nine are protected against discrimination because of age; people of other ages are not protected. Title VII outlaws discrimination for or against blacks *or* whites, men *or* women; the Age Discrimination in Employment Act is a one-way prohibition, outlawing only discrimination against older people.

2. Retirement is regulated. Section 4(f)(2) makes it illegal to force employees to retire before age seventy.[6] That provision reflects

legislative concern over mandatory retirement in debating the Age Discrimination Act and its later amendments.[7]

3. "Reasonable factors other than age" can be used. Section 4(f)(1) is more permissive than Title VII in allowing employers to differentiate among people because of some reasonable factor other than age.

The "reasonable factors" provision would seem to allow employers to engage in definition 2 discrimination. That is, a reasonable factor other than age may have a disparate impact on older and younger people. Speed, strength, and other physical standards are factors that could easily have an adverse effect on older candidates for a job. It seems easier to show that such a factor is "reasonable" than to show that it is a business necessity or job related. One company was even allowed to discriminate against older workers because it cost more to employ them.[8] Such a defense would be unthinkable in a case of race or sex discrimination.

In short, the Age Discrimination Act is more permissive than Title VII in allowing "reasonable factors" to affect decisions. However, the EEOC regulations interpreting the Age Discrimination Act say that job relatedness is required of practices having an adverse impact on people in the protected age group, just as it is required under Title VII. Employment tests may be particularly troublesome for older people. The EEOC regulations point out that many older people finished their schooling before the emphasis on testing began and may therefore lack "test sophistication," regardless of their ability to do the job.[9] Still, the "reasonable factors" provision does make it easier to comply with age discrimination rules than with Title VII.

### Age as a Bona Fide Occupational Qualification

The Age Discrimination Act also allows definition 1 discrimination: if age is a BFOQ, then employers may engage in disparate treatment because of age. In this regard, the Age Discrimination Act is theoretically like the sex discrimination prohibition in Title VII. However, while the courts seldom consider sex to be a BFOQ, they sometimes consider age to be. Particularly when safety is paramount, employers have been allowed to discriminate against older people. Case 4.1, the bus driver case, is an example: the courts have decided such cases in favor of employers.[10]

In other words, while it is illegal to use generalizations based on sex, it is not necessarily illegal to use generalizations based on age. But it is important for the employer to support its policy with factual evidence that the generalization is both true and job related; unsubstantiated assumptions about older people are not acceptable. Still, the fact that generalizations are allowable at all makes age discrimination regulation more lenient than race or sex discrimination regulation.

### Management Responses

Most instances of age discrimination, however, have none of the careful documentation or factual basis of Case 4.1. Instead, age discrimination is often unsubstantiated and surprisingly blatant. As one legal analysis put it, "When a personnel interviewer writes 'too old' on an application, it is hardly surprising that a jury later is not receptive to his testimony that the notation was a slip of the pen."[11] This situation occurs more frequently in court cases than one might imagine.[12]

Other more subtle forms of age discrimination also pose risks of adverse court judgments. For instance, an employer cannot expect to be successful in defending a preference for younger workers based on assumptions that they have more drive or ambition. Another common assumption about older job applicants is that some deficiency has prevented them from keeping pace with the career advancement of their peers. This assumption would also probably be indefensible; the older applicant could attribute the lack of advancement to luck or to shortcomings that have been overcome.[13]

In short, management cannot afford to ignore age discrimination regardless of the fact that regulatory burdens may not be as heavy as they are in other areas of discrimination. The same careful documentation and control is needed as that required in cases of race and sex discrimination. Also, it is important to reconsider the job relatedness of those selection requirements, such as physical standards, that are likely to affect older applicants adversely. Finally, the employer should be prepared to assign a reasonable value to the older applicants' greater experience when evaluating job candidates.[14]

## Handicap Discrimination

Like age discrimination, discrimination against handicapped people is not covered by Title VII. Instead, it is covered by the Vocational Rehabilitation Act of 1973, excerpts of which appear in Exhibit 4.2 The differences

**Exhibit 4.2**   Excerpts from the Vocational Rehabilitation Act of 1973

### Section 7

(6) (B) Subject to the second sentence of this subparagraph, the term "handicapped individual" means, for purposes of titles IV and V of this Act, any person who (i) has a physical or mental impairment which substantially limits one or more of such person's major life activities, (ii) has a record of such an impairment, or (iii) is regarded as having such an impairment. For purposes of sections 503 and 504 as such sections relate to employment, such term does not include any individual who is an alcoholic or drug abuser whose current use of alcohol or drugs prevents such individual from performing the duties of the job in question or whose employment, by reason of such current alcohol or drug abuse, would constitute a direct threat to property or the safety of others.

### Section 503

(a)   Any contract [or subcontract] in excess of $2,500 entered into by any Federal department or agency for the procurement of personal property and nonpersonal services (including construction) for the United States shall contain a provision requiring that, in employing persons to carry out such contract the party contracting with the United States shall take affirmative action to employ and advance in employment qualified handicapped individuals as defined in section 7(7).

between this law and the others considered thus far are immediately apparent. The Vocational Rehabilitation Act is much like Executive Order 11246 in two ways: it applies only to government contractors, and it requires affirmative action.

To understand employers' obligations under the Vocational Rehabilitation Act and how they differ from obligations under Title VII, it is necessary to consider both the definition of the handicapped individual and the act's affirmative action requirement.

## Definition of Handicap

As noted in section 7 of the act, the definition of handicapped individual is quite broad. The breadth of the definition reflects congressional intent to eliminate any narrowness or ambiguity in the reach of the law.[15] The definition's reference to "major life activities" has been interpreted by the Department of Labor to include communication, ambulation, self-care, transportation, and the like, as well as employment. The phrase "substantially limits" means that an individual is covered to the extent that the impairment affects employability. And the law makes it clear that its benefits extend to those who are incorrectly regarded as impaired and those who were impaired in the past, as well as to those presently impaired.[16]

While the term *handicap* is usually associated with physical impairments, the wording in section 7 makes it clear that mental problems such as retardation and emotional disorders are covered as well. So are certain illnesses that are often grounds for rejection for employment, such as diabetes, heart disease, epilepsy, and cancer.[17] Most notably, alcoholism and other forms of drug dependency are also covered, although subject to the proviso noted in section 7.

### Affirmative Action for the Handicapped: Reasonable Accommodation

In defining the obligations of government contractors to take affirmative action for the handicapped, the Department of Labor guidelines say:

> A contractor must make a reasonable accommodation to the physical and mental limitations of an employee or applicant unless the contractor can demonstrate that such an accommodation would impose an undue hardship on the conduct of the contractor's business. In determining the extent of a contractor's accommodations, the following factors among others may be considered: (1) business necessity and (2) financial cost and expenses.[18]

That excerpt identifies the relevant factors, but it still does not provide much guidance in distinguishing reasonable from unreasonable accommodation. Just how accommodating must employers be? Some possible definitions of reasonable accommodation are:

1. *Job access:* this is what most people think of as reasonable accommodation. Besides wheelchair ramps and braille signs on elevators, it can include day shift preference for the visually impaired, air conditioning for workers with respiratory problems, transportation for the immobilized and redesign of facilities for people with prosthetic devices.[19] The fact that many of these are costly has led some employers to take the financial cost provision in the guidelines above with a grain of salt.

2. *Job design:* this involves eliminating tasks that a handicapped person cannot perform. For example, tasks involving reaching might be removed from a job to accommodate a person confined to a wheelchair.

3. *Qualifications:* some prerequisites, such as passing a physical examination, may limit the entry of handicapped persons. Clearly, reasonable accommodation includes eliminating such prerequisites if they are not job related.

4. *Unprejudiced treatment:* some people may be frightened or disturbed by handicaps such as epilepsy and speech impairments. Hiring decisions should not be influenced by such feelings unless the impairment is demonstrably job related.

5. *Employee assistance:* professional help may be offered to employees to control handicaps such as alcoholism, drug dependency, or psychological problems.

6. *Preferential treatment:* handicapped persons may be favored over nonhandicapped employees.

Which of these accommodations is required by law is subject to some debate. Clearly, numbers 3 and 4 are required. Numbers 1 and 2 are often expected of recipients of federal funds, but the extent to which they are mandatory is uncertain. Number 5, employee assistance programs, is generally recommended but not always expected, particularly of smaller employers. Finally, number 6, preferential treatment, is not advocated by any court or compliance agency, yet many employers understandably assume that it is really what compliance investigators want. Given the reports of some observers that OFCCP is getting tougher,[20] it is not surprising that employers view this as the best way to stay out of trouble.

Still, it seems likely that employers have considerably more latitude than prevailing fears would suggest. Reasonable accommodation does not mean abandoning job-related requirements, even if those requirements result in the disqualification of persons with certain handicaps.[21] Case 4.2 provides an example. In deciding the case, the U.S. Supreme Court ruled that the complainant's handicap rendered her unqualified to do the work for which she sought training. While it is not certain that cases such as Case 4.2 can be generalized to cover other situations, they indicate that some consideration will be given to employers' arguments that certain handicaps are sometimes job related.

Likewise, there is a lamentable misunderstanding among some managers that they are not allowed to discipline the alcoholic or drug dependent employee for job performance problems. This reluctance leads the employer to treat the alcohol- or drug-dependent employee too leniently and that may prevent effective treatment of the dependence. Sometimes confronting the person with the problem and insisting that he or she participate in some programmatic approach to solve it is the only way to get through to the employee. [22]

In sum, reasonable accommodation does not mean that the employer must sacrifice productivity by tolerating lower job performance from handicapped employees, nor does it mean that the employer must endanger others by placing a handicapped employee in a position where the handicap would pose a threat. Indeed, being free of certain handicaps may be a "bona fide occupational qualification." It does mean, however, that employers should be aware that their interests may be served by recognizing the potential of those who have traditionally been thought unemployable because of their handicaps.

## Religious Discrimination

The two principal laws governing religious discrimination are Title VII and the U.S. Constitution. The relevant excerpts from those two are presented in Exhibit 4.3. Note the reference to reasonable accommodation in section 701(j) of Title VII.

The EEOC guidelines define religion to include "moral or ethical beliefs as to what is right and wrong which are sincerely held with the strength of traditional religious views." Paradoxically, then, atheists are protected under the definition of religion, as are others who sincerely practice a creed that is not recognized under the conventional heading of religion.

Historically, religious discrimination has been definition 1 discrimination, adverse treatment of an individual because of that individual's religion. Examples are refusing to hire or promote Catholics or Jews into managerial positions or preferring members of one's own church. More recently, however, religious discrimination has come to include unequal impact: the use of employment practices that make it more difficult for members of certain religions to practice their faith. The classic example is

## Exhibit 4.3    Laws Governing Religious Discrimination

---

### Title VII, 1964 Civil Rights Act

**Section 701** (j) The term "religion" includes all aspects of religious observance and practice, as well as belief, unless an employer demonstrates that he is unable to reasonably accommodate to an employee's or prospective employee's religious observance or practice without undue hardship on the conduct of the employer's business.

### U.S. Constitution

**First Amendment (1791)** Congress shall make no law respecting an establishment of religion, or prohibiting the free exercise thereof; or abridging the freedom of speech, or of the press; or the right of the people peaceably to assemble, and to petition the Government for a redress of grievances.

---

requiring work on the Sabbath day. Many employers require Saturday work, but some religions observe Saturday as the Sabbath and have rules against working on the Sabbath. Orthodox and conservative Jews, Seventh-Day Adventists, and members of the Worldwide Church of God generally may not work on Saturdays. Such conflicts between work rules and religious rules are more frequent nowadays than overt religious discrimination.

Direct, overt religious discrimination is illegal, with very few exceptions. It is condoned only when religion is a bona fide occupational qualification. The concept of BFOQ is interpreted narrowly, although not quite so narrowly as it is in the area of sex discrimination. For example, religion may be a BFOQ when hiring persons to teach in a denominational school. Generally, though, employers cannot use the BFOQ defense as a justification for religious discrimination.

The legal status of indirect discrimination or disparate impact, however, is less clear-cut. Practices such as Saturday work rules that adversely affect certain religious groups are excusable if the employer "is unable to reasonably accommodate . . . without undue hardship" (see Exhibit 4.3, section 701). The question here, as with the Vocational Rehabilitation Act, is what constitutes reasonable accommodation.

In Case 4.3, the employee claims that the airline did not make reasonable accommodation, that it could have done more without undue hardship. Indeed, compared to other things that companies have been required to do in the name of EEO, the employee's suggestions do not seem a great hardship. Yet they do incur some costs. In deciding a case similar to Case 4.3, *TWA* v. *Hardison,* the U.S. Supreme Court said:

> To require TWA to bear more than a *de minimis* cost in order to give Hardison Saturdays off is an undue hardship. Like abandonment of the seniority system, to require TWA to bear additional costs when no such costs are incurred to give other employees the days off that they want would involve unequal treatment of employees on the basis of their religion. By suggesting that TWA should incur certain costs in order to give Hardison Saturdays off the Court of Appeals would in effect require TWA to finance an additional Saturday off and then choose the employee who will enjoy it on the basis of his religious beliefs. [23]

By ruling as it did, the Supreme Court explicitly overturned the EEOC guidelines that required employers to do more than the airlines did. The opinion means that many members of sects with Saturday Sabbaths will continue to experience conflict between the demands of their religions and demands of their jobs.

If this judgment seems unsympathetic to religious minorities, the Court's action might be explained by the First Amendment to the U.S. Constitution, reprinted in Exhibit 4.3. Some observers have argued that the First Amendment prohibits Congress from mandating reasonable accommodation to a person's religion. If so, then Title VII's religious discrimination prohibition is unconstitutional. [24] Consider the following:

1. The First Amendment restricts Congress only. The Constitution governs government. Thus, the First Amendment does not say that it is illegal for a private party to affect the establishment of religion or prohibit the free exercise of religion, only that it is illegal for Congress to make laws having that effect.

2. Title VII does concern itself with religion. One could argue that its mandate for reasonable accommodation encourages religion and religious diversity by requiring employers to establish conditions conducive to the practice of religion by their employees. In that regard, Title VII is a "law respecting an establishment of religion." As one legal observer puts it, "when Congress forces some private citizens to conform their conduct with the religious demands of other citizens, serious [First Amendment] questions are raised." [25]

The reader may find these observations to be trivial, even perverse. Nevertheless, a serious reading of the First Amendment does raise genuine questions about whether Title VII is consistent with it.

This constitutional uncertainty over the status of Title VII's ban on religious discrimination makes vigorous enforcement of that ban difficult. When the concept of reasonable accommodation is interpreted as the Supreme Court interpreted it in *Hardison,* it is difficult for the EEOC to compel employers to establish working conditions that permit diversity of religious practices. Thus it is more difficult for Title VII to effect improvements in the status of religious minorities than for it to improve the status of the other groups it protects.

## Employment in the Public Sector

Like all the other classifications considered here, the classification of public employment is subject to all the regulatory activities and principles discussed in Chapter 2. However, two other bodies of law apply to the public sector that do not apply to employment in private industry: the Civil Service Reform Act and the Fifth and Fourteenth Amendments to the U.S. Constitution. Each adds certain EEO burdens that private sector employers are not required to shoulder.

### Civil Service Reform Act of 1978

This act states that "it is the policy of the United States . . . to provide . . . a federal workforce reflective of the Nation's diversity."[26] To implement this provision, the U.S. Office of Personnel Management has issued regulations requiring that federal agencies develop programs to increase the employment of all groups that are underrepresented in any of the agency's occupational categories. The regulations specify in detail the methods for determining underrepresentation, and they require vigorous recruiting and job redesign to make the agency's work force more representative.

While those regulations do not cover state and local governments, they do represent a principle that has been advocated for governments at all levels: the principle of representative bureaucracy. This principle holds that it is government's responsibility to ensure that public servants are representative of the citizenry, that the diversity of groups in the population e matched proportionally by diversity in public service. While the Office of Personnel Management guidelines do not cover enough societal groups to bring about total representativeness, they are certainly consistent with the spirit of representative bureaucracy.

## The United States Constitution

The concept of merit employment has been central to public sector personnel administration since the nineteenth century. The concept is too complex to discuss completely here, but its major guiding principle is that personnel decisions be made according to the candidate's merit rather than his or her political affiliation or some subjective criterion. This focus on objective merit represents a long tradition of reliance on objective criteria of the job candidate's competence.

Part of merit employment is a rejection of such criteria as race and sex that are irrelevant to competency. Laws exist at all levels of government requiring that the hiring and promoting of people be on objective bases rather than subjective ones. Of course, those laws serve EEO objectives. As Chapter 2 notes parenthetically, no similar laws mandate merit employment in the private sector.

The U.S. Constitution has two specific provisions that reinforce this emphasis on merit employment, the Fifth and Fourteenth Amendments. These are reprinted in Exhibit 4.4. The Fifth Amendment applies to the federal government, while the Fourteenth Amendment applies to state and local government. Those amendments mandate due process of law and equal protection of the law and thus require that any classification of persons used by any level of government must be one that serves legitimate state objectives.

The practical implication of that mandate is that public sector personnel managers must concern themselves not only with the handful of prohibited classifications discussed in Chapter 2, but also with any other arbitrary classification. Case 4.4, about the homosexual teacher, is an example. It is not illegal for a private sector employer to discriminate against homosexuals; Title VII applies to biological sex only.[27] However, it is illegal for a unit of government such as a school board to single out any class of people, homosexuals included, for unfavorable treatment without a sound justification. For Case 4.4, specific evidence (not emotions or common sense) is required to show that the teacher's reappointment as a schoolteacher would interfere with the orderly functioning of the school.

**Exhibit 4.4** Excerpts from the U.S. Constitution Governing Public Sector Employment

---

### Fifth Amendment (1791)

No person shall be held to answer for a capital, or otherwise infamous crime, unless on a presentment or indictment of a Grand Jury, except in cases arising in the land or naval forces, or in the Militia, when in actual service in time of War or public danger; nor shall any person be subject for the same offence to be twice put in jeopardy of life or limb; nor shall be compelled in any criminal case to be a witness against himself, nor be deprived of life, liberty, or property, without due process of law; nor shall private property be taken for public use, without just compensation.

### Fourteenth Amendment (1868)

*Section 1.* All persons born or naturalized in the United States, and subject to the jurisdiction thereof, are citizens of the United States and of the State wherein they reside. No State shall make or enforce any law which shall abridge the privileges or immunities of citizens of the United States; nor shall any State deprive any person of life, liberty, or property, without due process of law nor deny to any person within its jurisdiction the equal protection of the laws.

. . . .

*Section 5.* The Congress shall have power to enforce, by appropriate legislation, the provisions of this article.

---

The mere fact that a teacher is homosexual is ordinarily not sufficient justification for dismissal. However, the teacher in Case 4.4 openly proclaimed his homosexuality and attracted notoriety. If that disrupts school operations, then the court may find in favor of the school board.[28]

In sum, while it is generally easier to justify a classification on which personnel decisions are made under Constitutional standards than it is to justify one of the prohibited classifications enumerated in Title VII,[29] the open-ended Constitutional mandate for reasonableness of classifications tends to make public sector regulation more stringent than private sector regulation.

# Notes

1. Equal Employment Opportunity Commission, Guidelines on Discrimination Because of National Origin, 29 Code of Federal Regulations 1606.

2. See Paul S. Greenlaw and John P. Kohl, "National Origin Discrimination and the New EEOC Guidelines," *Personnel Journal*, 1981, 60, 634–36. See also *Frontera* v. *Sindell*, 522 F.2d 215, 11 FEP 1132 (6th Cir. 1975).

3. *Espinoza* v. *Farah Manufacturing Co., Inc.*, 414 U.S. 86 (1973). But see *Guerra* v. *Manchester Terminal Corp.*, 498 F.2d 641, 8 FEP 433 (5th Cir. 1974).

4. Glen Elder, "Age Differentiations and the Life Course," *Annual Review of Sociology* Palo Alto, Calif.: Annual Reviews, 1975), pp. 165–90; James Kelly, "Women, the Handicapped, and Older Workers," in Joseph Famularo, ed., *Handbook of Modern Personnel Administration* (New York: McGraw-Hill, 1972), Chap. 70; and "Aging and the IQ: The Myth of the Twilight Years," *Psychology Today* (March 1974):35–40.

5. See Robert Fjerstad, "Is It Economical to Hire the Over Forty-Five Worker?" *Personnel Administration*, 28, No. 2 (1965):22–28.

6. There are few exceptions to this prohibition: see Sec. 12 of the act.

7. Edward T. O'Donnell, Marshall D. Lasser, and Kermit G. Bailor, "The Federal Age Discrimination Statute: Basic Law, Areas of Controversy, and Suggestions for Compliance," *Wake Forest Law Review*, 15 (1979):1–37.

8. *Mastie* v. *Great Lakes Steel Corp.*, 424 F. Supp. 1299 (E.D. Mich. 1976).

9. Code of Federal Regulations, Part 1625 at Sec. 1625.7.

10. *Usery* v. *Tamiami Trail Tours, Inc.*, 531 F.2d 224 (5th Cir. 1976); *Hodgson* v. *Greyhound Lines, Inc.*, 499 F.2d 859 (7th Cir. 1974).

11. O'Donnell, Lasser, and Bailor, "Federal Age Discrimination Statute," p. 32.

12. Ibid., p. 33. For example, *Hodgson* v. *First Federal Savings and Loan Association*, 455 F.2d 818 (5th Cir. 1972); and *Brennan* v. *Ace Hardware Corp.*, 495 F.2d 368 (8th Cir. 1974).

13. O'Donnell, Lasser, and Bailor, "The Federal Age Discrimination Statute."

14. Ibid.

15. Barbara Lindemann Schlei and Paul Grossman, *Employment Discrimination Law* (Washington, D.C.: Bureau of National Affairs, 1976), p. 225.

16. Code of Federal Regulations, Part 60-741, Appendix A.

17. Leslie B. Milk, "The Key to Job Accommodations," *Personnel Administrator*, 24, No. 4 (1979):31–33, 38.

18. Code of Federal Regulations, Part 60-741.6(d). Also see D. P. Jackson, Affirmative Action for Handicapped and Veterans: Interpretive and Operational Guidelines," *Labor Law Journal*, 29 (1978):107–17.

19. Milk, "Key to Job Accommodations."

20. Gopal C. Pati and John I. Adkins, Jr., "Hire the Handicapped—Compliance Is Good Business," *Harvard Business Review* 58 (January 1980):14–22.

21. *Coleman* v. *Darden*, 595 F.2d 533 (10th Cir. 1979); *Hoffman* v. *Ohio Youth Commission*, 13 FEP Cases 30 (D.C. Ohio 1975).

22. Robert D. Dugan, "Affirmative Action for Alcoholics and Addicts?" *Employee Relations Law Journal*, 5 (1979):234–44.

23. *Trans World Airlines, Inc.* v. *Hardison*, 432 U.S. 63 (1977).

24. Civil Rights Act of 1964, Title VII, Sec. 701(j).

25. Ibid.

26. Civil Service Reform Act of 1978, Sec. 3(1).

27. See *Smith* v. *Liberty Mutual Insurance Co.*, 569 F.2d 325 (5th Cir. 1978); and Sch▓ and Grossman, *Employment Discrimination Law*, p. 368.

28. *Acanfora* v. *Board of Education of Montgomery County*, 359 F. Supp. 843 (U.S. Dist. C▓ Md. 1973). See also *Norton* v. *Macy*, 417 F.2d 1161, 9 FEP 1382 (D.C. Cir. 1969); *Gayer* Schlesinger, 490 F.2d 740, 750 (D.C. Cir. 1973); and *Safransky* v. *Personnel Board*, 215 N.W.▓ 379, 9 FEP 1391 (Wis. 1974).

29. See *Washington* v. *Davis*, 426 U.S. 229 (1976).

# 5

# Evidence and Proof in EEO Cases

*Case 5.1*   The federal government sued a nationwide trucking line and its union for discrimination against black and Hispanic Americans in hiring intercity truck drivers. These minorities, the government claimed, were relegated to lower-paying local driving jobs by the existence of separate bargaining units (local unions) for intercity and local drivers. Protection from layoffs and competition for vacancies were determined by bargaining unit seniority, so that intercity runs were given to the applicant who had been an intercity driver the longest.

To support its argument, the government presented the following statistics on the company work force:

|                   | *White* | *Black and Hispanic* |
|-------------------|---------|----------------------|
| Intercity drivers | 1802    | 13                   |
| Local drivers     | 1117    | 167                  |

Moreover, the government introduced population statistics that showed further disparities. Some company terminals in areas of substantial black population had no black intercity drivers.

The company's response was that statistics can never establish a prima facie case of discrimination, and that population comparisons ignored the fact that much of the population was unqualified. For its part, the union conceded that the seniority system perpetuated past discrimination. But the union also argued that, since the seniority system was free from any discriminatory purpose in its history and its application, it was a bona fide seniority system under section 703(h) of Title VII and should not be overturned.

***Case 5.2***   The federal government sued a suburban school district for discriminating against black schoolteachers in its hiring practices. The government pointed out that, while the U.S. census showed that 15.4 percent of the schoolteachers in the metropolitan area were black, only 1.8 percent of the schoolteachers employed by the district were black. The school district replied that there were relatively few black teachers in the district because there were relatively few black pupils there. Besides, the metropolitan area included a center city with a relatively large black population and a school district that had made efforts to maintain a 50 percent black teaching staff. In light of that competition, the suburban district asserted that it was unreasonable to expect it to hire black teachers in proportion to their availability in the labor market. Excluding the center city, only 5.7 percent of the teachers in the metropolitan area were black. Finally, the low percentage of blacks on the teaching staff reflected hiring that took place before Title VII was made applicable to the school district (1972); since then, 3.7 percent of the teachers hired were black. To summarize the statistics:

| | |
|---|---:|
| Total number of teachers employed by the school district | 123 |
| Percent of black teachers employed by the school district | 1.8 |
| Total number of teachers hired by the school district after 1972 | 405 |
| Percent of teachers hired by the school district after 1972 that are black | 3.7 |
| Percent of teachers in metropolitan area that are black | 15.4 |
| Percent of teachers outside center city that are black | 5.7 |
| Percent of pupils in the school district that are black | 2.3 |

***Case 5.3***   A construction company specializing in firebrick installation in steel mills was charged with discrimination against blacks in its hiring of bricklayers. The company delegated that hiring entirely to its supervisors, some of whom simply hired people they knew to have the skills or people who had been recommended to them. The company did not hire people who applied at the gate. The plaintiffs were fully qualified black bricklayers who were turned down at the gate. They said that the hiring policy unnecessarily cut the company off from black bricklayers, which was particularly unjustifiable in light of the history of discrimination against blacks in the construction trades. The company responded that placing the responsibility for hiring in the supervisor's hands and refusing gate applicants was the best way to ensure

that its new workers were competent, and thus the best way to avoid the costly losses caused by incompetent work in the firebrick contracting business. Besides, while 5.7 percent of the bricklayers in the relevant labor market were black, 13.3 percent of the hours worked by company bricklayers were worked by black bricklayers. Also, a study by the union showed that 20 percent of the bricklayers hired by the company were black.

Chapter 2 has already introduced the basic ideas of evidence and proof in a Title VII case:

> The plaintiff must present some evidence that unequal treatment occurred or that an employment practice had unequal impact on the groups covered by Title VII.

> The defendant must then present evidence of job relatedness to justify having engaged in a practice having unequal impact.

Exhibit 2.7 outlines this sequence and shows how the burden of proof shifts between plaintiff and defendant in a Title VII case.

Evidence of unequal treatment is generally straightforward and will not be discussed at length here. Evidence of unequal impact, however, is a matter that demands close attention. In discussing evidence of unequal impact, this chapter examines the Supreme Court's opinion in an important case similar to Case 5.1. That case concerns seniority systems as well as evidence and proof. Therefore, the legal status of seniority systems under EEO law will also be considered in this chapter, even though it is not strictly relevant to evidence and proof.

Evidence of job relatedness involves the *validity* of employment practices and the methods that industrial psychologists use to determine validity. The legal document that covers validity is the federal agencies' Uniform Guidelines on Employee Selection Procedures, which gives the standards used by federal EEO agencies in determining whether an employment practice is valid. This chapter outlines the most important legal and managerial implications of those guidelines.

## Chapter Objectives

To summarize, then, this chapter is organized around the following objectives:

1. To indicate the importance of evidence and proof and the importance of the manager's role regarding such evidence in deciding the outcome of an EEO case.

2. To examine in detail the statistical evidence required by a court as part of a prima facie case of discrimination presented by the plaintiff. Two types of analysis will be presented: *stock analysis*, designed to determine whether the employer's work force is sufficiently *representative* of the various groups in the labor market; and *flow analysis*, designed to determine whether employment practices have an adverse *impact* on any sex or ethnic group.

3. To discuss briefly the kind of evidence that indicates discrimination in pay.

4. To outline the evidence of job relatedness discussed in the Uniform Guidelines on Employee Selection Procedures and to review professional opinion about certain provisions of those guidelines.

5. In the process of considering impact evidence for a prima facie case, to review the provision of the *Teamsters* case regarding seniority systems.[1]

Before reading this chapter, it is important to understand the material in Chapter 2 fully, particularly the last section on basic principles of evidence and proof.

## Why Study Evidence and Proof?

There is only one reason for managers to concern themselves with the intricacies of evidence and proof in Title VII cases: those intricacies determine the outcome of the case. Unfortunately, the common managerial approach to EEO neglects evidence and proof, focusing instead on what employment practices are legal. In short, the typical approach goes no further than Chapter 4 of this book. The problem with such an approach is that legality is largely a matter of evidence that is specific to an individual case, rather than a matter of generalizations about the practices that apply from case to case. And the manager has an important role in the gathering of such evidence.

For example, recall Case 2.3, the case regarding conviction records. It is all too tempting to conclude from that case that it is illegal to use convictions as a screening device. But that is true only if using the conviction record has an adverse impact on one of the groups covered by Title VII and cannot be shown to be job related. Indeed, some cases have upheld screening that takes account of conviction records.[2] So it is inaccurate to make a generalization about whether such an employment practice is legal or illegal; the outcome of any case will rest on the evidence regarding its impact and job relatedness.

The manager is the source of much of this evidence. At a minimum, the manager keeps the personnel files from which race and sex data are derived. Ideally, the manager has also processed those data to determine how many employees in each job classification belong to each of the groups covered by Title VII. Also, the manager should know how many applicants from each group are hired and how many are rejected. An organization that is not keeping those basic statistics is making a mistake. Even if no one has ordered the organization to collect the data, it may be only a matter of time before the organization is sued by an employee charging discrimination. Once that happens, the organization will be compelled to produce the necessary statistics. It is a painful process for management to respond to such demands for evidence if it has not been keeping these figures all along.

In addition, it is advisable for management to keep track of other data that are instrumental in court verdicts. This chapter discusses some of the information that is relevant. Data on the number of women and minorities in the labor market are essential in determining whether a plaintiff might be successful in presenting a prima facie case of discrimination to a court. And analysis of the requirements of a job and of employees' performance in the job are often essential in determining whether the employer might be successful in defending against that prima facie case. Without such information, the manager has no basis for determining whether the organization's employment practices would be found illegal.

## The Prima Facie Case: General Considerations for Statistical Proof of Discrimination

Regardless of whether an EEO case involves allegations of unequal treatment or unequal impact, statistical proof is relevant.[3] When the court decided Case 2.3 in *Green* v. *Missouri Pacific Railroad*, it listed three types of unequal impact statistics that are relevant as evidence:[4]

1. *Impact on actual applicants:* a comparison between the proportion

of black applicants that was hired and the proportion of white applicants that was hired.

   2. *Impact on potential applicants:* this kind of information is used when information on actual applicants is unavailable. An example is the *Griggs* case, where the court made a comparison between the percentages of blacks and whites with high school diplomas in North Carolina.[5] With the assumption that applicants for a position at Duke Power Company were a random cross section of the North Carolina population, a high school diploma requirement could be expected to have the same impact on black and white applicants that is reflected in the statewide education figures.

   3. *Representativeness of the employer's work force:* a comparison between the proportion of the organization's work force that is black and the proportion of some outside reference population that is black. To illustrate somewhat simplistically, the proportion of an organization's computer programmers that is black could be compared with the proportion of the qualified and available computer programmers in the labor market area that is black.

   Representativeness measures such as number 3 have been referred to as *stock* statistics, while the two applicant measures, number 1 and to a lesser extent number 2, have been referred to as *flow* statistics.[6] A *stock* is a count of people that occupy a position at a given time. Stock measures can be looked at as the inventory of people in the organization—the personnel balance sheet of the organization. Stock measures indicate discrimination when they show that some group is not proportionately represented in the organization. A flow, on the other hand, is a count of the people that move from one position to another between two points in time—promotions, demotions, transfers, and other personnel actions. Flow measures indicate discrimination when personnel policies restrict the flow of one group more than that of another. If stocks are balance sheets, then flows are income statements, in that they count transactions. The next two sections cover stock and flow measures.

## Stock Analysis: Representativeness

Stock analysis is a complex topic. This section covers that topic primarily by discussing the evidence implications of three court cases. The first case,

*Teamsters* v. *U.S.*, explains the justification for using stock statistics as evidence of discrimination in Title VII cases. *Teamsters* also defines the conditions under which an employer is allowed to use a seniority system that has a disparate impact on the groups covered by Title VII, and this section parenthetically discusses what the case says about that. Next, the case of *Hazelwood* v. *U.S.* is discussed. That case considers the question of what figures the organization's stock statistics should be compared to in determining whether a group is underrepresented. The case also addresses the quantitative question of how much underrepresentation is too much—how great a disparity does the plaintiff have to show in order to advance a prima facie case? Finally, the case of *Furnco Construction Corp.* v. *Waters* establishes how an organization can use stock statistics to advance its side of the case.

Stock analysis is the most commonly used analysis in EEO cases and is often crucial to the outcome of the case. It is based on a comparison between two numbers, one describing the employer's work force and one describing the relevant population or labor market that the employer's work force is supposed to mirror. The important questions are how the numbers are derived and how much of a difference between them is too much.

To take a simple example, the figure for the employer may be 25 percent black, and the figure for the labor market may be 30 percent black. There is a difference between these two figures. Is it a large enough difference to be significant? And are the figures themselves valid? How is the labor market figure determined? Generally, labor market figures are derived by counting certain types of people in a certain geographical area. What geographical area defines the labor market? Are there alternate geographical areas that could be advanced as a definition? And who is to be counted in that geographical area? The entire population? The entire civilian labor force? Only those who have the qualifications for the job in question? Who is counted in the employer's figure? Full-time employees only, or part-time employees as well? Employees in all job classes, a subset of job classes, or just one job class? Employees in just one department, an entire facility, or nationwide across all facilities? While this chapter cannot give conclusive answers to all those questions, the importance of such questions to the ultimate outcome of the case should be evident.

Case 5.1 presents an elementary question of representativeness. This situation was resolved by the U.S. Supreme Court in *Teamsters* v. *U.S.*, a case that is second only to *Griggs* in its importance for EEO. The Court opinion in *Teamsters* made three points unmistakably clear:

1. Representation statistics can establish a prima facie case and shift the burden of proof in an EEO trial from the complainant to the defendant.

2. In some cases, the appropriate labor market figure is the total population, despite the provision in section 703(j) of Title VII about statistical imbalances (Exhibit 2.3):

> Statistics showing racial or ethnic imbalance are probative in a case such as this one only because such imbalance is often a telltale sign of purposeful discrimination; absent explanation, it is ordinarily to be expected that nondiscriminatory hiring practices will in time result in a work force more or less representative of the racial and ethnic composition of the population in the community from which employees are hired. Evidence of longlasting and gross disparity between the composition of a work force and that of the general population thus may be significant even though § 703(j) makes clear that Title VII imposes no requirement that a work force mirror the general population.[7]

3. Where disparities are overwhelming, it is irrelevant to quibble over the niceties of statistical analysis. The defendants challenged the government's statistics largely on technical grounds. However, the Court observed:

> At best, these attacks go only to the accuracy of the comparison between the composition of the company's work force at various terminals and the general population of the surrounding communities. They detract little from the Government's further showing that Negroes and Spanish-surnamed Americans who were hired were overwhelmingly excluded from line-driver jobs. Such employees were willing to work, had access to the terminal, where healthy and of working age, and often were at least sufficiently qualified to hold city-driver jobs. Yet they became line drivers with far less frequency than whites.
>
> In any event, fine tuning of the statistics could not have obscured the glaring absence of minority line drivers. As the Court of Appeals remarked, the company's inability to rebut the inference of discrimination came not from a misuse of statistics but from "the inexorable zero."[8]

By these holdings, the *Teamsters* case made it possible for plaintiffs to advance their cases by demonstrating a disparity between the employer's work force and the general population.

# Teamsters *on Seniority*

Nevertheless, the Supreme Court ruled that the company and the union could keep their seniority system, despite its adverse impact on minorities. The important holdings on seniority were, first, that in passing section 703(h) of Title VII, Congress wished to protect bona fide seniority systems, even including systems that perpetuate the effects of "pre-Act" discrimination, discrimination committed before the effective date of Title VII:

> In sum, the unmistakable purpose of § 703(h) was to make clear that the routine application of a bona fide seniority system would not be unlawful under Title VII. As the legislative history shows, this was the intended result even where the employer's pre-Act discrimination resulted in whites having greater existing seniority rights than Negroes. Although a seniority system inevitably tends to perpetuate the effects of pre-Act discrimination in such cases, the congressional judgment was that Title VII should not outlaw the use of existing seniority lists and thereby destroy or water down the vested seniority rights of employees simply because their employer had engaged in discrimination prior to the passage of the Act.[9]

Second, a system is bona fide if it is created and maintained free from discriminatory purposes. Specifically, the Court said:

> The seniority system in this litigation is entirely bona fide. It applies equally to all races and ethnic groups. To the extent that it "locks" employees into non-line driver jobs, it does so for all. The city drivers and servicemen who are discouraged from transferring to line-driver jobs are not all Negroes or Spanish-surnamed Americans; to the contrary, the overwhelming majority are white. The placing of line drivers in a separate bargaining unit from other employees is rational, in accord with the industry practice, and consistent with National Labor Relations Board precedents. It is conceded that the seniority system did not have its genesis in racial discrimination, and that it was negotiated and has been maintained free from any illegal purpose. In these circumstances, the single fact that the system extends no retroactive seniority to pre-Act discriminatees does not make it unlawful.[10]

Third, those who were discriminatorily denied employment *after* the effective date of Title VII are entitled to retroactive seniority back to the date they would have been employed had the company not discriminated.[11]

The practical impact of these holdings is that a seniority system with disparate impact does not have to be defended in the way that other employment practices with disparate impact must be defended. Section

703(h) expressly protects seniority systems, but that section also expressly protects professionally developed ability tests, and *Griggs* established that the disparate impact of a test cannot be excused simply by showing that there was no discriminatory purpose behind the test's adoption or use. Thus, the Supreme Court has established separate rules for seniority systems and tests under section 703(h).

### *More on Stock Analysis:* Hazelwood *and the Relevant Labor Market*

Identifying the relevant labor market in an EEO case is complex. Theoretically, it involves enumerating those that are willing and able to perform the job in question. Practically speaking, though, it is impossible to obtain an estimate of how many blacks and whites are both willing and able. One cannot readily send a team of interviewers throughout the area in which potential employees might live to ask whether residents of the area would be willing to take a particular job or to assess the abilities of those who are willing.

As a workable approximation, then, some courts have more or less adopted the following definition of the relevant labor market for jobs that require skills not possessed by the general population: those living within a reasonable commuting or recruiting area for the facility who are in the same occupational classification as the job in question. While this definition may not be universally applicable, it is a practical definition, for various government agencies have collected occupational data and provide separate enumerations by sex, ethnic group, and occupation for a variety of geographical units encompassing the entire nation. Both the United States Bureau of the Census and the United States Department of Labor provide such statistics, which are used as evidence in many EEO cases. There are other definitions and other sources of data as well: enumerations by professional associations, licensing boards, vocational schools, and the like. Besides those, a court could consider unemployment statistics, records of state employment service applicants, and data on training program graduates.

Case 5.2, concerning the racial composition of a teaching staff, raises more complicated questions of representativeness than Case 5.1 does. The main issues are:

1. Should the employer's percentage of blacks be based on the total teaching staff or those hired since Title VII became effective?

2. Should the labor market percentage of blacks be based on the pupils in the district, the census enumeration of teachers in the metropolitan area, or the census enumeration of teachers in the metropolitan area outside the center city?

3. When those questions are answered, what determines whether the disparity between the two figures is great enough to constitute a prima facie case?

The U.S. Supreme Court decided these issues in *Hazelwood School District v. U.S.* Regarding the first question, the Court said:

> Racial discrimination by public employers was not made illegal under Title VII until March 24, 1972. A public employer who from that date forward made all its employment decisions in a wholly nondiscriminatory way would not violate Title VII even if it had formerly maintained an all-white work force by purposefully excluding Negroes. For this reason, the Court cautioned in the *Teamsters* opinion that once a prima facie case has been established by statistical work force disparities, the employer must be given an opportunity to show that "the claimed discriminatory pattern is a product of pre-Act hiring rather than unlawful post-Act discrimination."[12]

Regarding the second question, the Court totally rejected pupils in the district as the standard of comparison for the district's teaching staff. But the Court left the remaining choice up to the lower court, saying:

> In determining which of the two figures [overall metropolitan area or metropolitan area outside St. Louis, the center city]—or, very possibly, what intermediate figure—provides the most accurate basis for comparison to the hiring figures at Hazelwood, it will be necessary to evaluate such considerations as (i) whether the racially based hiring policies of the St. Louis City School District were in effect as far back as 1970, the year in which the census figures were taken; (ii) to what extent those policies have changed the racial composition of that district's teaching staff from what it would otherwise have been; (iii) to what extent St. Louis' recruitment policies have diverted to the city teachers who might otherwise have applied to Hazelwood; (iv) to what extent Negro teachers employed by the city would prefer employment in other districts such as Hazelwood; and (v) what the experience in other school districts in St. Louis County indicates about the validity of excluding the City School District from the relevant labor market. [Footnote omitted.][13]

Finally, in answering the third question, how to tell whether the disparity is large enough to constitute a prima facie case of discrimination and shift the burden of proof to the school district, the Court used a rule of thumb from the field of statistics:

> It involves calculation of the "standard deviation" as a measure of predicted fluctuations from the expected value of a sample. Using the 5.7% figure as the basis for calculating the expected value, the expected number of Negroes on the Hazelwood teaching staff would be roughly 63 in 1972–1973 and 70 in 1973–1974. The observed number in those years was 16 and 22, respectively. The difference between the observed and expected values was more than six standard deviations in 1972–1973 and more than five standard deviations in 1973–1974. . . .
>
> As a general rule for such large samples, if the difference between the expected value and the observed number is greater than two or three standard deviations, . . . then the hypothesis that teachers were hired without regard to race would be suspect.[14]

The standard deviation is a routine statistical tool, but the fact that the Court advanced this rule of thumb is noteworthy, for at least two reasons. First, the Supreme Court committed itself to specific numbers, albeit a range of numbers instead of a single number. Second, in specifying the standard deviation, the Supreme Court was using a measure that objectively took into consideration the size of the employer's work force. Previously, courts generally looked at the two black percentages and more or less intuitively decided whether the disparity was an important one. Often they did consider the fact that a given disparity was more likely to be due to chance rather than to discrimination when fewer employees were involved, but they usually did so subjectively. The standard deviation makes that determination objectively.

In other words, the standard deviation measure allows us to state precisely how confident we are that the difference did not arise by chance. For example, with a difference of two standard deviations between the employer's black percentage and the relevant labor market's black percentage, we can be nearly 98 percent confident that the difference did not arise by chance; with a three standard deviation difference, we are almost 99.9 percent confident.[15] If a difference does not arise by chance, then it arises by the operation of some systematic process—a process such as discrimination. Of course, some process besides discrimination may account for it, but that is up to the employer to prove.

## The Use of Labor Market Statistics by an Employer to Demonstrate Good Faith

Case 5.3 presents a situation in which the stock statistics make the employer look good. Technically, though, such statistics are part of the *plaintiff's* case, the prima facie case. So can an employer ever use them? The Supreme Court said that employers can use them in certain situations. The case, *Furnco Construction Corp.* v. *Waters*, was one of disparate treatment (see Exhibit 2.7), so the employer's motives were relevant:

> The employer must be allowed some latitude to introduce evidence which bears on his motive. Proof that his work force was racially balanced or that it contained a disproportionately high percentage of minority employees is not wholly irrelevant on the issue of intent when that issue is yet to be decided. We cannot say that such proof would have absolutely no probative value in determining whether the otherwise unexplained rejection of the minority applicants was discriminatorily motivated. Thus, although we agree . . . that in this case such proof neither was nor could have been sufficient to *conclusively* demonstrate that Furnco's actions were not discriminatorily motivated, the District Court was entitled to *consider* the racial mix of the work force when trying to make the determination as to motivation. The Court of Appeals should likewise give similar consideration to the proffered statistical proof in any further proceedings in this case.[16]

In short, *Furnco* established that employers can use statistics as evidence of good motives.

## Flow Analysis: Impact on Actual and Potential Applicants

Both the *Teamsters* case and the *Hazelwood* case were decided on the basis of stock analysis (representativeness) rather than flow analysis (impact). However, other cases (for example, *Green* v. *Missouri Pacific*) apply flow analysis to actual applicants. The relevant ingredients of a flow analysis are the number of candidates and the number of those candidates selected. The *selection ratio,* or *passing rate,* is the ratio of the number selected to the number of candidates. If the difference in selection ratios between groups is too great, the court will infer discriminatory impact. Once again, the question here is, How much is too much? Several methods for determining the answer have been proposed:

1. *Intuition:* adverse impact exists if the difference between the selection ratios of the two groups offends the judge's subjective notion of fairness.

2. *The four-fifths rule:* adverse impact exists if the ratio of the discriminated-against group's selection ratio to the selection ratio for the majority group is less than four-fifths:

$$\frac{S_d}{C_d} \Big/ \frac{S_m}{C_m} < 0.8$$

where $S$ = number selected; $C$ = number of candidates; $d$ = discriminated-against group; and $m$ = majority group. This is the standard used by the federal EEO agencies in the Uniform Guidelines for Employee Selection Procedures, which are discussed starting on page 105. In addition, some courts have recognized the four-fifths rule also.[17]

3. *The 95 percent confidence level:* adverse impact exists if the difference between the selection ratios is one which, statistically speaking, would not be expected to arise by chance alone more than 5 percent of the time. Basic statistics provides methods for determining the confidence level of a difference between two selection ratios. The figure of 95 percent is arbitrary; what is important is the fact that some courts acknowledge the legal status of a relatively technical concept such as confidence level.

4. *The two or three standard deviation rule:* adverse impact exists if one selection ratio differs from the other selection ratio by more than two or three standard deviations. This simply applies the *Hazelwood* rule to an analysis of impact on actual applicants.

Although impact on actual applicants seems like the most pertinent statistical evidence in a case of disparate impact, it may actually be a biased indicator of discrimination. For instance, if an organization discourages women or minorities from applying, that would cause the applicant impact statistics to make the organization look better than if it had turned them down after they had applied. The organization could underemploy women or minorities without showing adverse impact on actual women or minority applicants. Further, organizations would be discouraged from making efforts to attract more women and minority applicants, for fear that too many of them would have to be turned down as unqualified, and the actual applicant statistics would therefore look bad.

Impact on potential applicants is used infrequently, despite the fact that *Griggs* and *Green* v. *Missouri Pacific* mention it. One reason may be that it is simply not possible to evaluate data on potential applicants by means of standard statistical significance tests because the number of potential applicants is large. With large numbers of people, as in the *Griggs* example with high school graduates, virtually any difference in impact percentages would be statistically significant, and the employer would thereby fail the test no matter how small the race or sex difference in impact might be.

## Pay Analysis

There are also methods for determining whether differences in pay between groups are discriminatory. The pay differences of major concern are those between men and women. Pay discrimination is covered by Title VII and also by the Equal Pay Act of 1963, excerpted in Exhibit 5.1. Notice that the act permits pay differences that are due to differences in:

skill

effort

responsibility

working conditions

seniority

merit

quantity of production

quality of production

any other factor other than sex

The significance of the list is that if the employer can demonstrate that pay differences between male and female employees can be attributed to any of those factors, then the employer is not in violation of the Equal Pay Act.

There is a statistical method, called multiple regression analysis, for

**Exhibit 5.1**   Excerpts from the Equal Pay Act of 1963

---

### Section 3

(d) (1) No employer having employees subject to any provisions of this section shall discriminate, within any establishment in which such employees are employed, between employees on the basis of sex by paying wages to employees in such establishment at a rate less than the rate at which he pays wages to employees of the opposite sex in such establishment for equal work on jobs the performance of which requires equal skill, effort, and responsibility, and which are performed under similar working conditions except where such payment is made pursuant to (i) a seniority system; (ii) a merit system; (iii) a system which measures earnings by quantity or quality of production; or (iv) a differential based on any other factor other than sex: Provided, That an employer who is paying a wage rate differential in violation of this subsection shall not, in order to comply with the provisions of this subsection, reduce the wage rate of any employee.

---

determining whether the pay differences between men and women can be attributed to legitimate factors. It is not possible to discuss such methods thoroughly here. However, it can be said that if the pay differences between men and women are perfectly predictable from differences between them on the legitimate factors, then there is nothing left to be attributed to illegal discrimination. If not, then it is up to the employer to show some allowable reason for the pay difference between men and women. Multiple regression analysis determines whether there is any difference between men's and women's average pay levels after the variance due to legitimate factors has been removed systematically.

The main dispute over laws governing pay lies in the definition of the term *equal work* in the Equal Pay Act. Traditionally, pay differences between men in one job and women in another job have been defensible if the employer can demonstrate that the jobs did not involve "substantially equal work." Employers cannot pay men and women at different rates for essentially the same work simply by calling the women's job by one title and the men's job by another. However, in this view the act does allow employers to justify pay differences when there are actual dissimilarities in the work. This would allow work traditionally done by women to be paid less than work traditionally done by men—as long as the work is truly different.

Now, however, the EEOC is advancing the idea that EEO law mandates equal pay for work of comparable worth. By that criterion, even two jobs involving substantially different tasks must be paid the same if the worth in the work done in the two jobs is the same. This attitude attacks the problems of low pay for "women's work" such as nursing, teaching, and secretarial work. The problem with the standard of comparable worth, however, is that it is difficult to come up with a method for computing worth that does not perpetuate sex differences, much less to reach a general consensus that such a method should be legally mandated.[18]

## Proof of Job Relatedness: The Uniform Guidelines on Employee Selection Procedures

When the complainant in an EEO case succeeds by stock or flow analysis to establish a prima facie case, the employer must defend by presenting evidence that the practice in question was a business necessity or job related. What kind of evidence is sufficient to defend a practice having unequal impact has been the subject of hundreds of court cases. The most significant case is, of course, *Griggs* v. *Duke Power Co.* (see Chapter 2). In an important footnote to the *Griggs* opinion, the Court pointed to guidelines published by the EEOC as a source of information on the requirements a test would have to meet in order to be considered job related. Those guidelines, the Court said, were "entitled to great deference."[19]

The version of the guidelines that existed at that time was relatively straightforward—not entirely free from controversy, but rather moderate and reasonably intelligible to the informed manager. Since then, however, these guidelines have undergone several changes and have become quite technical and controversial.[20] A background in psychological measurement and industrial psychology is necessary to interpret the current guidelines fully. Still, it is imperative to attempt to understand the basics, no matter how complex the guidelines may be. This section of the chapter organizes and summarizes the main points and implications of those guidelines. It is not a thorough analysis, but it does provide a coherent overview.

Essentially, the guidelines cover three broad areas:

1. *Scope:* the practices that are covered by the guidelines

2. *Impact analysis:* what numerical criteria will be used to determine whether employment practices have adverse impact on one of the groups covered under the law
3. *Acceptable management alternatives:* the steps that management can take upon finding adverse impact

Each of these is discussed in turn.

## The Scope of the Guidelines

One aspect of scope is the laws that the selection guidelines interpret. Those laws are Title VII, Executive Order 11246, and the Inter-Governmental Personnel Act, a law covering public-sector employees. Any employer subject to any of those laws is required to abide by the guidelines.[21]

Another aspect of coverage is the employment practices that are covered. The selection guidelines apply to all staffing decisions—not just tests, but all other bases for employment decisions. That includes even subjective decision making, as discussed in Chapter 2. However, the selection guidelines do not cover employee recruitment, since recruitment is not a matter of selection decision making.[22]

It is easy to overlook the fact that these guidelines apply to more than just tests. Often employers make the mistake of abandoning their tests in favor of less formalized, alternative selection procedures because they believe that the alternatives will allow them to avoid the burden of compliance with the Uniform Guidelines.[23] Clearly that is not the case. Interviews and casual methods of personnel selection are covered as well. In fact, because tests are the most objective, best documented, and most completely validated means of personnel selection, it may be easier to reconcile them with the guidelines than to reconcile other selection procedures.

## Determination of Adverse Impact

Basically, the standard for determining adverse impact in the selection guidelines is the four-fifths rule discussed on page 102. In it, the government gives employers something rare—a specific rule. However, sometimes what the government gives with its right hand, it takes away with its left:

> Smaller differences in selection rate may nevertheless constitute adverse impact, where they are significant in both statistical and practical terms or where a

user's actions have discouraged applicants disproportionately on grounds of race, sex, or ethnic group. Greater differences in selection rate may not constitute adverse impact where the differences are based on small numbers and are not statistically significant, or where special recruiting or other programs cause the pool of minority or female candidates to be atypical of the normal pool of applicants from that group.[24]

In short, the agencies reserve their right to excuse an employer that fails the four-fifths rule or hold in violation an employer that satisfies the four-fifths rule. What determines when the agencies will bend the rule? The agencies have attempted to answer that question in a supplemental document called "Questions and Answers on the Uniform Guidelines." Of relevance is the following excerpt:

20. Q. Why is the 4/5ths rule called a rule of thumb?
A. Because it is not intended to be controlling in all circumstances. If, for the sake of illustration, we assume that nationwide statistics show that use of an arrest record would disqualify 10% of all Hispanic persons but only 4% of all whites other than Hispanic (hereafter non-Hispanic) the selection rate for that selection procedure is 90% for Hispanics and 96% for non-Hispanics. Therefore, the 4/5 rule of thumb would not indicate the presence of adverse impact (90% is approximately 94% of 96%). But in this example, the information is based upon nationwide statistics, and the sample is large enough to yield statistically significant results, and the difference (Hispanics are 2½ times as likely to be disqualified as non-Hispanics) is large enough to be practically significant. Thus, in this example the enforcement agencies would consider a disqualification based on an arrest record alone as having an adverse impact.[25]

The agencies' hedging is not surprising. When small numbers of employees are involved, a violation of the four-fifths rule will frequently arise by chance alone. On the other hand, when large numbers of employees are involved, systematic discrimination may exist even when the ratio of the passing rates is safely above four-fifths. We are left, then, with considerably less certainty about the directions that agency enforcement will take than the four-fifths rule in the guidelines might suggest. Nevertheless, the four-fifths rule stands as a center of gravity of sorts regarding the likelihood of agency acceptance of a selection procedure.

A second important principle is the *bottom line principle.* The guidelines explain this principle as follows:

C. *Evaluation of selection rates. The "bottom line."* If . . . the total selection process for a job has adverse impact, the individual components of the selection process should be evaluated for adverse impact. If . . . the total selection process does not have an adverse impact, the Federal enforcement agencies, in the exercise of their administrative and prosecutorial discretion, in usual circumstances, will not expect a user to evaluate the individual components for adverse impact, or to validate such individual components and will not take enforcement action based upon adverse impact of any component of that process, including the separate parts of a multipart selection procedure or any separate procedure that is used as an alternative method of selection.[26]

For example, consider the selection screening system depicted in Exhibit 5.2. Assume that an applicant cannot be processed by any step until completing the preceding step. Simple arithmetic shows that the *test* fails the four-fifths rule. However, the hiring process considered as a whole does satisfy the four-fifths rule, because the interviewer refers for testing a larger proportion of blacks than whites. The guidelines state that under such circumstances the agencies will be governed by the overall ratio of acceptance rates: the bottom line of the number actually hired. This provides some reassurance to employers that they can make up for adverse effect against a group in one part of the selection procedure by counterbalancing it with favorable treatment of that group in another step.

Faced with such reasonableness, the cynic will ask what the catch is. The catch is that the agency will recognize the claim of an applicant who is screened out by a procedure having adverse effect against members of his

**Exhibit 5.2** Selection System: The Bottom Line

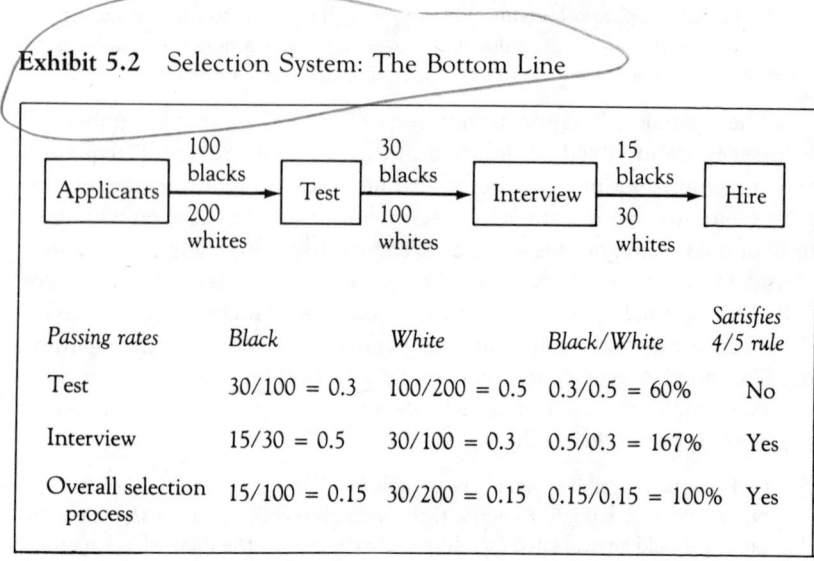

| Passing rates | Black | White | Black/White | Satisfies 4/5 rule |
|---|---|---|---|---|
| Test | 30/100 = 0.3 | 100/200 = 0.5 | 0.3/0.5 = 60% | No |
| Interview | 15/30 = 0.5 | 30/100 = 0.3 | 0.5/0.3 = 167% | Yes |
| Overall selection process | 15/100 = 0.15 | 30/200 = 0.15 | 0.15/0.15 = 100% | Yes |

or her group, regardless of whether the employer makes up for that impact by favoring other members of the group at another step in the selection process. The principle is that rights are individual, not collective, and the unfortunate victim of a procedure having adverse impact is comforted little by the realization that others of the group are getting preferential treatment in some other phase of the hiring process.

### Alternatives for Selection Procedures Having Adverse Impact

Boiling down all that the selection guidelines have to say concerning what an employer should do if faced with a selection procedure having adverse impact, there seem to be two basic alternatives:

1. *Eliminate the unequal impact.* Repeatedly, the guidelines invite the organization to avail itself of the bottom line principle. For example:

> Sec. 6. *Use of selection procedures which have not been validated.*
> A. *Use of alternative selection procedures to eliminate adverse impact.* A user may choose to utilize alternative selection procedures in order to eliminate adverse impact or as part of an affirmative action program. . . . Such alternative procedures should eliminate the adverse impact in the total selection process, should be lawful and should be as job related as possible.[27]

Two simple expedients that are suggested, more or less, in the guidelines are adjusting the impact of the test,[28] and establishing an affirmative action goal.[29] Adjusting the impact can be carried out as illustrated in Exhibit 5.2, or it can be effected by adding points to the scores of members of one group, so that the average scores of the group are equal.

2. *Present evidence that the test is valid.* The organization can do this either by conducting its own validity studies or by using information on the test's validity collected elsewhere. Conducting a validity study is an expensive, technical process that will be discussed briefly in the next section; the magnitude of the undertaking has naturally made employers interested in the second alternative. The opportunity to borrow a validity study is attractive. However, the selection guidelines set stringent requirements on employers wishing to generalize from other validity studies. To summarize them, the employer borrowing the study must demonstrate a similarity between its situation and the situation that exists in the organization where the study was conducted. That means a similarity between the jobs for which the candidates are being selected, between the char-

acteristics of the applicant pools, and between any other factor that might conceivably affect the validity of the test.[30]

## Guidelines Requirements for Validity Studies

For most practical purposes, job relatedness can be equated with validity. Validity is essentially a demonstration of the connection between the test and the job. Some of the requirements for a validity study are:

1. *Job analysis:* if validity is a connection between the test and the job, then some analysis of the job is necessary in order to demonstrate that the connection exists.[31]

2. *Quickly acquired skills:* a test is not considered valid if it tests for knowledge, skills, or abilities that are learned after a short time on the job.[32]

3. *Scoring:* cutoff scores must be reasonable, based on the expected level of performance of individuals receiving various scores on the test.[33] Also, the guidelines limit the use of scores to rank applicants:

> Evidence which may be sufficient to support the use of a selection procedure on a pass/fail (screening) basis may be insufficient to support the use of the same procedure on a ranking basis, and that method of use has a greater adverse impact than use on an appropriate pass/fail basis. . . . The user should have sufficient evidence of validity and utility to support the use on a ranking basis.[34]

4. *Using higher level tests:* it is not acceptable to use tests validated on a higher level job to select applicants for lower level jobs, except when there is a reasonable likelihood that the individual in the lower level job will be promoted to the higher level job.[35]

5. *Alternative tests with less adverse impact:* the guidelines say:

> B. *Consideration of suitable alternative selection procedures.* Where two or more selection procedures are available which serve the user's legitimate interest in efficient and trustworthy workmanship, and which are substantially equally valid for a given purpose, the user should use the procedure which has been demonstrated to have the lesser adverse impact. Accordingly, whenever a validity study is called for by these guidelines, the user should include, as a part of the validity study, an investigation of suitable alternative selection procedures and suitable alternative methods of using the selection procedure which have as little adverse impact as possible, to determine the appropriateness of using or validating them in accord with these guidelines.[36]

The possible open-endedness of such an investigation of suitable alternatives has led this section of the guidelines to be called the "cosmic search" requirement.

The guidelines follow traditional principles of psychological measurement in recognizing three methods for conducting a validity study: criterion, content, and construct validation.

**Criterion Validity**   Simply speaking, *criterion validity* is demonstrated when a correlation is shown between the test score and some measure of job performance, such as sales figures or supervisory ratings. Thus, the test has validity to the extent that individuals with higher test scores perform better on the job. The name *criterion validity* comes from the terminology of psychological measurement, which calls the job performance measure against which a test is correlated a "criterion" measure.

Criterion validity can be assessed either by giving the test to existing employees and correlating scores with a job performance measure (a *concurrent* validation study), or by giving the test to all applicants and determining the correlation between test scores and job performance only for those applicants that are finally hired (a *predictive* validation study). A predictive study is generally preferred, but it is more expensive than a concurrent study.

Some of the guidelines requirements for an acceptable criterion validity study are:

The job performance (criterion) measure should tap an important aspect of the job. [37]

The employer should attempt to make the job performance measure as free from bias as possible. For example, if supervisor ratings are used as the criterion measure, the employer should be aware that vague judgments of employees' performance may be more susceptible to bias than other measures (see pages 43–45). [38]

The sample of employees upon which the validity study is conducted should be representative of those available for employment for the job. Most obviously, the proportion of women and minorities in the sample must be adequate. [39]

The relationship between the test and its job performance criteria should be statistically significant, with a probability of no more than one in twenty of having occurred by chance. [40]

If it is technically feasible to do so, the employer should demonstrate the "fairness" of the test by showing that the test predicts job performance in the same way for all groups involved.[41] For example, if blacks with a test score of fifty have a job performance rating of ninety, then whites with a test score of fifty should have a job performance of ninety also. If this is not the case, then the employer should adjust the scoring so that individuals from different groups with the same test scores will have the same predicted job performance.[42]

***Content Validity***    A test is content valid if the content of the test constitutes a fair sample of the content of the job. To simplify, the procedure for constructing a content valid test is to identify the "content" of the job, that is, specify the tasks involved. Then randomly select a sample of those tasks and incorporate those tasks into the test. Finally, devise a scoring procedure which weights each task according to its relative importance to the job.

A simplified example of a content valid test is a typing test for a secretarial position. Such a test can roughly replicate conditions on the job: the applicant can be given a typical sample of typing work under typical working conditions, and his or her performance on that sample can be evaluated. Assuming that the tasks on the test constitute a random sample of the tasks on the job (ordinarily a dubious assumption at best), the test is content valid.

The selection guidelines requirements for content validity studies include these:

The job analysis, which is even more important for content then for criterion validity, must enumerate the work behaviors required, their relative importance, and the products that result.[43]

The test should measure *observable* work behavior or products rather than abstract traits considered important in a job. A selection procedure based on inferences about mental processes cannot be supported solely or primarily on the basis of content validity. Thus, a content strategy is not appropriate for demonstrating the validity of selection procedures which purport to measure traits like intelligence, aptitude, personality, common sense, judgment, and leadership.[44]

In short, the thrust of the guidelines is to minimize the inferential leap between the test and job performance. The less the content of the selection procedure resembles a work behavior, or the setting and manner of the administration of the selection procedure resemble the work situation, or the result resembles a work product, the less likely the selection procedure is to be content valid, and the greater the need for other evidence of validity.[45]

***Construct Validity*** A construct is a trait; a test is construct valid when it measures a trait that is important for a job. To take a simplified example, if the trait of leadership is important to the position of a police sergeant, a test that measures leadership would have construct validity for that position. To prove construct validity, an employer has to prove that the test actually does measure the trait, and that the trait actually is necessary for the job. Those two elements are often very difficult to prove. As an indication of that difficulty, the Uniform Guidelines establish three rather stringent general steps that a construct validity study must follow:

> The job analysis must systematically define both the work behaviors involved in the job and the constructs that are believed to be important to job performance.[46]

> The test must measure one of those constructs. In the example of the police sergeant, there must be evidence that the test validly measures leadership.[47] This evidence may be obtained from previous validity studies. For example, scores on the test might have correlated with leadership ratings given to other employees in other organizations upon previous administration of the test.

> The construct must be related to the performance of critical work behaviors.[48] For example, it must be shown that leadership ability is correlated with job performance for the position of police sergeant. In essence, this implies that a *criterion* validity study between leadership and job performance be conducted, or that such data be borrowed from an employer with a similar job situation.[49]

Understandably, then, organizations have not rushed to embrace construct validation as a means of satisfying the selection guidelines.

## Selection Guidelines: A Summary

Even though the above discussion is too brief to do justice to the Uniform Guidelines on Employee Selection Procedures, it does illustrate one important problem, that is that the selection guidelines impose such complex, stringent requirements on selection procedures having adverse impact that many employers elect not to bother attempting to validate their selection procedures. Instead, they hire by the numbers. If they sense that the government desires them to hire a given percentage of minorities or women, they attempt to hire that percentage; they impose a quota on themselves. With the quota, concern over validity is not legally mandated and tends to be forgotten. Indeed, the emphasis on hiring by the numbers is naturally taken as a sign that true ability, as measured by valid tests, is irrelevant. Many employers suspect that, even if they were to select their employees with unassailably valid tests, the government would find a way to harass them if their hiring practices had an adverse impact against one of the groups covered by the law. The tendency to ignore validation and hire by the numbers, then, is quite understandable.

The misfortune is that it is possible to have it both ways. It is possible to hire by the numbers *and* to employ a test that identifies the most competent of the applicants. That can be done by giving the test to all applicants as a measure of competency. Then, if a fixed number of individuals from each race and sex group were to be hired, the highest scoring members of each group would be selected. Some individuals would be turned down despite having scores higher than those from another group who were hired. But an employer would turn down no one whose score was higher than someone of the same race or sex who was hired. In short, while employers may feel obliged to hire a fixed number of women or minorities, there is no reason why those hired can't be the most competent women or minorities who apply.

## Notes

1. *International Brotherhood of Teamsters* v. *U.S.*, 331 U.S. 324 (1979).

2. *Richardson* v. *Hotel Corporation of America*, 332 F.Supp. 5119 (E.D. La. 1971). See also *Lane* v. *Inman*, 509 F.2d 184 (5th Cir. 1975).

3. There is an extensive literature on this topic. For example, see David C. Baldus and James W. L. Cole, *Statistical Proof of Discrimination* (New York: McGraw-Hill, 1980), with annual supplements; Frank C. Morris, Jr., *Current Trends in the Use (and Misuse) of Statistics in Employment Discrimination Litigation*, 2nd ed. (Washington, D.C.: Equal Employment Advisory Council, 1980); H. C. Hay, "The Use of Statistics to Disprove Employment Discrimination," *Labor Law Journal*, 29 (1978):430–40; W. H. Holley, Jr., and H. S. Feild, "Using Statistics in Employment Discrimination Cases," *Employee Relations Law Journal*, 4 (1978):43–58; E. W. Shoben, "Probing the Discriminatory Effects of Employee Selection Procedures with Disparate Impact Analysis under Title VII," *Texas Law Review*, 56 (1977):1–45.

4. *Green* v. *Missouri Pacific R.R. Co.*, 523 F.2d 1290 (8th Cir. 1975).

5. *Griggs* v. *Duke Power Co.*, 401 U.S. 424 (1971), n. 6.

6. Neil C. Churchill and John K. Shank, "Affirmative Action and Guilt-Edged Goals," *Harvard Business Review*, 54, No. 2 (March-April 1976):111–16.

7. *Teamsters* v. *U.S.*, p. 20.

8. Ibid., n. 23.

9. Ibid., pp. 352–53.

10. Ibid., pp. 355–56.

11. Ibid., Sec. III *et passim*. See also *Franks* v. *Bowman Transportation Co.*, 423 U.S. 814 (1976); P. I. Weiner, "Seniority Systems in the Post-Teamsters Era," *Labor Law Journal*, 30 (1979):545–58; *Watkins* v. *United Steelworkers of America, Local 2369*, 516 F.2d 41, 10 FEP 1297 (5th Cir. 1975); *Waters* v. *Wisconsin Steel Works of International Harvester Co.*, 502 F.2d 1309, 8 FEP 577 (7th Cir. 1974), *cert. denied*, 424 U.S. 997 (1976); *Franks* v. *Bowman Transportation Co.*, 424 U.S. 727, 12 FEP 549 (1976); and *Albemarle Paper Company* v. *Moody*, 422 U.S. 405 (1975).

12. 433 U.S. 299 (1977), pp. 309–10.

13. Ibid., pp. 311–12.

14. Ibid., n. 14. Here, the formula for the standard deviation of a percentage or a proportion is:

$$sd = \sqrt{pq/n}$$

where: $p$ = proportion of population that is black; $q$ = proportion of population that is not black $(1 - p)$; and $n$ = number of employees.

15. Technically, this is for a one-tail statistical test. It is used because, in an EEO case, the employer is accused of discrimination against a certain group, which is tantamount to a directional hypothesis requiring a one-tail test.

16. 438 U.S. 567 (1978), p. 580.

17. See *Firefighters Institute for Racial Equality* v. *City of St. Louis*, 616 F.2d 350 (8th Cir. 1980); *U.S.* v. *City of Chicago*, 21 FEP cases 200 (N.D. Ill. 1979); and Baldus and Cole, *Statistical Proof*, 1981 supplement.

18. L. Smith, "The EEOC's Bold Foray into Job Evaluation," *Fortune*, September 11, 1978, pp. 58ff. See also R. G. Blumrosen, "Wage Discrimination, Job Segregation, and Women Workers," *Employee Relations Law Journal*, 6 (1980):77–136; R. Blumrosen, "Wage Discrimination, Job Segregation, and Title VII of the Civil Rights Act of 1964," *University of Michigan Journal of Law Reform*, 12 (1979):397–502; and B. A. Nelson, E. M. Opton, Jr., and T. E. Wilson, "Wage Discrimination, and the 'Comparable Worth' Theory in Perspective," *University of Michigan Journal of Law Reform*, 13 (1980):233–301.

19. *Griggs* v. *Duke Power Co.*, 401 U.S. 424 (1971).

20. The current Selection Guidelines are at 29 Code of Federal Regulations, Part 1607. See also T. G. Abram, "Overview of Uniform Selection Guidelines: Pitfalls for the Unwary Employer," *Labor Law Journal*, 30 (1979):495–502.

21. Ibid., Sec. 2.A.

22. Ibid., Sec. 2.C.

23. See, for example, Hal Lancaster, "Job Tests Are Dropped by Many Companies Due to Antibias Drive," *Wall Street Journal*, September 3, 1975, pp. 1, 19.

24. Selection Guidelines, Sec. 4.D.

25. Questions and Answers on the Uniform Guidelines on Employee Selection Procedures, 44 Federal Register 11996 (March 2, 1979), question 20.

26. Selection Guidelines, Sec. 4.C.

27. Ibid., Sec. 6.A.

28. Ibid., Sec. 6.B(2).

29. Ibid., Sec. 17(2)(a).

30. Ibid., Sec. 7.

31. Ibid., Secs. 14.A and 14.B(2).

32. Ibid., Sec. 5.F.

33. Ibid., Sec. 5.H.

34. Ibid., Sec. 5.G.

35. Ibid., Sec. 5.I.

36. Ibid., Sec. 3.B. Also see R. C. Robertson, "The Search for Alternatives—The Need for Research Under the Uniform Guidelines on Employee Selection Procedures," *Labor Law Journal*, 30 (1979):483–88.

37. Ibid., Sec. 14.B(3).

38. Ibid., Sec. 14.B(2).

39. Ibid., Sec. 14.B(4).

40. Ibid., Sec. 14.B(5).

41. Ibid., Sec. 14.B(8). As mentioned on page 50, this provision would usually have an adverse effect on black employment.

42. Questions and Answers, question 67.

43. Selection Guidelines, Sec. 14.C(2).

44. Ibid., Sec. 14.C(1).

45. Ibid., Sec. 14.C(4). See also R. M. Guion, "Content Validity—The Source of My Discontent," *Applied Psychological Measurement*, 1 (1977):1–10; and R. M. Guion, "Scoring of Content Domain Samples: The Problem of Fairness," *Journal of Applied Psychology*, 63 (1978): 499–506.

46. Ibid., Sec. 14.D(2).

47. Ibid., Sec. 14.D(3).

48. Ibid.

49. Ibid., Sec. 14.D(4).

# 6

# Affirmative Action

*Case 6.1*  Three truck company employees, two whites and one black, were charged with misappropriating sixty one-gallon cans of antifreeze that were part of a shipment the company was carrying. The company fired the two whites but let the black employee off with a warning. The whites charged the company with discriminating against them because of race, in violation of Title VII. The company responded that Title VII was passed to solve problems of economic inequality and discrimination suffered by blacks; thus the congressional purpose of the statute indicated that it afforded no protection to whites.

*Case 6.2*  A chemical company and its union included an affirmative action provision in their collective bargaining agreement. Under that provision the company's on-the-job craft training programs, admission to which was governed by seniority, were subject to the requirement that 50 percent of the openings be given to black employees until the percentage of black craft workers in the company approximated the percentage of blacks in the local labor force. A white employee was turned down for the training program and charged the company with a violation of Title VII, because it admitted black employees with less seniority than he into the training program. The company and union said that such preferences were legal as a method for making up for the prior discrimination that blacks faced in the world of work.

The term *affirmative action* reveals almost nothing of its true meaning to those unfamiliar with EEO. We do know that many employers are expected to undertake affirmative action, but it is unclear exactly what that action should be. As it turns out, the term has a variety of meanings; this chapter explores those meanings.

## Chapter Objectives

One purpose of this chapter is to review the various definitions of affirmative action and indicate the legal status of each. In doing so, it distinguishes between the kind of affirmative action that a federal court can order (*involuntary* affirmative action) and the kind that can be undertaken in the absence of a court order (*voluntary* affirmative action).[1] Then the chapter examines the legal status of one definition that is sometimes given for affirmative action: preferential treatment of underrepresented groups.

The last half of the chapter discusses affirmative action planning requirements for government contractors. We will discuss the requirement for setting goals and timetables to increase the employment of underutilized groups. Setting affirmative action goals is a complicated task if done properly; its complexity explains in part why there has been so much dissatisfaction with affirmative action.

## Definitions of Affirmative Action

Affirmative action has meant different things to different people. Among the possible definitions that have emerged over the years are these:

1. *Recruitment of underrepresented groups:* seeking applicants from groups that are underrepresented in the employer's work force

2. *Changing management attitudes:* trying to eliminate conscious and unconscious prejudices that individual managers and supervisors may have toward groups that are underrepresented in the employer's work force

3. *Removing discriminatory obstacles:* identifying those employment practices that work to the disadvantage of groups that are underrepresented in the employer's work force and replacing them with practices that do not work to the disadvantage of those groups

4. *Preferential treatment:* hiring and staffing preferentially for groups that are underrepresented in the employer's work force

The first three definitions are straightforward and not particularly controversial, and they are certainly legal for an employer to undertake. The fourth definition is more controversial, and so more attention will be devoted to it than to the others.

## The Legal Status of Preferential Treatment

The legality of preferential treatment depends in part on whether the affirmative action is involuntary (court ordered) or voluntary (all preferences that are not court ordered are considered voluntary, including preferences an employer includes in its affirmative action plan). Most involuntary affirmative action has its origin in section 706(g) of Title VII:

> *If the court finds* that the respondent has intentionally engaged in or is intentionally engaging in an unlawful employment practice charged in the complaint, the court may enjoin the respondent from engaging in such unlawful employment practice, and order such *affirmative action* as may be appropriate, which may include, but is not limited to, reinstatement or *hiring* of employees, with or without back pay (payable by the employer, employment agency, or labor organization, as the case may be, responsible for the unlawful employment practice), *or any other equitable relief* as the court deems appropriate [emphasis added].

It is clear that the clause predicates affirmative action upon a finding of guilt by a court. The consensus of the courts is that this kind of affirmative action could include hiring preferences for discriminated-against groups.[2] Involuntary affirmative action is seen as a *remedy* for prior illegal behavior on the part of the employer. One might look at it as a means of redressing an imbalance that was caused by the employer's past discriminatory treatment of the group in question.

At first, this interpretation of section 706(g) may seem to conflict with section 703(j) of Title VII, which says, "nothing contained in this title shall be interpreted to require any employer . . . to grant preferential treatment to any individual or to any group" because of race, color, religion, sex, or national origin. However, a careful reading reveals that the two do not conflict. Specifically, section 703(j) does not *prohibit* preferential treatment; it only makes it clear that Title VII shall not be interpreted to require it. And the section deals only with preferential treatment that might be required "on account of an imbalance which may exist," not with preferential treatment that might be required on account of other reasons—for instance, on account of prior acts of discrimination by the employer.

However, there is a clearer statement in Title VII regarding preferential treatment than section 703(j). Section 703(a)(1) explicitly prohibits discrimination because of race, religion, sex, or national origin. Presumably that includes "reverse" discrimination, that is, discrimination against the majority caused by preferential treatment of a minority. The discussion of legislative history in Chapter 2 supports that view. When one group is preferred, someone will *not* be hired, placed, or promoted *because* he or she was not a member of that group. Clearly, then, preferential treatment because of race, religion, sex, or national origin violates the wording of section 703(a) of Title VII of the 1964 Civil Rights Act. This would seem to threaten voluntary preferences.

Case 6.1 presents a clear example of the kind of preferential treatment that seems to be prohibited by section 703(a). Perhaps the company decided not to discharge the black employee because it was concerned about the EEO implications. The company may not have wanted to lose any of its black employees, and it certainly did not want to provoke a charge of discrimination against the company. The fact that the white employees filed the discrimination charge is one of the ironies that federal regulation holds for employers. The U.S. Supreme Court decided this issue in favor of the white employees in *McDonald* v. *Santa Fe Trail Transportation Co.*:

> Title VII of the Civil Rights [Act] prohibits the discharge of "any individual" because of "such individual's race." . . . Its terms are not limited to discrimination against members of any particular race. Thus although we were not there confronted with racial discrimination against whites, we described the Act in *Griggs* v. *Duke Power Co.* . . . as prohibiting "discriminatory preference for *any* [racial] group, *minority or majority*" (emphasis added). Similarly the EEOC, whose interpretations are "entitled to great deference," *Griggs* v. *Duke Power Co.*, . . . has consistently interpreted Title VII to proscribe racial discrimination in private employment against whites on the same terms as racial discrimination against nonwhites. . . . This conclusion is in accord with uncontradicted legislative history to the effect that Title VII was intended to "cover all white men and white women and all Americans," . . . and create an "obligation not to discriminate against whites."[3]

That decision left employers in a quandary. As Chapter 5 pointed out, a statistical imbalance can stand as evidence of discrimination. Thus employers are under pressure to make their work forces numerically representative of the relevant labor market through special efforts to hire and promote members of underrepresented groups. To make such efforts without occasionally lapsing into preferential treatment of members of a group is to walk a fine line. Understandably, then, employers were fearful that, whatever they might do, they would be subjected to legal attack—either for not employing enough women and minorities or for discriminating against white males in their efforts to employ more women and minorities. Understandably too, the *McDonald* case and others like it[4] were viewed as a barrier to the progress of women and minorities in the world of work, because they discouraged employers from making vigorous efforts to hire and promote them.

Case 6.2 indicates the nature of the potential conflict between minority employment and Title VII. How is the employer to improve the position of blacks without giving them preferential admission to the training program?

In 1979, the Supreme Court decided the issue in favor of the company. The case, *Weber* v. *Kaiser Aluminum and Chemical Corp.,* is one of the most important EEO cases decided by the courts. To decide in favor of the company's affirmative action plan, the Court had to confront two seemingly contradictory pronouncements: their own earlier holding in *McDonald* (Case 6.1) and the wording of section 703(a) of Title VII. The Court disposed of the *McDonald* case easily by pointing to a footnote in *McDonald* that expressly stated that the Court was not passing judgment on affirmative action plans.[5] The *McDonald* case concerned discrimination in discharge procedures, so the court did not view it as governing how they should decide a case such as *Weber* that involved affirmative action placements in training programs.

It was not so easy for the Supreme Court to resolve the apparent contradiction between section 703(a) of Title VII and Kaiser's numerical preference system. The Court's treatment of this issue was unusual and noteworthy in that it overruled the words of the law:

> It is a "familiar rule, that a thing may be within the letter of the statute and yet not within the statute, because not within its spirit, nor within the intention of its makers."[6]

Seldom does a court reject the words of a statute, even in the name of legislative intent. Ordinarily, courts try to *reconcile* the words of the law and the intentions of the lawmaker. But this was far from an ordinary case, and the issues it raised were extraordinary ones as well:

> The prohibition against racial discrimination in §§703(a) and (d) of Title VII must therefore be read against the background of the legislative history of Title VII and the historical context from which the Act arose. . . . Examination of those sources makes clear that an interpretation of the sections that forbade all race-conscious affirmative action would "bring about an end completely at variance with the purpose of the statute" and must be rejected. . . .
>
> Congress' primary concern in enacting the prohibition against racial discrimination in Title VII of the Civil Rights Act of 1964 was with "the plight of the Negro in our economy." . . . "The relative position of the Negro worker [was] steadily worsening." . . .
>
> Congress feared that the goals of the Civil Rights Act—the integration of blacks into the mainstream of American society—could not be achieved unless this trend were reversed. . . .
>
> It plainly appears from the House Report accompanying the Civil Rights Act that Congress did not intend wholly to prohibit private and voluntary affirmative action efforts as one method of solving this problem. . . .
>
> Given this legislative history, we cannot agree with respondent that Congress intended to prohibit the private sector from taking effective steps to accomplish the goal that Congress designed Title VII to achieve. . . . It would be ironic indeed if a law triggered by a Nation's concern over centuries of racial injustice and intended to improve the lot of those who had "been excluded from the American dream for so long," 110 Cong. Rec., at 6552 (remarks of Sen. Humphrey), constituted the first legislative prohibition of all voluntary, private, race-conscious efforts to abolish traditional patterns of racial segregation and hierarchy.[7]

The Court's majority focused on the fact that Kaiser's affirmative action plan was a result of deliberation and negotiation between the company and the union. This voluntary collaborative aspect of the quota was important to the Court, which said that Congress desired to protect such voluntary actions by employers when it passed Title VII in 1964. Ironically, the Court cited conservative critics of Title VII in justifying their approval of the quota system:

> Title VII could not have been enacted into law without substantial support from legislators in both Houses who traditionally resisted federal regulation of private business. Those legislators demanded as a price for their support that "management prerogatives and union freedoms . . . be left undisturbed to the greatest extent possible." . . . In view of this legislative history and in view of Congress' desire to avoid undue federal regulation of private businesses, use of the

word "require" rather than the phrase "require or permit" in §703(j) fortifies the conclusion that Congress did not intend to limit traditional business freedom to such a degree as to prohibit all voluntary, race-conscious affirmative action.[8]

However, the *Weber* case does not legitimate all quota systems, only those that are part of a "bona fide affirmative action plan." It is not exactly clear what makes an affirmative action plan bona fide, but the Court's opinion seems to imply that employers should be reluctant to use:

1. a numerical standard more stringent than the 50 percent quota used by Kaiser, or otherwise less accommodating to majority rights[9]

2. a plan that breaks down old discriminatory patterns less than Kaiser's[10]

3. a plan that is less voluntary than Kaiser's, more of an imposition on labor or management[11]

4. any quota that is not clearly designed to end when numerical balance is attained in the employer's work force.[12]

Those points were not stated explicitly by the Court as a precise set of rules; they are only some of the factors that seem important.

The dissenting opinion in the *Weber* case was forceful. The minority pointed to evidence in the Congressional Record that Congress did intend Title VII to prohibit preferential treatment designed to achieve racial balance. Some of that evidence was reviewed in Chapter 2. The opinion quoted many legislators who apparently did not view the law they were passing as condoning even benign preferences for victims of discrimination. Whether one accepts the majority's view that the historical context in which Title VII was passed dictates that it be interpreted to allow preferential treatment in order to solve the social problems it was designed to solve, or the minority's view that the legislators themselves did not desire it to be interpreted to allow preferential treatment, it seems safe to say that the debate over the wisdom, if not the legality, of preferences is still alive.

Exhibit 6.1 summarizes the legal status of preferential treatment. Though an oversimplification, it provides a general overview of the law of preference. The major uncertainty is what constitutes a "permissible" affirmative action plan. The four *Weber* case cautions above provide some guidance. Another source of guidance might be found in the regulations governing affirmative action by federal contractors. Those regulations are discussed in the following pages.

**Exhibit 6.1** Is Preferential Treatment Legal?

| Type of Preference | Answer | Reason |
|---|---|---|
| *Involuntary* (court ordered) | | |
| Ordered because of an imbalance | No | Section 703(j) of Title VII |
| Ordered because of Title VII violation | Yes | Section 706(g) of Title VII |
| *Voluntary* | | |
| Part of a permissible affirmative action plan | Yes | *Weber* v. *Kaiser* |
| Not part of a permissible affirmative action plan | No | *McDonald* v. *Santa Fe* |

## Affirmative Action for Government Contractors

It is widely conceded that government contractors are required to engage in all four forms of affirmative action discussed at the beginning of this chapter, including preferential treatment. However, nothing in the regulations specifies that preferences are required; instead, euphemisms are used. Contractors are not told to set quotas; they are told instead to set "goals and timetables."[13] They are not told to engage in preferential treatment; they are told instead to engage in a "good faith effort to make [their] overall affirmative action program work." Whether that adds up to a mandate for preferential treatment is a matter of debate. However, it seems safe to say that most employers regard it as such.

The regulation outlining the required ingredients of affirmative action for federal contractors is Revised Order No. 4, issued by the Office of Federal Contract Compliance Programs, a subdivision of the U.S. Department of Labor. Revised Order No. 4 is a detailed regulation. Most of it lists the required and suggested steps that management should take in the name of affirmative action. This discussion organizes the main items in that list in an attempt to show what the major components of affirmative action planning are.

Revised Order No. 4 can be divided into three main planning steps:

1. Conduct a *utilization analysis,* a comparison of employment of

women and minorities in the employer's work force with the availability of women and minorities in the labor market.

2. Establish *goals and timetables* to eliminate any instances of underutilization of women and minorities in the employer's work force. Goals and timetables are numbers showing the expected levels of utilization and the dates when those levels will be attained.

3. Plan *action steps* to be taken by management as means of reducing underutilization and thus attaining the goals and timetables.

Those three components, and the problems involved in carrying them out, are discussed below.

## Utilization Analysis

The utilization analysis called for in Revised Order No. 4 includes two steps: an analysis of the employer's work force and an analysis of the available labor supply.[14] The outcome of each step is a set of numbers: two numbers for each job, one showing the percentage of the employer's work force that belongs to the group in question and the other showing the percentage of the available labor supply that belongs to that group. If there is a disparity between the two numbers, then that group is said to be "underutilized" and the employer is expected to establish goals and timetables to eliminate the underutilization. Clearly, utilization analysis is significant because it determines the magnitude of the goal.

There is a similarity between a utilization analysis and a labor market analysis pursuant to a prima facie case, as discussed in Chapter 5. The objective of both is to compare the utilization of groups in the employer's work force with the representation of those groups in some external population. One might include, perhaps naively, that the same rules apply to both—that the same statistical standard for determining whether a disparity between the employer's work force and the relevant labor market is great enough to shift the burden of proof to an employer in a court case might also determine whether the degree of underutilization is great enough to require goals and timetables in an affirmative action plan. The government does not make it that easy, however; the rules are different.

The major difference between a utilization analysis and a labor market analysis pursuant to a prima facie case can be seen in this description of a utilization analysis from Revised Order No. 4:

In determining whether minorities are being underutilized in any job group the contractor will consider at least all of the following factors:

(i) The minority population of the labor area surrounding the facility;

(ii) The size of the minority unemployment force in the labor area surrounding the facility;

(iii) The percentage of the minority work force as compared with the total work force in the immediate labor area;

(iv) The general availability of minorities having requisite skills in the immediate labor area;

(v) The availability of minorities having requisite skills in an area in which the contractor can reasonably recruit;

(vi) The availability of promotable and transferable minorities within the contractor's organization;

(vii) The existence of training institutions capable of training persons in the requisite skills; and

(viii) The degree of training which the contractor is reasonably able to undertake as a means of making all job classes available to minorities.[15]

A similar list of factors is used to determine whether women are being underutilized.

Immediately evident from that list is the multitude of data sources that must be considered in determining the availability of women and minorities in affirmative action planning. Usually those sources lead to conflicting conclusions about underutilization in the organization. By contrast, in a court case a single factor can determine whether the burden of proof is shifted to the defendant—for example, population in the *Teamsters* case and the number of licensed schoolteachers in the *Hazelwood* case. Moreover, in affirmative action planning there is no authoritative guide to combining and weighing the eight factors to determine whether underutilization exists. While a list of specific weights has been provided by the OFCCP, those weights seems somewhat arbitrary, and the agency does not insist upon them. Thus, the organization is left with a degree of uncertainty about whether its eight-factor analysis adds up to a verdict of underutilization and a mandate for goals and timetables.

The analysis of the composition of the employer's work force is the other component of the utilization analysis. Revised Order No. 4 requires an enumeration by race, sex, and ethnic group for each job group. A *job group* is defined as "one or a group of jobs having similar content, wage rates and opportunities."[16] When the task of collecting information about each of the eight factors for each job group is added to that of determining how the eight factors are to be weighed and combined for each job classification, the analysis becomes a major personnel undertaking.

## Goals and Timetables

Goals and timetables specify the percentage of a job group to be filled by women or minorities and the date by which that percentage is to be attained. Goals and timetables are required for all job groups in which underutilization is found.[17] Usually there is a sequence of year-by-year goals for each job group, and the OFCCP expects those goals to lead to complete elimination of underutilization.[18] Revised Order No. 4 adds the following requirements:

> (a) . . . in establishing the size of his goals and the length of his timetables, the contractor should consider the results which could reasonably be expected from his putting forth every good faith effort to make his overall affirmative action program work.
>
> . . . .
>
> (e) Goals may not be rigid and inflexible quotas which must be met. . . .
>
> (f) In establishing timetables to meet goals and commitments, the contractor will consider the anticipated expansion, contraction and turnover of and in the work force.[19]

The first requirement, that the goals be attainable with a good faith effort, depends on the definition of good faith effort. The reader's common sense notion of what the term means is probably as good as any definition the author could give. Presumably, in ascertaining whether an organization has put forth a good faith effort, the OFCCP looks for evidence that the organization at least tried to do what it planned to do, perhaps that its heart is in the right place when it comes to EEO. The requirement that goals not be inflexible quotas is often taken with a grain of salt by cynics, especially considering the decision in the *Weber* case. Finally, the requirement to consider expansion, contraction, and turnover is essential, if for no other reason than to avoid setting goals that are impossible to attain. Unfortunately, consideration of those factors is seldom as careful and accurate as it should be.

## Action Steps

Most of Revised Order No. 4 is concerned with listing steps that contractors can take to reduce underutilization and achieve their goals. Some of those steps specify management roles in the affirmative action process. Revised Order No. 4 gives top management the responsibility for legitimating affirmative action by making it clear to the entire organization that the chief executive officer is committed to the task.[20] However, the order also emphasizes the importance of involvement by all management levels in the planning process, particularly in setting goals.[21]

Other steps involve communication to encourage underutilized groups to seek positions with the organization.[22] One type of communication involves publicizing the contractor's affirmative action policy, both inside and outside the organization. The contractor is expected to publicize its affirmative action posture internally by means of meetings, training programs, and company newspapers. The contractor is expected to publicize it externally by maintaining contact with minority and women's organizations, by participating in programs designed to increase the employment opportunities of underemployed groups, and by including women and minorities among people pictured in company advertising. Besides that sort of publicity, another important form of communication is announcing job opportunities, both internally and externally. Contractors are expected to post openings on bulletin boards and establish formal procedures for competitive bidding on those openings. And they are expected to publicize job openings to the outside world in ways that would reach women and minority applicants. Recruitment should include women's and black schools as well as predominantly white schools. Managers are also expected to reach out beyond the predominantly white or male civic organizations that they have traditionally been affiliated with. Job vacancies are expected to be listed with employment agencies such as state employment services that are likely to reach members of underutilized groups.[23]

Also recommended are steps designed to increase employment opportunities by removing unnecessary barriers to employment.[24] Job specifications and selection methods must be validated if they screen out women and minorities disproportionately. Also, managers making employment decisions should be selected and trained to ensure freedom from bias. In addition, the contractor should, whenever possible, use public training programs that are likely to reach members of underutilized groups. Other suggestions are career counseling programs for employees, job rotation, and child care and transportation programs for employees.

Finally, part of the order covers auditing and controlling the affirmative action process.[25] The contractor is expected to conduct a thorough analysis of the organization to identify problem areas—practices that violate EEO laws and units of the organization in which there is underutilization. Also, various levels of management are expected to be involved in the process of planning and executing solutions to those problems. The effectiveness of the solutions must be monitored regularly. Auditing and controlling is by no means a simple matter: the expectations of the federal government are so detailed and the scope of affirmative action so wide that it is difficult to devise a system to monitor the entire operation.

## The Main Problem: Setting Goals

Many written plans reflect something less than a wholehearted commitment to the ideals of affirmative action. Many are largely copied verbatim from Revised Order No. 4 or from some model affirmative action plan. Understandably, affirmative action often seems a combination of going through the motions and getting the numbers to look good enough to keep the OFCCP off the organization's back. And often the result is unattainable goals.

Ideally, then, affirmative action planning involves the following steps:

1. Identify areas of underutilization in the organization by means of the utilization analysis.
2. Determine how the organization's employment policies might be contributing to that underutilization.
3. Plan for changes in those policies (action steps).
4. Set affirmative action employment goals.
5. Later, note the organization's successes and failures in meeting those goals.
6. Try to identify the reasons for the failures.
7. Take those reasons into account in the next cycle of planning and goal setting.

All too often, however, affirmative action follows these steps:

1. Conduct the utilization analysis, making every effort to minimize the reported disparity between the employer's work force and the available labor market.
2. Where disparities do exist, set affirmative action goals and timetables, but keep them as lenient as possible, yet stringent enough to avoid the wrath of the OFCCP.
3. For "action steps," give as much preference to underutilized groups

as possible in hiring and promoting decisions, but do not make the preferential treatment so blatant as to precipitate discontent in the organization.

4. Later, identify successes and failures in goal attainment.

5. Where failures exist, try to think of excuses that will sound plausible to the OFCCP.

6. Pray for mercy.

7. If prayers are not answered, set more difficult goals for the next planning cycle.

One cause of these problems lies in the nature of the regulations themselves. As the discussion of Revised Order No. 4 above suggests, the requirements for affirmative action planning are sometimes unclear and other times so burdensome as to invite evasion. An examination of the order will reveal why it is so difficult to comply with. Also, the order implies that goals are set before action steps are planned—as in the second list of seven steps, rather than in the first list—which raises the risk that the goals cannot be attained by means of any reasonable set of action steps.

A number of writers have suggested that the problems can be remedied in part by certain steps that are not required by Revised Order No. 4.[26] While the order specifies detailed planning steps, it does not specify a complete and coherent approach. Specifically, the problem of unattainable goals often results from a factor not covered adequately in Revised Order No. 4 and not addressed in the affirmative action planning systems used by most organizations: *internal mobility.* Internal mobility is the movements of employees within the organization's work force: the promotions, demotions, and transfers that employees ordinarily expect in most organizations. Clearly, internal mobility affects the attainability of affirmative action goals.

One way to incorporate the impact of internal mobility on affirmative action is to project the number of external hiring opportunities the organization will have. For each job class, the expected number of promotions and terminations are subtracted from the current number of employees to arrive at a count of expected hiring opportunities. Those hiring opportunities are then allocated among the race, sex, and ethnic groups, and the resulting new hiring figures for each group are added to the number of employees from that group who are expected to remain in the job classification or to move in from another job classification within the organization.

However, a little thought will show why this method may be impractical in some situations. First, the manager must estimate how many people from each race, sex, and ethnic group will leave the organization—a difficult task to carry out accurately in many organizations. Second, the people who are promoted or transferred *out* of a job class must be added *in* somewhere, and it is often difficult for managers to make certain the promotions out of all the jobs add up to the promotions in. Third, the promotion and transfer rates may differ among race, sex, and ethnic groups within any job class. In fact, if women and minorities are less likely to get promoted than males from the majority, they may get discouraged and may be more likely to leave the organization. Not only could that complicate goal setting, but also it would mean that the organization's affirmative action problems are caused in part by the promotions process, and promotion goals as well as hiring goals are required.

Even simple situations get complicated. With only 5 job classes, there are 6 possible places where employees may be at the time for which the goals are set: the same job, one of the 4 other job classes, or outside the organization. That applies to both sexes for at least 2 races, black and white. The *total number of personnel flows*, or movements to keep track of, would be 5 job classes × 6 possible destinations × 2 sexes × 2 races = 120 personnel flows or movements. For 10 job classes and 4 race/ethnic groups, the figure would be $10 \times 11 \times 2 \times 4 = 880$ flows. It is no wonder that managers throw up their hands in despair.

A computer can help keep track of movements and forecast future personnel flows, as some organizations have demonstrated.[27] The manager can use the computer to test various affirmative action strategies and forecast their effects on the employment of underutilized groups. For example, the manager can ask the computer what would happen if a certain number of blacks were hired into a certain position or if a training program increased the number of women qualified for promotion. Once the manager finds a feasible mix of affirmative action strategies, one that is forecast to produce acceptable results, the forecast results can become the affirmative action goals.

Notice how the use of the computer brings the process of goal setting somewhat closer to the ideal set of eight steps listed above. By basing affirmative action goals on a set of specific action steps designed to produce specific changes in staffing patterns, the organization might persuade the OFCCP to judge its "good faith" by the criterion of whether it takes the steps it planned rather than whether it achieved the numerical goals it set. Both the employer and the agency can diagnose more easily the reasons for failure to obtain goals, separating the failures due to bad faith from those due to unanticipated staffing changes that took place despite the fact that the planned action steps were taken (for example, black turnover rates not dropping despite the organization's well publicized efforts to provide promotion opportunities).

Finally, compared with typical approaches to goal setting, the approach advanced here is clearly more consistent with what the *Griggs* case tells us about congressional intent: only if the manager examines the movements of employees into, through, and out of the organization can there be any hope of removing the "artificial and arbitrary barriers" that have caused the underemployment of women and minorities.

## Notes

1. Certainly, however, there are degrees of compulsion in "voluntary" affirmative action. An employer does not feel free to ignore an agency's recommendation for an affirmative action goal simply because it is not backed up by the authority of a court.

2. *Rios* v. *Enterprise Association Steamfitters, Local 638,* 326 F. Supp. 198 (S. Dist. N.Y. 1971); *Franks* v. *Bowman Transportation Co.,* 423 U.S. 814 (1976).

3. At 427 U.S. 273, pp. 278–80 (1976).

4. *Brunetti* v. *City of Berkeley,* 12 FED Cases 937; 11 CCH Employment Practices Decisions Par. 10,804 (N. Dist. Cal. 1975); *Watkins* v. *United Steelworkers of America, Local No. 2369,* 516 F.2d 41 (5th Cir. 1975); *Chance* v. *Board of Examiners,* 534 F.2d 993 (2d Cir. 1976); *Weber* v. *Kaiser Aluminum and Chemical Corp.,* 564 F.2d 216 (5th Cir. 1976), *reversed,* 443 U.S. 193 (1979).

5. 423 U.S. 923, n. 8 (1976).

6. 443 U.S. 193, p. 201 (1979); quoting *Holy Trinity Church* v. *United States,* 143 U.S. 457, p. 459 (1892).

7. Ibid., pp. 201–4.

8. Ibid., pp. 206–7.

9. Ibid., pp. 199, 201.

10. Ibid., p. 201.

11. Ibid., p. 200.

12. Ibid., p. 201.

13. Revised Order No. 4, 41 Code of Federal Regulations, Part 60, at Sec. 2.10 (1979).

14. Ibid., Sec. 2.11.

15. Ibid., Sec. 2.11(b)(1).

16. Ibid., Sec. 2.11(b).

17. Ibid., Sec. 2.10.
18. Ibid., Sec. 2.12(g).
19. Ibid., Sec. 2.12.
20. Ibid., Sec. 2.20(a).
21. Ibid., Sec. 2.22(b).
22. Ibid., Sec. 2.21.
23. Ibid., Sec. 2.24.
24. Ibid.
25. Ibid., Secs. 2.23 and 2.25.
26. James Ledvinka, "Technical Implications of Equal Employment Law for Manpower Planning," *Personnel Psychology* 28 (1975):299–323; Neil C. Churchill and John K. Shank, "Affirmative Action and Guilt-Edged Goals," *Harvard Business Review* 54, no. 2 (March–April 1976):57–70; William B. Chew and Richard L. Justice, "EEO Modeling for Large Complex Organizations," *Human Resource Planning* 2 (1979):57–70; George T. Milkovich and Frank Krzystofiak, "Simulation and Affirmative Action Planning," *Human Resource Planning* 2 (1979):71–80.
27. For example, General Motors (see Chew and Justice, "EEO Modeling"); and AT&T (Lee Dyer and Elizabeth C. Wesman, "Affirmative Action Planning at AT&T, *Human Resource Planning* 2 (1979):81–90).

# II

# Employee Safety and Health

# 7

# Workers' Compensation Laws

*Case 7.1*   A male production supervisor asked one of his female workers to work overtime. The worker answered that it would make her miss her carpool ride home. Since company rules required the supervisor to stay on the job whenever subordinates work overtime, and since the worker lived only a few miles from the supervisor, the supervisor offered to drive her home. By the time they left work, it was dark and the roads were icy. The supervisor's car skidded off the road, and the force of the skid pushed the worker over into the arms of the supervisor. One thing led to another, and the worker hit the supervisor and caused an injury that hospitalized him for an extended period. The supervisor filed a workers' compensation claim against his employer for lost pay and medical expenses.[1]

*Case 7.2*   A supervisor repeatedly reprimanded a worker, who retaliated with threats against the supervisor. Shortly thereafter, the supervisor took a position with another company. Later, in a tavern, he met the worker he had reprimanded, who made good on his earlier threats. As a result of the brawl, the supervisor suffered a disabling injury. He sued his former employer for workers' compensation.[2]

*Case 7.3*   A textile mill employee complained to a fellow worker that his back hurt when he did a certain lifting task one day on the job. He reported to the company physician, who diagnosed his complaint as a strain of the lower back muscles. The employee returned to work immediately, but left a month later with the same problem. He died not too long thereafter from cancer, which he had been unaware that he had had. Medical examiners concluded that the back strain had caused the cancer to spread more rapidly than it would have otherwise. Thus his widow filed for death benefits under workers' compensation, on the grounds that the job-induced back strain contributed to and hastened the employee's death.[3]

***Case 7.4*** Mackinac Island in Lake Superior is a resort of great beauty, offering recreational activities in a charming, isolated setting. Part of the attractiveness of the island is that motor vehicles are not allowed on it. Much of the travel on the island is by bicycle, and the bicycling is looked upon as one of the principal leisure activities as well. A new employee of the hotel, while enjoying a bicycle sight-seeing tour of the island one day after work, was injured in an accident and filed a workers' compensation claim against the hotel for the losses suffered due to the injury.[4]

***Case 7.5*** Some years ago, a textile mill worker in a small town noticed that she had difficulty breathing. Her superior thought it might be an allergy. The company doctor told her she had "bronchial trouble." Later, she developed a severe cough and went to her family doctor, who checked her for tuberculosis but could not determine what was wrong with her. Later, the family doctor became the mill doctor. Finally, twenty years later she was so seriously debilitated that she had to quit and seek hospitalization. Her personal doctor said it would be "better for her nerves" if she could get back to work. However, she heard about an independent screening clinic for byssinosis, a disease that often caused symptoms similar to hers in textile workers exposed to cotton dust in the mills. It was the first time she had heard that her problem might be job related. Further medical examination at the clinic supported the notion that her problem was byssinosis. When she informed the hospital that her condition might be work related, the hospital told her that her company-provided medical insurance could not cover work-related illnesses. Yet workers' compensation covers only work-related illnesses. Because she had heard that employers appealed byssinosis workers' compensation claims endlessly, she decided not to forego her medical insurance benefits; she relinquished her claim that her condition was work related and with it any hope of collecting workers' compensation.[5]

This chapter covers state laws that provide compensation to victims of occupational injuries and illnesses: income replacement for those who cannot work, medical care for the injury or illness, and other forms of financial relief. The chapter does not cover the federal programs that provide such compensation for specific industries, such as the Federal Black Lung program (mining), the Longshoreman's and Harbor Worker's Compensation program (shipyards), and the Federal Employers' Liability

Act (federal government agencies). Strictly speaking, then, this chapter is not about federal regulation.

However, the chapter is relevant to federal statutes regulating job safety and health, particularly to the Occupational Safety and Health Act (OSHA). OSHA was passed in part as an attempt to solve some of the inadequacies that were thought to exist in state workers' compensation laws. Thus it is important to understand the nature of workers' compensation in order to appreciate fully the intention of Congress in passing OSHA. The history of federal regulation in the area of job safety and health can be traced back to the origins of state workers' compensation laws in the nineteenth century. This chapter covers that early history and describes the operation of those state laws, while the next chapter covers the more recent forces leading up to the passage of OSHA.

## Why Workers' Compensation Is a Personnel Concern

Workers' compensation is often handled by personnel departments as part of their overall responsibility for safety programs. There are several reasons why safety programs are assigned to personnel. First, safety sometimes just does not seem to fit anywhere else in the organization, so personnel gets stuck with it (along with the watermelon). Second, safety management is regulated by government, and government regulation is not as unfamiliar to the personnel manager as it may be to other managers in the organization. As Chapter 1 stresses, the personnel manager has to cope with EEO regulation, union-management relations law, and the regulatory areas covered later in this book. So the rest of the organization may look upon the personnel manager as an expert of sorts in dealing with government regulation and hope that this expertise can be applied to safety management. Third, safety programs often involve safety training, and training is often a personnel department responsibility. Finally, safety may be assigned to personnel because it is seen as a people problem, and the personnel department is often responsible for solving people problems by designing training, compensation, and discipline systems to evoke the desired behavior from employees.

Workers' compensation in particular is important to management because it costs money. The cost is over $10 billion per year,[6] and the employer is the source of that money, one way or the other. Either the employer compensates the employee directly, or the employer pays premiums to a workers' compensation insurance fund. Those premiums are based in part on the organization's safety and health record. Thus, a good safety and health record pays off directly, and alleviating safety and health problems on the job is a way in which personnel and human resource managers can justify their existence to management on a cost-benefit basis.

Still, much of the subject of workers' compensation is technical and more a concern of attorneys and insurance people than of personnel managers or general managers. This book does not cover those technical matters, but limits itself to issues of relevance to personnel management. The law of workers' compensation is far more detailed and voluminous than this chapter suggests. The reader who wishes a thorough grounding in those details should consult the references listed at the end of this chapter.

## Chapter Objectives

This chapter, then, is designed to give enough of a background for the reader to:

1. Know the historical motivation behind workers' compensation laws
2. Be aware of the system through which those laws are administered
3. Understand the principles behind the application of those laws, particularly the obligations that those laws place on management
4. Understand the cost of those obligations
5. Understand how the nation's experiences under state workers' compensation laws provided the background for the federal Occupational Safety and Health Act

The regulatory model again serves as a vehicle for the presentation of that material (see Exhibit 7.1). Chapter 8 then applies the regulatory model to the Occupational Safety and Health Act. Together the two chapters can be regarded as an overview of the structure of government regulation of job safety and health.

## Problems Leading to the Laws

We begin our discussion on the left-hand side of the model, the problems that led to the laws. The origins of workers' compensation laws can be

**Exhibit 7.1** The Regulatory Model Applied to Workers' Compensation

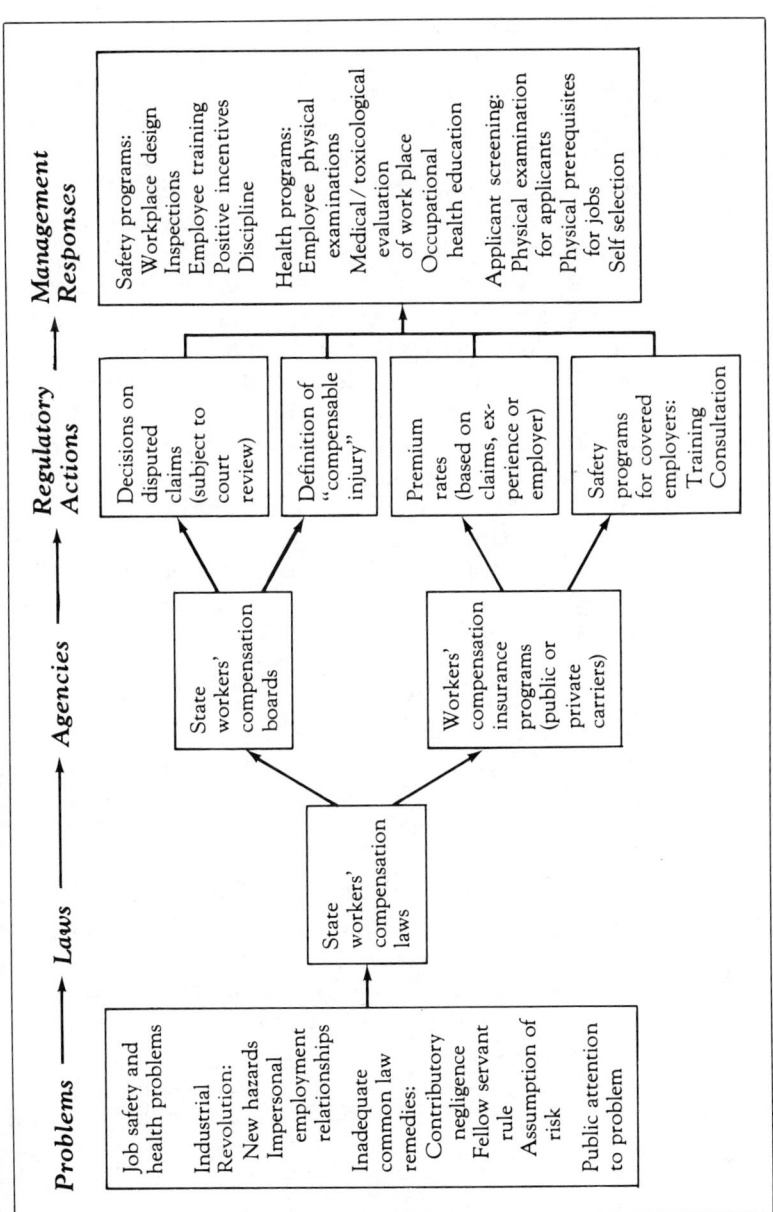

traced to the Industrial Revolution. Besides increased mechanization and an increased scale of production, the Industrial Revolution brought about major changes in the relationship between workers and management. Before the Industrial Revolution, when production was carried out by small proprietorships and family enterprises, workers had closer ties to the owners of business. When an injury or illness kept a worker away from the job, those personal ties often led the employer to assume voluntarily some responsibility for the support of the worker and the worker's family.

With the Industrial Revolution came a shift from small enterprises to large factories as a locus of production, and ownership came to be separated from management. With those changes, the relationship between employer and employee lost some of its personal qualities, and the worker lost the assurance of care in time of need. Also, with the increased urbanization that the Industrial Revolution brought, there were fewer personal ties in the community, thus less likelihood of assistance from close, long-time friends than would be the case in a small town. In sum, the Industrial Revolution brought about changes that made more visible the personal risks attached to participation in the world of work and dissolved some of the social ties that previously assisted workers in managing those risks.[7]

A related problem was the nature of the existing legal remedies for victims of occupational injuries and illnesses. Those remedies were called *common law remedies*; they were grounded not in statutes passed by legislative bodies but in the traditions of court precedents passed down ever since the days of the Magna Carta. Common law is no less the law for not having been passed by a legislature. It is common law that makes a personal liable for damages if his or her dog bites someone; similarly, it was common law that made employers liable for damages if their employees were injured at work.

But this system was not adequate. First, lawsuits were time consuming, expensive, emotionally taxing, and not at all prompt in providing relief. Second, some fine print in the common law, the common law defenses, often excused an employer from liability when workers sued for losses due to job-related injuries and illnesses.[8] Three common law defenses were used with great success by employers:

1. *Contributory negligence:* the employer was not liable to the extent that the loss was caused by the employee's negligence. Many injuries are caused at least in part by the employee's being less than wholly diligent,

and thus many victims' compensatory awards in such suits were reduced accordingly. While this defense apportioned damages according to the degree of responsibility that each party bore, it resulted in workers having to bear a burden they often could ill afford to bear.

2. *Fellow servant rule:* the employer was not responsible to the extent that the loss was caused by the action of a fellow employee. When other employees were responsible in part for an accident, the victim's recourse was to sue those employees. However, considering the fact that those employees were likely to be no better off financially than the victim, it was often pointless to initiate such suits.

3. *Assumption of risk:* the employer was not responsible to the extent that the loss was part of the usual risks involved in the kind of work that the employee was doing. In essence, this defense assumed that people took jobs with their eyes open, voluntarily accepting any dangers that were evident in the jobs. Presumably, the evidently dangerous jobs were responsible for more than their share of injuries and illnesses; thus the net effect of this defense was to remove protection for those workers who needed it the most.

Taken together, those three defenses served to make common law remedies for occupational injuries and illnesses largely illusory.

All these problems surfaced toward the end of the nineteenth century—the muckraking era—when journalists were increasingly inclined to be critical of business. The plight of workers at the hands of a dangerous and impersonal industry and their inability to gain legal redress for injuries was well publicized. As a result several states passed laws designed to provide relief. In 1911, the first of the laws bearing resemblance to modern workers' compensation laws was passed in Wisconsin. In the next ten years, the majority of states followed suit, and by 1948 every state had its own workers' compensation law. [9]

Such a major legal restructuring could not have taken place without a quid pro quo, some benefit for employers as well as for the workers. The benefit for employers was limitation of liability. Limits for the maximum allowable compensation were part of each state's workers' compensation law. Considering today's enormous settlements and damage awards in liability cases outside the employment arena, such a quid pro quo cannot be taken lightly.

## The Nature of Workers' Compensation Laws

Workers' compensation laws vary somewhat from state to state, in ways described in detail elsewhere.[10] However, there are some features of the workers' compensation system that are common to virtually all states:

1. The laws generally provide for replacement of lost income, medical expense payment, rehabilitation of some sort, death benefits to survivors, and lump-sum disability payments. Many states have higher benefits for minors who suffer job injuries.[11]

2. The worker does not have to sue the employer to get that compensation—in fact, covered employers are exempt from such lawsuits.

3. The compensation is mostly paid through an insurance program, financed through premiums paid by employers.

4. Workers' compensation insurance premiums are based on the accident and illness record of the organization. The more the claims paid to an employer's employees, the higher the employer's premiums are.

5. There is an element of co-insurance in the workers' compensation coverage. Co-insurance is insurance under which the beneficiary of the coverage absorbs part of the loss that is covered. In automobile collision coverage, for example, there is often co-insurance in the amount of a $100 deductible for each accident. In workers' compensation coverage, there is co-insurance in that the worker's loss is usually not fully covered by the insurance program. For example, most states provide for a maximum payment of only two-thirds of wages lost due to the accident or illness. As of 1981, only six states covered a higher percentage of lost pay.[12]

6. Medical expenses, on the other hand, are usually covered in full under workers' compensation laws.

7. It is a no-fault system: all job-related injuries and illnesses are covered, regardless of whose negligence caused them.

Still, there are significant differences among states.

1. While workers' compensation coverage is compulsory in most states, it is voluntary in South Carolina, New Jersey, and Texas. In those states, any employer electing not to be covered can be sued by workers, but without the protection of the three common law defenses noted above.

2. In some states, public employment is fully covered; in other states, none or only part is covered.

3. Six states plus the Commonwealth of Puerto Rico require that employers participate in state-administered workers' compensation insurance funds; twelve states allow the employer to choose between state-run coverage and coverage from private insurance companies. The remaining states have private coverage only. [13]

4. Most states permit employers to insure themselves against worker compensation claims; six states do not permit self-insurance.

Most of all, states differ in the extent of their workers' compensation coverage. There is great variation in the amount paid for permanent disabilities, the ceilings on amount of income replaced, the ease with which workers can collect for occupational illnesses, and the likelihood that disputed workers' compensation claims will be resolved in favor of claimants.

This unevenness of coverage has led to vigorous criticism of workers' compensation. [14] Inconsistency can cause problems because a state that is less generous toward claimants is also likely to be a state in which workers' compensation costs employers less. The result is that states can, and do, use their low cost of coverage in an attempt to attract industries from other states. For example, the state of Indiana has advertised its low workers' compensation cost in the *Wall Street Journal*. [15] Naturally, this results in complaints from higher-cost neighboring states, and this problem has already come to the attention of Congress. [16]

## The Regulatory Apparatus Applicable to Workers' Compensation

In most states the main administrative body is the state workers' compensation board. The board's main function is to decide disputed claims for compensation. In a few states, however, that decision is made by the courts. [17] Often the board's decision is written and published as a court case is. The body of workers' compensation decisions provides guidance in determining how new disputed claims should be resolved; in other words, it provides precedent for determining what constitutes a *compensable injury*. The definition of compensable injury is the principal legal question in most workers' compensation disputes.

Another component of the administrative apparatus of workers' compensation is the insurance system that pays the compensation. Two important regulatory actions are involved, *premium rates* and *safety programs* by insurance carriers for covered employers. The premium rates, as already noted, are based on the employer's claim experience and are intended to be an incentive for employers to improve safety and health conditions on the job.[18] To aid in improving safety, and to keep claims payments down, the workers' compensation insurance carriers offer various safety program services to the employers they cover. Those services include training, consultation regarding work-site alterations to improve job safety or health, and advice on methods of motivating employees to follow safe work procedures.

## Interpretation of the Law: What Is a Compensable Injury?

Employers are liable only for losses due to a compensable injury. To understand the limits of employer responsibility under workers' compensation laws, then, it is necessary to understand the concept of a compensable injury.

To the uninitiated, the most notable thing about the concept of compensable injury is how broad it is. Workers' compensation laws limit their coverage to those injuries "arising out of and in the course of . . . employment."[19] Thus, a compensable injury is a job-related injury. What is surprising is how tangential to the job an injury can be and still be considered job related. The following discussion gives some examples of how the concept of compensable injury is defined.

### Job Relatedness

How close in time and space to the work place must an injury happen in order to be considered compensable? Frequently, workers have been awarded compensation for accidents occurring off the job premises and after working hours. For example, injuries received at the company picnic, or while playing for the company baseball team are often deemed compensable. The guiding factors include the degree of employer initiative in organizing the activity, the degree to which employees are required, implicitly or explicitly, to participate, and the amount of benefit that the employer derives from the activity. If the company baseball team is organized by the company, and if the company gains favorable publicity from it, then injuries connected with participation on the team may be compensable.[20]

Case 7.1 illustrates how far-fetched valid workers' compensation claims can seem. The major consideration governing compensability is whether the accident arose "out of and in the course of . . . employment." In this case, the workers' compensation board decided that it did. The occasion of the accident resulted from the foreman's request for overtime work. The foreman would not have stayed on the job and driven the worker home had it not been for the company's rule and the need to have the employee work overtime. Because the accident was caused by the demands of work and occurred in the course of meeting those demands, the claim was granted.

An injury can be compensable even if it occurs after the worker quits working for the employer against whom the claim is filed. Case 7.2, involving the fight in the tavern, is in example. Despite the delay between the claimant's employment and the injury, and despite the fact that the employer had no reasonable way to assume responsibility for the injury, the injury was held to be compensable. The guiding principle behind that decision was that the worker's former employment created a danger that accompanied the worker even after he terminated his employment. The important point is that the condition of employment set in motion a chain of events that culminated in the injury. That is what is meant by "*arising out of* and in the course of . . . employment."

Case 7.2 also illustrates the employer's liability for the actions of its employees. Just as an employer is responsible for the employment practices of its supervisors in EEO cases, particularly where sexual harassment is alleged (see Chapter 3), so an employer is responsible for the safety hazards created by the misbehavior of its employees. Workers' compensation awards for injuries arising out of improper employee behavior are commonplace. Even instigators of horseplay can win compensation if horseplay is a regular feature of life at the work place.[21] This underscores the need for enforcement of work rules regarding employee behavior when safety is at stake. Whenever the work situation exposes workers to increased risks of injury, the employer is responsible for such injuries, whether or not the injury occurs at the work place, and whether or not it is caused by employee misbehavior in violation of company rules.

## Acts of God

Workers' compensation does *not* cover injuries that are caused by acts of God. An *act of God* is an accident that is neither caused by employment nor made more likely to occur because of employment. Natural disasters such as tornadoes are usually considered acts of God, and employers are generally not liable for injuries due to them, even if the injury occurs on the job. The exception is work that increases the risk of injury. The employer is generally liable even in the event that a worker is struck by lightning, if the worker was working on a utility pole or if the job otherwise increased the risk of being struck by lightning. In sum, to be considered an act of God, the injury must have entirely natural causes, such that no action the employee could have taken—including quitting work—would have lessened the likelihood of the injury's occurring.[22]

## Cumulative Disability

A cumulative disability is one that is created or made more severe by repeated incidents or repeated exposure to harmful situations. Perhaps the clearest example is employees who work where noise levels are too high and consequently suffer progressive hearing losses. Employers are responsible for such disabilities despite the fact that it is difficult to point to any single incident that caused the disability. It may be difficult to prove that the work contributed to the condition, but the worker is generally given the benefit of the doubt. For instance, when the job causes unusual stress and anxiety, the employer may be held liable for mental and emotional problems that might have resulted from those job conditions.[23]

### Aggravation of Preexisting Disability

What about situations such as Case 7.3, where the worker's back strain was alleged to have exacerbated his cancer condition? The conditions of work are not those that are ordinarily fatal, but the injured employee was not an ordinary employee. He had a disability, cancer, that put him at a greater risk of death. Although it may seem unjust to hold employers responsible for such situations, they are indeed held responsible; in this case, the company paid the death benefits. The basic rule is, "you take them the way you get them." If the employer hires an employee having a condition that increases the likelihood of an injury, the employer is still liable for that injury should it occur. In short, managers hire workers "as is," and the moral for managers is caveat emptor.

That raises some interesting EEO issues: If employers, cognizant of liabilities in situations such as Case 7.3, screen new applicants for conditions that might predispose them to injury if hired, the result is that people with certain physical handicaps may be rejected. Employer liability may give the employer the justification for refusing to hire diabetics and people with heart problems. Diabetics can die from a bruise, and heart disease raises the risk from many environmental conditions. Sadly and paradoxically, then, one area of regulation, workers' compensation, militates against the purposes of another, EEO for the handicapped.

The decisions in the three cases already discussed suggest that claims are decided in favor of the worker even when management can do nothing to prevent the problem. That is what is meant by the no-fault principle. The practical effect of no-fault coverage is to make management responsible for things it can do little to prevent. It also extends the concept of job-related injuries far beyond what one might expect. Case 7.4 stands at just about the extreme in that regard, for it was decided in favor of the employee. The logic was that off-the-job recreational activities such as bicycling were one of the inducements that attracted people to work at the resort. In a sense, the bicycling was an employee benefit, so the accident was job related.

While those cases show what workers' compensation covers, they do not show what it fails to cover. One major criticism of workers' compensation laws has been that they have excluded too many claims from coverage and that they have been inadequate in the compensation provided for the claims that are covered. This criticism, along with others, is discussed below.

Also, lest the reader despair of being able to do anything constructive about reducing workers' compensation claims, it should be pointed out that the vast majority of claims do arise from preventable incidents. Most of the undisputed claims, the ones that break no new legal ground, are caused by conditions that management can alter. The somewhat atypical cases discussed above are presented because they give an indication of how far the workers' compensation authorities will go in holding management responsible.

## Management Responses

The most typical steps taken to reduce the likelihood of workers' compensation claims are those listed in the management responses column of Exhibit 7.1 and discussed further in Chapter 8. Occupational injury prevention programs might include the following elements:

Appraisal of work place design, with possible changes in that design

Safety inspection of the work place and removal of any hazard that can be found

Employee safety training, to teach safe work procedures and increase safety awareness

Motivational programs and policies including positive incentives, such as safety awards and bonuses for employees of departments or work groups with good safety records, and negative incentives, such as punishment for violations of safety rules

Occupational health programs are somewhat more recent in origin. Some possible elements are:

Inspection of the work place for health risks, such as high levels of exposure to toxic substances, and appropriate corrective action

Physical examinations for employees

Education programs for employees, designed to increase occupational health awareness, convey health information, and persuade employees to identify health problems and get them treated before they become more serious

Prevention-oriented (health maintenance) employee medical benefits programs

Other responses include selection and screening methods for new employees:

Physical examinations for applicants

Appropriate physical requirements to identify employees with disabilities that might be aggravated by the job

Counseling to advise candidates and current employees of potential hazards in certain positions, so that they might select themselves out of such positions if the hazards pose risks to them due to specific medical problems they might have

Refusing to hire minors (because compensation payments are higher for them)

## Has Workers' Compensation Worked?

To evaluate the record of workers' compensation it is first necessary to examine the purposes that workers' compensation is intended to serve.[24]

The following list seems a reasonable summary of what workers' compensation was supposed to have accomplished:

1. *Adequate compensation:* provide reasonable income, as well as reasonable medical and disability benefits, to victims.

2. *Adequate rehabilitation:* provide services to reclaim the victim's capabilities. This was an important objective that led to the passage of the workers' compensation laws.[25]

3. *Improve the system for delivering compensation:* provide a single dependable source for compensation awards of predictable magnitude, reduce the delays and costs of the old court-administered common law approach, and eliminate the attendant legal expenses.

4. *Encourage prevention:* establish an insurance premium based on the employer's safety record to persuade the employer to seek the causes of occupational accidents and illnesses.

The record of workers' compensation laws is not very impressive by those criteria. The record on adequate compensation is mixed. While medical payments have been adequate in recent years, they were not so in earlier years. And the principle of co-insurance has been carried to such lengths that in many states the maximum weekly income benefit puts a family of four well below the official poverty level.[26] Regarding rehabilitation, workers' compensation has been criticized as totally inadequate.[27] Workers' compensation laws have been more successful in improving administration, the third objective. While there are inevitable administrative problems in the enforcement of any statute, the situation is much better than when the courts handled the problem as a matter of common law.

Finally, it is clear that the financial incentive of the experience-based premium system is inadequate to motivate the kind of health and safety improvements that are necessary in order to bring about a significant improvement in occupational illnesses and injuries. It is apparent now that such improvements often involve significant capital expenditure for new equipment and redesigned production processes. Those expenditures far outweigh the potential savings from the lower workers' compensation premiums that would result.

The disappointing record of workers' compensation has led to widespread calls for reform of the system. In a 1972 report, the National Commission on State Workmen's Compensation Laws enumerated nineteen essential criteria of an adequate workers' compensation system and concluded that not one of the state laws met all nineteen conditions. The average state complied with fewer than twelve. The commission recommended comprehensive federal legislation to insure adequate coverage if states did not revise their laws in line with the essential recommendations.[28] As a consequence of the commission's report, many states have upgraded the workers' compensation coverage. Four years later, however, a task force from the federal agencies concluded that there was still need for reform.

One area in which workers' compensation systems have been criticized most is their coverage of occupational illness. Case 7.5, involving byssinosis, is an example. Often workers lose their claims outright at the first step in the claims process, the state workers' compensation board. Or, if they should win these, their employers file repeated appeals. As a result, remarkably few cases such as Case 7.5 ever result in awards to the employee.[29] Contrast that with the liberal decisions reached in Cases 7.1 through 7.4.

Several provisions of the law in some states make it hard for an employee to be compensated for an occupational illness. Also, it is difficult for some workers to get expert medical witnesses to testify that the illness is job related; other workers die before the lengthy claims adjudication process is complete.[30] This has been particularly true for victims of diseases such as byssinosis, the pulmonary disease in Case 7.5 that affects so many textile workers after extended exposure to cotton dust. Some of the provisions of some state workers' compensation laws that have made it difficult to collect compensation are:

*Exposure requirements:* in South Carolina, a major textile state, a victim of byssinosis has to show seven years of exposure to the disease-causing condition on the job in order to collect benefits, despite medical evidence that byssinosis can be contracted in less than five years.[31]

*Time limits for filing claims:* generally there is a time limit for filing workers' compensation claims, but sometimes diseases cannot be diagnosed until after the time limit has expired.

*Disease lists:* in some states, victims of diseases that were not on the state's list of compensable diseases were not eligible for workers' compensation for those diseases—and at one time byssinosis was not on the list in either North or South Carolina.[32]

Other problems mentioned by workers' compensation critics are the fact that employers frequently contest illness claims and that medical opinion is often divided on whether a claimant's illness was caused by working. Either situation can make it difficult for the claimant to win compensation.

As a consequence, bills have been introduced in Congress to increase state workers' compensation coverage. This legislation addresses most of the problems mentioned above. Some of those opposing the proposed legislation point out that the states have been upgrading their programs in response to the criticisms of the 1972 report of the National Commission. They also point out that the restrictive treatment of occupational illness is beginning to ease as well. This trend, they say, suggests that many of the problems of workers' compensation laws are already being solved without federal intervention (although it is by no means clear that the motivation to continue solving them would persist if the threat of federal intervention were removed). Finally, the critics note that other federal efforts to regulate compensation for occupational injuries and illnesses have not been models worthy of emulation. For instance, the Longshoreman's and Harbor Worker's Compensation Act was also an effort to liberalize compensation coverage and to increase benefit levels, but it has resulted in enormous cost increases for those industries. The National Association of Stevedores estimates that the average cost of the Longshoreman's and Harbor Worker's Compensation Act to its members amounts to 6 percent of gross revenues.[33]

Nevertheless, the failure of workers' compensation seemed evident enough by the 1960s to convince many that federal intervention was necessary. The incomplete coverage of workers' compensation, coupled with the evidence that work was becoming increasingly unsafe, lent support to the movement that led to the passage of the 1970 Occupational Safety and Health Act. The next two chapters discuss that law.

## Further Information on Workers' Compensation

Several legal publishers provide periodically updated treatises on workers' compensation law. One highly regarded source is Arthur Larson, *Workmen's Compensation Law* (New York: Matthew Bender), a 10-volume service. Also available is a 2-volume desk edition, *Larson's Workmen's Compensation.* These are updated annually and include summaries of workers' compensation court cases. A 1-volume service that includes case summaries and summaries of state and federal statutes is *Workers' Compensation Law Reporter,* published by Commerce Clearing House.

## Notes

1. Russell L. Greenman and Eric J. Schmertz, *Personnel Administration and the Law,* 2d ed. (Washington, D.C.: Bureau of National Affairs, 1979), p. 201.

2. *Thornton v. Chamberlain Manufacturing Co.,* 62 N.J. 235, 300 A.2d 145 (1973), discussed in Greenman and Schmertz, *Personnel Administration,* pp. 205–6.

3. *Celeste v. Progressive Silk Finishing Co.,* 72 N.J. Super. Ct. 125 (1962), discussed in Greenman and Schmertz, *Personnel Adminstration,* pp. 197–198.

4. See Ann Davis, "Workman's Compensation," in Joseph J. Famularo, ed., *Handbook of Modern Personnel Administration* (New York: McGraw-Hill, 1972), chap. 51.

5. Hearings on H.R.5482 Before the Subcommittee on Labor Standards of the House Committee on Education and Labor, 95th Congress, 2d Session (1980); see pp. 71–75.

6. Robert M. McCaffery, "Benefits and Services—Statutory," in Dale Yoder and Herbert G. Heneman, Jr., eds., *ASPA Handbook of Personnel and Industrial Relations* (Washington, D.C.: Bureau of National Affairs, 1979), chap. 6.6; *Analysis of Workers' Compensation Laws—1980 Edition* (Washington, D.C.: Chamber of Commerce of the United States, 1979); Wayne F. Cascio, *Human Resource Costing* (Boston: Kent, 1982).

7. See Wilbert E. Moore, *Industrial Relations and the Social Order,* rev. ed. (New York: Macmillan, 1951).

8. See Robert J. Paul, "Workers' Compensation—An Adequate Employee Benefit?" *Academy of Management Review* 1, no. 4, 1976:112–23.

9. See *Analysis of Workers' Compensation Laws—1980 Edition; The Report of the National Commission of State Worker Compensation Laws* (Washington, D.C.: National Commission on State Worker Compensation Laws, 1972); Paul, "Workers' Compensation."

10. For a good summary, see *Analysis of Workers' Compensation Laws—1980 Edition.*

11. Ibid.

12. *Workers' Compensation Law Reporter* (Chicago: Commerce Clearing House).

13. *Analysis of Workers' Compensation Laws—1980 Edition.*

14. See, for example, Hearings on H.R.5482.

15. *Wall Street Journal,* August 16, 1976.

16. Hearings on S.3060 Before the Subcommittee on Labor of the Senate, Committee on Human Resources, 95th Congress, 2d Session (1978), pp. 376–79.

17. *Analysis of the Workers' Compensation Laws—1980 Edition.*

18. Paul, "Workers' Compensation."

19. See McCaffery, "Benefits and Services"; and Greenman and Schmertz, *Personnel Administration.*

20. Greenman and Schmertz, *Personnel Administration;* and Arthur Larson, *Larson's Workmen's Compensation Law* (New York: Matthew Bender).

21. Larson, *Larson's Workmen's Compensation Law.*

22. Ibid.

23. Ibid.

24. Paul, "Worker's Compensation."

25. Ibid.

26. Statement by Andrew J. Biemiller, in Hearings on S.3060.

27. Paul, "Worker's Compensation."

28. *The Report of the National Commission on State Worker Compensation Laws.*

29. Presentation of the Panel Representing the Carolina Brown Lung Association; in Hearings on H.R.5482, pp. 69–90.

30. Ibid.

31. Statement of Essie Briggs, in Hearings on S.3060, pp. 117–25.

32. Ben Bowen, in Hearings on S.3060, p. 163.

33. Statement of the Alliance of American Insurers, in Hearings on S.3060, pp. 223–59.

# 8

# The Occupational Safety and Health Act

*Case 8.1* By 1976, several research studies linked benzene exposure to cancer. Benzene is used in manufacturing fuel, solvents, and other products. The existing OSHA regulation mandated a maximum occupational exposure level of ten parts per million (ppm) for benzene. While the research studies had not found conclusive evidence that cancer was caused by exposure at a level of 10 ppm, the secretary of labor took the position that, where cancer-causing agents are concerned, no safe exposure level can be determined. Therefore, OSHA lowered the standard to 1 ppm, the minimum that could be detected without highly sophisticated monitoring equipment. The agency calculated that the new standard would require capital investments in engineering controls of approximately $266 million, first year operating costs of $187 to $205 million, and recurring annual costs of about $34 million. OSHA concluded that such costs were not likely to threaten the financial welfare of the affected firms, and that the benefits of the proposed benzene standard were likely to be appreciable. The petroleum industry trade association filed suit to overturn the new standard, claiming that the benefits of the proposed standard were not likely to be appreciable enough to justify the costs. Few employees would benefit, and in the petroleum industry the standard would cost $82,000 per employee who benefited. An industry witness offered expert testimony, which OSHA disputed, that the new standard would prevent at most two deaths per year.

***Case 8.2*** Protracted exposure to cotton dust among textile workers appears to be responsible for a chronic respiratory disease known as byssinosis, or brown lung (see Case 7.5). One study found a 25 percent incidence of byssinosis among workers in cotton preparation and yarn manufacturing. Initially, OSHA had adopted a maximum permissible cotton dust exposure level of 1 milligram per cubic meter (1 mg/$m^3$). Later, OSHA reduced that to 0.2 mg/$m^3$ because of evidence that the reduction would reduce the incidence of byssinosis. The textile industry challenged the reduction, saying that OSHA had failed to demonstrate that the costs of the new standard bore a reasonable relationship to the benefits. Indeed, the costs were estimated to be as high as \$2.7 billion, a considerable burden for the industry to have to bear. OSHA replied that the \$2.7 billion cost estimate was exaggerated and that, in any event, there was no reason to believe that the new standard would threaten the survival of the industry. OSHA also argued that cost-benefit analysis was not required—the Act requires that hazards be removed "to the extent feasible" (see section 6(b)(5) of Exhibit 8.2). While the new cotton dust standard might have been costly, OSHA reasoned that it was still "feasible."

***Case 8.3*** At the time of OSHA hearings on the hazards of vinyl chloride, there were thirteen confirmed deaths from liver cancer among employees exposed to vinyl chloride. The maximum exposure standard that existed was 500 ppm. Animal experiments showed that concentrations as low as 50 ppm caused cancer, but most of the scientific testimony stated that one could not extrapolate those animal findings to humans. Also three studies conducted on humans indicated no adverse effects from exposure levels that low. Still, there was no guarantee that levels even lower than 50 ppm were safe. Finally, OSHA settled on a standard of 1 ppm. Industry groups objected to the new standard as unreasonable. In the words of the president of a major vinyl plastics producer, "the proposed permanent standard is not technologically feasible and, if adopted, would shut down the industry." Indeed, a study commissioned by OSHA agreed that a 1 ppm ceiling was not feasible for the industry with its present technology.

***Case 8.4*** An OSHA inspector appeared at an electrical and plumbing firm to conduct an inspection. The proprietor, after learning from the inspector that no one had complained about his company and that the inspector had no search warrant, refused to admit the inspector to his place of business, claiming that he was protected by the unreasonable search and seizure provision of the Bill of Rights. OSHA filed suit to force the proprietor to admit the inspector, arguing that the Bill of Rights was not intended to prevent the kind of search that the OSHA inspector wanted to conduct.

***Case 8.5*** An OSHA inspector at a seaport discovered that hardly any longshoremen were wearing hard hats. An OSHA safety regulation required all of them to wear hard hats. OSHA cited the company for a violation and levied a fine of $455 on the company. The company appealed, testifying that it had already undertaken strenuous but unsuccessful measures to obtain compliance with the hard-hat rule: encouraging their use at safety meetings, posting hard-hat signs, and putting hard-hat messages in pay envelopes. The company strongly believed that firing the violators would precipitate a wildcat strike. Considering the fact that such a strike took place earlier over the same issue at another port, the company concluded that compliance with the regulation was simply not achievable.

***Case 8.6***    To protect employees from objects falling from conveyor belts, an appliance assembly plant installed a mesh guard screen twenty feet above the work floor. Maintenance of the screen sometimes required walking out on it, a dangerous procedure that led to injuries. Eventually, a maintenance employee fell to his death while working on the screen. The company then forbade maintenance employees from walking on the screen. Nevertheless, a foreman ordered two employees to perform the usual maintenance work on the screen. The employees refused, claiming the screen was unsafe. The foreman sent them to the personnel office, where they were given written reprimands and ordered to punch out without being paid for the remainder of their shift.

This chapter discusses one of the most controversial pieces of legislation passed in recent history, the 1970 Occupational Safety and Health Act (OSHA). Both OSHA and the workers' compensation laws discussed in Chapter 7 govern employee health and safety, but there are some important differences between the two:

1. Workers' compensation laws are state statutes; OSHA is a federal statute.

2. Workers' compensation laws are designed to compensate employees for injuries and illnesses they have already received; OSHA is designed to remove the hazardous conditions that give rise to those injuries and illnesses. OSHA provides no compensation.

3. Workers' compensation uses workers' compensation insurance premiums as incentives to motivate employers to improve job safety and health; OSHA uses a system of inspection, citations, and cash penalties.

4. Workers' compensation has no mandates for safety; OSHA mandates that employers establish working conditions that meet certain written standards of safety.

# Chapter Objectives

The purpose of this chapter is to lay a foundation for the understanding of OSHA by using the regulatory model. While OSHA is controversial and consequently in flux, that foundation has remained stable even as the details of OSHA regulation change. The chapter first traces the social problems and political events leading up to the passage of OSHA. Then it enumerates the main provisions of OSHA, identifies the various regulatory agencies having OSHA responsibilities, and indicates the regulatory activities of those agencies.

However, the overall objectives of this book's coverage of OSHA, in this chapter and in Chapter 9, are much more modest than the objectives of its coverage of EEO. Safety is a technical field that is often turned over to staff specialists with engineering backgrounds. EEO, on the other hand, is nontechnical enough that it can be comprehended by managers who have no special expertise—and EEO permeates so many facets of people management that it usually *must* be comprehended by managers throughout the organization. Further, the volume of printed regulations from OSHA is so immense that the regulatory area is impossible to cover as thoroughly as this book covers EEO. Nevertheless, OSHA merits close attention, if for no other reason than that it has probably generated more controversy than any other area of law covered in this book.

Exhibit 8.1 presents the regulatory model for OSHA. In this chapter, the entire regulatory model is covered, except for management responses, which are covered in a section at the end of Chapter 9. Most of Chapter 9, however, evaluates OSHA's record as a regulatory agency and presents some of the varying political opinions regarding OSHA.

# Problems Leading to the Law

Several problems, and the response of various political forces to those problems, were responsible for the passage of the 1970 Occupational Safety and Health Act.

## The Inadequacies of Workers' Compensation Laws

Chapter 7 provides evidence of the ineffectiveness of workers' compensation laws as a means of solving safety and health problems. Workers'

**Exhibit 8.1**  The Regulatory Model Applied to OSHA

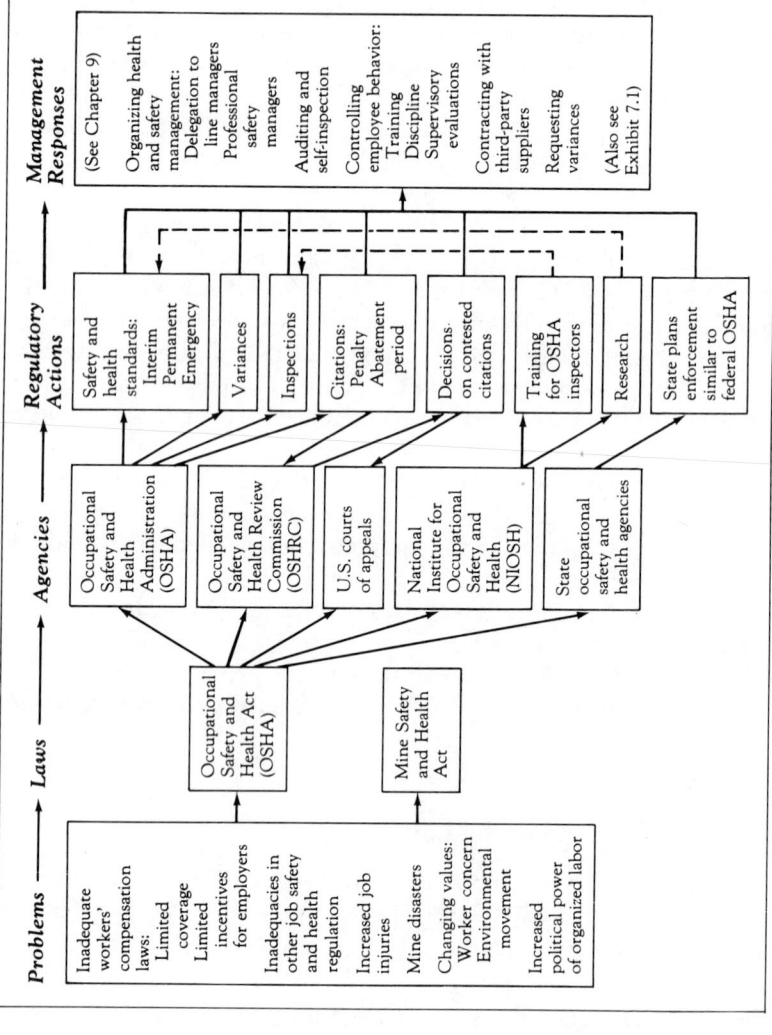

compensation not only fails to motivate employers to remove hazards in the work place but also fails to provide adequate compensation to victims of those hazards.

Actually, coverage was worse in the years preceding the passage of OSHA in 1970 than Chapter 7 suggests. Workers' compensation improved considerably during the 1970s. Before that, at the time of its inception in the first two decades of this century, workers' compensation was severely limited: coverage was fragmentary, benefits were of short duration, and job health coverage was even worse than job safety coverage.[1] Little attention was paid to those inadequacies in the years following as the nation became preoccupied with the problems of the Depression and World War II.

Inadequate prevention was a different problem. Workers' compensation simply did not offer enough of an economic incentive for employers to improve safety and health. In fact, workers' compensation perhaps *reduces* the incentives. This may seem strange, since the lure of lower premiums for workers' compensation was supposed to motivate the organization to improve conditions. But because workers' compensation is an insurance program, it operates to limit risks, and that reduces the incentives for the employer to prevent accidents and illnesses. In short, with workers' compensation, employers may make less of an attempt to remedy safety and health hazards because there is less at stake.[2]

Compounding that inadequacy is the fact that workers' compensation makes the employee and society at large bear some of the costs of job injuries and illnesses. It shifts the burden to the employee in that it provides only partial income replacement—co-insurance. It shifts the burden to society in that social security and other welfare programs bear much of the cost of supporting and rehabilitating the victims. Thus, in 1970, state workers' compensation programs replaced an average of less than one-half of lost income. It seems reasonable to question whether that limited liability is enough to stimulate employers' concern over safety and health problems.[3]

A related economic argument against workers' compensation is that the normal operation of the labor market would naturally result in employers' paying workers more for more hazardous jobs. The idea is that employers, in order to attract sufficient numbers of workers, must pay a risk premium to people taking hazardous jobs. To the extent that workers' compensation insurance already compensates employees on risky jobs, employers do not have to pay as much of a risk premium as they would were there no workers' compensation laws. Moreover, if employees can be kept ignorant of their rights to compensation, the costs of hazards to employers is reduced still further.[4]

Economic incentives for employers are even less adequate in the case of occupational illness than in the case of occupational injury. Sometimes it is difficult to determine the extent to which an illness, such as cancer, is caused by work hazards rather than non-work conditions such as smoking. Also, occupational disease is often not diagnosed until long after the person has been exposed to the illness-producing hazard on the job—decades after, in the case of atomic radiation exposure and certain other cumulative occupational diseases. Thus workers' compensation benefits begin so late that the cost to the employer is discounted considerably. In other words, discounting liabilities for diseases to present value further reduces the incentive for the employers to remedy the problem that created the illness.[5]

In sum, the economics of workers' compensation seemingly does little to decrease the likelihood of job hazards.[6] Considering the fact that in 1970, when OSHA was passed, the coverage of workers' compensation laws was worse than the more current situation described in Chapter 7, it is understandable that there was widespread dissatisfaction with workers' compensation as a method for improving safety and health on the job.

## Existing Federal Safety and Health Regulation

When OSHA was being deliberated in Congress, other job safety and health regulation existed, but it was widely regarded as inadequate. As early as the 1890s, laws were passed governing coal mine safety.[7] In 1936, the Walsh-Healey Act was passed, requiring government contractors to comply with safety and health standards. Federal employees have been covered by workers' compensation since 1916.[8] Also, in 1914 the Public Health Services Office of Industrial Hygiene and Sanitation was created.

However, just as state workers' compensation lawmaking activities slowed during the 1930s and 1940s, so did federal job safety lawmaking.[9] Some states had passed their own occupational safety and health laws, but those laws did little to address occupational health problems and little to penalize offending employers.[10] In general, the state laws were pale predecessors of the later federal Occupational Safety and Health Act.

### Increased Industrial Injuries

According to Nicholas A. Ashford, the increase in occupational injuries between 1961 and 1970 was probably the most important single factor behind the passage of OSHA.[11] During that period, the reported injury rate in industry increased nearly 29 percent with fourteen thousand deaths attributed to accidents on the job.

An additional impetus came from a number of highly publicized work site disasters that occurred during this period. Most notable among them was the Farmington, West Virginia mine explosion in November 1968, in which seventy-eight miners died.[12] More than any other single incident, the Farmington disaster can be seen as the event that prompted increased federal involvement in occupational safety and health.

### Changing Values

In the years preceding OSHA, the educational level of the work force in the United States had steadily increased. Some observers believe that this increase in education, along with increased wage levels in the manufacturing sectors, brought about a change in the values and priorities of workers, with job safety and health concerns becoming more important and bread-and-butter, paycheck issues receding by comparison.[13] Political values and social issues were changing as well, particularly during the 1960s, with environmentalism beginning to emerge in the latter part of the decade as a significant concern. This new environmental concern coincided with new research findings indicating that chemicals found in many work places were hazardous to health. Those findings sensitized the public to the environmental problems of the world of work and fostered a climate that was receptive to legislation dealing with occupational safety and health problems.[14] Generally, by making the public conscious of the changes industrial pollution wrought in the general environment, the environmental movement increased the awareness that such pollution might well be far more serious in the work environment.[15]

Thus in 1965 the National Advisory Environmental Health Committee prepared the Frye Report, a study of critical occupational health needs. While the federal government did not respond immediately to the challenge, the Frye Report was endorsed by both labor and management representatives on the committee.[16] This broad consensus of concern over the occupational environment helps explain why it was possible to reach agreement on a law as stringent as OSHA.

## Organized Labor

Clearly a major explanation for the passage of OSHA was the increased political power of labor unions and their increased interest in job safety and health. At the time of deliberation over OSHA, 65 percent of collective bargaining agreements contained some provision for health and safety.[17] Generally, organized labor welcomed OSHA.

Some have questioned the depth of union commitment to safety and health issues,[18] but the prospect of legislation on the matter had some attraction for unions. For one thing, if a law were to mandate safety on the job, then unions would not have to bargain for safety to be included in labor contracts. Also, many union contracts cover only a single firm, so any contract provision that is costly may put that firm at a competitive disadvantage, to the detriment of the union as well as management.[19] Further, if an entire industry has the hazard, it may be difficult for a single company to eliminate it, because a single company alone often cannot afford the research and development necessary to devise and implement a solution. For that matter, the union too probably lacks the technical expertise and research facilities to propose solutions.[20] A national law would solve these problems.

Finally, unions supported legislation because the agency responsible for that legislation was likely to be the U.S. Department of Labor, which had a history of being friendly to union interests. This fact provided some assurance that any law dealing with safety and health problems would be enforced in a manner responsive to organized labor.[21]

## Legislative History of OSHA

Still, efforts to pass job safety and health legislation were unsuccessful during the 1950s. Some limited measures did get passed in the 1960s, however. In 1965, Congress passed the McNamara-O'Hara Public Service Contract Act, which extended the Walsh-Healey Act's safety and health provisions to cover the providers of government services. Then, the Metal and Nonmetallic Mine Safety Act of 1966 was passed, which provided inspections and established health and safety standards for mining. In 1969, a tougher mining law was passed, the Federal Coal Mine Health and

Safety Act. Finally, the Occupational Safety and Health Act was passed in 1970.

OSHA's legislative history can be traced back to 1968, when President Lyndon B. Johnson submitted to Congress an occupational safety and health bill containing some of the elements of what was later to become OSHA. That bill was strongly opposed by business interests, with the U.S. Chamber of Commerce arguing that enforcement of safety standards was a state function, not a federal one. In the view of many, unions did not support the measure very strongly either. Finally, when Johnson announced that he was withdrawing from the presidential race, the bill languished along with much of the rest of his legislative program.[22]

However, after the coal mine explosion in Farmington, West Virginia, in November 1968, the unions, particularly the steelworkers, became more active in lobbying for job safety legislation. Ralph Nader also lent his support to the movement for legislation. Finally, after considerable partisan controversy, a surprisingly stringent Occupational Safety and Health Act was signed into law at the end of 1970.

John Mendeloff remarks that one of the most notable characteristics of the legislative history of OSHA is the general lack of manifest congressional concern over the costs of compliance. This is understandable; how could management raise before Congress cost objections to legislation that promised to save lives and prevent injuries and illnesses? From the written record, then, there is little evidence that Congress regarded cost as a reason to hold back on regulation. That fact is not lost on OSHA's administrators when they interpret congressional intent regarding how costly their standards are permitted to be.[23]

# The Law:
## Obligations of Employers and Employees

The Occupational Safety and Health Act itself is reasonably brief and straightforward; what is truly voluminous and technically complex are the written regulations issued pursuant to OSHA. Because of that complexity, little attention is devoted in this book to the OSHA regulations; the remainder of this chapter covers the act itself. First, the obligations of both management and employees are discussed; following that is a discussion of the regulatory apparatus that OSHA establishes.

Exhibit 8.2 includes some of the more significant OSHA provisions.

**Exhibit 8.2** Excerpts from the Occupational Safety and Health Act

### Section 3

(8) The term "occupational safety and health standard" means a standard which [is] . . . reasonably necessary or appropriate to provide safe or healthful employment. . . .

### Section 5

(a) Each employer

(1) shall furnish to each of his employees employment and a place of employment which are free from recognized hazards that are causing or are likely to cause death or serious physical harm.

(2) shall comply with occupational safety and health standards promulgated under this Act.

(b) Each employee shall comply with occupational safety and health standards and all rules, regulations, and orders issued pursuant to this Act which are applicable to his own actions and conduct.

### Section 6

(a) . . . the Secretary [of Labor] shall . . . promulgate as an occupational safety or health standard any national consensus standard, and any established Federal standard. . . .

. . . .

(b)(5) The Secretary, in promulgating standards dealing with toxic materials or harmful physical agents under this subsection, shall set the standard which most adequately assures, to the extent feasible, on the basis of the best available evidence, that no employee will suffer material impairment of health or functional capacity even if such employee has regular exposure to the hazard dealt with by such standard for the period of his working life. . . .

(b)(6)(A) Any employer may apply to the Secretary for a temporary order granting a variance from a standard or any provision thereof promulgated under this section. . . .

### Section 8

(a) In order to carry out the purposes of this Act, the Secretary, upon presenting appropriate credentials to the owner, operator, or agent in charge, is authorized

(1) to enter without delay and at reasonable times any workplace or environment where work is performed by an employee of an employer; and

(2) to inspect and investigate . . . any such place of employment . . . and to question privately any such employer, owner, operator, agent or employee.

. . . .

(c)(1) Each employer shall . . . make available . . . such records regarding his activities relating to this Act as the Secretary . . . may prescribe by regulation as necessary or appropriate. . . .

. . . .

(f)(1) Any employees or representative of employees who believe that a violation of a safety or health standard exists that threatens physical harm, or that an imminent danger exists, may request an inspection.

### Section 9

(a) If, upon inspection or investigation, the Secretary or his authorized representative believes that an employer has violated a requirement of . . . this Act, he shall with reasonable promptness issue a citation to the employer. . . . The citation shall fix a reasonable time for the abatement of the violation. . . .

Section 5(a) of Exhibit 8.2 specifies the obligations of management. Part (1) of that section is usually referred to as the "general duty" clause because it imposes upon management not simply the obligation to comply with certain specific safety standards, but also the general duty of eliminating those hazards that may not be covered by any standard.

The purpose of the general duty clause is to cover the omissions that are inevitable in any body of specific safety and health standards. Considering the inherent complexity of the problem, total coverage of all hazards is inconceivable in a set of specific regulations. The general duty clause places upon employers the burden of identifying the problems that the government does not identify.

Compliance with the specific regulations, mandated in part (2) of section 5(a), presents a different kind of burden, the burden of comprehending an exceptionally detailed and lengthy set of mandatory standards. This is discussed further below. Two other employer obligations under the Occupational Safety and Health Act are to allow the government to inspect the work place, as specified in section 8(a), and to keep relevant records, as discussed in section 8(c)(1) of the act. OSHA inspections are also discussed in greater detail below.

The obligations of employees are stated in section 5(b) of Exhibit 8.2. Superficially, the law imposes a broad set of obligations on employees as well as on employers. However, OSHA provides no penalties for violations of employee obligations. For all practical purposes, then, the federal government regulates employer compliance but not employee compliance. This relative imbalance in OSHA's impositions on employers and employees is consistent with organized labor's support of the law. It too is discussed further below.

## The Regulatory Apparatus

The Occupational Safety and Health Act is administered and enforced by a rather complicated regulatory apparatus, with responsibilities divided among five entities: (1) the Occupational Safety and Health Administration (OSHA), the main enforcement agency; (2) the Occupational Safety and Health Review Commission (OSHRC); (3) the National Institute for Occupational Safety and Health (NIOSH); (4) the federal courts of appeals; and (5) those states having approved occupational safety and health plans.

### The Occupational Safety and Health Administration (OSHA)

This agency, a branch of the U.S. Department of Labor, has the following responsibilities:

Establishing *safety standards,* as set forth in section 6 of OSHA

Allowing *variances* from those standards as provided in section 6(b)(6)(A) of OSHA

Conducting *inspections* of work places, as discussed in section 8(a) of OSHA

Issuing citations for OSHA violations, as noted in section 9 of OSHA

There are three kinds of *standards* issued by the administration: interim, permanent, and emergency.[24] Interim standards are the ones that OSHA adopted just after the act was passed. Permanent standards are established by a procedure so intricate and time-consuming that the results ought well to be "permanent." It is beyond the scope of this book to detail the numerous steps of the adoption procedure for permanent standards. But the existence of the procedure makes it abundantly clear why it takes so long to get permanent standards adopted and why it is so difficult to remove permanent standards once they are adopted.[25] Emergency standards are temporary regulations issued by the secretary of labor when it is determined that employees are being exposed to grave danger from some job hazard. Once an emergency standard is issued, OSHA must begin hearings designed to replace it with a permanent standard within six months.

A *variance* can be sought by an employer who is unable to comply with a standard. Two types of variances can be sought, temporary and permanent. A temporary variance is designed to give the employer time in which to comply with a new permanent standard. A permanent variance, on the other hand, is designed to give an employer a permanent exemption from a standard. To get a temporary variance, employers must (1) present evidence that they are unable to meet the standard by the deadline, (2) establish plans and timetables for meeting the standard, and (3) certify that they have informed the employees of their right to contest the application for the temporary variance.[26] A permanent variance, on the other hand, is granted only when the employer can show that it can obtain the same degree of safety by some method other than the one called for in the standard. For example, if an OSHA standard specifies a railing of a certain minimum thickness, and an employer can show that superior materials can provide the same degree of safety without being that thick, the employer would have a case for a permanent variance allowing the use of thinner railing made out of the superior material. Variances represent an opportunity for management to relieve unnecessarily burdensome requirements and thus are a strategy, albeit a difficult one, for making life under OSHA easier.[27]

*Inspections* by OSHA are the first step in the process of enforcing compliance with standards. Because of its limited resources for inspecting the enormous number of work places subject to its authority, OSHA has established a set of priorities for determining which work sites to inspect. In decreasing order of importance, the priorities are: (1) facilities in which an employee has complained of a hazard (see section 8(f)(1) in Exhibit 8.2), (2) facilities at which an accident has been reported, and (3) any facility that is part of an industry on OSHA's list of target industries, whose safety records are particularly poor.

Inspections generally follow an established procedure. The OSHA inspector is legally entitled to enter the employer's premises and is bound by law not to notify the employer in advance of the inspection.[28] Both the employer and the employees are entitled to have a representative accompany the inspector, and the employee representative is entitled to "walk-around pay" for time spent accompanying an inspector during his or her visit to the facility.[29] The inspector is entitled to enter any place at the facility to determine whether a violation exists. After the inspection, a closing conference is held.

The final step in the Occupational Safety and Health Administration's involvement is the issuance of *citations*. Citations are a determination by the agency that the employer has violated a standard. Along with a specification of the nature of the violation, a citation includes a statement of *penalties* to be levied against the employer and an *abatement period*, or period during which the employer is expected to eliminate, or "abate," the hazard. Oftentimes the abatement period is of greater concern than the penalty. The penalties can be quite severe, but they are seldom imposed at their maximum levels. Imprisonment is included among the possible penalties for willful violations that result in death, for giving advance notice of an inspection, or for making false statements in any reports. For repeated violations, a penalty of up to one thousand dollars per day may be levied.

## The Occupational Safety and Health Review Commission (OSHRC)

Citations by the Occupational Safety and Health Administration can be appealed to OSHRC, which operates as a trial court of sorts, similar to the way in which the U.S. district courts operate in cases involving Title VII EEO violations (see Chapter 2). OSHRC functions independently of the rest of the OSHA regulatory apparatus. Proceedings before OSHRC are rather complicated, but recent moves have been made to simplify them.[30] The case load before OSHRC has been steadily increasing, with about 6800 cases handled during fiscal year 1979. This increase reflects an increasing tendency for employers to contest OSHA citations. For instance, at the beginning of fiscal 1979, 9.5 percent of OSHA inspections were contested, while at the end of the fiscal year, about 12 percent were contested.[31]

## U.S. Courts of Appeals

Like district court findings in an EEO case, the findings of OSHRC in an OSHA case can be appealed directly to the federal courts of appeals. This follows the same set of procedures outlined in Chapter 1, with the possibility of Supreme Court review of the appellate court decision.

## National Institute for Occupational Safety and Health (NIOSH)

NIOSH has two principal functions, training and research. Training is carried out mostly for the benefit of OSHA inspectors and other personnel associated with the enforcement of the Occupational Safety and Health Act. Research into job safety and health is conducted principally for the purpose of creating new safety and health standards to be adopted by OSHA. In carrying out its research function, NIOSH has the right to enter work places and the right to subpoena information. Generally, the major function of NIOSH is to provide necessary information for the adoption of new standards and to provide a source of trained personnel for OSHA enforcement.[32]

## Delegating OSHA Compliance Activities by Means of Approved State Plans

Section 18 of OSHA permits the states to take over responsibilities for occupational safety and health, provided that certain conditions are met.[33] One major condition is that the state program is "at least as effective in providing safe and healthful employment and places of employment as the standards promulgated" under the federal OSHA law.[34] The process for getting a state plan approved is probably as lengthy and cumbersome as the process for getting a new safety standard adopted. This discourages states from adopting plans. Besides, the U.S. secretary of labor can withdraw OSHA's approval of a state plan whenever there is evidence that the state has failed to comply with any of the provisions or assurances of the state plan.[35] Still, for those states that wish to go through the procedure, the federal government will fund up to 50 percent of the operation of the state program.

Why would a state want to assume responsibility for occupational safety and health enforcement in return for just half a rebate? One reason is to get OSHA out of the regulation business in the state. As Chapter 9 indicates, OSHA probably has a worse reputation than any other federal regulatory program. A more substantial reason for a state to adopt a plan is that a state plan, unlike the federal OSHA, can offer state safety and health consultation to employers without threatening to call for an inspection when the consultants find a potential violation. OSHA, however, believes that it cannot offer consultation with that assurance. Consequently, employers view OSHA not as an organization to assist in overcoming safety and health problems, but purely as an adversary. By providing consultation services, state OSHA programs could conceivably do much to reduce work hazards.

## Controversies

This discussion of OSHA provisions raises some questions that have been the source of much criticism and controversy. The two main issues are (1) the appropriateness of the specific safety standards adopted by the Occupational Health and Safety Administration and (2) the relative balance of employee rights and employer rights.

### *Appropriateness of the Safety Standards*

Immediately upon adoption of OSHA, questions arose about specific standards. From the first, the agency was mandated to adopt standards (see section 8(a) of Exhibit 8.2). How was that to be accomplished? Safety is an exceptionally complex and technical area that differs from industry to industry. Regulating it was a task of immense proportions. How was OSHA to ensure a set of standards at the outset that would provide adequate protection to workers in all industries?

The answer was that OSHA was directed by section 8(a) to adopt *consensus* standards, safety and health standards that safety and health specialists in industry had devised well before OSHA. During congressional debate over the passage of OSHA, business groups generally favored adoption of the consensus standards in order to minimize the discretion of the Department of Labor in determining safety standards. However, Democrats criticized the consensus standards as watered down and out of date. As a compromise, the final version of OSHA did incorporate the consensus standards, but only as interim standards. It was envisioned that the Department of Labor would eventually adopt permanent standards after further study and deliberation.

What was not generally realized at the time was that consensus standards were seldom followed by industry. Industry regarded consensus standards as desirable, but many industrial facilities failed to meet those standards. Understandably, business groups did not want to admit that during congressional debate. In Mendeloff's words, "to oppose adherence to the mild and innocuous-sounding 'consensus' standards, which had essentially been developed by industry, would have spoiled the image they were trying to project."[36]

In developing permanent standards to replace those interim consensus standards, the greatest controversy concerns feasibility. Section 6(b)(5) of OSHA clearly establishes feasibility as a criterion, but many OSHA standards are widely regarded as infeasible. How is feasibility defined?

Clearly, it would be infeasible "to protect employees by putting their employers out of business," as the court said in one case.[37] Yet it is equally true, according to the court in the same case, that "Standards may be economically feasible even though from the standpoint of employers, they are financially burdensome and affect margins adversely."[38] Where on the continuum between financial burdens and bankruptcy do the courts draw the line? As might be expected, the question cannot be answered precisely. The same case also held that the standard does not have to be so feasible as "to provide a route by which recalcitrant employers or industries may avoid the reforms contemplated by the act," and that the standard cannot be so financially burdensome that "only a few leading firms" could comply within the deadlines.[39]

Case 8.1 on benzene raises the issue of whether the standard must be one that considers costs and benefits. In *Industrial Union Department, AFL-CIO v. American Petroleum Institute*, the Supreme Court rejected OSHA's benzene standard, but not because of OSHA's failure to weigh its benefits against its costs.[40] OSHA's error was its failure to find sufficient evidence that the exposure reduction from 10 ppm to 1 ppm would reduce the incidence of cancer, or even solid evidence that existing work place exposure levels were hazardous. Thus, the benzene case left unanswered the question of whether cost-benefit analysis was required for OSHA standards.

The Supreme Court did answer the cost-benefit question in a cotton dust case similar to Case 8.2. The Court's opinion in *American Textile Manufacturers Institute, Inc.* v. *Donovan* upheld OSHA. The agency was required only to show feasibility, not to show a balancing of costs and benefits:

> The plain meaning of the word "feasible" supports respondents' interpretation of the statute. According to Webster's Third New International Dictionary of the English Language, "feasible" means "capable of being done, executed, or effected," . . . . Accord, The Oxford English Dictionary ("Capable of being done, accomplished or carried out"); Funk & Wagnalls New "Standard" Dictionary of the English Language ("That may be done, performed or effected"). Thus, §6(b)(5) directs the Secretary to issue the standard that "most adequately assures . . . that no employee will suffer material impairment of health," limited only by the extent to which this is "capable of being done." In effect then, . . . Congress itself defined the basic relationship between costs and benefits, by placing the "benefit" of worker health above all other considerations save those making attainment of this "benefit" unachievable. Any standard based on a balancing of costs and benefits by the Secretary that strikes a different balance than that struck by Congress would be inconsistent with the command set forth in §6(b)(5) [references omitted].[41]

The key to understanding the difference between Case 8.1 and Case 8.2 is that in the former case there was no evidence that the more stringent benzene exposure level would alleviate a hazard, while in the latter case there was some evidence that the more stringent cotton dust requirement would reduce the incidence of byssinosis.

Is a standard unfeasible when the technology does not exist by which to comply with it? Case 8.3 presents the example of vinyl chloride. The plastics industry was claiming that existing technology did not permit compliance without essentially bankrupting the entire industry. And, apparently, the OSHA standard did not seem to be well founded on the scientific research that preceded it. The logic behind the rejection of the benzene standard might well have dictated rejection of the vinyl chloride standard as well. Nevertheless, in *Society of the Plastics Industry* v. *OSHA*, a court of appeals upheld the standard.[42] Considering the thirteen deaths, said the court, the standard was a reasonable one, despite any doubts one might have about its scientific soundness. Concerning the evident lack of technology, the court said:

> In the area of safety, we wish to emphasize, the Secretary [of Labor] is not restricted by the status quo. He may raise standards which require development

of new technology, and he is not limited to issuing standards based solely on devices already fully developed.[43]

The vinyl chloride standard is an example of a technology-forcing standard, one that may be technologically infeasible for the industry to follow initially but that the industry could in time meet by developing new technology. Indeed, that is precisely what the industry was forced to do, once the standard was upheld by the courts. Once the technology was developed, the industry discovered that its earlier predictions of financial disaster were greatly exaggerated. The actual cost of compliance to users was $300 million and the cost to producers was only $25–35 million.[44]

Needless to say, the vinyl chloride incident did nothing to enhance the credibility of industry claims that OSHA standards would lead to the financial demise of American business. Currently, even a well-founded fear of the financial consequences of an OSHA standard is no assurance that the government will see fit to withdraw or moderate the standard. Neither cost nor the lack of technology is necessarily an adequate justification for refusal to comply.[45]

## Rights of Employers and Employees

Cases 8.4 and 8.5 give examples of recent judicial determinations regarding two *employer* rights: the right to be free from warrantless OSHA inspections and the right to discipline employees for refusal to obey the firm's safety rules.

The right to be free from warrantless search is guaranteed by the U.S. Constitution, but imposing this on OSHA enforcement can present an obstacle to efficient enforcement. Requiring search warrants forces the agency to spend time and effort petitioning for the warrant, perhaps having the petition denied, perhaps in the process tipping off the employer in enough time for safety violations to be corrected before the warrant is finally obtained. The U.S. Supreme Court attempted to reconcile these considerations in *Marshall* v. *Barlow's*, a case similar to Case 8.4.[46] While agreeing that the employer had the right to demand a search warrant, the court also said that OSHA would not have to follow the same rigorous procedure that a police department must follow in obtaining a search warrant in a criminal case. OSHA is usually entitled to a warrant whenever an inspection is based on either an employee complaint or a reasonable administrative policy, such as "inspect the worst industries first." While that tends to mitigate the burden of obtaining warrants on OSHA somewhat, employers have filed many lawsuits challenging the legitimacy of OSHA inspection warrants since the Supreme Court's decision in the *Barlow* case. The outcomes of those cases tend to uphold OSHA's basic right to conduct a reasonable inspection, but they have also forced certain unanticipated procedural requirements on OSHA and have invalidated several OSHA inspections.[47] OSHA may have to document its case with such evidence as details concerning the grounds for the employee's complaint, the justification for any deviation from the "worst first" list, and the like. And two federal courts have recently issued decisions that threaten OSHA's right to keep their request for a search warrant a secret from the employer.[48] Evidently, the issue of search warrants is a long way from resolution by the courts.

The right to discipline employees for violation of company safety rules is well established.[49] OSHA regulations specifically permit an employer to discipline an employee in situations such as presented in Case 8.5. But Case 8.5 raises a different issue: the employer's *obligation* to discipline. The situation in Case 8.5 was decided against the employer in *Atlantic and Gulf Stevedores, Inc.* v. *OSHARC.*[50] Regardless of the threat of a wildcat strike, the employer was responsible for employee compliance with the hard-hat regulation. The court suggested some approaches that the employer might have taken to solve their problem:

> Bargain with the union: the law gives the employer the right to "insist to the point of impasse upon the right to discharge or discipline disobedient employees" in safety and health situations.

> Get an injunction: if the strike happens anyhow, the employer is legally entitled to a court injunction against it under most union contracts.

> Ask OSHA for an exemption from the standard: section 6(b)(6)(A) allows employers to seek a variance.

But this reasoning has been criticized as unrealistic and impractical.[51] Unions often refuse to bargain on such issues, a court injunction is often ineffective against a wildcat strike, and obtaining a variance is often infeasible because the company cannot meet OSHA's stringent criteria. Apparently, considering the realities of modern day labor-management relations, an employer in such a predicament must choose between a fight with OSHA and a fight with its workers.

Employees are guaranteed certain rights as well. The principal employee right is defined by the principal employer obligation: the right to a work place free from recognized hazards. Second, OSHA has a reasonably straightforward section giving employees the right to participate in enforcement proceedings,[52] and recent cases have made it clear that the right is quite broad.[53]

A third employee right raises new issues: the right to refuse hazardous work. Case 8.6 presents the classic situation. Employers have long insisted on their authority over work assignment, and labor arbitrators have consistently held that refusal to accept a work assignment is a justifiable grounds for discharge.[54] However, deciding Case 8.6 in favor of the employer would force employees who were convinced that the work would be hazardous to choose between their livelihood and their physical well-being. The Supreme Court decided this matter against the employer in *Whirlpool Corporation* v. *Marshall.*[55] The key issue in the case was the reasonableness of the workers' concern:

> Circumstances may sometimes exist in which the employee justifiably believes that the express statutory arrangement does not sufficiently protect them from death or serious injury. Such circumstances will probably not often occur, but such a situation may arise when (1) the employee is ordered by his employer to work under conditions that the employee reasonably believes pose an imminent risk of death or serious bodily injury, and (2) the employee has reason to believe that there is not sufficient time or opportunity either to seek effective redress from his employer or to apprise OSHA of the danger.
>
> . . . .
>
> The Act does not wait for an employee to die or become injured. It authorizes the promulgation of health and safety standards and the issuance of citations in the hope that these will act to prevent deaths or injuries from ever occurring. It would seem anomalous to construe an Act so directed and constructed as prohibiting an employee, with no other reasonable alternative, the freedom to withdraw from a workplace environment that he reasonably believes is highly dangerous.[56]

In the *Whirlpool* situation, there was clear evidence that a specific hazard posed a threat to life. Short of that, the right of employees to refuse work they consider to be hazardous is more debatable. Still, the case does stand as a major exception to the employer's basic right to discipline employees. In that regard, the case is testimony to the importance Congress attached to job safety and health in debating and passing the Occupational Safety and Health Act.

While the importance of job safety and health is undisputed, and while the courts are beginning to settle some of the uncertainties regarding the proper interpretation of the Occupational Safety and Health Act, the controversies over OSHA continue. Critics still regard many of the safety standards as ill advised, and some still regard the balance of employee rights and employer rights as tilted too much in favor of the employee. The Supreme Court's decision in the cotton dust case may have ended claims that the law mandates cost-benefit analysis, but it did not silence those who argue that OSHA should be enforced with due regard for costs and benefits. Because that argument may yet come to influence future legislators as well as future enforcement of existing legislation, it is discussed with other criticisms of OSHA in Chapter 9.

## Further Information on OSHA

Among the subscription information services on OSHA is the *Occupational Safety and Health Reporter,* published by the Bureau of National Affairs, which also publishes the full texts of OSHA court opinions in *Occupational Safety and Health Cases.* A periodical published by the U.S. Department of Labor, *Job Safety and Health,* deals with OSHA issues extensively. Also, *Employee Relations Law Journal* and *Labor Law Journal* cover occupational safety and health regulation issues.

## Notes

1. Nicholas A. Ashford, *Crisis in the Workplace: Occupational Disease and Injury* (Cambridge, Mass.: MIT Press, 1976), p. 49.

2. Ibid., p. 407.

3. John Mendeloff, *Regulating Safety: An Economic and Political Analysis of Occupational Safety and Health Policy* (Cambridge, Mass.: MIT Press, 1979), p. 11.

4. Ashford, *Crisis*, p. 408.

5. Mendeloff, *Regulating Safety*, p. 12.

6. Ashford, *Crisis*, p. 417.

7. *The Job Safety and Health Act of 1970* (Washington, D.C.: Bureau of National Affairs, 1971), p. 14.

8. Ashford, *Crisis*, p. 51.

9. Ibid.

10. Mendeloff, *Regulating Safety*, p. 153.

11. Ashford, *Crisis*, p. 3.

12. Ibid., p. 46.

13. Ibid., p. 4.

14. *The Job Safety and Health Act of 1970*, p. 15; also see Ashford, *Crisis*, p. 52.

15. Ashford, *Crisis*, p. 21.

16. Ibid., p. 57.

17. *The Job Safety and Health Act of 1970*, p. 14.

18. Mendeloff, *Regulating Safety*, p. 16.

19. Ibid., pp. 16–17.

20. Ibid.

21. Ibid.

22. See Ashford, *Crisis*, pp. 52–53; Mendeloff, *Regulating Safety*, p. 17.

23. Mendeloff, *Regulating Safety*, pp. 20–22.

24. *The Job Safety and Health Act of 1970*, pp. 2–3.

25. See *Occupational Safety and Health Law 1980* (New York: Practising Law Institute, 1980), pp. 24–35 for a description.

26. *The Job Safety and Health Act of 1970*, p. 38.

27. See Paul I. Weiner, "Variance Under OSHA: An Update," *Labor Law Journal* 28 (1977):161–65.

28. Sec. 17(f), Occupational Safety and Health Act.

29. *Occupational Safety and Health Law 1980*, p. 19.

30. Ibid., pp. 139–40.

31. Ibid., p. 131.

32. Sec. 22, Occupational Safety and Health Act.

33. For an excellent overview, see *Occupational Safety and Health Law 1980*, pp. 157–93.

34. Sec. 18(c)(2), Occupational Safety and Health Act.

35. Sec. 18(f), Occupational Safety and Health Act.

36. Mendeloff, *Regulating Safety*, p. 38.

37. *Industrial Union Dept. AFL-CIO v. Hodgson*, 499 F.2d 467 (D.C. Cir. 1974); also see *Occupational Safety and Health Law 1980*, p. 41.

38. Ibid.

39. Ibid.

40. 448 U.S. 607 (1980).

41. 9 Occupational Safety and Health Cases 1913 (U.S. Supreme Court 1981), p. 1920.

42. 509 F.2d 1301 (2d Cir. 1974).

43. Ibid., p. 1309.

44. Basil J. Whiting, "Regulatory Reform and OSHA: Fads and Realities," *Labor Law Journal* 30 (1979):514—27.

45. See Herbert R. Northrup et al., *The Impact of OSHA* (Philadelphia: University of Pennsylvania Press, 1978); and *Occupational Safety and Health Law 1980*, pp. 137ff.

46. *Marshall v. Barlow's, Inc.*, 436 U.S. 307 (1978).

47. *Occupational Safety and Health Law 1980*, pp. 9–10.

48. Ibid., p. 10.

49. 29 Code of Federal Regulations, Part 197, at Sec. 22.

50. 434 F.2d 541 (3rd Cir. 1976).

51. Roger B. Jacobs, "Employee Resistance to OSHA Standards: Toward a More Reasonable Approach," *Labor Law Journal* 30 (1979):219–30.

52. Sec. 10(c), Occupational Safety and Health Act.

53. See *Occupational Safety and Health Law 1980*, p. 138.

54. Lawrence Stessin, *The Practice of Personnel and Industrial Relations: A Casebook* (New York: Pitman, 1964).

55. 8 *Occupational Safety and Health Cases* 1001 (1980). The Court ruled that employers could not discriminate against employees who refuse to perform their assigned tasks in the face of imminent danger. While the reprimand was held to constitute "discrimination," the Court declined to rule on whether the denial of pay was. See n. 31 of the case, p. 1007.

56. *Whirlpool Corporation* v. *Marshall*, 445 U.S. 1, pp. 10–12.

# 9

# The Impact of OSHA

One reason OSHA is so controversial is the belief among many that OSHA does more harm than good, that it has had an adverse impact on safety as well as on profits. Regardless of whether that belief is well founded, it is widespread and angrily held. Consequently, the impact of OSHA deserves more extended treatment than does the impact of regulation in other areas.

There is actually little evidence that leads to solid conclusions one way or the other regarding OSHA's performance. Both critics and supporters confine themselves to using data that advance their side of the debate, and both advance plausible arguments that the other side's data are really attributable to something besides OSHA. For example, critics can claim that any improvements in safety statistics are due to technological developments and not to OSHA, and supporters can claim that any worsening in such statistics is due to more vigilant accident reporting and not to deficiencies in OSHA. All in all, evaluation of OSHA is far more difficult and equivocal than either side seems willing to concede.

Still, OSHA has few defenders. Understandably, management has opposed it. In academic circles, the verdict has gone strongly against OSHA, with economists in particular attacking it.[1] Some unions have supported OSHA, but aside from them, about the only defenders of OSHA are OSHA officials, and even they have conceded that OSHA's record was dismal in its early stages. Others who support federal regulation of job safety and health in principle also seem disappointed with the way OSHA has discharged its regulatory responsibilities.

If OSHA has failed in its safety objectives, then personnel and human resources managers should know about it. Safety is a product of people interacting with things. Safety problems occur when the people are ill-trained or unmotivated, or when the things on the job are hazardous, or when the procedures governing the interaction of people and things are unsafe. In large part, those problems are problems of personnel and human resource management.

## Chapter Objectives

This chapter begins with a discussion of problems of OSHA regulation. Some of these are little more than start-up problems, transitory embarrassments that occurred during what may have been the most inauspicious beginning of an agency in the history of federal regulation. Because those problems have passed, most observers now believe that OSHA no longer deserves the bad publicity it received from some of those initial missteps. However, other problems of OSHA's are more enduring, and they too are discussed in this chapter.

Next, the chapter asks whether, despite its problems, OSHA's benefits outweigh its costs. The chapter acknowledges the difficulties of undertaking a cost-benefit analysis of OSHA. Nevertheless, most analysts find OSHA's failures more prominent than its accomplishments, and it is important to understand that point of view. The chapter presents a model interrelating many of the negative observations about OSHA scattered throughout the literature and provides an account of the dynamics underlying OSHA's disappointing record. Finally, the last part of the chapter identifies some of the management responses to OSHA.

## Start-Up Problems

Even its director conceded that OSHA's record was poor at the outset.[2] Part of the problem was OSHA's standards themselves, and part was the enforcement of those standards.

The main problem with the standards originated in section 6(a) of the act (see Exhibit 8.2), which mandates the adoption of consensus standards and federal agency standards as interim OSHA standards. The consensus standards were so voluminous that the agency did not have the time or staff to review their appropriateness, but instead adopted them more or less wholesale.[3]

The resulting problems were legendary. The consensus standards included several provisions that were so trivial as to make a laughingstock of the agency. For example, one mandated that "each water closet shall occupy a separate compartment with a door and walls or partitions between fixtures sufficiently high to assure privacy." Such solemn declarations by a federal agency cannot do much to enhance public respect for regulation.[4]

Other regulations struck many observers as foolish. For instance, Murray Weidenbaum quotes the regulations that took more than a paragraph to define *exit*, while the dictionary gave a five-word definition.[5] Another regulation required that work places having walking areas marked off with white paint be repainted yellow.[6] Still another regulation prohibited employers from providing ice water to employees. Why? Because back in the days when ice was cut in blocks from rivers, ice water was unsanitary. The regulation had outlived its usefulness, but that didn't keep OSHA from adopting it with all the rest.[7]

Bathroom regulations raised the most laughs: the one already mentioned on partitions, another that required coathooks on bathroom doors, another requiring that bathrooms be located no more than two hundred feet from any employee's work place, and the famous regulation that mandated split toilet seats and prohibited round ones.[8] Ronald Reagan told this story about a bathroom standard in a campaign speech:

> The owner of a small business in one western state was told to install separate men's and women's restrooms for his employees. He had only one employee—at home—in the same bed. It was his wife.[9]

OSHA standards were criticized on other grounds as well. Some were thought to be overly strict, tolerable as voluntary benchmark standards, but never intended to serve as legal minimums. (This was the same complaint that critics of the EEOC Selection Guidelines made—see Chapter 5.) Some standards were considered too vague (for example, the requirement that management offer first aid training where there is no medical facility in "near proximity" to the work place);[10] others were considered too specific (for example, the mandate that fire extinguishers having a weight of less than 40 pounds be installed no more than 5 feet above the floor).[11] The fact that such requirements were originally standards promulgated by industry seemed to be forgotten by some of the critics.

The problems with enforcement of the standards might be considered misjudgments. OSHA inspectors seemed to seize on the most trivial standards for the greatest enforcement effort. The agency made firms spend as much as $8,000 to install bathroom stall doors,[12] and it made Dow Chemical spend $60,000 per plant to lower all railings eight inches to comply with an OSHA standard—even though Dow studies showed the higher level to be safe.[13] During OSHA's first five years, more than 98 percent of its citations were for "non-serious" cases, and the average fine was under $27.[14]

In part, the enforcement problems were due to OSHA not wanting to appear indecisive[15] while waiting for sounder permanent standards to be adopted. And in part those problems were due to a lack of qualified people in the labor market to hire as inspectors. Early on, the government moved "to broaden and relax" the qualification standards for industrial hygienists.[16] Another cause of OSHA's ineffectiveness may have been President Nixon's move toward decentralization of government functions and his evident reluctance to support strong OSHA enforcement.[17]

In time, OSHA began to change for the better. NIOSH began turning out trained inspectors, and qualifed professionals began filling OSHA positions. Eventually, complaints about inspections declined. Also, OSHA reordered its priorities to stress serious hazards and deemphasize nuisance citations. Most recently, some of the more trivial rules and regulations have been deleted. As a result of such steps, OSHA's image has improved considerably.

## More Enduring Problems

Other problems seem less transient than trivial standards and untrained staff. These more enduring problems seem destined to be the problems of the 1980s for OSHA. Four symptoms of OSHA's difficulties have been frequently examined: (1) the costs of compliance, (2) the inadequacy of OSHA's regulation of occupational health, (3) the labor-management conflict created by OSHA; and (4) the points of conflict between OSHA and other regulatory areas.

## Costs of OSHA

The most common criticism of OSHA is that it is too costly. Critics have put forth many specific estimates of compliance costs. Like Senator Joseph McCarthy's figure of fifty-seven communists in the State Department, those figures make one skeptical, but they all seem high. Weidenbaum estimated the 1973 compliance cost to industry at over $3 billion.[18] The anticipated compliance cost of just one OSHA standard, the 90-decibel noise-level standard, was estimated at $13 billion.[19] Leigh estimated the cost of the coke-oven emission standard to the steel industry at about $240 million per year.[20] For the plastics industry, Northrup estimated the capital cost of compliance with the vinyl chloride standard to be over $20,000 per employee, with additional noncapital expenses of over $1,000 per employee per year.[21] For the textile industry to comply with the cotton dust exposure standard, he estimated the cost of equipment installation alone at over $2 billion.[22]

While the vinyl plastics industry is apparently healthy enough to survive the impact of the vinyl chloride standard, the textile industry may not be healthy enough to withstand the cotton dust standard. Textiles face heavy foreign competition, and the cotton dust standard would cause estimated price increases ranging from 22 to 625 percent.[23]

Lost productivity is one reflection of those costs. Northrup estimated the loss in productivity to the vinyl plastics industry due to the vinyl chloride standard at 6 percent. For those vinyl plastics facilities that existed at the time the regulation was adopted, the loss was estimated at 10 to 15 percent. There is also evidence that OSHA affects strategic planning decisions. For example, some chemical firms have rejected new product ventures explicitly to avoid OSHA compliance problems.[24]

Small businesses face greater problems, for they cannot afford OSHA regulations as well as large businesses can. Not only are they at a disadvantage from the standpoint of economies of scale, but also their chronic shortage of capital makes it difficult for them to undertake the large capital investment in safer equipment that OSHA compliance requires. While the Occupational Safety and Health Act authorizes the Small Business Administration to make loans to small businesses for OSHA compliance purposes, such indebtedness, like any other, adversely affects a firm's capital position.[25] When Richard Saunders of Wichita, Kansas, was told by OSHA that compliance for his foundry would require electrical work costing $500,000, he closed the business. Borrowing the money, he explained, "would be starting down the road to bankruptcy."[26]

## Inadequate Regulation of Occupational Health

During congressional hearings on OSHA, both labor and management agreed that health hazards, not safety hazards, were the major problem warranting government regulation. The most notable evidence of that was the research indicating that between 60 and 90 percent of cancers were caused by factors in the environment, presumably the work environment.[27] Yet by the middle of 1975, only about 10 percent of OSHA's inspections touched on health matters.[28]

Two explanations have been given for the inattention to health: lack of personnel and lack of progress in developing new standards. OSHA originally planned on a staff of one thousand health standard compliance officers, yet there were only two thousand qualified industrial hygienists in the entire country.[29] The situation can be expected to improve gradually as more people become trained in industrial hygiene. But the lack of progress in adopting standards may be harder to solve. For one thing, OSHA mandates an elaborate standard development procedure, as noted in Chapter 8. Also, the very nature of some occupational illnesses causes delays in standards relating to those illnesses. Illnesses often have multiple causes, and often their causes are unknown.[30] That makes it more difficult to arrive at firm conclusions regarding the efficacy of possible work environment standards.

## Labor-Management Conflicts

OSHA has changed the relationship between management and unions regarding work hazards. Before OSHA, job safety was voluntarily negotiated by unions and management. As a result, 31 percent of all labor contracts in 1971 provided for joint union-management safety committees.[31] Since OSHA, however, an adversary relationship between labor and management seems more prevalent.

Labor-management conflict over safety usually arises in three areas, employee discipline, OSHA's process for adopting new standards, and OSHA inspections. Discipline is a safety issue because OSHA places responsibility for unsafe employee behavior in the hands of the employer. This increases the likelihood that employers will enforce safety rules by taking disciplinary action against employees who violate them. Such disciplinary action, however justifiable, tends to strain labor-management relations.

Regarding new OSHA standards, labor generally advocates stringent standards, while management has a natural interest in more relaxed standards. The resulting conflict is one cause of delay in the adoption of standards. It also makes OSHA hearings over standards into political battlegrounds, and the standards that emerge are more likely to be subjective or political in nature rather than objective or scientific.[32] Finally, OSHA inspections are an issue because employees can threaten to complain to OSHA about health and safety conditions on the job, a step that usually leads to an OSHA inspection.

## Conflict with Other Regulatory Areas

Two areas have been singled out as conflicting with OSHA: privacy legislation and regulations prohibiting sex discrimination against pregnant women.

The Occupational Safety and Health Act raises privacy issues in section 8(c) (see Exhibit 8.2). That section gives OSHA agencies widespread access to records that are likely to contain confidential information. In the case of *E. I. du Pont deNemours* v. *Finklea*,[33] a court ruled that NIOSH was entitled to see confidential medical records. The court also put stringent restrictions on the way NIOSH was to handle the records, in order to limit the potential for disclosure. Nevertheless, the decision is far from a firm assurance that confidential information on employees or applicants will not become public as discussed in Chapter 12.[34]

Furthermore, OSHA requires private sector employers to collect certain health information without requiring them to treat such information confidentally. That is a problem, for employers frequently agree to exchange medical records of workers who are known to have been exposed to health hazards.[35] Unions have already complained that employers discriminate against such workers because of the possibility that the previous exposures might lead to a disability for which they would be liable under workers' compensation.[36] Yet depriving employers of the opportunity to exchange such information prevents the new employer from avoiding job assignments that expose employees to hazards that previous exposures in their old jobs have made them more susceptible to.

Pregnancy poses an occupational health problem because some otherwise harmless substances in a work place are demonstrably hazardous to pregnant women or to their unborn children. But, as Chapter 3 points out, exclusion of pregnant women is ordinarily considered illegal sex discrimination. This has been a major problem in the vinyl plastics industry. Essentially, that industry must choose between risking EEO problems by excluding women from jobs that expose them to vinyl chloride or risking liability for damages suffered by pregnant women if they are allowed to take such jobs. It is possible that a major proportion of production jobs in the vinyl plastics industry will be closed to pregnant women because of that problem.[37]

## Do Benefits Outweigh Costs?

### Some Likely Gains from OSHA

Not all of OSHA's effects have been negative. Whiting noted that federal regulation can sometimes shake companies out of their rigidity and lethargy, with beneficial effects on their long-term survival and profit.[38] For instance, the vinyl chloride standard made the vinyl plastics industry develop the technology necessary to comply, and that technology has also resulted in a more cost-effective product. Another example is the technology being devised to meet the health standards in the copper industry.[39] Also, one study found that health and safety regulations similar to OSHA in four western European countries and Japan have tended to be a catalyst to technological innovation.[40] Weidenbaum lists seven benefits that can be expected to result from health and safety regulation:

1. productivity gains from those who would have otherwise been injured or ill
2. greater enjoyment of life by those persons
3. reduced costs of treatment and rehabilitation
4. reduced costs of administering worker compensation and insurance and training replacements
5. reduced need for private sector efforts to encourage job safety and health
6. reduced damages to plants and equipment
7. reduced disruption of work[41]

## The Difficulty of Evaluating OSHA

Evaluating OSHA by comparing its costs and benefits is quite controversial. Cost-benefit analysis attempts to evaluate programs objectively by expressing impact in net dollars, but many observers suggest that it is inherently impossible to do that with OSHA. Most of those who are pessimistic about the possibility of cost-benefit analysis have been pro-OSHA—not surprising, since most of the cost-benefit evaluations of OSHA that have been done have been negative. Some of the pro-OSHA reservations are:[42]

1. Those who criticize the high costs of OSHA seldom make clear *whose costs* are involved. While the costs of OSHA regulations are borne by employers, the costs of no regulations would be borne by workers.

2. Most analysts neglect the *benefits* of OSHA. Benefits are harder to quantify. Thus the verdicts on OSHA come out somewhat one-sided.

3. Despite the apparent objectivity of cost-benefit analysis, *value judgments* are unavoidable. For example, Whiting points out that the discount rates used to measure future costs of hazards are value judgments: the higher the discount rate, the lower the importance attached to events in the future. Considering the fact that so many anticipated OSHA benefits, such as improved health of the nation's work force, are long range in nature, Whiting's criticism is significant.

4. Most of the costs of OSHA are *one time* costs, capital investments in new equipment or modification of facilities. But if those are absorbed in operating budgets rather than financed over time, cost estimates for OSHA are inflated.

5. *Other influences* besides OSHA can affect cost and benefit measures. For example, if the measure of OSHA's impact upon safety is the number of reported accidents, a lack of improvement may be due not to OSHA's ineffectiveness but to the improvements in worker compensation benefits that have taken place over the past few years. Improved benefits give workers more incentive to report accidents, and the resulting increase in the reported accident rate would tend to make OSHA look bad.

6. As with any evaluative technique, some *arbitrary assumptions* must be made in cost-benefit analysis. For instance, when there is no information available about the indirect costs of work injuries (costs aside from worker compensation liabilities that were incurred by the companies), some studies have arbitrarily set them equal to the direct costs.

## Impact on Safety and Health

Despite those difficulties, many attempts to evaluate OSHA's impact have been made. The majority appear to conclude that OSHA, on balance, has not been effective. For example, Northrup's extensive study concluded that OSHA was not effective in the aerospace and chemical industries.[43] In the vinyl plastics industry, Northrup figured the benefit of the controversial vinyl chloride standard to be approximately twenty-two lives saved over the next four decades at a total cost of $200 million, for a cost of over $9 million per life saved. Other OSHA standards may fare better, but the general picture is not encouraging. Overall injury figures give an inconclusive verdict. While the injury rate actually increased during the first four years of OSHA's existence, the severity of those injuries decreased. During the following year the opposite occurred.[44] While John Mendeloff's study indicated some positive outcomes,[45] Nicholas A. Ashford concluded that OSHA had failed to live up to its potential,[46] and Robert S. Smith reported that the effects of OSHA on injuries were not significantly different from zero.[47]

One should not accept those dismal conclusions without bearing in mind the questionable validity of the accident data used to measure impact. For example, those data include accidents due to strain and exertion, a problem that OSHA was never meant to solve. Strain and exertion are caused by fatigue due to increased overtime work, and overtime increases during economic good times, regardless of OSHA. Thus, if strain and exertion injuries are removed from the data, accident rates show a decrease since OSHA came into being.[48]

Moreover, one should not jump to the conclusion that OSHA's inspections are ineffective simply because research shows that accident rates do not fall after an OSHA inspection. OSHA might well be effective in promoting company concern over safety out of a *fear* of inspection.[49]

Considering the unreliability of accident data[50] and the existence of explanations besides OSHA for any changes in accident and health data, it seems premature to write off OSHA. The measures of effectiveness used in the research to date may be insensitive to some true, significant impact of OSHA. Nevertheless, many observers are willing to conclude that OSHA has been ineffective. One thing is certain: the clear-cut beneficial impact of OSHA that was hoped for has not materialized.

## Causes: The Dynamics of OSHA's Ineffectiveness

Many explanations have been offered to account for OSHA's failures. While it is difficult to keep track of the points raised by the authors, common themes do emerge. Exhibit 9.1 depicts some of the more prominently mentioned factors that have been said to contribute to the perpetuation of problems despite (or because of) the existence of OSHA. While no pictorial representation can do justice to the complexity of explanations, Exhibit 9.1 attempts to bring some order to the subject.

Before discussing Exhibit 9.1, it is useful to examine three major themes that emerge from the commentary about OSHA's failures. One is that the bureaucratic barriers to standard adoption and the inherent difficulty of solving occupational safety and health problems conspire to make enforcement ineffective.

A second theme concerns economic forces. Northrup, for instance, believes that OSHA underestimates the potential of the market to solve occupational safety and health problems and overestimates the potential of government regulation to solve those problems. Part of OSHA's error is an overreliance on specific safety standards, which is said to force employers to allocate resources in ways that are less than ideal for solving safety and health problems. The recommended alternative to specific standards is an *injury tax*, based on the employer's safety record. By penalizing employers with the worst records, it would provide an economic incentive for adopting the safety steps that would be most effective.[51]

A third theme is labor-management conflict. Some ingredients of this conflict have already been mentioned. Generally, labor-management conflict has resulted in OSHA's being used as a club. Thus OSHA's regulatory approach is punitive, as exemplified by the fact that because of a provision in the act, OSHA cannot conduct courtesy inspections to help management identify hazards, but instead must issue a citation whenever a violation is found.[52]

**Exhibit 9.1**  The Dynamics of OSHA Ineffectiveness

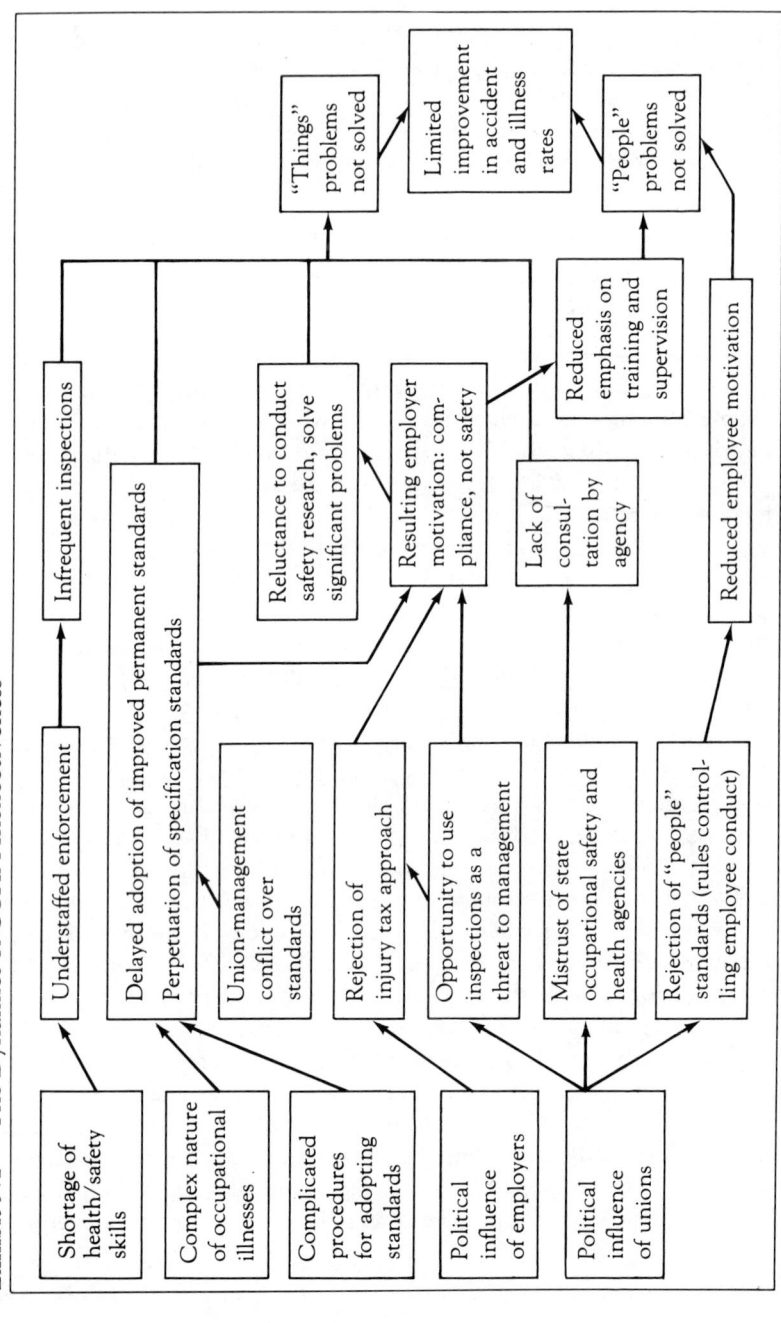

These three themes and others are explored and interrelated in the following discussion.

## What Causes Occupational Accidents and Illnesses?

To understand OSHA's problems, it is helpful to consider the causes of occupational accidents and illnesses. It is very easy to present statistics suggesting that accidents are caused by people: their carelessness, their lack of training, or some other personal deficiency. An alternate explanation is that accidents are caused by things: physical hazards in the work environment. Actually, much of the current research suggests that accidents on the job are generally caused by an interaction between people problems and thing problems.[53]

For example, fatigue is a major cause of accidents. But fatigue is a not purely personal characteristic or a purely environmental one, but rather an interaction between the person and the demands of work. Likewise, higher accident rates have been found to be associated with greater overtime work,[54] regardless of the personal characteristics of employees. New work also increases the risk of accidents, because it presents a set of demands to which employees are unaccustomed and for which they are often untrained. In sum, accidents, like most human behavior, are properly regarded as a product of both the person and that person's environment.

The problem is that OSHA's standards focus on environmental factors to the near exclusion of personal factors. They regulate things in the work environment that may pose hazards, but they rarely regulate the behavior of employees. Where OSHA standards do govern employee behavior, they provide no sanctions for employees.

## Failure to Address People Problems

OSHA's emphasis on things rather than people can be expected to have effects on motivations of employers as well as the motivations of employees. Employers get the message that they should be more concerned with engineering controls and less concerned with training, discipline, and improved work procedures. That message is reinforced by reports that OSHA, while lavishing its attention on the work place as a physical environment, neglects safety standards for personal protective equipment such as hard hats and safety shoes. OSHA does not even require employers to note whether injured workers were wearing protective equipment at the time of their injuries. A NIOSH testing laboratory chief was quoted in the

*Wall Street Journal* as saying, "We can't tell whether a worker with a head injury had a helmet on, let alone where he was hit."[55]

The effect on employees is predictable. With no OSHA penalties for unsafe working behavior, employees have no motivation aside from self-protection for following safety rules, unless the employer applies sanctions or incentives. As Weidenbaum notes, OSHA standards appear to have shifted responsibility for the employee's protection from the employee to the employer.[56]

### Inadequate Approach to Thing Problems

Even the safety problems that do reside in the work environment cannot be satisfactorily addressed given OSHA's difficulties. The shortage of qualified staff makes inspections infrequent and impedes the enforcement of the standards that do exist. And the standards that exist are of questionable effectiveness.

The main criticism is that most OSHA standards are *specification* standards rather than *performance* standards. A specification standard states the type of equipment and facilities that must be used. For example, a specification standard might state that a railing must have a certain minimum diameter. A performance standard, on the other hand, might state that the railing must withstand a certain weight applied to it without breaking. The objective of both the specification standard and the performance standard is the same: to ensure that the railing is strong enough. However, a railing that achieves that objective (that is, one that met the performance standard) would violate a specification standard if it achieves it the wrong way, for example, if it did not have the minimum diameter. The only way out for an employer in such a situation is to petition OSHA for a variance, a cumbersome and risky way to gain approval for a situation that is just as safe as the one mandated in the standard.[57]

There are other problems with the standards. One is that the long time required to replace the consensus standards and to develop standards to cover new hazards causes numerous gaps in the OSHA standards. At the time of a major grain elevator explosion in New Orleans, OSHA had no standards governing the dust hazard that caused the explosion, despite the fact that dust was a well-known danger in grain elevator operation.

Two factors explain why OSHA's "thing" standards are so inadequate. One is the difficulty of moving new standards through the bureaucratic maze. The difficulty is greatest when the standard concerns a complex problem. Complex problems are more likely to be the subject of detailed, conflicting, and incomplete research findings,[58] which slow down the deliberations over new standards considerably.

The second problem is the political nature of the standard development process.[59] As noted above, the process is an adversary one. While business attempts to make the standard as permissive as possible, unions urge a strict standard. The self-interest on the business side is evident. The self-interest on the union side, in addition to the obvious concern for protecting union members, is often (1) to have the government impose a safety requirement that would otherwise have to be bargained for at contract negotiation time, and (2) to gain another weapon against management. A strict standard is a weapon, because it is one more thing that the employer could be cited for violating if the facility is inspected by OSHA. Political conflicts over standards cause delays in the standard development process and thus account in large measure for the prevalence of the old consensus standards, particularly the specification standards involving expensive engineering controls. They also help explain why health standards take so long to be adopted.

## The Plight of State Programs

Chapter 8 discusses the role that states can play in taking over OSHA enforcement from the federal government and cites some advantages for employers of their doing so. Yet progress in this area has been disappointingly slow to some observers. One reason is that unions mistrust state programs. A complete state takeover would mean that unions would have to deal with fifty-one occupational safety and health agencies instead of with just one federal agency. Besides, the one federal agency has always been regarded as a friend to organized labor. Aside from union mistrust, another factor is the unpopularity of OSHA. Some states are reluctant to take over the work of a federal agency that has been as soundly criticized as OSHA has been, particularly since they are only given a 50 percent subsidy for undertaking such a controversial program. Furthermore, the states that do choose to get involved face difficult barriers imposed by the Occupational Safety and Health Administration.[60] The result of those factors is that few states have programs, which means that few businesses have access to the risk-free courtesy inspection programs that state agencies, but not the federal agency, are allowed to provide.

## Standards Versus Incentives: The Injury Tax Alternative

Perhaps the most significant problem in all of this is that OSHA's regulations motivate employers to be more concerned with compliance than with safety. OSHA's sanctions are for failure to meet standards, not for failure to attain a desired accident and health record.

While one might not expect the motive to comply with standards to conflict with the motive to achieve a good safety and health record, sometimes it does. Consider a company decision on whether to undertake research on health and safety problems. Such research would be expected to improve occupational safety and health, yet OSHA makes it risky. If the research uncovers new problems, OSHA could impose new standards or schedule more inspections. The vinyl plastics industry learned an expensive lesson about that: industry-financed research uncovered the link between vinyl chloride and cancer, and that in turn precipitated the stringent vinyl chloride exposure standard adopted by OSHA.[61] Because the standard was regarded by the industry as unreasonable, the incident caused some second thoughts about the advisability of embarking on safety research.

Another conflict between compliance and safety occurs when trivial or otherwise inferior standards force employers to divert resources from activities that might be more effective in improving safety and health. For example, aerospace firms were forced to change the height of a multitude of fire extinguishers by three or four inches throughout facilities that were often the size of several football fields. As Northrup observed, the money might have been better spent on something with a more substantial impact on safety.[62]

A frequently suggested solution is to replace the standards with an injury tax on employers, based on safety records. An injury tax would not work with occupational illnesses, because their onset often occurs many years after the exposures that caused them. But in the area of accident prevention, an injury tax would allow employers to achieve a good safety record by whatever means they saw fit. It would eliminate the need for the often trivial OSHA standards.

The political opposition to an injury tax is overwhelming. Neither business nor labor supports the idea. The business community is reluctant to support a proposal that would subject it to an added tax burden. Unions are opposed because a tax would eliminate the necessity for standards and inspections and deprive unions of a major threat over management. Finally, unions fear that an injury tax might encourage employers to reduce injury rates by transferring or firing those workers that have more accidents.

In conclusion, OSHA's apparent ineffectiveness is a product of several underlying political and economic forces. While OSHA's problems do not demonstrate conclusively that government regulation of job safety and health is doomed to fail, they do suggest that the political process presents formidable obstacles to success.

## Management Responses to OSHA

OSHA has changed the way that organizations manage their safety and health programs. These management responses are reflected in the right-hand column of the regulatory model in Exhibit 8.1. The changes have occurred in several areas.

1. *Organizing:* OSHA has led to a more formally organized safety and health function in firms covered by OSHA. Responsibilities and lines of authority have become clearer, and the threat of inspections and citations has made it apparent that top management control and support for safety and health programs is essential. Likewise, OSHA has brought about an increased involvement of line managers in safety programs, both to diagnose safety problems and to implement solutions.[63] Also, since OSHA, employers have been more likely to hire safety specialists with professional safety backgrounds.[64]

2. *Auditing and self-inspection:* OSHA has also made it more important for the organization to review its own safety status and identify problem areas. Facilities that are too small to hire their own safety and health professionals can usually get assistance from the corporate headquarters staff or from their worker compensation insurance carriers. There are other sources of help as well: equipment manufacturers, other employers, trade associations, and the like.

3. *Controlling employee behavior:* While OSHA is directed at things rather than people, it has called attention to the potential use of training, discipline, and rewards to improve safety records. Another control approach is to take safety into account in evaluations of both supervisory and non-supervisory personnel. The most controversial control method is discipline. Management has the right to discipline employees for safety

violations, but, as Chapter 8 indicated, management may not be able to exercise that right without risking worker dissatisfaction or outright retaliation.

4. *Contracting with third parties and suppliers:* One problem that employers face is hazards created by equipment, material, and services provided by outside suppliers or subcontractors. Mason suggests controlling for that problem by writing the contracts for the goods or services in such a way that the suppliers and subcontractors assume the risk for work stoppages and delays that result from OSHA violations attributable to whatever good or service they provide. Another approach is to write OSHA requirements into specifications and to deal only with providers who agree to warrant compliance with OSHA standards.[65]

5. *More active approaches:* One more active approach is to request variances from OSHA, as discussed in Chapter 8. Variances represent one way to replace specification standards with performance standards on an ad hoc basis. If a company can demonstrate that its own situation is as safe as the one envisioned in the regulation, OSHA ordinarily grants the variance.

Another approach is somewhat more aggressive: going to court. OSHA is regarded as such a threat to the business community and such a symbol of regulatory excess to conservatives that it has become a major target of business-oriented law firms such as the National Chamber Litigation Center. Lobbying for a loosening of OSHA restrictions is another element in the strategies of businesses and trade associations. It seems likely that such efforts would increase if the business community becomes more aware of OSHA's vulnerable points, but it also seems likely that they would decrease if OSHA were to become as effective in solving its current problems as it was in solving its start-up problems.

# Notes

1. For example, see Herbert R. Northrup et al., *The Impact of OSHA* (Philadelphia: University of Pennsylvania Press, 1978); John Mendeloff, *Regulating Safety: An Economic and Political Analysis of Occupational Safety and Health Policy* (Cambridge, Mass.: MIT Press, 1979); Nicholas A. Ashford, *Crisis in the Workplace: Occupational Disease and Injury* (Cambridge, Mass.: MIT Press, 1976); Murray L. Weidenbaum, "Four Questions for OSHA," *Labor Law Journal* 30 (1979):528–31; and J. Paul Leigh, "Wages, Regulation, and the Economics of Risk," *Los Angeles Business & Economics* 5, no. 3 (Summer 1980):24–28.

2. Eula Bingham, "OSHA: Only Beginning," *Labor Law Journal* 29 (1978):131–36.

3. Ashford, *Crisis*, pp. 145–46.

4. 29 Code of Federal Regulations, Part 1910, at Sec. 141(2); Northrup, *Impact of OSHA*, p. 50.

5. Murray L. Weidenbaum, *Business, Government, and the Public* (Englewood Cliffs, N.J.: Prentice-Hall, 1977), pp. 64–65.

6. *Wall Street Journal*, May 19, 1977, p. 48.

7. Fred K. Foulkes, "Learning to Live with OSHA," *Harvard Business Review* 51, No. 6 (November–December 1973):57–67.

8. Ibid.; also see Bingham, "Only Beginning."

9. "Why Nobody Wants to Listen to OSHA," *Business Week*, June 14, 1976, p. 64.

10. Foulkes, "Learning to Live with OSHA."

11. Northrup, *Impact of OSHA*, p. 51.

12. Ibid., p. 50.

13. *Wall Street Journal*, May 19, 1977.

14. "Foundations for a National Policy to Preserve Private Enterprise in the 1980s," a study prepared for the Subcommittee on Economic Growth and Stabilization of the Joint Economic Committee, U.S. Congress (Washington, D.C.: Government Printing Office, 1977), p. 19.

15. Frank J. Thompson, *Health Policy and the Bureaucracy* (Cambridge, Mass.: MIT Press, 1981).

16. Ibid.

17. "Why Nobody Wants to Listen to OSHA."

18. Weidenbaum, *Business, Government, and the Public*, p. 67.

19. Ibid., p. 68.

20. Leigh, "Wages," p. 24.

21. Northrup, *Impact of OSHA*, p. 284.

22. Ibid., p. 515.

23. Ibid., pp. 1, 513.

24. Ibid., pp. 284–85.

25. "Foundations for a National Policy to Preserve Private Enterprise in the 1980s," p. 22.

26. *Wall Street Journal*, September 15, 1980.

27. Ashford, *Crisis*, p. 518; Bingham, "Only Beginning."

28. Mendeloff, *Regulating Safety*, p. 41.

29. Northrup, *Impact of OSHA*, p. 539; "Foundations for a National Policy to Preserve Private Enterprise in the 1980s," p. 19.

30. See Albert L. Nichols and Richard Zeckhauser, "Government Comes to the Workplace: An Assessment of OSHA," *The Public Interest* 49 (Fall 1977):39–69.

31. Walter Jensen, Jr., Coenraad L. Mohr, and Duke Nordlinger Stern, "Administration of the OSH Act in the Face of Criticism from Industry and Labor," *American Business Law Journal* 11 (1973–74):37–54.

32. Northrup, *Impact of OSHA*, p. 412.

33. 442 F. Supp. 821 (S.D.W.Va., 1977).

34. See Susan Pettee Maguire, "OSHA Records and Privacy: Competing Interests in the Workplace," *American University Law Review* 27 (1978):953–80.

35. Ibid.

36. Ibid.

37. Northrup, *Impact of OSHA*, p. 416.

38. Basil J. Whiting, Jr., "Regulatory Reform and OSHA: Fads and Realities" *Labor Law Journal* (August 1979):514–27.

39. Ibid.

40. Cited in Weidenbaum, *Business, Government, and the Public*, p. 68.

41. Weidenbaum, *Business, Government, and the Public*, p. 66.

42. Whiting, "Regulatory Reform," p. 526.

43. Northrup, *Impact of OSHA*.

44. See Murray L. Weidenbaum, "The Costs of Government Regulation of Business," in Hearings on the Cost of Government Regulation Before the Subcommittee on Economic Growth and Stabilization of the Joint Economic Committee, 95th Congress, 2d Session (1978); also see Mendeloff, *Regulating Safety*.

45. Mendeloff, *Regulating Safety*, pp. 164–67.

46. Ashford, *Crisis*.

47. Cited in Weidenbaum, "Costs of Government Regulation," p. 51.

48. See Northrup, *Impact of OSHA*, pp. 51, 82; Mendeloff, *Regulating Safety*, p. 164.

49. Mendeloff, *Regulating Safety*, p. 165.

50. See Northrup, *Impact of OSHA*, p. 4.

51. Ibid., pp. 79, 537.

52. Jensen et al., "Administration of the OSH Act."

53. See Dale S. Beach, *Personnel: The Management of People at Work* (New York: Macmillan, 1980), pp. 636ff.

54. Northrup, *Impact of OSHA*, p. 82.

55. *Wall Street Journal*, November 18, 1977.

56. Weidenbaum, *Business, Government, and the Public*, p. 70.

57. Ashford, *Crisis*, p. 179; Ronald H. Davis, "Safety and OSHA," *The Personnel Administrator* 25, No. 11 (1980):53–54.

58. *Wall Street Journal*, May 19, 1977.

59. Mendeloff, *Regulating Safety*; Northrup, *Impact of OSHA*, p. 412.

60. Davis, "Safety and OSHA."

61. Weidenbaum, *Business, Government, and the Public*, p. 68.

62. Northrup, *Impact of OSHA*, p. 51.

63. Foulkes, "Learning to Live with OSHA."

64. Robert E. McClay, "Professionalization of the Safety Function," *Personnel Journal* 56 (1977):72–77.

65. Joseph Barry Mason, "OSHA: Problems and Prospects," *California Management Review* 19, No. 1 (1976):21–27.

# III

# Employee Pension
# And Benefit Plans

# 10

# Regulation of Employee Pension and Benefit Plans: Origins

## Case 10.1

Dear Senator Javits:

I don't know if you can do anything for me or not but this is my problem.

I joined the _____Union on October 25, 1952. At that time we were told at the age of 65 and with 15 years of service in the union shop we could get a pension. A short time later the union officials changed the time from 15 to 20 years.

I was a steady member until November 1968 when I was taken sick. I paid my dues for 26 weeks hoping my health would improve so I could go back to work but it did not. I applied for a pension but was turned down because I did not have 20 years in. I think I am entitled to at least partial pension by our first agreement. If I could only get something I would not have to have Medicaid as I do now for the doctor and medicine. My social security is not enough to pay all I have to pay by the time I pay my mortgage payment, lights, heat, and telephone. I do not have anything left. If it were not for the Food Stamps I would not be able to have enough food.

I hope you can look into this for me.

## Case 10.2

Dear Senator Javits:

I read with interest your recent press release concerning pension plans in industry.

I am a recent victim of one of these cancellations of right to participation in one of these plans. I worked for 40 years in the _____Plant at Elizabethton, Tennessee. _____was owned by _____which in turn is owned by _____, a Texas corporation. Then in December 1970 they closed down the _____Plant and it has now reopened under new ownership. My rights to the retirement plan were terminated. It is now too late to build anywhere else. I have been hurt and other longtime employees of this plant have also been hurt.

I checked with the Social Security Administration and found that my benefits at the age of 62 after 40 years of work would be $134.80. Now a bill is being readied to give a minimum of $200 monthly on welfare. This is disgusting. It puts a premium on laziness and irresponsibility and penalizes the man who works. I realize that answers are difficult and hard to find but unless found, I fear for the existence of our nation.

### Case 10.3
Hon. Jacob K. Javits

Dear Sir:

After having been employed by the _____Company for more than twenty-nine (29) years, I have been notified that my employment is being terminated. At the time this notification was given to me, my superiors stressed that my work was entirely satisfactory and that I should not feel that the action was a reflection on my performance. In fact, throughout the entire period of my _____employment, which began March 23, 1942, all of my superiors have, without exception, rated my work performance entirely satisfactory, and, in most cases, as outstanding.

Needless to say, the termination notice comes as a jolt! My employment with _____covers "years of plenty" when other employment opportunities as well as education opportunities were readily available, and when job offers were declined in favor of continued employment with _____. One of the major influencing factors in reaching the decision to remain with _____in each instance was the pension which eventually would be available to me under the _____Plan for Employees' Pensions, Disability Benefits, and Death Benefits. The anticipated pension naturally has always been considered by me to be a part of my compensation, especially during periods when comparatively low salaries were being received by _____employees. The pension was always stressed by _____to both existing and new employees as a major employment benefit. It seems significant that my employer has elected to terminate my employment after these many years of service and only two years before I become eligible to receive the pension.

It is a frightening thing, after having devoted a lifetime to _____, to find myself in the ranks of the unemployed and to be thrust suddenly into the position of job seeking at a time when the economic situation is very unfavorable; when my age (47) is not considered the most desirable by most prospective employers; and when my years of experience with _____are not readily adaptable to another field.

In view of your involvement with the Senate Labor and Public Welfare Committee and its recent investigation of private pension plans, I urgently appeal to you, as my representative in the U.S. Senate, for any assistance and/or advice you can provide me with in regard to recourse available to me.

### Case 10.4

Dear Senator Javits:

I am a former New York City resident who has read with deep interest your recent comments concerning workers' pension abuses.

I should like to call your attention to an abuse that makes those mentioned pale in comparison.

My father was a dues-paying member in good standing of the _____Union, Local _____, virtually from its very inception. For eighteen solid years he faithfully paid into the pension fund. He then dropped out of the union for two years to open a small shop of his own. It failed and he returned to the union and paid dues for an additional ten years before being told by his doctor that he must move to a warmer climate. Upon applying for his pension he was told by the union that he was entitled to no pension whatsoever because he had not contributed to the fund for 20 consecutive years. He therefore lost everything he had contributed for 28 years and now subsists on what amounts to near poverty.

Under the rules of this union (ostensibly formed to protect the members) it is theoretically possible for a member to contribute to the pension fund for more than 39 years and receive nothing.

On behalf of my father, and other members of that union, I am asking you to include in your investigation these unions and their pension practices. In fact, I am making a personal plea to you to make a special investigation of the _____ Union, Local _____. Perhaps through your interest the lives of some old and poor workers can be made a bit brighter in their last few years.

### Case 10.5

The president of a company was a member of the committee that administered the company pension plan and a director of the bank that invested the plan's funds. Of the plan's $622 million assets, 53 percent was invested in securities of the company. As the company encountered financial problems, it began turning to the pension fund for financing. Eventually, the company went bankrupt.

### Case 10.6

A large city hired a securities analyst, without checking his résumé, to manage $39 million in annual stock market investments made by the city employees' pension fund. The analyst succeeded in taking responsibility for the stock investments away from a large bank and placing it in his own hands. Some brokers reported that the analyst knew little about the stock market; others claimed he was a genius. The latter group must have been correct, for he succeeded in making more money in broker's commissions than the bank had made. Subsequently, the analyst was indicted for taking bribes from stock brokers.

**Case 10.7**     Corporate officers of a retailing company were also trustees of the company pension fund. They purchased company stock for the fund while selling their own shares in the company. When the fund stopped buying, the value of the stock dropped to a third of its previous price, reducing the penion fund's assets by more than $4.5 million.

**Case 10.8**     The largest plant of the main division of an automotive manufacturer closed down permanently. The pension plan covered 10,437 employees. Its assets at closing were $24 million; its liabilities to current retirees were $21.7 million. That left about $3.3 million for those not yet retired. The final settlement paid full benefits to 3,457 employees age 60 and over. But only 15 percent of benefits was given 4,080 workers age 40 to 60, a group whose average company service was around 23 years. For example, the typical worker of age 40 with 20 years' service received a lump sum payment of $350 in lieu of a pension. No benefits at all were given to the 2,090 workers under 40.

The cases at the beginning of this chapter are a sample of pension problems that happened before the passage of the Employee Retirement Income Security Act (ERISA). ERISA is a federal law governing the operation of private retirement income plans. It is a more complex law than any of the others discussed thus far in the book, and it probably has a greater overall impact on business as well. EEO may have a greater impact on personnel management, and OSHA may be the subject of more spirited ideological debate, but ERISA has more significance for the financial management of an organization. The reason for ERISA's impact on finance is that large sums of money are invested in pension funds. The regulation of those sums, particularly the favorable tax status that can be granted to them, is of obvious importance to the organization. Indeed, ERISA is as much a tax law as it is anything else.

The fact that the law governing pensions is also a tax law explains why it is so bafflingly complex. A career could easily be devoted to understanding ERISA tax law alone, and organizations rarely attempt to comply with ERISA without professional assistance. The generalist manager can hope to understand enough about EEO and OSHA to avoid obvious illegalities, but that hope is in vain when it comes to ERISA. Even compensation specialists usually must call on pension experts when they undertake benefit planning.

Accordingly, this book's treatment of ERISA is a limited one. It assumes that the reader's interest in ERISA is that of the general manager or the personnel manager, not the financial manager, the tax expert, or the risk analyst. Therefore, it focuses on the implications of ERISA for people management, particularly for compensation and communication.

## Chapter Objectives

This chapter covers the problems leading to the passage of ERISA. It examines the failure of many retirement plans to provide adequate compensation before ERISA and the failure of many employers to inform employees adequately about retirement plan provisions. The cases at the beginning of this chapter are examples of such failures, which Congress attempted to solve by passing ERISA.

Do the cases present a fair picture of retirement plans before ERISA? Out of necessity, they are a biased sample. Most plans quietly went about their business of providing retirement income without generating inequities and improprieties such as depicted in the cases. But constituents do not write angry letters to legislators when they are pleased with their pensions. Consequently, congressional deliberation dwelled on the worst side of retirement plans, and this chapter dwells on that too.

The chapter also discusses how politics and the complexities of retirement plan problems combined to delay the passage of ERISA. As with other areas of federal regulation discussed in this book, the regulatory model is used to organize the material. This chapter concerns the problems column of the regulatory model; other parts of the model are discussed in Chapter 11.

Before that, however, it is important to understand how retirement plans operate. The first part of this chapter discusses some elementary principles of retirement plans. These principles help clarify why pensions are susceptible to the types of problems that led Congress to pass ERISA.

## How Retirement Plans Operate

Entire books and college courses are devoted to retirement plan operations;[1] only a minimal introduction is given here. To understand the significance of federal regulation of retirement plans, it is necessary to understand (1) what a retirement plan is, (2) who pays for a retirement plan, (3) how employees become eligible for retirement income, (4) how the money is provided to pay those employees, and (5) how that money is taxed by the federal government.

## What Is a Retirement Plan?

According to ERISA,[2] a pension or retirement plan is a program, established or maintained by an employer or an employee organization, that either provides retirement income to employees or results in a deferral of income by employees. But here, for purposes of clarity, it is probably better to define it as a payment of income for life beginning at retirement.

There are many ways in which retirement income can be paid to an employee upon retirement. Perhaps the most familiar is by means of an *annuity*. Generally, an annuity is a periodic payment of an allowance, beginning and ending at specified times. Retirement annuities ordinarily begin upon retirement and end at either the employee's death or the employee's spouse's death. If the annuity pays until the employee's spouse dies, it is called a *joint and survivor's annuity*.

Annuities are insurance policies of sorts. In fact, many life insurance policies are structured so that benefits can be paid as an annuity. An individual can purchase an annuity either by a lump sum payment or, more commonly, by a periodic premium payment (such as the familiar monthly contribution to a pension fund). As with any form of life insurance, the cost of the annuity depends upon the life expectancy of the insured party. Also, the cost depends upon the *discount rate*, or the rate of interest deducted from a future payment, which reflects the amount that the insurer expects to make by investing the individual's premium payments.

In the typical retirement plan, however, individual payments are not made in an employee's name. Instead, the employer makes a periodic contribution reflecting the anticipated retirement income obligations to its employees as a group. Forecasts are made regarding the expected retirement dates of current and future employees, along with the life expectancies of employees and retirees, taking due account of several other factors, such as the possibility of an employee terminating before becoming eligible for a pension. All those forecasts are translated into a lump sum contribution for all employees, not separate contributions for individual employees.

Often overlooked in discussions of retirement plans is the fact that any retirement plan must embody implicit value judgments about who is to be rewarded, and those value judgments may make it more difficult for some people than others to reap benefits. For instance, plans vary in the value they place on seniority: some plans favor long-term employees, while others make no preferences. Such value judgments have been a source of controversy over retirement plans.

### Defined Benefit Versus Defined Contribution Plans

One important distinction among retirement plans is that some plans guarantee the amount of the benefit paid to the employee while others guarantee the amount of the contribution made by the employer toward the employee's pension. The former kind of plan is called a *defined benefit plan,* the latter a *defined contribution plan.*

This distinction is important. With a defined benefit plan, the objective is to provide a certain fixed income after retirement. The income is based on a formula, and there is a wide variety of formulas in use. The employer agrees to pay whatever it will cost to guarantee that amount of income. With a defined contribution plan, on the other hand, the employer agrees to make a defined periodic contribution to the pension fund. Upon retirement, the employee receives a pension income that is dependent upon the retiree's life expectancy at the time of retirement and upon the earnings of the employer's contributions to the fund over the years.

The defined benefit plan is usually referred to as a pension plan. The amount of the employee's retirement income is predictable, generally being fixed by formula. The most common formula makes the pension a function of the employee's salary at or near retirement and the number of years that the employee has worked for the organization. For example:

$$\text{Salary} \times \text{Years of service} \times 0.02 = \text{Retirement income}$$

An employee with 30 years of service making $20,000 upon retirement would have a retirement income of:

$$\$20,000 \times 30 \text{ years} \times 0.02 = \$12,000/\text{year}$$

The important feature is that the benefit is guaranteed, and the employer is obligated to put in as much money—and only as much money—as is required to provide that guaranteed benefit.

A defined contribution plan basically operates as though the employer were depositing a certain defined sum of money periodically into a retirement account established in the employee's name. The amount of money deposited periodically may be fixed (for example, $10 for each week worked during the year); such an arrangement is called a *money purchase plan*. Or the contribution may depend on the organization's profits—a *profit-sharing plan*. Another arrangement is the *savings plan*, in which the organization typically agrees to contribute a fixed proportion of whatever savings an employee contributes. There are other types of defined contribution plans, but they are of less importance to this discussion. The significant point about defined contribution plans is that the employer's contribution is allowed to accumulate in the employee's account, and the employee's retirement benefit depends on the balance that happens to be in that account at the time of retirement.[3]

The crucial distinction between defined benefit and defined contribution plans lies in who bears the greater risk. In a defined benefit plan, the employer bears more risk, while in a defined contribution plan, the employee bears more risk. Put another way, things are more predictable for the employee in a defined benefit plan, while things are more predictable for the employer in a defined contribution plan.

Predictability, then, is the chief advantage of the defined benefit plan for the employee. Of course, the employee in a defined contribution plan can capitalize on any unexpected appreciation in the value of the pension account. But the employee must also bear the burden of any disappointing earnings in that account, and employees are usually less able to absorb such disappointments than employers. On the other hand, a defined contribution plan may be more advantageous to younger employees.

### Who Pays?

The employer almost always pays into the retirement fund, but the employee does not always do so. Retirement plans that provide for employee contributions are called *contributory* plans, while those for which all funds are provided by the employer are called *noncontributory* plans. In contributory plans, the amount to be contributed by the employee is generally expressed as a percentage of the employee's compensation, usually no more than 6 percent of the employee's salary or wages. Most employee contributions are made automatically through payroll deductions; some plans provide for lump-sum contributions by employees as well.[4]

## When Are Employees Eligible?

The term *eligible* is vague; it could refer to any of three significant milestones that can be reached during the course of an employee's association with a retirement plan: participation, vesting, and retirement.

*Participation* takes place when the employer begins contributing to the retirement plan in the employee's name. New employees usually do not participate in retirement plans immediately. Most plans have a waiting period of one year or so before the employer establishes an account in the employee's name and contributes money to the account.

*Vesting* occurs when the employee acquires a *nonforfeitable* right to a retirement benefit. Nonforfeitability means the employer is obligated to pay that employee the benefit. Even if the employee quits before the minimum retirement age, the employer must start paying retirement income whenever the employee does reach retirement age. Of course, when the employee eventually reaches that age, the benefit is almost always less than it would be if the employee had worked to the minimum retirement age, but it is still worth something. Prior to vesting, if the employee terminates, the employer is obligated to pay nothing. After vesting, the employer is obligated to provide whatever retirement income the organization's benefit formula would dictate. In the simplified example above, if a plan provides for vesting after 10 years of service, and if an employee making $20,000 a year terminates immediately after having been vested, that employee would ultimately be entitled to a retirement income of $20,000 \times 10$ years $\times 0.02 = \$4,000$ per year upon reaching retirement age. A vested employee can change employers, acquire vested rights in a similar pension plan with the new employer, and retire with a pension from both employers.

*Retirement* is the date at which the employee can terminate employment and start collecting retirement income. Often the plan will allow a range of permissible retirement dates, with lower benefits for employees electing to retire at earlier dates.

## How Are Retirement Plans Funded?

If the plan is a defined benefit plan, the employer contributes enough to the retirement fund to finance the anticipated payments that would be made to beneficiaries, in accordance with whatever pension benefit formula is in use. If the plan is a defined contribution plan, the employer contributes a specified amount, and the payment made to beneficiaries fluctuates with the earnings of the fund.

The main funding problems occur with defined benefit plans. Besides making constant payments to existing retirees, a defined benefit plan also sets aside funds for future benefit payments, both to existing retirees and those employees who have not yet retired. A pension program can avoid setting money aside for those future benefit payments and still live up to its obligations by paying pensions on a cash basis—if the pension program survives. If it goes out of existence, however, it can cover those future payments only to the extent that it has built up sufficient assets; beyond that, some future benefit payments that were promised will not be made.

### Tax Treatment of Retirement Fund Contributions

One important factor in the funding of retirement plans is the tax status of contributions made to those plans. If the Internal Revenue Service determines that a retirement plan is "qualified," then the employees are not taxed on the contributions that the employer makes to the plan, even if they are vested, and the employer may deduct those contributions. Also, the earnings on the retirement fund are tax exempt during the period they are held in the fund. Later, retirement benefits are taxed as personal income when they are distributed to employees.

This opportunity for employers to deduct contributions many years before they show up as income is a significant financial advantage. If the money that the employer contributes to the retirement plan were instead given to the employee directly, the employee would have to pay taxes on that money, as well as on anything earned from investing that money, and earnings would build up much more slowly. Tax qualification, then, allows the employer to offer a more valuable compensation package than would be possible otherwise.

The Internal Revenue Service's rules for tax qualification are part of the regulatory apparatus governing retirement plans. Also, while ERISA covers both qualified and nonqualified retirement plans, it establishes additional conditions for qualification as well, conditions that are enforced by the Internal Revenue Service. All this contributes to the complexity of ERISA enforcement.

# Problems with Retirement Plans

From this discussion one might sense some problems inherent in retirement plans, problems that might move Congress to pass corrective legislation.

Throughout the 1960s, Congress witnessed growing criticism of private pension plans. Most of the criticism was based on personal experiences of participants who had problems with their funds. Gradually Congress held hearings, commissioned studies of the problem, and introduced legislation to deal with it. In the opinion of Senator Jacob Javits of New York, a prominent supporter of pension reform legislation, pension plans operated on the basis of three dangerously obsolete assumptions:

> The first of these assumptions is that an employee is going to work for one company all or most of his working career. The second assumption is that the company can and should use the pension plan as a club to prevent the employee from seeking job opportunities elsewhere. The third assumption is that the company will stay in business forever in substantially the same or expanded form as when it installed the pension plan.[5]

These three assumptions relate to two general problems that concerned Congress during the years before ERISA. The first two assumptions concern involuntary *forfeiture* of retirement benefits. Vesting rules were sometimes so strict and complicated that employees found themselves involuntarily giving up pension rights as they changed jobs, took leaves of absence, and the like. At the time ERISA was being debated, the rate of pension forfeitures was over 50 percent.[6] The third assumption concerns the problem of *termination*—retirement plans going out of existence. Sometimes a company went out of business or shut down operations at a facility; other times a conglomerate acquired a facility and closed down the pension plan for financial reasons.

## Forfeiture

The fact that employees do not work for one company all or most of their working careers means that employees may leave an employer before they become vested in that employer's benefit plan, thus forfeiting their right to retirement benefits. This in turn makes it possible for employers to use the retirement plan as a club, to keep employees from leaving, for the employee who leaves before becoming vested leaves with nothing.

Forfeiture can be a tragedy; it means no retirement income. Often retirees have no other source of income, for people at retirement age can rarely find employment. The result is often personal financial devastation.

Clearly, the problem Congress faced was serious, and the letters to Congress from those affected were often moving. It is hard to imagine a legislator sending a form letter in response to the kind of correspondence shown in the cases at the beginning of this chapter. And there was much correspondence. Senator Javits received five hundred letters a year for the four or five years before ERISA hearings were held in 1971 and over five hundred during the three weeks immediately following the release of a Senate Labor Subcommittee report on pension problems.[7] These cases suggest that involuntary forfeiture is caused by stringent, complex standards for employee vesting.

One forfeiture problem is *forfeiture due to illness.* Case 10.1 is an example.[8] The writer of that letter could have done nothing to avoid ineligibility. Note that the longer an employee must work before being vested, the more likely that advancing age will bring the sort of medical problems that force the employee to quit before becoming vested. If the union in Case 10.1 had not raised its vesting period from fifteen years to twenty years, the writer of the letter would have received a pension.

Another type of vesting problem outside of the control of the employee is *forfeiture due to changes in management.* The writer of the letter in Case 10.2 was the unfortunate victim of an acquisition of one company by another.[9] In such situations, the employee loses not only the job but also the service credit toward a pension.

A more abusive forfeiture problem is *discharging employees shortly before they vest.* In Case 10.3,[10] we are entitled to suspect that the company terminated the employee in order to avoid paying him a retirement income. As Chapter 4 points out, the Age Discrimination in Employment Act now makes that illegal. Nevertheless, it was a common occurrence in the 1960s, and it drew attention to the fact that stringent vesting requirements of those programs could give employers a motive to discriminate.

Another vesting problem was *forfeiture due to lack of portability.* Portability means that the employee is entitled to carry service credits from the old employer's retirement plan to the new employer's plan without first having been vested in the old employer's plan. Portability is important in very mobile occupations, occupations that usually take a person from employer to employer. Without portability, the repeated job changing can keep a person from accumulating enough service time with one employer to acquire vested rights to a retirement income. Even if a highly mobile individual does manage to vest in one employer's plan, that individual still may end up with substantial nonvested time with other employers. The result is a total retirement benefit that is smaller than what individuals in less mobile occupations would receive. This situation constitutes a disincentive for people to enter highly mobile occupations.

Another forfeiture problem comes from *complicated vesting rules.* Oftentimes there is fine print in a retirement plan, so that individuals inadvertently make job choices that deprive them of opportunities for vesting. For example, it seems likely that the person in Case 10.4 would not have made the career change he did if he had realized that he would be depriving himself of a pension.[11] Aside from the question of whether the rule in Case 10.4 was a reasonable one, there is the question of why the rule was not communicated to participants clearly enough for them to understand the implications of their job changes.

Underlying most forfeiture problems is the fact that many employers made a value judgment that retirement benefits should favor more senior employees. Thus, they set vesting limits high enough to keep short-term employees from collecting retirement income. Also important is the simple fact that it saves money for employers to make vesting as hard to get as possible. That is not to say that before ERISA all, or even most, employers were motivated by the prospect of pension-savings when they made employment decisions about older employees. But some were, and that provided a strong justification for Congress to seek an end to pension abuses.

## Retirement Plan Termination

Other employees lost retirement benefits because their plans went out of existence. If the funding of a retirement plan is adequate to cover the plan's liabilities, then commitments can be honored even when the plan ends. Unfortunately, adequate funding was the exception. Most plans were able to cover current costs of retirement income to the existing retirees out of their current revenues, but usually they could not afford to pay full benefits to the nonretired vested employee if the fund went out of existence.

Moreover, some plans were subject to outright funding abuses. Sometimes retirement plan assets were invested in questionable ways. Occasionally, individuals having control over assets misappropriated them for their own personal gain.

One misuse of retirement plan funds was to regard them as a source of capital during times of economic hardship for the company. Sometimes this kind of investment strategy works well, as with the Sears retirement plan. But Case 10.5, a composite of several actual cases, presents a classic example of why it often does not succeed. The problem is obvious: as the company's financial picture becomes more and more precarious, it turns more and more to the retirement plan fund as a source of investment capital. Consequently, the fund's assets come to have less and less value. If the company goes out of business, the ultimate result is that the fund is worth far less than it would have been had the fund been invested prudently.

Other retirement fund investments were even more obviously inappropriate. Some involved conflict of interest between the fund and the individuals who made decisions regarding the fund's assets. Case 10.6 was a particularly famous example that also illustrates another pension abuse known as *churning,* excessive buying and selling of retirement fund assets to generate commissions for securities brokers.[12] And situations such as Case 10.7 resulted in calls upon Congress to pass legislation outlawing such blatant conflicts of interest.[13]

Terminations are also brought about by business reorganization. Sometimes one company would acquire another company because of surpluses in the second company's pension funds and then close the pension plan, use the plan's assets to buy annuities for the employees who were vested, and pocket what was left over. Often it was stringent vesting rules that made such moves profitable,[14] and sometimes the stringent vesting rules made it even more profitable for the conglomerate to close down the acquired concern entirely.[15]

Many plan terminations raised no questions of abuse, but their inadequate funding still hurt beneficiaries. In congressional hearings prior to passage of ERISA, the United Automotive Workers union presented a study on the termination of retirement plans, the conclusion of which was, "No matter how carefully plans may be negotiated and developed, no matter how soundly conceived and financed, large numbers of persons covered will not receive all—in some instances, any—of their expected benefits."[16] The implication was that more was needed than a law that would prevent abuses. Some means of guaranteeing benefits was necessary.

## Retirement Income: Right or Privilege?

A central issue underlying any consideration of proposals to deal with the retirement income problems discussed above is the question of whether employees have a right to the benefits that are provided for in their plans, or whether an employer can legitimately withhold those pensions. Case 10.3 raises this question most clearly. The employer clearly led the employee to believe that a pension was forthcoming; indeed, the employer used the pension program as an inducement to work. In Congress the sentiment was strong for regarding the payment of whatever pension was promised as an obligation. Some legislators referred to pensions as *deferred wages*. For example, Congressman John H. Dent of Pennsylvania said during the 1971 hearings on pension reform legislation:

> I read in the papers that one union negotiated a $1.25 increase for a 3-year period. When I looked at it closely, I found that the major part of that negotiated contract was for welfare, pension benefits and not actually money in the pocket of the workers. I am led to make the determination that this is, indeed, part of the wages of the worker, and as such, they must be insured or they will not be paid. [17]

In the same hearings, Republican Representative Jack C. Kemp of New York, then a freshman legislator, observed:

> Every fringe benefit is, in fact, a part of the wage structure, and the right of the employee to be able to insure and guarantee that right is the purpose of this legislation. I think it is of great interest and concern to Congress, and I will be watching this legislation and following it with great interest, and plan to be actively involved in furthering the goals. I don't think there is any greater need today than to protect the rights of the employees in this regard. [18]

Clearly, if retirement income is to be regarded as deferred compensation, then the abuses reported in the cases above are intolerable.

## The Politics of Pension Reform

The complaints about retirement plans discussed above had been well known for many years before the passage of ERISA in 1974. In 1962, President John F. Kennedy appointed the President's Committee on Corporate Pension Funds. That committee recommended legislation to require universal vesting. Even earlier there was concern over the lack of legislative standards. During the 1950s, a series of flagrant financial abuses were highlighted by extensive congressional hearings. Then, in 1958, Congress passed the Welfare and Pension Plans Disclosure Act, based on the premise that adequate disclosure of pension plan finances would be sufficient to prevent such financial abuses. [19]

The report of President Kennedy's committee focused attention on the fact that the 1958 law had not solved retirement plan problems. Yet ERISA was not passed until 1974. What was responsible for the delay in passing comprehensive pension reform legislation? The answer lies partly in politics, partly in the fact that pension reform is an inherently difficult matter to legislate.

One factor that impeded legislative pension reform was a change in administrations. When Kennedy's committee reported its results in 1965, Lyndon B. Johnson was president, and Johnson was persuaded by Henry Ford II not to endorse legislation to implement the Kennedy committee proposals. Ford personally argued that further government regulation would inhibit the growth of pension funds and alienate the business community. As a result, while a pension reform bill eventually emerged with the backing of the labor department, it did not have the support of the president.[20]

### The Studebaker Plant Closing

One event which may have done more than any other to influence the course of federal regulation of personnel and human resources management was the closing of the Studebaker Division of the Studebaker-Packard Corporation in 1964. Case 10.8 presents some details of that closing.[21] The division's facility was located in South Bend, Indiana, a city of about 130,000 people. The Studebaker plant was the economic mainstay of the community, and the impact of its closing on the local economy was enormous; large numbers of people were thrown into the labor market. Many Studebaker workers were too old to compete for the few jobs that were available. The closing came to be regarded as a case study of the economic problems of older workers, and the plight of the Studebaker employees was well publicized.

The Studebaker closing had a marked impact on congressional deliberation. Coming as it did on the heels of other, smaller pension fund terminations, it provided an important stimulus to the ultimate passage of ERISA.

### Reasons for Delay

Nevertheless, pension reform legislation did not come quickly. Despite dramatic situations such as the Studebaker closing, the issue had not drawn widespread popular support.[22] Most notably, organized labor did not support the idea wholeheartedly. Some unions supported it, and others supported various ideas for addressing one problem or another, but in general labor was not regarded as enthusiastic.[23] Evidently, the reason was that some plans managed by unions had been susceptible to problems: note, for example, Cases 10.1 and 10.4. That fact was not lost on legislators. During congressional testimony by I. W. Abel, president of the United Steelworkers union, Representative Dent pointedly noted the questionable funding arrangements in some union pension plans:

> Mr. Abel, I think we ought to discuss, if you don't mind, for the few minutes we have left, something that has been brought up, a loose end up in the air. The clothing workers were mentioned—[their union does] have an industry-wide plan, but because of the industry-wide aspects of it, they have felt very secure in having a partially funded plan. They go along on what they call sort of a pay-as-you-go or level of payments plus interest. That is the only funding they do. However, we have found upon investigation that that particular fund, the clothing workers, has $80 million worth of assets but $350 million of unfunded liabilities. Now, in days not too long ago, they could feel rather secure, in my opinion, in that kind of industry-wide operation because it was inconceivable in a nation of over 250 million people that all of a sudden there would be such a demand on the pension funds by retiring persons, and also a diminution of major industries. Today the clothing industry finds itself in the position where they can't be assured of having even 50 percent of the clothing industry intact in the next 2 years because they are impacted by cheap imports. In the last 5 years, for the first time, the clothing workers who have been in the forefront in the fight for free trade in this country, have almost completely turned around in their position and are now fighting not only for protectionism, but for the survival of the clothing industry. The steel industry finds itself in the same position. . . .
>
> [Mr. Abel:] . . . organized labor isn't pushing extra hard this year for pension reform. I want the record to show that insofar as the Steelworkers are concerned, and I am sure all industry workers, if we could secure the law next week, we would welcome it. Those that have joined me today are here to not only let the members of this committee know, but also to let their respective congressmen and senators know that they are quite interested in this problem.[24]

Another reason for the delay was caution on the part of the executive branch. As already noted, President Johnson withdrew his support of a pension reform bill. The next president, Richard Nixon, was also reluctant to support certain elements of the proposed legislation. Nixon particularly opposed the idea of insuring pension benefits against plan termination.

Also, up until late 1971, the Nixon administration did not endorse a federal standard for vesting and funding. However, the administration did take certain steps to facilitate the passage of pension reform legislation, particularly by adding some provisions to increase the attractiveness of pension reform to certain influential groups. As a result, in the early 1970s, support for the legislation gradually grew. More unions began to add their support for the legislation, and even some pension plan administrators decided that the industry could benefit from additional federal regulation.[25]

However, in 1972 a new problem arose. It became evident that pension reform legislation could not be passed without the involvement of two committees in each house of Congress instead of the usual one. Bills are ordinarily turned over to a single committee for deliberation and hearings. If the bill concerns personnel management, that committee is usually the one that deals specifically with labor legislation: the House Education and Labor Committee and the Senate Labor Committee. However, as already noted, the regulation of retirement plans inevitably involves taxation issues, since any such legislation inevitably affects the rules by which tax deferral of contributions is granted.

As a result, the tax-writing committees became involved: the House Ways and Means Committee and the Senate Finance Committee. This created further delays in moving the legislation through Congress. It is not difficult to imagine the delicate negotiations that were necessary to get four committees instead of the usual two to agree. Consequently, it was not until late 1973 that both Senate committees approved a bill for consideration by the full Senate, and not until February 1974 that both House committees had approved a measure for that body to consider. Finally, after extensive work resolving the differences, Congress passed ERISA in August of 1974.[26]

Thus ERISA seems to have been the product of compromise even more than most federal regulations. An important result of the compromise was that, while ERISA mandates that certain standards be observed by all retirement plans, it does not mandate that employers provide a retirement plan in the first place.[27] Besides the four legislative committees, a major factor accounting for the unusual amount of compromise in passing ERISA was the numerous interest groups involved in the operation of the private pension system. With the other areas of federal regulation discussed in this book, business and labor are the interest groups, along with civil rights and women's rights groups in the case of EEO. With ERISA, however, accountants, actuaries, bankers, and pension consultants also have a stake.[28] Besides those groups, a sizeable community of attorneys had become established around the pension system, and they had their own interests in ERISA.

It is abundantly clear, then, why the politics of pension reform were more elaborate and involved than the politics of equal employment or the politics of job safety and health. And, as Chapter 11 makes clear, the resulting law is fully as complicated as the political process that gave rise to it.

# Notes

1. See Jeffrey D. Mamorsky, *Pension and Profit-Sharing Plans: A Basic Guide* (New York: Executive Enterprises, 1977); and Barbara B. Creed, *ERISA Compliance Reporting and Disclosure* (New York: Practising Law Institute, 1981).

2. Sec. 3.2, Employee Retirement Income Security Act.

3. See Mamorsky, *Pension and Profit-Sharing Plans,* chap. 11.

4. Ibid., p. 44.

5. Statement of Senator Jacob K. Javits, Hearings on H.R. 1269 Before the General Subcommittee on Labor of the House Committee on Education and Labor, 92d Congress, 1st Session (1972), p. 85.

6. Ibid., pp. 56–57.

7. Ibid., p. 57.

8. Hearings on H.R. 1269, p. 138.

9. Ibid., p. 139.

10. Ibid., p. 144.

11. Ibid., p. 145.

12. Ibid., p. 97.

13. Ibid.

14. Statement of Rep. Robert H. Mollohan, Hearings on H.R. 1269, p. 150.

15. Rep. John H. Dent, Hearings on H.R. 1269, pp. 43–44.

16. Jacob C. Hurwitz and Willie L. Burris, "A Study of the Termination of UAW Pension Plans," in Hearings on H.R. 1269, p. 170.

17. Hearings on H.R. 1269, p. 44.

18. Ibid., pp. 50–51.

19. Peter Henle and Raymond Schmitt, "Pension Reform: The Long, Hard Road to Enactment," *Monthly Labor Review* 97 (1974):3–12.

20. Hearings on H.R. 1269, p. 95.

21. Hurwitz and Burris, "Termination of UAW Pension Plans," p. 167.

22. Statement of I. W. Abel, Hearings on H.R. 1269, p. 53.

23. See the statements of Leonard Woodcock, Rep. John N. Erlenborn, and I. W. Abel, Hearings on H.R. 1269, pp. 45–48.

24. Hearings on H.R. 1269, pp. 51–52.
25. Henle and Schmitt, "Pension Reform."
26. Ibid.
27. Ibid.
28. Ibid.

# 11

# The Employee Retirement Income Security Act: Provisions and Impact

Personnel directors who have spent their adult years trying to cope with the U.S. Labor Department Regulations say that they have never seen anything quite like ERISA. ERISA can be viewed as the regulator's masterpiece, a law of infinite reach and complexity that nobody fully understands and nobody can ignore.[1]

That statement from *Fortune* magazine suggests it is unrealistic to attempt to describe ERISA's provisions in a single chapter. However, ERISA is much less forbidding when viewed only in terms of its implications for personnel and human resource management. While ERISA's provisions relating to taxation and financial management are quite complex, its impact on people management can be readily conveyed in a chapter.

## Chapter Objectives

Accordingly, this chapter provides an overview of ERISA. Obviously, it cannot prepare the reader to undertake much management responsibility or to design a retirement plan. Rather, it is intended to provide enough information for the manager to do two things: (1) understand the likely impact of ERISA on the organization's choice of retirement plan, and (2) serve as the communication link between the pension plan and its participants. As this chapter points out, the responsibility for communication with employees has definite legal implications.

## How ERISA Responds to Retirement Plan Problems

Exhibit 11.1 shows the regulatory model applied to ERISA. The left-hand column reviews Chapter 10's discussion of the major retirement plan problems and political forces that came to bear upon Congress during the time that ERISA was being debated. Each problem was a call for action, and the action called for differed from problem to problem. ERISA can perhaps be best understood as a law written in response to those problems, with separate sections addressing each. The complexity of pension problems, then, accounts in part for the complexity of ERISA.

But there are other complicating factors as well. One is the inherent complexity of the federal tax system, particularly the system of tax qualification that determines whether a private retirement plan is eligible for tax deferral. Another is the immense diversity that characterizes the private retirement income system. Many different provisions had to be written into the law to accommodate the various forms that pension plans took.

Exhibit 11.2 outlines the main provisions of ERISA as responses to the retirement plan problems that concerned Congress. ERISA attacks some of those problems more vigorously than others and thus reflects the political realities that made compromise on some problems necessary and the realities of the plans that made it inherently hard to solve some problems through the regulatory process.

### Forfeiture

A common problem causing forfeiture was the kind of stringent eligibility requirements that arose in Cases 10.1 and 10.4. ERISA's solution is to mandate minimum eligibility standards that are more generous than the ones prevailing at the time ERISA was passed. ERISA requires that employees be eligible to participate after one year's service, or at age twenty-five, whichever comes earlier.[2] ERISA also mandates vesting

**Exhibit 11.1** The Regulatory Model Applied to ERISA

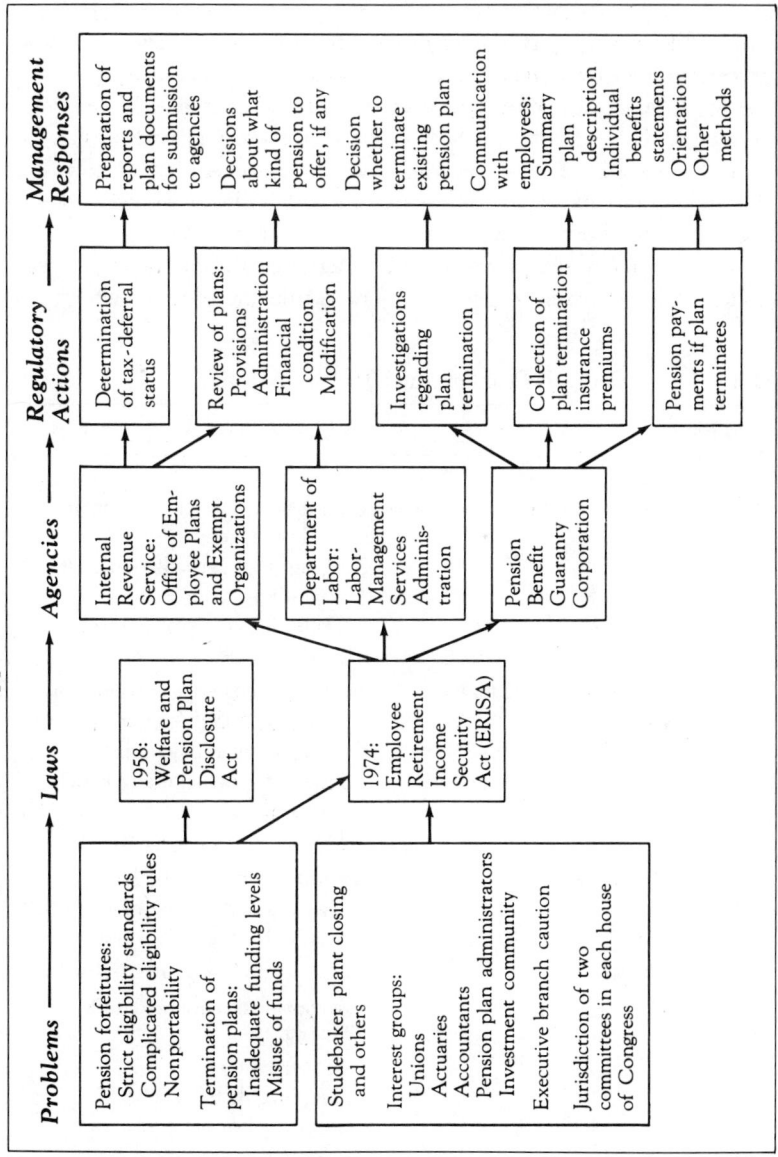

standards that are more generous than existed in many plans. Several vesting options are permissible, perhaps the most popular being one that confers full vesting upon the employee after ten years of service. Another option provides for graded increases in vesting: 25 percent after five years of service, 50 percent after ten years, and 100 percent after fifteen years of service. A third option, called the *rule of forty-five*, provides full vesting when the sum of the employee's age and years of service equals forty-five.[3] The multiplicity of vesting options is one of the ERISA complexities that accommodates the diversity in the private pension system.

A related ERISA provision is a liberalized definition of a "year of service" and a "break in service." The former determines whether the

**Exhibit 11.2** Pension Problems and ERISA Solutions

| *Problem* | *ERISA Provision* |
|---|---|
| *1. Forfeitures* | |
| Caused by strict eligibility standards | *Participation and vesting provisions* (Title I, section 2): |
| | Options for participation and vesting |
| | Definitions of "year of service" and "break in service" |
| Caused by complicated eligibility standards | *Information and employee communication* (Title I, section 1): |
| | Summary plan description |
| | Financial statement and benefits information |
| | Understandable language |
| Caused by nonportability | *Limited portability* (Title II): |
| | Tax-deferred contributions to IRA at old employer's option |
| *2. Terminations* | |
| In general | *Plan termination insurance* (Title IV): |
| | Coverage limits |
| | Employer liability up to 30 percent of net worth |
| | Vesting of all accrued benefits at termination |

**Exhibit 11.2**   Pension Problems and ERISA Solutions   *(Continued)*

| *Problem* | *ERISA Provision* |
|---|---|
| Caused by inadequate funding levels | *Minimum funding provisions* (Title I, section 3): |
| | Funding of current costs on current basis |
| | Amortization of past service liabilities |
| | Amortization of changes and experience |
| Caused by misuse of funds | *Fiduciary responsibilities* (Title I, section 4): |
| | Prudent man rule |
| | Diversification to minimize large losses |
| | Prohibited transactions with parties-in-interest |
| | 10 percent limit on investment in employer securities or real property |
| | Bonding |

participant is given credit for a year of employment; the latter determines when the employer can consider the employee's participation in the plan to be interrupted. Recall the problems of the employee in Case 10.4, who left the union for a few years to try business for himself. Under ERISA, the retirement plan rules that caused those problems would be illegal. ERISA mandates credit for a year of service whenever the employee works for one thousand hours during the year, and it prohibits a break in service unless the employee works for less than five hundred hours during the year. Even after a break in service, ERISA requires that the employee be allowed to resume participation after one year of reemployment, with full credit for all years of service prior to the break.[4]

How are hours counted? Different employers have different systems; some do not keep track of hours at all. Accordingly, ERISA provides several options for counting hours.[5] The variety of alternatives is baffling, and it takes some study for the manager to pick the one that is best suited to the enterprise and figure out how to comply with it.[6] This is another example of how diversity in management practices creates complexity in ERISA.

Another problem causing forfeitures was complicated pension rules, which made it easy for employees to forfeit benefits inadvertently, as in Case 10.4. This is a communication problem. ERISA requires that retirement plan provisions must be communicated clearly to participants. ERISA also includes an elaborate set of requirements for reporting and disclosing aspects of the plan to participants and to the government. These requirements were designed largely to bring questionable practices to light. Three reporting requirements are worth noting: (1) *the summary annual report,* a financial statement of the plan that must be prepared every year; (2) *the summary plan description,* a description of the provisions of the plan that must be provided to each participant; and (3) *an individual benefit statement,* a summary of the participant's own status regarding benefits that must be provided upon request to the participant as often as once a year. [7]

Not only does ERISA mandate that this information be provided, but it also mandates that it be provided in a way that does the participant some good. ERISA requires that the summary plan description be communicated both *thoroughly* and *clearly.* For anyone who is aware of the complexities of employee benefit plans, particularly retirement plans, the difficulty of being both thorough and clear should be apparent.

A final forfeiture problem, the lack of portability, is more difficult than the other problems. As noted in Chapter 10, employees without portable pensions who change employers are not entitled to service credits from the old employer's plan to the new employer's plan. An effective solution to the portability problem would seem to necessitate a government-administered retirement fund into which employers would deposit their contributions. Clearly, such a fund would have been hard to pass into law. Accordingly, ERISA provides only a limited solution to the portability problem. What ERISA offers is the opportunity for employers, if they choose, to deposit at an employee's request their contributions into an *individual retirement account* when a vested employee leaves. An individual retirement account (IRA) is a device created by ERISA to allow people who do not participate in a tax-qualified pension plan to enjoy the advantages of tax qualification. The IRA provision allows them to establish their own individual tax-deferred funds financed by their own tax-deferred contributions. While the main purpose of the IRA was to give individuals who do not participate in tax-qualified pension plans the same tax shelter as those who did, it also offers that opportunity to people who leave qualified retirement plans. [8]

While better than nothing, the IRA transfer hardly solves the problem of nonportability, as the following example makes clear. Consider an employee who works for ten years with company X, then leaves to work ten years for company Y, and then retires. Because most people's salaries increase over time, we might suppose that the employee's ending salary with company X was $10,000 a year, while the ending salary with company Y was $20,000 per year. Also, because most defined benefit retirement income plans base the payment on the employee's salary at or near the time of termination, we might realistically assume a benefit formula like the one given in Chapter 10: terminal salary × years of service × 0.02. With a truly portable retirement income, the employee's account would be transferred from company X to company Y and the income would be:

$$\$20{,}000 \times 20 \text{ years} \times 0.02 = \$8{,}000 \text{ per year}$$

However, with the IRA transfer, company X would deposit an amount that would provide an income based on the $10,000 terminal salary with company X. That would be added to the company Y income based on the terminal salary with company Y, to yield:

$$\$10{,}000 \times 10 \text{ years with company } X \times 0.02 = \$2{,}000 \text{ per year}$$
$$\$20{,}000 \times 10 \text{ years with company } Y \times 0.02 = \underline{\$4{,}000 \text{ per year}}$$
$$\text{Total} = \underline{\$6{,}000 \text{ per year}}$$

### Termination

One cause of retirement plan termination was *inadequate funding.* ERISA requires more accelerated funding of liabilities than was generally the case prior to ERISA. Even before ERISA, the employer had been required by law to fund all current liabilities on a current basis (that is, contribute an amount of money equaling the cost of benefits accruing currently). [9] For example, if a vested employee under a defined benefit plan accumulated another year of service, then the employer became liable for the amount that the employee's entitlement was increased by the additional year of service, and the employer had to contribute money to cover that liability to the fund.

What ERISA added was a requirement that existing plans start amortizing *past service* liability over a period of forty years.[10] Past service liability is the company's liability for employees' years of service prior to ERISA or to adoption of the plan. If an employer does not set aside money year by year to cover its obligations for past employee service (and most employers did not before ERISA), then the fund cannot cover its obligations if it terminates. That was precisely the problem with plan terminations such as Studebaker's: the plans had not set aside enough money to cover past service liabilities. ERISA requires new plans—those initiated after the passage of ERISA—to fund their past service liabilities in thirty years. Changes in the pension plan must be amortized over thirty years. Also, ERISA requires fifteen years' amortization of "experience" gains or losses: unplanned changes in the fund's financial picture. For example, if the fund's investments do better (or worse) than expected, the employer's contribution must be adjusted accordingly. [11] All these ERISA funding requirements have increased the operating costs of retirement plans.

A second cause of plan terminations is misuse of funds. This is not a matter of having inadequate money, but rather a matter of putting that money in the wrong places. Cases 10.5, 10.6, and 10.7 involved this problem. Such blatant mismanagement was not eradicated by the legal strictures that existed before ERISA. ERISA's approach is to mandate certain investment standards for the managers of funds' assets to follow. Known as *fiduciary standards,* those ERISA provisions govern the actions of all persons responsible for retirement plan administration.

ERISA's principal fiduciary standard is known as the "prudent man rule":

> A fiduciary shall discharge his duties . . . with the care, skill, prudence, and diligence under the circumstances then prevailing that a prudent man acting in a like capacity and familiar with such matters would use in the conduct of an enterprise of a like character and with like aims. [12]

In short, a fiduciary must act competently. That means exercising native good judgment, and it also means being knowledgeable. If a fiduciary does not have the knowledge to manage the fund, then he or she must acquire it.

ERISA also includes specific prohibitions regarding fund management. For instance, ERISA prohibits the investment of more than 10 percent of a fund's assets in the securities or real property of the employer. [13] It also requires that fund investments be diversified to minimize the risk of large losses. [14] Finally, ERISA prohibits various conflicts of interest. [15] A fiduciary may not use the fund's assets for his or her own purposes, nor engage in any dealings with company employees. And, of course, a fiduciary may not receive any bonus, commission, or other form of personal compensation from any party making transactions with the fund, such as the kickbacks from securities dealers in Case 10.6.

If a plan terminates despite the funding and fiduciary requirements, ERISA provides plan termination insurance for defined benefit plans. The insurance program pays the retirement income, up to a limit, when the liquidated assets of the terminated plan are insufficient. Plan termination insurance was included in ERISA despite the opposition of President Nixon because it seemed impossible otherwise to provide security to employees during events such as the Studebaker plant closing. ERISA's program is administered by a federal agency, the Pension Benefits Guaranty Corporation, and it is funded by premiums paid by employers. Upon termination of an insured plan, participants become vested immediately. To the extent that the fund's assets do not cover its liabilities, the employer is liable to the Pension Benefits Guaranty Corporation for the unfunded liabilities. The amount of the liability can be as much as 30 percent of the employer's net worth.[16]

This discussion omits much of the detail in the ERISA provisions. There are other provisions of ERISA dealing with matters such as the tax treatment of lump-sum distributions (payments to participants that are made all at once upon retirement rather than as an annuity)[17] and the maximum amount that an employer can contribute toward an employee's retirement income.[18] Also, ERISA makes it illegal to discriminate in favor of high-level employees.[19] Finally, ERISA includes provisions for integrating the employer's retirement payment with social security, which allow an employer to tailor the retirement income benefit from its own fund to fit social security benefits.[20]

## Agencies

Three agencies are listed in the Regulatory Agency column of Exhibit 11.1. The first two, the Internal Revenue Service's Office of Employee Plans and Exempt Organizations and the Department of Labor's Labor-Management Services Administration, have similar functions. The reporting requirements for each are quite extensive, with both requiring information about the financial status of the retirement income program and other aspects of program structure and operation.

Two main agencies exist because of the same issue of congressional committee jurisdiction that contributed to the delay in passing ERISA in the first place. Each committee works with its own agency; the labor committees work with the Department of Labor, while the tax committees work with the Internal Revenue Service. Relations between the committee and its agency are generally friendly, and each committee tends to support its respective agency. Considering the impulses toward empire building in government, it is understandable that the final ERISA bill gave substantial responsibilities to each agency.

Originally, it was thought that the Internal Revenue Service would handle the tax-qualification aspect of retirement plan funding, while the Department of Labor would handle other aspects of plans. However, it soon became apparent that no such neat division of responsibilites was possible. Consequently, the jurisdictions overlap, and so do the demands on employers.

The third agency, the Pension Benefit Guaranty Corporation (PBGC), administers the plan termination insurance program. The PBGC also has its regulations and record-keeping requirements, and there is a degree of overlap between PBGC and the other two as well.

The problem of overlap, duplication, and conflict among the agencies responsible for ERISA enforcement has not gone unnoticed in Congress. Legislation has been proposed to create a single ERISA agency, the Employee Benefits Administration, which would assume most of the functions now performed by the three existing agencies. Whether this proposal can overcome the natural tendencies toward self-preservation characteristic of federal agencies remains to be seen.

## The Impact of ERISA

As noted already, ERISA has had an impact on both financial management and people management. The impact on financial management has been enormous; it could hardly have been otherwise considering the amount of assets in private retirement funds and the comprehensiveness of ERISA's provisions regarding the appropriate management of those assets. While detailed, extensive coverage of the financial management aspects of ERISA is beyond the scope of this book, it is important for those concerned with people management to be aware of ERISA's financial impact. The major impact of ERISA on people management has been to increase the importance of communicating with employees about benefit plan provisions.

## Financial Impact

The question of ERISA's financial impact is a matter of some debate. It is difficult to tell whether any given assessment of ERISA is motivated more by emotion, ideology, and self-interest than by impartial appraisal of the evidence. The discussion here concerns ERISA's impact on investment strategies for retirement fund assets, the costs of providing retirement income, and the type of plan offered. These three aspects are considered because they suggest that ERISA may be encouraging management strategies that *reduce* retirement income security.

ERISA's impact on investments is best reflected by the prudent man rule. That rule is widely regarded as a mandate for caution as well as for competence.[21] It suggests investment in high grade bonds and other securities, not investments in growth stocks or speculative issues. This advice may have been appropriate at the time ERISA was passed, for intemperate investments seemed to be a common problem then. Nowadays, however, prudence may not be so prudent. With double-digit inflation and other factors, an overly "prudent" investment might have a disappointing yield compared to more speculative ones. This hardly advances the security of retirees. Accordingly, the Department of Labor has made it clear that it does not necessarily consider it imprudent to make a risky investment. The prudence of such an investment will be viewed according to the role it plays in the overall investment strategy for the plan.[22] Still, the impact of ERISA on investments is a conservative one.

ERISA's impact on the *costs* of having a plan is clear. Liberalized participation and vesting requirements have given retirement income rights to employees who would never have had them before ERISA. The minimum funding provisions have adverse effects on profits, in that they require employers to allocate a large portion of operating revenues toward amortizing retirement income liabilities. The 10 percent limit on fund investments in the employer's real property and securities also makes it more difficult for the employer to turn to the fund as a source of financing. PBGC presents problems too. While the insurance premium is relatively modest at present, the 30 percent liability provision is said to have a more serious impact on financing.[23] Investors, faced with a potential 30 percent liability, might tend to stay away from riskier investment opportunities more than they would without PBGC.

A final source of costs is ERISA's substantial paperwork, which includes not only detailed financial reports, but also much nonfinancial information. The burden is exacerbated by the fact that it comes from three agencies, with all the duplication and inconsistency that one might expect under such circumstances. While steps have been taken to relieve that problem, it will probably continue to exist as long as ERISA responsibilities continue to be divided among three separate agencies.[24]

In short, ERISA makes retirement income costly. Yet employers are not required to offer retirement plans. Consequently, some employers are abandoning such plans, and others are choosing not to create them. The magnitude of this withdrawal from the private retirement income system is open to debate, but there is no doubt that some exists.

Even if ERISA does not drive the employer away from retirement plans, it may drive the employer away from the type that is most desirable for employees. The reason is that some ERISA provisions do not apply to all kinds of plans:

> The minimum funding provisions, the participation and vesting provisions, and the 10 percent limit on investment in employer securities or real property apply only to *defined benefit* and *money purchase* plans.

> Plan termination insurance is required only for *defined benefit* pensions. Thus the 30 percent liability is not a factor with any kind of pension plan except defined benefit.

Ironically, then, ERISA discourages employers from offering the very kind of plan that provides the greatest retirement income security—the defined benefit plan. To an extent, it also acts to discourage the money purchase plan, which is second in security offered to employees.

As a reflection of the trend toward plans that offer less security, some analysts recommend that employers without plans consider more modest ones than they might in the absence of ERISA.[25] For example, shortly after the passage of ERISA, Donald G. Carlson offered seven recommendations for companies without retirement income plans. The first two were (1) not to adopt a pension plan but instead make discretionary pension payments, and (2) raise salaries and urge employees to put the extra money into individual retirement accounts or personal savings accounts. In short, don't offer a plan. Four of the remaining five recommendations were to offer plans that provide less security than the traditional defined benefit plan: profit-sharing retirement income, retirement income based on a savings plan, a money purchase defined contribution plan, and a very modest defined benefit plan supplemented by a profit sharing or savings plan. Only the last of Carlson's options was the traditional defined benefit plan, and Carlson qualified the recommendation by observing, "The question is whether the cost of this approach will soon become too high or too uncontrollable."[26]

In short, ERISA has some perverse consequences. By encouraging employers to choose a plan that places substantial risk on employees, or perhaps to choose no plan at all, ERISA hardly lives up to the words "retirement income security" in its title.

## Employee Benefit Communication

ERISA mandates that the employee benefit plan description be comprehensive and comprehensible. That mandate covers not just retirement income plans, but all forms of employee benefit plans, including medical and disability insurance plans. This discussion examines (1) what information ERISA requires employers to communicate to employees, (2) the standards that ERISA applies to those communications, (3) the extent of the employer's legal liability for failure to communicate adequately to employees, and (4) the nature of management responses to those legal considerations.

ERISA requires some information to be provided automatically to participants and some to be provided upon the request of the participant.[27] Among the information that must be provided automatically is:

A description of the plan

A description of any amendments made to the plan

An annual report of the financial status of the plan

For vested participants who terminate: a statement of benefits

For those whose claims are denied: an explanation of the denial

Among the information to be provided upon request is:

A personal retirement plan benefit statement giving the participant's total accrued benefits, along with either the participant's vested benefits or the date that the participant's benefits will become vested

Supporting documents, reports, and other descriptive materials on the plan

In sum, the employer must communicate the nature of the benefit plan, the financial status of the benefit plan, and the individual participant's status under the plan.

ERISA's standard for adequacy of communication is stated specifically in the statute:

> The summary plan description . . . shall be written in a manner calculated to be understood by the average plan participant, and shall be sufficiently accurate and comprehensive to reasonably apprise such participants and beneficiaries of their rights and obligations under the plan. [28]

However, pensions are complex; the burden of being both clear and complete is an extremely difficult one, and no management course of action will guarantee that both will be accomplished satisfactorily. Completely conveying the complexities of a benefit plan is almost certain to mystify the average plan participant at some point.

Miller and Dorenfeld suggest an approach that might minimize the inherent conflict between the twin ERISA mandates: (1) make the summary plan description as clear as possible by confining it to the *general* features of the benefit plan, and (2) establish a convenient procedure for employees to obtain nontechnical answers to any *specific* questions they might have about the plan. [29] Of course, the courts would have to agree that such a procedure constitutes an adequate fulfillment of the communications obligation quoted above, and it is not entirely certain that the courts will do so.

That raises the issue of legal liability for miscommunication. The legislative history of ERISA clearly indicates that Congress was concerned about the problem of a participant misunderstanding the provisions of the plans. Many of the letters to Congress concerned misunderstandings (for example Case 10.4). Indeed, the disclosure provisions of ERISA were motivated largely by such misunderstandings. [30]

Consequently, ERISA provides specific penalties for failure to supply a summary plan description within thirty days of a request for it. Furthermore, some have suggested that ERISA also establishes an *implied* liability to provide whatever level of benefit the employee was led by the faulty communication to expect, regardless of whether the actual plan provides for such benefit. Thus, if the employer misleads an employee into believing that a certain benefit is forthcoming, the employer would be obligated to provide that benefit.[31]

In addition, totally aside from ERISA, common law provides for recovery due to negligent misrepresentation, inaccurate communication caused by failure to exercise due care in the conduct of one's affairs. Since negligence is defined as "conduct which falls below a standard established by the law for the protection of others against unreasonable risk of harm," participants who were misled because a plan description did not live up to ERISA's standard would seem to have a possible legal recourse. Also, the courts may consider a statement about benefits to be an implicit contract. In that case, the employer would be liable to provide what any misleading statement indicated that the employer would provide.[32] While the courts do not always apply these theories of liability very vigorously, still there seems to be enough at stake in all this for employers to make every effort to provide employees with a full and accurate understanding of the provisions of their benefit plans.

A number of writers have suggested specific management responses to the provisions of ERISA.[33] Some observe that good benefit communication is worthwhile even without the legal mandates of ERISA, because it tells employees what their employer is doing for them. Often employees do not know enough about their benefit plan to realize its true value, and that leads them to undervalue their compensation. Nevertheless, it took ERISA to stimulate much of the recent interest in benefit plan communication.

Two types of communications are typically prepared with ERISA compliance in mind, the benefit plan description and the individualized statement of benefits. The benefit plan description, designed to satisfy the ERISA provision requiring a summary description for each benefit plan participant, is usually prepared in the form of a booklet. Often considerable effort and expense is lavished on it to make it attractive to employees. Since a major concern is that it be understandable, the technical terms and the complex grammar often found in official plan documents are eliminated. The objective is to make the summary description so appealing that employees will actually read it and so clearly written that employees will actually understand it.

The individualized statement of benefits is designed to comply with the ERISA mandate that participants be provided with a personal retirement income benefit statement upon request. Most such statements are prepared with the aid of a computerized employee record system, and they usually tell the employee more than the minimum required by ERISA. Some benefit statements report the exact amount of life insurance that the employee has, the expected amount of retirement benefits assuming some given future salary level, and the specific hospitalization insurance benefits to which the employee is entitled.

ERISA has been one of the factors accounting for the increased use of computers in personnel management. In many organizations, computers represent the only economical method for retrieving the detailed individual information necessary to provide the individualized report required by ERISA. Once the required reporting is computerized, it is a reasonably simple matter to expand it to include the other benefit information that might be of interest to the employee.

There is also an increasing awareness of the supervisor's importance in communicating employee benefits. The supervisor is the one who can most easily answer the employee's questions, and the supervisor is also the one who can most readily make misleading remarks. It is important, then, that the supervisor be able to serve as an accurate source of information. Besides, the supervisor is the one who can most readily detect misunderstandings, correct them, and alert the organization to the communication failure. Whether the supervisor is the main source of that feedback to the organization, or whether methods such as questionnaires and interviews are used as well, some source of feedback is essential. Even a clear message can be misunderstood, and that misunderstanding can cause problems.

ERISA was passed largely because employees were misled about their retirement benefit plans, so it is only natural that a significant part of ERISA's mission for management involves communication. It so happens that most employees are not well informed regarding their benefit programs in general; notably, they tend to underestimate the dollar value of those programs. Here, then, for once at least, the federal government might be mandating a course of action that helps the organization, because it makes employees more conscious of the value of the benefit programs that the organization is providing for them.

## Further Information on ERISA

Being a branch of tax law, ERISA is covered by a wide variety of books, periodicals, and information services. Useful for those without a background in taxation is Sheldon Mike Young's *Pension and Profit Sharing Plans* (New York: Matthew Bender), a 5-volume service that is periodically updated by the publisher. A 1-volume periodically updated treatise is Jeffrey D. Mamorsky, *Employee Benefits Law: ERISA and Beyond* (New York: Law Journal Services Press). The Bureau of National Affairs publishes the full texts of ERISA court opinions in *Employee Benefits Cases.* Among the journals that cover ERISA issues extensively are *Employee Relations Law Journal, Labor Law Journal,* and *Pension World.*

# Notes

1. *Fortune,* February 1977.

2. Employee Retirement Income Security Act, Sec. 202(a)(1)(A).

3. Ibid., Sec. 203(a).

4. Ibid., Sec. 202.

5. 29 Code of Federal Regulations, Sec. 2530.200.

6. See Richard G. Schreitmueller, "Living with ERISA Administration," *The Personnel Administrator* 22 (May 1977):26–34.

7. Employee Retirement Income Security Act, Secs. 102, 103, and 105.

8. Ibid., Sec. 408.

9. Jeffrey D. Mamorsky, *Pension and Profit-Sharing Plans: A Basic Guide* (New York: Executive Enterprises, 1977), p. 183.

10. Employee Retirement Income Security Act, Sec. 302.

11. Ibid., Sec. 1011.

12. Ibid., Sec. 404(a)(1)(B).

13. Ibid., Sec. 407.

14. Ibid., Sec. 404(a)(1)(C).

15. Ibid., Sec. 406.

16. Ibid., Sec. 4062.

17. Ibid., Sec. 2005.

18. Ibid., Sec. 2004.

19. See Mamorsky, *Pension and Profit-Sharing Plans,* pp. 133–39.

20. Ibid., chap. 7.

21. See Roger D. Blair, "ERISA and the Prudent Man Rule: Avoiding Perverse Results," *Sloan Management Review* 20, No. 2 (1979):15–25; Robert D. Paul, "Can Private Pension Plans Deliver?" *Harvard Business Review* 52 (September–October 1974):22–24ff. Some observers do not see the government's position as overly cautious: for example, Paul S. Greenlaw and Robert L. Monske, "ERISA and 'Prudent' Pension Plan Investment: A Decision-Theory Model," *Personnel Journal* 58 (1979):600–606.

22. 44 Federal Register 37222 (June 20, 1979).

23. See Donald G. Carlson, "Responding to the Pension Reform Law," *Harvard Business Review* 52 (November-December 1974):133–44.

24. John N. Erlenborn, "ERISA in the '80s," *Pension World* 16, No. 1 (January, 1980):38–45.

25. Carlson, "Pension Reform Law."

26. Ibid., p. 142.

27. See Mamorsky, *Pension and Profit-Sharing Plans;* and Barbara B. Creed, *ERISA Compliance Reporting and Disclosure* (New York: Practising Law Institute, 1981).

28. Employee Retirement Income Security Act, Sec. 102(a)(1).

29. Edward B. Miller and Marc A. Dorenfeld, "ERISA: Adequate Summary Plan Descriptions," *Houston Law Review* 14 (1977):835–52.

30. Ibid.

31. E.g., *Anthony v. Ryder Truck Lines, Inc.,* 611 F.2d 944 (3rd Cir., 1979).

32. Miller and Dorenfeld, "ERISA."

33. For example, Sandra Fleming, "Getting Your Money's Worth from ERISA," *Personnel* 52 (May–June 1975):32–43; Kathleen Doyle Gill, "Employee Communications and ERISA," *The Personnel Administrator* 20 (May 1975):23–26; Harold Dankner and Judith H. Frost, "ERISA Summary Annual Reports: An Employee Relations Opportunity," *Financial Executive* 45 (February 1977):40–44.

# IV

## Other Areas

# 12

# Other Regulations: Unemployment Compensation, Wage-Hour Law, and Privacy Legislation

## Chapter Objectives

The purpose of this chapter is to cover three additional areas of government regulation and to set forth a final opinion about the way regulation ought to be approached by both the regulators and those regulated. The three areas of government regulation are not as sweeping in their impact on personnel and human resources management as the areas already covered. Yet they are important enough to merit a brief discussion before the book concludes.

The first regulatory area, unemployment compensation, is administered by state governments. It provides income replacement for workers who are unemployed because of lack of suitable employment. Unemployment compensation is relatively straightforward; it does not leave managers with many questions about how to comply. Still, unemployment compensation is significant, not least because it can make the improper handling of employee termination an expensive matter.

The second area, wage and hour regulation, specifies minimum pay and maximum work hours for certain employees. Wage-hour law governs such matters as overtime pay, shift premiums, and the wage levels paid by government contractors. Wage-hour regulations are detailed and sometimes subtle, and the important ones differ among different types of organizations. As a consequence, a thorough discussion of wage-hour rules would be no more productive than a thorough discussion of the OSHA safety regulations. Besides, an important part of wage-hour law, the Equal Pay Act, is covered in Chapter 5. However, a brief consideration of wage-hour law is appropriate, because it is so basic to compensation management.

The final area, privacy legislation, concerns the proper treatment of employee information. In a sense, it concerns the question of whether the employer or the employee should control that information. Currently, federal privacy regulation is mostly limited to public sector employment, so it merits less attention than other regulatory areas do. Nevertheless, its impact is growing. Many state governments regulate the use of employee information, and Congress has been deliberating over more comprehensive legislation.

## Unemployment Compensation

As noted, unemployment compensation is state regulation. However, it is carried out under strict federal supervision, and it had its origin outside government entirely. The first unemployment compensation programs were private and voluntarily instituted, either by unions or by industrial concerns such as Eastman Kodak, General Electric, and Procter and Gamble. By 1923, the Procter and Gamble plan was able to guarantee forty-eight weeks of continuous unemployment compensation for its regular work force. By the end of 1930, some 110,000 union members participated in private unemployment compensation plans, with benefits funded by contributions from employers, union members, or both.[1]

The federal government entered the picture in 1935, with the passage of the Social Security Act. Title IX of the act made state unemployment compensation programs virtually inevitable by imposing a federal payroll tax on employers, but giving them a credit for almost all that tax if they were to pay taxes into a state unemployment compensation plan. In other words, for a state to keep its employers' money from going into general federal revenues, it had to enact an unemployment compensation program. As a result, within two years all states and the District of Columbia had adopted programs.[2]

To understand the managerial significance of unemployment compensation, it is necessary to understand the method used to finance the program and the criteria used to judge whether a person is entitled to compensation. Briefly, the program is funded by a tax on employers, with the tax rate based on employee turnover for the employer. Usually, however, the only turnover counted is that resulting in unemployment compensation payments to the terminating employee, so it is in the employer's economic interest to avoid terminating employees in a way that would make them eligible for unemployment compensation. Thus management action to avoid improper terminations is considered below, after which the impact of unemployment compensation is discussed.

## The Financing of Unemployment Compensation

The unemployment compensation tax system is often referred to as an *experience rating* system. In most states, the tax rate for an employer is based on the record of unemployment compensation that is paid to former employees because of their separation from the employer's work force. The general principle behind the experience rating system in most states is that each employer should contribute enough tax payments both to cover all unemployment compensation claims outstanding against that employer and to build up a reserve balance for the employer in the fund. This helps to keep the unemployment compensation fund solvent. Until the employer's reserve balance reaches a certain figure, contributions continue at the maximum tax rate. Once the reserve reaches the required amount, the tax rate is reduced, and thereafter the tax rate is set at whatever figure is necessary to maintain the reserve balance. A successful claim draws down the employer's reserve.

The difference in tax rates for employers with good experience ratings and those with poor experience ratings can be substantial. While the difference varies from state to state, the average minimum rate is 1.1 percent, and the average maximum rate is 4.4 percent.[3] This tax is paid on only a portion of the employer's payroll. On the average, employers are taxed on the first $5000 they pay each employee per year. Thus, the average cost of a bad experience rating amounts to approximately $165 per employee per year. It should be borne in mind that, despite the experience rating system, employers with better ratings still end up subsidizing unemployment attributable to employers with worse ratings.[4] Also, some employers are unable to do very much to reduce their tax rates. Still, the spread in taxation does give a general idea of what is at stake for employers.

## Criteria for Determining
## Unemployment Compensation Eligibility

The general criterion is that workers may receive unemployment compensation whenever they are unemployed due to lack of suitable employment. Two key questions are implicit in that definition: What is suitable employment? What determines whether someone is unemployed due to lack of such employment?

Basically, suitable employment is defined as any employment that is (1) in the worker's customary occupation, (2) located at a reasonable distance from the worker's residence, and (3) free from risk to health and safety. Any person out of work is expected to show a lack of suitable employment by making a reasonable effort to find a job and by periodically registering for work at the state agency that administers the unemployment compensation program (generally the state's department of labor). As one might expect, the states vary in their interpretation of those three criteria. But most states do expect employees to be willing to depart somewhat from their normal job classification if an opportunity should arise.[5]

The question of what constitutes a lack of employment presents other complications. The basic principle is that workers must be "able and available" for work. The practical implication of that principle is to deny eligibility to workers who voluntarily leave their work without good cause, workers who are discharged for misconduct connected with their work, and workers who refuse suitable employment.

Whether a person voluntarily leaves work without good cause may seem simple to determine, but often it is not. For example, some states consider leaving employment in order to accompany spouses who have been relocated as "good cause."[6] And if the evidence indicates that the worker was harassed into quitting, the termination is usually regarded as a *constructive discharge:* superficially voluntary, but for all practical purposes involuntary. In such cases, compensation is paid.

Perhaps the most important unemployment compensation question concerns discharge for misconduct connected with work. Some states are more reluctant than others to question management's disciplinary prerogatives. Most agree, however, that incompetence does not bar a discharged employee from compensation. When employees convince the compensation board that they were working to the best of their ability, their claims will usually be granted. The reasoning is that the termination was beyond the employee's control, so it was not voluntary, and therefore compensation should be given.

Generally, only *misconduct* can deny unemployment compensation to a terminated employee. Misconduct is behavior under the control of the employee—it *is* voluntary—which makes the firing of a willful rule violator simply another variety of voluntary termination (a "constructive quit," so to speak).

## Management Action

Management can take steps to defeat claims for unemployment compensation by employees who have been discharged because of misconduct. Most important is to be certain that the disciplinary system underlying the discharge is sound. If the system is not sound, then the organization may not be able to convince an unemployment compensation board that the discharge was actually due to misconduct rather than to some more arbitrary reason.

There is nothing particularly obscure about what constitutes a sound discipline system; most personnel management or labor arbitration texts cover this area adequately. Yet the principles of discipline are violated so often that it is worth stating some of the principles that seem to be significant for unemployment compensation:

The misconduct in question should be prohibited by an explicit rule of the organization.

The misconduct should be reasonably related to the employee's work, or to some other legitimate organizational objective.

The rule prohibiting the misconduct should be specific in its definition of the offense and in its setting forth of the punishment for infractions.

The rule should have been effectively communicated to all employees, including the employee filing the claim.

The infraction should be severe enough to warrant the punishment of discharge, or, if the infraction is less severe, it should be a repeated violation of the rule.

The rule should be enforced consistently.

The violation should be documented, as should *all* violations of the rule by *any* employee.

If the rule is one that was long ignored and then suddenly enforced, employees should have been given fair warning of the new policy.

When employers ignore those basic precepts, they reduce their chances of prevailing at an unemployment compensation hearing, even when an employee is fired for severe misconduct. For good reason, then, such employers often decline to contest claims.

However, other employers decline for the wrong reasons. They are convinced that it is hopeless to win in cases of disciplinary discharge, regardless of how good their disciplinary systems may be. While it may be harder to win in some states than in others, employers with adequate systems generally do have hope, if they follow their own systems consistently.

If an employer decides to contest a claim by a properly discharged employee, the first step is to recognize that the burden of proof in cases of misconduct is on the employer. The employer must be prepared to produce documentation and witnesses. The documentation should include all written reports and other material substantiating the decision to discharge an employee. The witnesses should include everyone having first-hand knowledge about the discharge or the incidents that led up to it.[7]

Establishing a sound, well-documented discipline system is costly, and so is preparing for an unemployment compensation claims hearing. But those costs should be weighed against the likely benefits. The obvious benefit is a potential reduction in unemployment compensation. A good discipline system has other benefits as well, totally aside from unemployment compensation. Not only does it help control problem behavior, but also it helps persuade employees that the rules are fair and that management has a sense of justice.

## The Impact of Unemployment Compensation

Unemployment compensation has been widely studied and its impact widely debated.[8] One common criticism comes from the evidence that it encourages people to remain unemployed by making unemployment less disadvantageous.[9] On the other side, unemployment compensation is also said to have some positive motivational effects on individual workers, but the evidence for that is equivocal.[10]

However, there is also evidence that unemployment compensation insurance has a positive motivational effect on *employers:* it encourages them to avoid laying off workers. To avoid unemployment compensation claims, employers tend to retain employees during recessions, when they would otherwise be tempted to let people go.[11] However, that too may be a mixed blessing: during good times, employers tend to have their existing employees work overtime rather than risk later unemployment claims by hiring new employees who may later have to be laid off.

It is hard to give a simple answer to the question of whether the overall impact of unemployment compensation has been beneficial. Yet the program has been relatively uncontroversial. It seems innocuous in comparison to the other regulatory areas considered in this book. But that too may change. In many states, recent amendments in unemployment compensation laws have increased the costs of the program, often by increasing the maximum tax rate for the employers that have the worst experience ratings. As the cost of this area of regulation increases, the program may become more controversial.

## Wage-Hour Law

Every state has a law governing minimum wages and maximum hours, and there are federal laws governing wages and hours for federal contractors as well.[12] But for most employers the law of main concern is the federal Fair Labor Standards Act (FLSA). The FLSA, administered by the Wage-Hour Division of the U.S. Department of Labor, was passed in 1938, when it mandated a minimum wage of twenty-five cents an hour for up to forty-eight hours per week. Overtime was to be paid at a rate of 1.5 times the regular rate. At the time, the FLSA covered only 33 percent of the nation's nonsupervisory work force.[13]

The FLSA was passed in the Great Depression, so naturally Congress intended it to solve some of the Depression's problems:[14]

*Deflation:* the FLSA was intended to attack deflation by increasing the purchasing power of low-paid workers.

*Unemployment:* the FLSA was intended to reduce unemployment by making it more expensive for employees to pay overtime to existing employees instead of spreading work around by hiring new employees.

*Labor disputes:* the FLSA was intended to lessen labor disputes by increasing pay in low paying jobs and by reducing long hours.

Those purposes must be borne in mind when attempting to understand the act, its interpretations, and subsequent amendments. The act has been remarkably durable. The problems of the Depression that gave rise to it were eventually abated. Yet, during World War II, when one might expect that any law limiting pay and overtime prerogatives would yield to wartime growth pressures, the strength of the law persisted. Since then, the scope and impact of the FLSA has been substantially expanded by Congress.

Currently, the FLSA's base minimum wage is $3.35 an hour for up to forty hours per week, and the law now covers a vastly larger segment of the nation's work force. (Workers who are not covered are referred to as *exempt* employees.) Other changes have taken place as well. Congress amended the FLSA in 1947 by passing the Portal-to-Portal Act, which specifies when the employee's compensable workday begins and ends. That in turn determines when the employee's time should be counted. In 1963, Congress amended it again by passing the Equal Pay Act, discussed in Chapter 5. In 1974, coverage was extended to state and local government employees. Later, that extension was declared unconstitutional by the U.S. Supreme Court in the only case to date where a congressional FLSA enactment was invalidated.[15]

The repeated amendments to the FLSA have made it difficult to pin down an interpretation of the act.[16] As soon as the distinction between exempt and nonexempt employees begins to emerge clearly from court cases, the act is amended, setting off a new round of court cases. However, the 1977 amendments simplified exemptions considerably.

The principal problems of wage-hour compliance are (1) counting the hours worked by the employee, (2) calculating the employee's regular rate of pay for nonovertime hours, and (3) determining whether an employee is exempt from the provisions of the FLSA.

## Hours Worked

To determine whether an employee is being paid below the hourly minimum, it is of course necessary to know how many hours that employee works. But some employers do not keep track of that.[17] Occasionally employees work more hours per day than their employer thinks, and their daily pay may be low enough to make their hourly rate less the FLSA minimum.

Even if the employer does count hours, the act may count them differently for purposes of determining compliance. For instance, the act counts time spent in "activities which are considered an integral part of the employees' jobs."[18] But what constitutes an integral part? The Portal-to-Portal Act specifies that travel to and from the job site is not an integral part, but other incidental preparatory activities are. Generally, if the activity in question is an indispensable part of the principal work activity, it must be counted.

There are other nuances built into the counting of hours. Greenman and Schmertz summarize a few:

Hours are counted even when the employer does not request the employee's services (as when an employee stays after to correct errors or fill out reports).

Time on call is counted, and so is the time when an employee is off duty, unless the employee can use that period of time effectively for his or her own purposes.

Brief rest periods are generally counted.

Meal periods are not counted, unless the employee is required to eat at his or her work place.

Voluntary attendance at lectures, meetings, or training sessions is not counted if it takes place outside of regular work hours and if it is not directly related to the employee's job.[19]

### Regular Rate of Pay

To determine whether employees are being paid the minimum overtime rate of 1.5 times their regular rate of pay, it is necessary to know what that regular rate is. But that is not always a straightforward matter, even when the hours are counted correctly. The FLSA states that the regular rate includes "all remuneration for employment paid to, or on behalf of, the employee," except for:

Overtime premiums

Weekend, holiday, or other extra-day premiums, if they are at least 1.5 times the nonovertime rate (if less than 1.5 times, they are counted as part of regular pay)

Premium rates that are agreed upon beforehand for work outside regular hours, if those rates are at least 1.5 times the rate for work during regular hours (if less than 1.5 times, they are counted as part of regular pay)[20]

On the other hand, shift premiums are included in the definition of regular rate of pay.

Other detailed rules govern the definition of regular rate in special situations, such as with employees who work on two jobs with different rates of pay and employees who work on commission. The act itself includes some of the rules; others are found in the *Interpretative Bulletins* of the Wage-Hour Division.[21] Those rules are generally regarded as the special province of compensation specialists in personnel and human resources management, and compensation managers usually make it a point to know the specific definitions of regular rate of pay that apply to their own organizations.

### Exempt Employees

The distinction between exempt and nonexempt employees is fundamental in personnel management. Employers do not have to follow FLSA standards for exempt employees. For the most part, exemption is limited to salaried professional, executive, administrative, and outside sales employees. The critical question is how to determine whether a given employee fits into one of those categories. This question seems to be a major area of uncertainty under the FLSA. Basic guidance can be found in the regulations and *Interpretative Bulletins* of the Wage-Hour Division.[22]

The major criteria of exempt status for *professionals* are that they:

Do work requiring knowledge generally acquired by prolonged specialized study, or engage in original and creative activity in a recognized artistic field

Consistently exercise discretion or judgment

Do work that is primarily intellectual and nonroutine

Devote at least 80 percent of their work hours to such activities[23]

The major criteria for *executives* are that they:

Primarily undertake management duties

Supervise two or more employees

Have control (or at least great influence) over hiring, firing, and promotion

Exercise discretionary powers

Devote at least 80 percent of their work hours to such activities[24]

There are comparable criteria for administrative and sales workers as well.[25]

The criteria for all classifications includes a minimum salary level that changes from year to year.

The exemption guidelines leave some uncertainties. Though detailed, they do not always permit a precise determination of an employee's exemption status. Sometimes investigators from the Wage-Hour Division visit a facility to determine status by means of observation and interview. One of the management problems with the encounter between the investigator and the employee on such visits is the employee's natural inclination to be modest. That can lead to an understatement of responsibility and authority, which in turn can result in the Wage-Hour investigator's incorrectly classifying him or her as nonexempt.[26]

### Impact of the FLSA's Minimum Wage Provision

Differences of opinion over the impact of the minimum wage have existed ever since the passage of the FLSA.[27] Opponents argue that the minimum wage works a hardship on business in low-wage rural areas, on labor intensive industries, and on marginal companies. The increase in wages at the lowest levels exerts a strong pressure to increase them at higher levels as well. When that is not done, the resulting wage compression discourages people from trying to improve their skills. Also, by raising the cost of labor generally, the minimum wage is said to encourage mechanization as an alternative to increased employment. The net result is said to be reduced employment of youth, the unskilled, and other marginal groups least able to afford it.

Those favoring the minimum wage argue that paying less than the minimum wage is unfair. Without a minimum wage, they say, businesses would compete against each other by cutting the pay of those groups of employees that have the least power to negotiate wages and that can least afford a lower income. The minimum wage provides by legislation what the marginal worker lacks in a free labor market. Moreover, even some business executives share the belief that repeal of the minimum wage would result in a return to exploitation of some workers.[28] Despite the arguments of opponents, the FLSA seems here to stay.

## Privacy Regulation

The concern over privacy is not a transitory phenomenon. It has its roots in the Bill of Rights and the Fourteenth Amendment to the U.S. Constitution. For instance, the Fourth Amendment's protection against unreasonable search and seizure could be read to prohibit government from unreasonably searching employee records. The Fifth Amendment's protection against self-incrimination could be read to prohibit government from examining any source of information that might be interpreted as incriminating, personnel file information included. Likewise, the notion of due process of law embodied in the Fifth and Fourteenth Amendments might be used to challenge any government action that deprives a person of privacy.

A number of diverse laws govern privacy. All are concerned in one way or another with the question of who should control information about employees or applicants. In a sense, this is a question of *who owns the information*. While there are some federal laws, most of the regulatory activity has been carried out by the states.

There are two reasons that privacy is relevant to federal regulation. One is that federal legislation to regulate privacy is continually being considered by Congress. The other is that privacy regulation tends to conflict with other federal regulatory mandates. Additionally, some organizations have made concerted efforts to comply with what they perceive to be the demands of government privacy regulation, and those management steps are worth examining.

Privacy regulation can be separated into two major areas: (1) the use of lie detectors and other devices to detect deception, and (2) the management of personnel records.

## Lie Detectors

The use of lie detectors by employers is now prohibited in seventeen states and the District of Columbia. Two other states require an employer to obtain the written consent of the employee before administering a lie detector examination. Those laws vary in scope and in their specific prohibitions, but their net effect is to make it illegal for employers to extract any information from employees or applicants that those persons do not want to provide voluntarily.

More recently, the U.S. Congress has considered legislation to make the use of polygraphs, voice analyzers, and other such deception-detection devices illegal in all states. The ultimate fate of such proposals is uncertain. However, they are regarded favorably by organized labor. Labor considers a polygraph examination to be a humiliating experience. On the other hand, employers have testified against such legislation. Employers want to avoid losing the right to use any method they might regard as a possible solution to their growing theft and security problems.[29]

The decisive factor, however, may be the widespread finding that all such forms of deception detection are disturbingly inaccurate.[30] The problem is with the "false positive"—the individual who is actually telling the truth but is falsely identified by the lie detector as lying. Employers may be grateful for any improvement over chance in identifying the culprit, but opponents point to the enormous personal costs of being a false positive. Considering that risk, they insist on very high accuracy, something that is not possible given the current state of the art.

Regardless of what happens to proposals for federal legislation, state regulation of lie detectors seems here to stay, and there is a reasonable chance that other states will pass laws in this area.

## Employee Records

In this area too, most of the regulation of private employers has been carried out by the states rather than by the federal government. However, the federal government does regulate itself, granting privacy rights to federal employees. The state laws vary, but they generally give employees in private industry the right of access to their files, the right to monitor the information that goes into them, and the right to limit the information that is released from them. Some states single out medical records for specific regulatory attention.

The federal law governing employment is the Privacy Act of 1974, which requires federal agencies to open their personnel files for employee inspection. Specifically, the Privacy Act gives federal employees the right to (1) determine what information is being kept about them, (2) review that information, (3) correct or amend that information, and (4) prevent the use of information for any purpose other than that for which it was collected.[31]

Other federal laws have an impact on privacy in the private sector. For instance, the Fair Credit Reporting Act controls the information that gets into credit reports that employers might request on employees or applicants, and the Family Educational Rights and Privacy Act controls student records at universities. However, those federal laws do not control private sector personnel actions.

The major significance of privacy regulation is not the existing laws but the laws that may be passed in the future. One section of the Privacy

Act of 1974 established the Privacy Protection Study Commission, which recently released a report including recommendations for further privacy legislation.[32] In 1975, a bill (aptly numbered House Resolution 1984) was introduced in Congress that would, essentially, extend the provisions of the Privacy Act to cover private industry.[33] While the Privacy Protection Study Commission stopped short of recommending that, it did recommend legislation to forbid the use of lie detectors by employers and to strengthen the provisions of the Fair Credit Reporting Act.[34]

Several legal issues are involved in the consideration of comprehensive privacy regulation:[35]

The right of access to personnel information

The opportunity to respond to derogatory information

The right to remove or correct erroneous information

The right to be notified that information is to be released to a third party

The right to know how the information is being used within the employer's organization

The right to require that the employer take reasonable precautions to insure that the information is reliable and not misused

While it is by no means certain that those rights will be enacted into law, the prospect seems to be greater than the prospects for other new regulations. Privacy is a concept that has appeal across the political spectrum. While political conservatives are less fond of new government regulation than political liberals are, personal privacy is a cornerstone of conservative belief. Indeed, most of the privacy bills currently pending in Congress have been introduced by a conservative legislator. So it is conceivable that conservatives might make an exception to their general opposition to federal regulation in the case of laws limiting intrusion into private affairs.

## Conflicts Between Privacy and OSHA Regulation

Recall from Chapter 8 that the Occupational Safety and Health Act gives its regulatory agencies broad rights of access to information regarding health and safety. Mostly, this involves medical information, which is considered to be among the most personal employee information. That fact has already caused problems for some companies. Prior to the passage of OSHA, du Pont Chemical had voluntarily kept health hazard evaluation records on its employees for many years. After the passage of OSHA, the National Institute of Occupational Safety and Health (NIOSH) requested that information from du Pont. Du Pont was willing to release it with employee identification deleted, but NIOSH was unwilling to accept it in that form. When NIOSH issued a subpoena for the documents, du Pont asked for the consent of the employees involved, and 631 refused. When du Pont went to court, the court upheld NIOSH.[36] A similar decision was made in a case involving General Motors.[37] With increasing attention being given to occupational disease, and with the resulting need for medical information on employees, it seems likely that such conflicts will continue.[38]

## Management Responses

The Privacy Protection Study Commission report included a set of recommendations for employers. Seven of the recommendations were:

Limit the collection of information to that which is relevant to specific personnel decisions

Give employees access to their personnel records

Inform employees and applicants about how their records will be used

Allow employees to correct inaccurate information

Limit the release of information to third parties without the employees' consent

Limit the internal use of employee records

Limit the external disclosure of employee information[39]

Even in the absence of federal regulation, private sector employers seem to be making a number of voluntary changes in their use of employees' records. Perhaps the most notable change has come in the use of reference information, information about an applicant from the applicant's former employer. There is no law regulating the use of references, but the growing concern over privacy and the threat of lawsuits by applicants and former employees is apparently leading employers to be more cautious, both about providing reference information to other employers and about using reference information provided by other employers. This concern seems well placed. Among the steps that observers recommend are,[40] for *users* of reference information:

> Ask for specific, job-related information only
>
> Do not use subjective information
>
> Obtain written consent from candidates before checking references

and for *providers* of reference information:

> Document all information released
>
> Release specific, objective information only
>
> Obtain written consent from employees before releasing information
>
> Do not give information over the telephone
>
> Do not blacklist employees
>
> Do not answer the question of whether you would rehire the employee—if your answer is "no," you would not want to be held responsible for the other party taking your advice

The effect of those recommendations is to objectify reference information. That in turn should improve the employer's EEO compliance as well as reduce the employer's vulnerability to lawsuits alleging the misuse of employee information.

## A Final Word

The most significant general statement that can be made about federal regulation is that it is *about problems*. Each regulatory area *attacks* problems and *creates* problems. In the heat of debate, people seem to forget that it does both. Those who approach regulation from a pro-regulation public policy perspective are quite conscious of the social problems that underlie regulation, but they are less sensitive to the management problems that regulation creates. Likewise, those who approach regulation from a management perspective are painfully aware of the management problems caused by regulation, but they often seem oblivious to the social problems that regulation is designed to attack.

Yet it is important for those concerned with each side of the regulatory model to be aware of the perspective of those concerned with the other side. If the regulators become more aware of the perspective of the manager, the result might be more effective regulation. And if the manager becomes more concerned with the perspective of the regulators, the result might be greater chances for survival in a highly regulated environment. Better yet, this mutual awareness might result in more voluntary efforts by employers to solve social problems without the compulsion of government regulation and in more voluntary efforts by regulators to recognize that a due concern for the management problems of the organizations they are regulating may do more than anything else to solve the social problems that the regulations were created to solve.

# Notes

1. Russell L. Greenman and Eric J. Schmertz, *Personnel Administration and the Law,* 2d ed. (Washington, D.C.: Bureau of National Affairs, 1979), pp. 161–62.

2. Ibid., pp. 162–63.

3. See Employment and Training Administration, U.S. Department of Labor, "Significant Provisions of State Unemployment Insurance Laws" (Washington, D.C.: U.S. Government Printing Office, 1977); also see the annual enumeration of changes in unemployment insurance laws, appearing in *Monthly Labor Review.*

4. Joseph M. Becker, *Experience Rating in Unemployment Insurance: An Experiment in Competitive Socialism* (Baltimore: The Johns Hopkins University Press, 1972).

5. Greenman and Schmertz, *Personnel Administration,* pp. 174–75.

6. Ibid., p. 172.

7. See H. C. Rockey, "A Briefer on Unemployment Compensation Hearings," *Supervisory Management* 21, No. 9 (1976):22–29.

8. For example, Arnold Katz, ed., "The Economics of Unemployment Insurance: A Symposium," *Industrial and Labor Relations Review* 30 (1977):431ff.

9. Raymond Munts, "Partial Benefit Schedules in Unemployment Insurance: Their Effect on Work Incentives," *Journal of Human Resources* 5 (1970):160–76.

10. Ronald G. Ehrenberg and Ronald L. Oaxaca, "Do Benefits Cause Unemployed to Hold Out for Better Jobs?" *Proceedings of the Twenty-Eighth Annual Meeting, Industrial Relations Research Association,* 1976.

11. David L. Edgell and Stephen A. Wandner, "Unemployment Insurance: Its Economic Performance," *Monthly Labor Review* 97, No. 4 (1974):33–39.

12. Among the more significant acts governing federal contractors are the Walsh-Healey Public Contracts Act, the Davis-Bacon Act, the Service Contract Act of 1965, and the Miller Act of 1935.

13. Peyton K. Elder and Heidi D. Miller, "The Fair Labor Standards Act: Changes of Four Decades," *Monthly Labor Review* 93 (1970):10–16.

14. Louis Weiner, *Federal Wage and Hour Law* (Philadelphia: American Law Institute, 1977), p. 14.

15. *National League of Cities* v. *Usery,* 426 U.S. 833 (1976).

16. See Greenman and Schmertz, *Personnel Administration,* p. 15.

17. See American Society for Personnel Administration, "What to Do When the Wage-Hour Investigator Calls."

18. 29 Code of Federal Regulations Sec. 785.34.

19. Greenman and Schmertz, *Personnel Administration*, pp. 25–26.

20. Sec. 7, Fair Labor Standards Act.

21. 29 Code of Federal Regulations, Chap. V, Secs. A.3–A.5.

22. Ibid., Chap. V.

23. Ibid., Sec. 541.3.

24. Ibid., Sec. 541.1.

25. Ibid., Secs. 541.2 and 541.500.

26. American Society for Personnel Administration, "What to Do."

27. Burton W. Teague, "The Minimum Wage—How Minimum Should It Be?" *Conference Board Record* 11 (January 1974):22–26.

28. Ibid.

29. Jerri L. Frantzve, "The Polygraph Bill (S.1945)—A Legislative Development of Significance to Industrial/Organizational Psychologists," *The Industrial-Organizational Psychologist* 15, No. 4 (1978):10–11.

30. See Paul R. Sackett and Philip J. Decker, "Detection of Deception in the Employment Context: A Review and Critical Analysis," *Personnel Psychology* 32 (1979):487–506.

31. See John D. Rice, "Privacy Legislation: Its Effect on Pre-Employment Reference Checking," *The Personnel Administrator* 23, No. 2 (1978):46–51.

32. Privacy Protection Study Commission, *Personal Privacy in an Information Society* (Washington, D.C.: Government Printing Office, 1977).

33. Ibid.

34. Philip G. Benson, "Personal Privacy and the Personnel Record," *Personnel Journal* 57 (1978):376–80, 395; also see John C. Fox and Paul J. Ostling, "Employee and Government Access to Personnel Files: Rights and Requirements," *Employee Relations Law Journal* 5 (1979):67–83.

35. See Rice, "Privacy Legislation."

36. *E. I. du Pont de Nemours* v. *Finklea*, 442 F. Supp. 821 (S.D. W. Va. 1977).

37. *General Motors* v. *Finklea*, 6 Occupational Safety and Health Cases 1976 (S.D. Ohio 1978).

38. See Fox and Ostling, "Employee and Government Access."

39. Ibid.; Benson, "Personal Privacy."

40. See Rice, "Privacy Legislation."

# Case Index

261

# Subject Index

discrimination *(continued)*
  *see also* Disparate impact/disparate treatment; Illegal classifications; *names of specific statutes and regulations*
disparate impact/disparate treatment, 41–42
  and the distinction between BFOQ and job relatedness, 60
  evidence and proof, 46–47, 91–93, 100–103, 106
  and race discrimination, 59
  and religious discrimination, 81–83
  and retirement plans, 64
  and seniority systems, 97–98
  and sex discrimination, 59, 64, 73
  and subjective personnel practices, 44
Dorenfeld, Marc A., 236
due process of law, 72, 85–86

Education Amendments of 1972, 26
education requirements for employment, 20, 38–42
EEO. *See* Equal employment opportunity (EEO)
EEOC. *See* Equal Employment Opportunity Commission (EEOC)
employee assistance programs, 80
Employee Benefits Administration, 232
employee records. *See* Records, personnel
employee selection, 33, 42, 110. *See also* Interviews; Job relatedness; Reference checking; Uniform Guidelines on Employee Selection
employer rights, 2
Employment Retirement Income Security Act (ERISA), 206–39
  on breaks in service, 226
  on communication of benefits, 207, 226, 228, 235–37

Employment Retirement Income Security Act *(continued)*
  compared to OSHA, 206–7
  congressional intent of, 213–22, 236
  duplication of agency authority over, 234
  on eligibility, 224
  on fiduciaries and fund management, 227, 230–31, 233
  financial impact of, 233–35
  on funding, 227, 229, 230, 234
  impact of, 234–35
  individual retirement accounts and, 228
  on integration of benefits with social security, 231
  on investment rules, 230, 233
  legislative history of, 213–14, 216–21
  management responses to, 233–39
  on participation, 226, 233
  Pension Benefits Guaranty Corporation and, 225, 231, 232, 233, 234
  and plan termination insurance, 219, 227, 231, 234
  and prudent man rule, 230–31, 233–34
  and regulatory model, 224–32
  on reporting and disclosure, 228
  rule of 45 and, 226
  Studebaker plant closing and, 218, 230
  union position on, 216, 219, 220
  on vesting provisions, 226, 232
  *see also* Retirement income plans
Environmental Protection Agency, 6
equal employment opportunity (EEO), 19–23
  compared to ERISA, 206, 220
  compared to OSHA, 159, 171
  in conflict with OSHA, 188

**DATE DUE**

| APR 1 1 1998 | | | |
|---|---|---|---|
| MAR 3 1 1998 | | | |
| | | | |
| | | | |
| | | | |
| | | | |
| | | | |
| | | | |
| | | | |
| | | | |
| | | | |
| | | | |
| | | | |
| | | | |
| | | | |
| | | | |

DEMCO 38-297

# POWDER KEG

# POWDER KEG

*Northern Opposition
to the
Antislavery Movement*

1831-1840

**Lorman Ratner**

BASIC BOOKS, INC., PUBLISHERS

*New York/London*

*To the memory of my mother and father*

234608

# *Preface*

This study of anti-abolition is limited to New England and the Middle Atlantic states during the period 1831–1840. This is not to imply that there was no anti-abolitionist sentiment in the Old Northwest (Ohio, Indiana, Illinois, and Michigan). However, because the Old Northwest was populated in part by southerners, there is in any study of that region the complicating factor of an ingrained sympathy for the slave system; the number of southerners who migrated to the Northeast, however, was negligible. Consequently, the presence of anti-abolitionist sentiment in the Northeast cannot be explained as a result of direct and sympathetic association either with slavery or with the South.

Antislavery appeals and the reaction against them were expressed before 1831 and continued after 1840; however, both the appeal and the reaction are of a special character in that decade. Abolitionists were better organized and made more concerted efforts to convince the northern public than ever before. Although the abolitionists' crusade continued after 1840, changes in the relationship between North and South caused northerners to view abolitionist proposals in a new light. Thus, though recognizing the long history of antislavery appeals and northern reactions to them, it is reasonable to consider the 1830's as a special era and to study the reaction to antislavery in that decade as a special case.

Anti-abolition was not an organized movement with prescribed principles and a definite leadership. It was a popular reaction against a set of principles and against proposed courses of action. The study of such a reaction presents methodological difficulties. The problems involved in assessing public opinion in a contemporary society are great, and the problems increase if the search is for the content of and the explanation for public opinion as it existed 125 years ago.

My objective was to discover views expressed by those who were involved with and reached some significant segment of the northern public. I examined newspapers, magazines, published sermons, and political speeches, as well as fictional and non-fictional popular writing. Private letters were not used both because public statements seemed more likely to indicate public sentiment, and because there was no reasonable way of determining whose papers should be consulted, as anti-abolition was not an organized movement. Recognizing that an individual's opinion might be shaped by his class, occupation, rural or urban surroundings, religious affiliation, or political allegiance, I selected sources reflecting the views of all such groups. The views uncovered were much the same regardless of group and so, though group affiliations are noted, the findings are of a consensus.

Having determined public opinion on a given question, there is still the problem of explaining why the public held these views. Northerners gave many reasons for their opposition to antislavery: reasons involving the Negroes' alleged inability to live in a white society, the general distrust of abolitionists because of their association with foreigners, concern for the preservation of the Union, the belief that slavery was a local not a national matter, and the general doubt that Negroes would benefit from abolition. Northerners believed their anti-abolitionist stand was logical. There were, however, other reasons, unexpressed but important in explaining anti-abolition. The last few pages of this book suggest the nature of those reasons. I am well aware of the importance of covert reasons. To attempt, however, to explore in depth that level of anti-abolition would force me to drop my primary purpose of identifying public opinion on abolition for a full-scale study of northern society in the 1830's, for anti-abolition was related to · economic, political, social, and cultural conditions of that society.

Instead, I have recorded and analyzed the expressed,

overt level of anti-abolition. Studying the subject at this level, I have uncovered much about northern views of the Negro, northern sentiments with regard to reform, northern views on the role of state and national government, and northern opinion on issues such as higher versus human law.

*New York*                                     LORMAN  RATNER
*January 1968*

# *Acknowledgments*

I have received assistance from many persons in the years since I began this investigation as a graduate student. My greatest debts are to David Brion Davis who directed my doctoral work and whose interest in antislavery led me into that area of study. I owe much to my friend and colleague George Wylie Sypher who provided invaluable help in rethinking, reorganizing, and rewriting the original dissertation, and to my wife to whom I am indebted for her hard work and patience through a number of difficult years.

I have profited from the suggestions and criticisms of Robin Williams, Edward Fox, and Paul Gates, all of Cornell University; Douglas Maynard and Thomas B. Davis, Hunter College; W. David Lewis, the State University of New York at Buffalo; Stanley Coben, Princeton University; and David W. Becker, Miami University of Ohio.

Much of the material examined in this project was rare, and I owe an unusually large debt to the reference-library staff of Cornell University who located and obtained the many books and microfilms I needed. I also wish to thank those librarians at the New York, New Jersey, and Pennsylvania Historical Societies, and at Harvard University, for their cooperation.

The Social Science Research Committee of Cornell University provided valuable financial assistance, as did Hunter College. Miss Audrey Schneiderman and Miss Sandra Ornstein handled typing chores efficiently and made editorial suggestions beyond the call of duty.

As anyone who has written a book knows, writing is in part a matter of endurance, and friends become almost as important as advisers. To those whose friendship I value so much, thank you.

Despite all the help and advice, I alone am responsible for any errors and shortcomings in the final product.

# Contents

# POWDER KEG

# 1

———•———

# *Racism Persists*

In the years from the Revolution to 1820 northern states
one by one emancipated the slaves within their borders.
Vermont's constitution outlawed slavery in 1777, Pennsylvania ended it in 1780, Massachusetts in 1783, Connecticut
in 1797, New York in 1799, and New Jersey in 1804. The
founding of the New England Anti-Slavery Society in
1831 and the American Anti-Slavery Society in 1833 were

in one sense logical results of these developments.[1] The existence of these groups establishes that some northerners were eager to work for the total abolition of slavery in America. Yet these organizations were better known through their denunciation by their northern opponents than through any widespread distribution of their literature or their success in winning adherents. In large measure the abolitionists' problem was that most northerners were convinced of Negro inferiority and that, whatever abolitionists may have claimed their objective to be, northerners believed the antislavery men sought to make whites and blacks equal. As part of his reaction to the abolitionists' appeal Massachusetts Attorney General James T. Austin expressed an extreme racist view that one heard often in this decade:

> Is it supposed they [Negroes] could amalgamate? God forbid. . . . But I fearlessly aver that if this be the tendency and the result of our moral reformation, rather than our white race should degenerate into a tribe of tawny-colored quadroons, rather than our fair and beauteous females should give birth to the thick-lipped, woolly-headed children of African fathers, rather than the Negro should be seated in the Halls of Congress and his sooty complexion glare upon us from the bench of justice, rather than he should mingle with us in the familiar intercourse of domestic life and taint the atmosphere of our homes and firesides—I WILL BRAVE MY SHARE OF ALL RESPONSIBILITY OF KEEPING HIM IN SLAVERY.[2]

This racism, as vehement as any found in the South in this period, cannot be dismissed as the rantings of one isolated northern extremist. It is, in fact, the purpose of this book to demonstrate that these and related opinions were widely held in the North, and to explain how they related to and stimulated anti-abolitionism in the North of the 1830's.

It is misleading to trace a relatively rapid and steady northern progression from slavery to freedom, and from freedom to the founding of the abolitionist societies of the 1830's. In fact, the legal history of abolition in the North is deceptive unless it is borne in mind that legal emancipation alone could not, did not, and was not intended to give the Negro full citizenship. There was, and had been since the seventeenth century, a widespread and deeply planted belief in the inferiority of the Negro, whether slave or free. This chapter will examine the evidence and results of this racism, and its continuation into the 1830's. Other chapters will examine why the abolitionists of the 1830's met with opposition of an unprecedented size and virulence. Racism joined with and intensified northern fears that a national antislavery policy endangered the Union, threatened states' rights, imperiled existing political parties and churches, and would lead to catastrophic civil strife in the form of rebellions and race war. Emancipation by single northern states had not raised these problems because of the small number of their Negro population, and emancipation had not entailed federal action or foreign intervention. There had been the comforting assumption, borne out in practice, that the freed Negroes would be kept at the lowest political, social, and economic levels of society. The abolitionists of the 1830's, however, encountered opposition of unexpected intensity and extent, for their program raised broader issues and new fears.

As noted above, this opposition had its most intangible yet perhaps its strongest basis in racism. A number of historians, most recently Leon Litwack in his *North of Slavery*, have collected convincing proof of this northern racism. Nevertheless, it may be useful to review this theme briefly, in order to establish the tradition which continued into the 1830's and which was strengthened by the reaction to abolitionism.

In Massachusetts, by the end of the seventeenth century, slavery existed both in fact and in law. There, as elsewhere, whites justified slavery on the basis of the supposed natural inferiority of the Negro or Indian, or because the nonwhite was not a Christian. Northern communities excluded the unbaptized slave from their activities and found other grounds for excluding the free Negro even if he was baptized.[3]

All of the New England and Middle Colonies legally restricted the activities of free Negroes. Whites in these colonies feared that the free Negroes might serve as leaders of a slave insurrection or perhaps foment a race war. And such fears had some foundation in fact. In 1712 Negro slaves revolted in New York City, killed several whites and burned some homes. The city court sentenced several Negroes suspected of rioting to be burned to death.[4] In 1741 another slave revolt rocked New York. In its aftermath 143 free Negroes were arrested, 13 burned, 18 hanged, and 21 transported to Africa.[5]

Even before these insurrections New York and other colonies showed their concern lest Negroes and other nonwhites become a menace to person and property. In 1710 New York City passed a law prohibiting Negroes, Indians and Mulattoes from being on the street at night unless carrying a lantern.[6] The law did not distinguish between free Negroes and slaves. In 1703 the Massachusetts legislature prohibited free Negroes from being on the street after nine o'clock.[7] Four years later that colony passed an act giving free Negroes restricted military duty and refusing to allow them to entertain slaves unless the master gave permission.[8] Rhode Island had similar restrictions on Negroes traveling after dark and prohibited Negroes from assembling in private homes or public places.[9]

By drafting such laws the colonists sought to lessen the danger of race violence. But this fear was not the only source of laws restricting the rights of Negroes; legal discrimination reflected widespread racial prejudice. New Jersey, which granted the Negro more legal rights than any other colony, provided in 1713 that "no Negro, Indian or Mulatto that shall thereafter be made free shall hold any real estate in his own right in fee simple or fee tail. And whereas it is found by experience that free Negroes are idle slothful people, and prove very often a charge to the place where they are . . . owners manumitting shall give security." [10]

In 1705–1706 the Pennsylvania colonial legislature marked the Negroes off as a distinct class, whether free or slave.[11] In 1725 that legislature subjected the Negro to a number of special regulations, among them a law, later adopted in many other colonies, prohibiting interracial marriage.[12] In 1717 the Connecticut lower assembly sought to prohibit Negroes from purchasing land and even living together as families without the express consent of the town.[13] These are a few examples of the manner in which northern colonies, before 1750, invoked discriminatory legislation against the Negroes.

After the Revolution northern states one by one ended slavery; but discrimination in the shape of voting prohibitions and social prejudice remained, and where discrimination had not been formalized before, it was now.

In 1780 Pennsylvania became the first state to institute gradual abolition of slavery. But despite this antislavery sentiment the transition from slave to freeman was difficult. The vote on gradual emancipation had been close; in fact, a minority protest was filed by 21 members of the state legislature.[14] In 1790 the state drafted a constitution which established the voting right of all freemen; but the state's constitution excluded the Negro from those desig-

nated as freemen and so denied him the vote.[15] In 1837 the
state legislature seriously considered a bill to prevent free
Negroes from entering the state and in the same session
formally and directly refused the Negro the vote.[16] New
Jersey, whose constitution of 1776 allowed all free males
the right to vote, ruled in 1820 that suffrage should be ac-
corded to white males only.[17] Connecticut enacted the same
provision in 1814, and a high property qualification for
Negro voters remained in New York's new constitution in
1821.[18]

This denial of political rights was coupled with a general restriction on the activities of free Negroes. In Massachusetts racial discrimination impelled free Negroes to establish their own Masonic order, schools, and social clubs.[19]
The state outlawed marriage between Negroes and whites,
and churches and ship owners adopted a policy of segregation. Negroes were even excluded from burial in the grave-
yards of the whites. The situation in other northern states
was much the same. Whites displayed prejudice against
Negroes even as they showed an awareness that slavery
was an evil and that the institution ought to be abolished.[20]

This construction of barriers against the admission of the
Negro into white society was the result of a long tradition
of race prejudice. Thus emancipation of Negroes in the
North, though it demonstrated the strong sentiment
against slavery, did not reflect a willingness to accept the
Negro into northern society. Racism or the conviction that

racism was an insurmountable barrier to racial harmony, had characterized the thinking of many northerners for a long time.

As early as 1700 Samuel Sewall of Massachusetts wrote a pamphlet attacking slavery and the slave trade.[21] Sewall criticized the men who engaged in the slave trade or held slaves; yet even he maintained that Negroes were inferior beings for whom there was no place in white society. As the explanation for Negro inferiority Sewall cited the biblical curse of Ham. The New Englander wrote: "There is such a disparity in their conditions, colour, and hair, that they can never embody with us, grow up into orderly families, to the peopling of the land; but still remain in our body politick as a kind of extravasate blood." [22]

Even this moderate attack on slavery, tempered by its expression of belief in Negro inferiority, found opponents. John Saffin, a Boston merchant, challenged Sewall's statements regarding the slave trade and insisted there was nothing immoral about taking captives in war and making them slaves. The Negroes transported to America, Saffin said, were prisoners of war; he then proceeded to defend the slave trade on the grounds that such prisoners were better off as slaves in America than in Africa.[23]

In addition to Sewall's work, the Pennsylvania Quakers Benjamin Lay and Ralph Sandiford wrote some antislavery tracts and were consequently expelled by their meeting. Other than those few protests, antislavery activity languished before 1750.

By the latter part of the eighteenth century a growing interest in missionary work, the considerable attention given to the rights of man at the time of the American Revolution, and the increasing reform activities of the Society of Friends all served to arouse interest in the abolition of slavery and the slave trade. The slave trade was cruel, its evils were obvious, and its abolition seemed only just. Men like Jefferson, Madison, and Franklin considered slavery a contradiction of American principles. But even in an era so marked by idealism Americans wondered and worried about the prospect of a multiracial country. Racial inferiority, or practical problems involved in emancipation, or both, were grounds for hesitancy.

The first President of the new republic was one of the many Americans whose statements about slavery reflected that concern. In 1786 Washington wrote to Robert Morris concerning the attempt made by Quakers in Philadelphia to free all slaves:

> this Society is not only acting repugnant to justice so far as its conduct concerns strangers, but, in my opinion extremely impolitickly with respect to the State, the City in particular; and without being able, (but by acts of tyranny and oppression) to accomplish their own ends. . . . [*sic*]
>
> I hope it will not be conceived from these observations, that it is my wish to hold the unhappy people, who are the subject of this letter, in slavery. I can only say that there is not a man living who wishes more sincerely than I do, to see a plan for the abolition of it; but there is only one proper and effectual mode by which it can be accomplished, and

**11**

> that is by legislative authority. . . . But when slaves who are contented with their present masters, are tampered with and seduced to leave them . . . it is oppression . . . and not humanity . . . because it introduces more evils than it can cure.[24]

A month later, in a letter to Lafayette, Washington wrote that "some petitions were presented to the [Virginia] assembly at its last session, for the abolition of slavery, but they could scarce obtain a reading." Washington feared that if such petitions were considered at the time, they could only lead to difficulties. He did feel, however, that eventually emancipation should be considered.[25]

In both letters and elsewhere in his correspondence Washington made clear that, though he favored emancipation, freedom for the Negro slave must come gradually and slaveholders' rights must be upheld. Washington supported the clause written into the Constitution prohibiting Congress from abolishing the slave trade until 1808. This apparently suited his belief that only by legislation could slavery safely and justly be ended.

Thomas Jefferson was more concerned with slavery and with the broader question of the Negro in America than any other political leader of the Revolutionary era. Though Jefferson thought emancipation desirable, he rejected the proposition that the Negroes, once freed, should be allowed to remain in America. In *Notes on Virginia*, written in the 1780's, Jefferson considered the question of the compatibility of the races:

> The deep-rooted prejudices entertained by the whites, as well as the ten thousand recollections by the Blacks, of the injuries they have sustained . . . distinctions which nature has made; and many other circumstances will divide us into parties and produce convulsions which will probably never end but in the extermination of our race or the other.[26]

In 1789, in answer to a letter questioning him about the advisability of immediate emancipation, Jefferson noted that some Virginia Quakers had freed their slaves and put them to work as tenant farmers, but rather than work, the slaves chose to steal. Jefferson felt this was inevitable: "A man's moral sense must be unusually strong, if slavery doesn't make him a thief. He who is permitted by law to have no property of his own, can with difficulty conceive that property is founded in anything but force." [27]

Jefferson maintained that living as slaves made it impossible for the Negroes to become part of American society; but he also pointed to the inferiority of the black race as a reason for their exclusion. He gave a biological explanation for the inferiority of the Negro and went into great detail in describing how color and general physical make-up made the Negro inferior to the white. Jefferson insisted there was evidence that the Negro lacked the white's mental powers.[28] In *Notes on Virginia* he observed:

> never yet could I find that a black uttered a thought above the level of plain narration; never seen even an elementary trait of painting or sculpture. In music they are generally more gifted than the whites. . . . Whether they will be

equal to the composition of a . . . melody . . . is yet to be proved. . . . Their love is ardent, but it kindles the sense only, not the imagination.[29]

For Jefferson, who detested slavery and felt compassion for the slave but believed the races were incompatible, colonization provided the only solution to the race problem. The colonizationists called for purchasing slaves, giving them their freedom and transporting them out of the country.

Even those who rejected the contention that Negroes were inferior recognized that the strong race prejudice of northern whites would make it impossible to bring the races together as equals. James Madison, Samuel Stanhope Smith, John Adams, and Hezekiah Niles are examples of antiracists who nevertheless came to accept the impossibility of any emancipation plan that would leave Negroes in white society.

By the 1820's James Madison agreed with Jefferson that colonization was the only way both to help the Negro and avoid racial conflict, though in his younger days he had been more optimistic than Jefferson regarding the future of the Negro in America. As late as 1790 Madison spoke out against slavery and advocated the immediate outlawing of the slave trade—a view he expounded during the Constitutional Convention. Madison was disappointed when the Convention gave the slave trade 20 years before it must cease. He told the delegates that 20 years "will produce all the mischief that can be apprehended from the liberty to import slaves. So long a term will be more dishonourable to the national character than to say nothing about it in the Constitution." [30]

The "Father of the Constitution" disagreed with Washington on this question just as the two men had disagreed years before on the question of using Negroes in the Revolutionary army. At that time Madison called for the emancipation of slaves in return for their service in the army. This would provide much-needed troops and would strengthen the colonists' ideological position.[31] In 1780 Madison wrote: "It [emancipation of slaves] would certainly be more consonant to the principles of liberty, which ought never to be lost sight of in a contest for liberty. . . ." [32] In all cases Madison stood in the minority until 1820; by then, years of observing the treatment of free Negroes in all the states caused him to take the popular stand favoring colonization. He noted the "unalterable prejudices in the U.S.," which caused him to favor the settlement of all Negroes beyond the bounds of any white settlement. Madison now concluded that the races were unable to live peacefully together since the blacks would always be dissatisfied with their inferior position and resentful of the wrongs done them as slaves. These past injustices would prevent the Negroes from becoming good citizens and would lead them to plot violence against the whites.[33] Though he rejected the argument for racial in-

**15**

feriority, Madison allowed his name to appear on the list of honorary officers of the recently formed American Colonization Society.

Samuel Stanhope Smith, one-time president of Princeton, was one of the few who shared Madison's early optimism regarding the prospects of an America in which Negroes and whites would live harmoniously together. In 1787 Smith published *An Essay on the Causes of the Variety of Complexion and Figure in the Human Species*. In this essay he objected to the idea, then generally accepted, that Negroes and Indians were biologically inferior to whites, and hence these races could not be granted equal status with white Americans. Smith sought to prove the common origin of all men. He accepted the physical differences between the races, but he attributed these differences to the Indians' and Negros' long residence in a primitive environment. Smith maintained that if the Indian and Negro races were exposed long enough to the white man's civilization, they would change their habits, color, and general physical appearance. Smith claimed there were records of such transformations.

In 1810 Smith brought out a second edition of this essay. In a new preface he observed that slavery prevented both the physical and social amalgamation of the Negro. Smith's associates at Princeton rejected his environmentalist theories, and there is no evidence that his views received widespread hearing or support.

John Adams, like Smith and Madison, opposed slavery

but feared the consequences of national abolition. Adams wrote in 1819 that he opposed slavery but, like so many Americans, he rejected proposals for immediate emancipation, fearing it would lead to racial violence. In a letter written in 1819 Adams made clear his position on the questions of slavery and the Negro in America:

> The turpitude, the inhumanity, the cruelty, and infamy of the African commerce in slaves have been so impressively represented to the public . . . that nothing I can say would increase the just odium in which it is and ought to be held. Every measure of prudence, therefore, ought to be assumed for the total extirpation of slavery from the United States. If, however, humanity dictates the duty of adopting the most prudent measures for accomplishing so excellent a purpose the same humanity requires, that we should not inflict severer calamities on the objects of our commiseration reducing them to despair, or to the necessity of robbery, plunder, assassination, and massacre, to preserve their lives. . . . The same humanity requires that we should not by any rash or violent measures expose the lives or property of our fellow citizens, who are so unfortunate as to be surrounded with these fellow-creatures, by hereditary descent, or by any other means without their own fault.[34]

Hezekiah Niles, editor of one of the most widely read periodicals in America, was another supporter of colonization for practical, rather than racial, reasons. In 1829, in Baltimore, Niles wrote in his paper, *Niles's Register:*

> No one can hate slavery more than I do. . . . But I can make great allowances for those who hold slaves in districts

where they abound—where in many cases, their emancipation might be an act of cruelty to them, and of most serious injury to the white population. Their difference of color is an insuperable barrier to their incorporation within the society; and mixture of free blacks with slaves is detrimental to the happiness of both.[35]

Madison, Smith, Adams, and Niles, believing whites would never accept free Negroes, reluctantly supported colonization. Men like Eliphalet Nott, president of Union College, or William Duer, president of Columbia University, saw colonization as the means of removing an inferior element from American society. Nott insisted that free Negroes "have remained already to the third and fourth, as they will to the thousandth generation—a distinct, a degraded, and a wretched race." [36] Duer considered the freedmen improvident and reckless.[37] Duer and Nott were but two of many influential northerners who, in the 1830's, commented publicly on the inferiority of the Negro and linked this belief to their rejection of abolition.

In 1835 a novel entitled *A Sojourn in the City of Amalgamation in the Year of our Lord 19—* was published anonymously in New York. *Sojourn* was written as an autobiographical piece in which the author, like Washington Irving's Rip Van Winkle, fell asleep and awoke many years later. His first observation was that blacks and whites were socializing and that amalgamation had been forced on society. As the writer saw it, the result was disastrous. The blacks became the most respectable part of the community.

Though still vulgar in dress and manners, they had attained a position of complete equality and now were in the process of subjugating the whites. Privilege after privilege was granted the Negro, and still he asked for more. White men were actually forced to marry Negro women, and fathers now came to look upon the marriage of their daughters to Negro men with great favor, though the author assured his readers that the white girls entered such unions against their wills. The scene depicted resembled a pagan orgy. Society had degenerated; people had become lazy, and the country was in a state of decline. This was the future the abolitionists were promising America: the inferior Negro destroying the superior white race.[38]

Anti-abolitionists constantly warned that racial amalgamation would result from emancipation of the slaves. Novelist and prominent politician James Kirke Paulding of New York agreed; emancipation, he insisted, would mean intermarriage. "The project of intermarrying with the blacks is a project for the debasing of the whites by a mixture of that blood, which wherever it flows, carries with it the seed of deterioration."[39] Paulding remarked that there were whites who would intermarry, but they were traitors to their race who would be universally condemned for their action. He then discussed at length the racial history of the Negro, a history that proved their inferiority. He noted that even when given educational opportunity the Negro failed to respond: "The mind of the African . . . seemed in great degree divested of this divine attribute of progressive improvement." [40] Whites were naturally superior and should not sacrifice this superiority for the sake of some abstract principle.

Concern was expressed often that abolition meant the freeing of an inferior people to mix with and degrade the white race. The editor of the influential *North American Review* was one of many northerners to issue such a warning.[41] When racial violence flared up in Philadelphia in 1838, racial mixing was cited as the immediate cause. After three days of racial violence the Philadelphia *Pennsylvanian* commented that white abolitionist women had been seen in the company of Negro men. The editor referred to the abolitionists' "socializing" with Negroes as a first step toward establishing the equality of the "African race." [42]

In March 1836 the *National Trades Union,* journal of the labor union of the same name, carried a lengthy review of James Kirke Paulding's book *Slavery.* The reviewer criticized English abolitionists who decried slavery and at the same time were willing to see children work 14 or 15 hours a day. He denounced the Irish reformer Daniel O'Connell, who supported the abolitionists, for having done nothing for English laborers but "could not bear to have his ebony brethren whipped even enough to arouse them to a sufficient degree of exertion to digest their hominy, pigs and poultry. So with our loving brethren [the abolitionists] to whom a dark skin and musky perfumes are no objections. . . ." [43]

The writer went on to accuse the abolitionists of being

wealthy men who preferred "to scatter firebrands" in their efforts to free slaves who were an inferior race, while leaving white Americans oppressed.[44] The reviewer noted that the Negro was actually better off as a slave in America than as a free man in Africa, and that the Negro slave was content in his condition. Then followed a discussion of the Negro's place in the American economy. The *National Trades Union* writer argued that certain tasks were too low for whites to perform, but that Negroes were fit and happy to perform them—shoe shining, for example. Some 15 years later George Fitzhugh, the southern apologist for slavery, made this last argument a main point in his defense of slavery.[45]

From many quarters came open expressions of strongly felt racism. An author who called himself "A Connecticut man" remarked of the Negro "That he partakes in an eminent degree of the indolence and propensity for animal indulgence . . . cannot be questioned. . . . They almost universally drink to excess, and are otherwise in gross debasement [*sic*]." [46] In the debates of the Pennsylvania State Constitutional Convention of 1837 a delegate referred to Negroes as "a race of criminals," a simple-minded people who would be used by "evil forces." [47]

In *The Last of the Mohicans* novelist James Fenimore Cooper made much of the racial characteristics of his characters—for example, Uncas, the Indian who was in love with a white girl. Cooper made it plain that marriage would have been improper between the two had not the girl a touch of Negro blood; even then the two had to die before their love could be consummated. And Cooper indicated that this trace of Negro blood had attracted the Indian to the mulatto girl.[48] Though Cooper drew the image of "the noble savage," many of the Indians in his novels showed cruelty and cunning. In his personal correspondence Cooper made clear that he considered the Indian civilization inferior to "Christian civilization," and the white race superior to any other.

Discussing Negro slavery, Cooper insisted that the great difference between American slavery and slavery in Europe (by which he meant serfdom) was that the American slave was "a variety of the human species, and was marked by physical peculiarities so different from his master, as to render future emalgamation improbable. . . . Nature has made a stamp on the American slave that is likely to prevent this consummation, and which menaces much future ill to the country." [49]

The popularity of minstrel shows added another, though indirect, comment on the belief in Negro inferiority. T. D. "Jim Crow" Rice created a stereotyped Negro comic figure for the northern stage public.[50] While playing in a theater in Cincinnati, he had seen an old Negro stablehand dancing and singing. He mimicked the Negro, adopted his name of "Jim Crow," and wrote a song "Jim Crow" based on a few words the old Negro had sung. Rice was the sensation of the northern theaters in the early 1830's. A whole series of plays about Negroes were written for him, and in

January 1833 Rice starred in a "black-face opera" called "Long Island Juba, or Love by the Bushel."[51] At the same time James Kirke Paulding's very popular play *The Lion of the West* was performed in New York. The hero, a Kentuckian called Nimrod Wildfire, made several references to how "lazy the niggers are" and the Negro servant in the play was a comic figure.[52]

For years before Rice began to appear, northern theater audiences had been used to seeing Negro clowns and black-face performers. Most circuses had a black-face clown in their troupe, and the circus performer George Washington Dixon became a stage success with his Negro act.[53] By the early 1830's many plays, even some tragedies, included a Negro song act. Northerners must have been impressed by this stereotype comic Negro, entertaining because he was so different, so inept. These caricatures revealed and must have intensified a common northern belief that the Negro was incapable of full citizenship in American society.

Racism may well have been the heart of anti-abolition, but many northerners insisted there were other grounds for rejecting antislavery. Northern critics saw in antislavery far more than just the danger of giving citizenship to racially inferior people. Abolition aroused fears for the future of the Union, the Constitution, political parties, churches—in other words, for the whole structure of American society. The next chapters will consider these various themes in anti-abolitionism.

## NOTES

1. Henry W. Farnam, *Chapters in the History of Social Legislation in the United States to 1860* (Washington, D.C., 1938), pp. 218–219.
2. James T. Austin, *Remarks on Dr. Channing's Slavery by a Citizen of Massachusetts* (Boston, 1835).
   Following a mass meeting at Faneuil Hall, Boston, in December 1837 to protest the Lovejoy murder, Austin attacked the protesters and insisted that the mob that had killed Lovejoy was blameless. He compared that mob to the patriots who took part in the Boston Tea Party.
3. George W. Williams, *History of the Negro Race in America, 1619–1880* (New York, 1883), I, 121.
4. Herbert Aptheker, *Slave Insurrections in the United States, 1800–1860* (Boston, 1938), p. 14.
5. *Ibid.*, p. 15–17.
6. Williams, *op. cit.*, p. 142.
7. *Ibid.*, pp. 194–195.
8. *Ibid.*, p. 194.
9. *Rhode Island Colonial Records*, III, 492–493, quoted by Williams, *op. cit.*, p. 264.
10. Williams, *op. cit.*, p. 284.
11. Edward R. Turner, *The Negro in Pennsylvania: Slavery-Servitude-Freedom, 1639–1861* (Washington, D.C., 1911), p. 26.
12. *Ibid.*, p. 27.
13. Robert A. Warner, *New Haven Negroes, A Social History* (New Haven, 1940), p. 7.
14. Turner, *op. cit.*, p. 78.
15. *Ibid.*, pp. 174–175.
    Negroes in Pennsylvania, as elsewhere in the North, were in the lowest position on the economic scale. Their only educational opportunities were afforded them in Negro schools. Negroes were admitted into some Episcopal and Moravian churches, but not on an equal basis with whites; in most churches, they were excluded. Thus, Negroes had to form their own religious organizations. In a

footnote in *Democracy in America* (Vintage ed.; New York, 1957) I, 271, Alexis de Tocqueville relates a conversation with a Pennsylvanian in which the Frenchman asked why Negroes failed to vote. The reply was that Negroes had the right to vote but were afraid to exercise it. The majority of citizens were so prejudiced against Negroes that judges were unable to protect them.

16. *Ibid.*, pp. 190–192.

17. Farnam, *op. cit.*, p. 218.

18. *Ibid.*, pp. 218–219.

19. In the 1790's Massachusetts Negroes established their own Masonic lodges. For the most useful discussion of the subject see Lorenzo J. Greene, *The Negro in Colonial New England* (New York, 1942), pp. 299–302.

20. C. Vann Woodward, *The Strange Career of Jim Crow* (revised ed., New York, 1957), pp. 6–7.
    Vann Woodward argues convincingly that prejudice translated into social action has come as formal institutional governing of race relations ended. Thus, Jim Crow replaced slavery in the South after the Civil War. A similar development took place in the North in the 1820's and 1830's. A long history of prejudice made it necessary for northerners to seek to define the place of the Negro; though, as the success of the American Colonization Society in attracting northern support shows, many northerners hoped the task would be unnecessary.

21. Samuel E. Sewall, *The Selling of Joseph*, selections quoted in *Massachusetts Historical Society Collections*, 1863–1864, pp. 161–165.

22. Quoted in Charles Wesley, "Negro Inferiority in American Thought," *Journal of Negro History*, XXV (October, 1940), 542.

23. Quoted in Elizabeth Donnan, *Documents Illustrative of the Slave Trade to America* (Washington, D.C. 1931), III, 18.

24. John C. Fitzpatrick, ed., *Writings of George Washington* (Washington, D.C., 1931), XXVIII, 407–408.

25. *Ibid.*, XXVIII, 424.

26. Paul L. Ford, ed., *Works of Thomas Jefferson* (New York, 1904), III, 379–380.

27. *Ibid.*, V, 447.

28. *Ibid.*, IV, 50–60.

29. *Ibid.*, IV, 58–69.

30. Gaillard Hunt, ed., *Writings of James Madison* (New York, 1900), IV, 303.

31. *Ibid.,* I, 106–107.

32. *Ibid.,* I, 107.

33. *Ibid.,* IX, 439–441.

34. Charles F. Adams, ed., *Writings of John Adams* (Boston, 1856), X, 379–380.

35. From *Niles's Register.* Quoted in Allan Nevins, *American Press Opinion, Washington to Coolidge* (New York, 1928), p. 60.

36. Quoted in Early L. Fox, *The American Colonization Society 1817–1840* (Baltimore, 1919) pp. 32–33.

37. *Ibid.,* pp. 33–34.

38. Oliver Bolokitten [pseud.], *A Sojourn in the City of Amalgamation in the Year of Our Lord 19—* (New York, 1835), *passim.*

39. James K. Paulding, *Slavery in the United States* (New York, 1836), p. 61.

40. *Ibid.,* p. 63.

41. *North American Review* (Boston), XXXV (1832), 118–164.

42. *Pennsylvanian* (Philadelphia), May 18, 1838.

43. *National Trades Union* (New York), March 12, 1836.
   The National Trades Union had its headquarters in New York and included local unions from all over the Northeast. Ely Moore was its first president. In 1839, while a member of Congress, Moore, in a speech before the House of Representatives, accused the Whigs of trying to destroy the power of the northern workingman by freeing Negroes "to compete with the Northern white man in the labor market." Quoted by Arthur Schlesinger, Jr., *The Age of Jackson,* p. 425.
   Microfilm of all issues of the Union's newspaper are available at the library of The New York School of Industrial and Labor Relations, Cornell University.

44. *National Trades Union,* March 12, 1836.

45. George Fitzhugh, *Cannibals All! Or Slaves Without Masters!* (Richmond, Virginia, 1857.)

46. [Anon.], *An Inquiry into the Condition and Prospects of the African Race in the United States and the Means of Bettering Its Fortunes* (Philadelphia, 1839), pp. 14, 24.

47. *United States Gazette* (Philadelphia), June 21, 1837.

48. James Grossman, *James Fenimore Cooper* (New York, 1949), pp. 44–46.
49. James Fenimore Cooper, *The American Democrat* (new ed.; New York, 1931), p. 166.
50. George C. Odell, *Annals of the New York Stage* (New York, 1928), III, 628–632.
51. *Loc. cit.*
52. James K. Paulding, *The Lion of the West* (new ed., Stanford, Calif., 1954), p. 37.
53. Carl Wittke, *Tambo and Bones* (Durham, N. C., 1930), p. 19.

# 2

*Meddling Outsiders*

Despite their prejudice toward the Negroes, northerners accepted the end of slavery in their own states on a local, state-by-state basis. But the abolitionism of the 1830's called for men of one state to impose their will upon men of other states and, at least in the eyes of the northern public, for men of one country to interfere with the affairs of another.

The English antislavery movement achieved a major victory when, in 1833 Parliament set forth steps to end slavery in the Empire. The English abolitionists played an important role in helping to organize the American antislavery groups. English tracts were distributed by American abolitionists. English and other European writers criticized America for permitting slavery and, on occasion, English abolitionists spoke from American platforms. The American abolitionists were closely associated with English antislavery men. As the New England antislavery leader Samuel May asserted, George Thompson and other English abolitionists crossed the ocean to show Americans their transgressions.[1]

In the 1830's, however, American abolitionists found this association with the English antislavery movement a costly one. The decade was characterized by an extreme sensitivity to foreign criticism and supposed foreign conspiracy. In an age when Americans, troubled by political and economic problems, feared for the future of their institutions and were overly quick to defend them, such an association could only arouse public ire.

In the 1830's European observers wrote articles and books decrying the state of American society.[2] Such critics as Harriet Martineau, Frances Trollope, Thomas Brothers, Basil Hall, and Gustave de Beaumont singled out slavery as a notable fault and criticized Americans for permitting it to continue. Americans were highly sensitive to such attacks; they answered their critics with counterarguments and even with outbursts of mob violence against foreigners or those connected with them. Both northerners and southerners associated American abolitionists with foreigners and denounced the antislavery men as un-American. The abolitionists, who welcomed help from their English counterparts, were attacked verbally, and at times with physical violence, as foreign conspirators or dupes of those conspirators.

In articles, novels, and travel accounts European critics made plain their dislike of slavery and their low regard for Americans who condoned it. The works of these European writers circulated in the North and were often attacked by northern writers.[3] Foreigners frequently wrote unfavorable accounts of their visits to this country, which made Americans even more hostile to foreign censure of slavery. Americans were already belligerent toward foreign observers who often pointed out the high incidence of violence in the United States, decried the lack of culture, the maltreatment of the Indians, and the corruption in American politics. A few samples from the vast foreign travel literature will demonstrate the kind of criticism Americans received with regard to slavery and the way they reacted to it.

In her *Domestic Manners of the Americans,* Frances Trollope made clear her distaste for American manners and institutions. Her commentary on the crudeness of American men, the gaudiness and general bad taste displayed by the women, and the lack of culture presented a grim picture of the Republic. In America, she remarked, "that polish which removes the coarser and the rougher parts of our nature is unknown and undreamed of." [4] Though she rather enjoyed the gracious plantation life of the South, Mrs. Trollope condemned the institution of slavery, especially what she termed "its licentious aspects." [5] Americans were acquainted with *Domestic Manners,* and both James Kirke Paulding, in *The Lion and the West,* and Asa Greene, in his satirical novel *Travels in America,* ridiculed Mrs. Trollope.[6] Paulding created Mrs. Wollope, a stuffy Englishwoman who criticized everything American. Though she said she disliked slavery, she treated her servants worse than slaves, and slaves she met worse than their masters would treat them. Paulding contrasted Mrs. Wollope's hypocrisy with the candor of his frontier hero, Nimrod Wildfire.[7] Greene dedicated his work to Mrs. Trollope, sarcastically assuring her that to place his name on the same page with hers was sure to give him immortality.[8]

Another English traveler, Harriet Martineau, wrote much more flattering accounts of America than Mrs. Trollope. In *Society in America* Mrs. Martineau praised many aspects of American life, but she, too, criticized our tolerance of slavery.[9] From 1835 to 1837 the abolitionists prevailed upon her to write a series of articles supporting their crusade. These articles were collected and published in 1838 as *The Martyr Age.* In these articles Mrs. Martineau wrote of her dislike of slavery and stated that England had imposed the institution on America, and that it was a carry-over of corrupt institutions Americans were in the process of eliminating. It was a measure of American sensitivity that this moderate position did not prevent Mrs. Martineau from being denounced as violently and often as were George Thompson, Daniel O'Connell, and other foreign critics. The northern press attacked her for praising William Lloyd Garrison and for supporting the antislavery movement in general, and referred to her as a meddling foreigner and a threat to the Republic.[10]

During the eighteenth century French writers had been the most prominent apologists for America. But in time the French, especially those of the "romantic school," came to look upon America as a society that had lost its golden chance.[11] Pastoral, virtuous America of the natural man without the fetters of institutions to bind him had been lost, and French critics now pictured America as a dull, money-conscious, middle-class society, similar to the France of the July Monarchy.[12] Americans, instead of communing with nature, had transformed their country into the counterpart of the well-mowed lawns of the eighteenth-century landscape.[13]

When those two most famous French travelers to America, Gustave de Beaumont and Alexis de Tocqueville, returned home, they each set about to record their experiences and make public their observations. While Tocqueville sought to analyze all aspects of American life, Beaumont wrote *Marie, or Slavery in the United States.* Here he expressed his disillusionment with America which had resulted from his observations of the treatment of the Negro.[14] Beaumont stressed that white Americans believed the Negroes were inferior. Marie, the heroine of his story, had a drop of Negro blood. She married a white, and because of this miscegenation, husband and wife both suffered and eventually were killed. In the course of the narrative Beaumont wrote of the many Americans who, though opposed to slavery, were so prejudiced that they would consider emancipation only if the Negroes were transported to Africa. He maintained that these antislavery, yet prejudiced, people felt slavery was a stain on the nation's honor. But, Beaumont noted, they resented any foreigner pointing this out, and he believed that their opposition to slavery was motivated by self-interest. "They are ridding themselves of an annoyance, an embarrassment . . . they have worked for themselves, not for the slaves." [15] Beaumont made clear to his French readers that the southern slaveholder was an unromantic figure who served as an example of feudal corruption, lacking both gallantry and honor.[16]

Beaumont joined with the English writers in condemning America as a society of hypocrites who preached democracy while they sanctioned slavery. Naturally, Americans resented these attacks, and defenders of the country, like Asa Greene or the influential New Yorker Calvin Colton, answered the charges.

In 1833 Calvin Colton, while a newspaper correspondent in London, published *The Americans*.[17] In this book he developed a line of defense that was reiterated time and again in the northern press and magazines of the 1830's.

Colton began by assuring his English readers that, despite the frequent reference to the Revolution in Fourth-of-July oratory, Americans actually felt no animosity toward the British.[18] He also denied that Americans were overly sensitive to foreign criticism. After refuting Mrs. Trollope's and Captain Hall's fallacies in regard to American manners, he discussed American institutions. Colton, a supporter of the American Colonization Society, which sought to free slaves and send them and all free Negroes to Africa, chided the British for being so critical of America when it was they who had introduced slavery into the Colonies. Though he confessed that the republic had done less than it should have to promote emancipation, he noted that many states had in fact outlawed slavery. Circumstances in the United States, he said, made emancipation less simple than it had been in England, but the American Colonization Society, was making real progress toward that goal. Colton pointed out that criticism of slavery in America was actually being used by English politicians for their own ends. The English radicals cited American institutions in their fight for reform, and more conservative English politicians countered by pointing out the weaknesses and failures of those institutions. In this way, Colton denied that there was any substance in the British criticism and insisted that Americans were handling the slavery problem adequately.[19] Returning to the subject of slavery in a long appendix, Colton defended colonization, accepted the basic inferiority of the

Negro, and warned that in all good projects there are always some mischief-makers, i.e., the abolitionists.[20]

Sometimes specific European writers on slavery were the target, but usually northern writers simply denounced foreign interference in general. John Quincy Adams, though he aided the abolitionists, noted in his diary in 1835:

> It [the abolitionist movement] has linked itself with religious doctrines and religious fervor. Anti-slavery associations are formed in this country and in England, and they are already cooperating. . . . They have raised funds to support and circulate inflammatory newspapers and gratuitously . . . send multitudes of them into the Southern country, into the midst of swarms of slaves. . . .[21]

Catherine Beecher, daughter of the prominent clergyman and reformer Lyman Beecher, wrote that the general disposition of the people in America was to believe the English were interfering in American affairs through the abolitionist societies.[22] The *Boston Transcript* denounced all foreign criticism of American slavery and proposed that foreigners should be refused the right to speak on the subject.[23] Miss Beecher and the editor of the *North American Review* both noted that the English had introduced slavery into America and so had no right to be critical.[24] William Lloyd Garrison's presence in New York, on his return from England in 1833, helped to touch off a riot in that city. One New York paper implied that Garrison had gone to England to learn how to undermine the institutions of his own country.

Some northerners went beyond simply rejecting foreigners as legitimate critics of America. By the 1830's stories of an English abolitionist conspiracy circulated in the North —indicating indeed how highly sensitive Americans were in the 1830's to criticism of their institutions. By 1835 some newspapers were carrying stories claiming that abolitionists were part of a foreign plot. Since these stories circulated in a number of northern newspapers, the idea of a foreign plot in which abolitionists were involved seems to have struck a responsive chord in northern society. In the 1830's Americans were generally prone to the belief that, in any case, they were beset by all sorts of foreign threats and plots.

In 1834 the painter, writer, and inventor, Samuel F. B. Morse began publishing a series of letters in the *New York Commercial Advertiser,* writing under the pseudonym "Brutus." These letters described a foreign conspiracy, master-minded by Prince Metternich in collusion with the papacy and aimed at the overthrow of republican government in America. By 1844 all 12 letters, collected in book form and entitled *Foreign Conspiracy Against the Liberties of the United States,* had gone through six editions.[26]

The fact that Morse had traveled in Europe seemed to give his story added validity. Also, many writers before him had conditioned Americans to accept the idea of conspiracies at work, especially foreign conspiracies. For centuries

European Protestants had feared a Catholic plot to destroy Protestantism, and after the Bavarian Illuminati scare of the 1790's Americans were particularly concerned about the existence of such plots.[27] The signs of anti-Catholic feeling in the 1830's are well-known.[28] Many believed the Catholics were conspiring to destroy both Protestantism and democracy. These same Americans were susceptible to anti-Masonic and anti-Mormon appeals.[29]

Since northerners often spoke of foreign powers seeking to destroy the republic, opponents of antislavery found this appeal to the fear of conspiracy an excellent way to arouse public sentiment against the abolitionists. Furthermore it was an effective means by which to silence the antislavery advocates, for conspirators were considered unworthy of the right even to be heard.

James Watson Webb, editor of the *New York Commercial Advertiser,* and James Gordon Bennett, of the *New York Herald,* were leading proponents of the idea of an abolitionist conspiracy. Both editors told similar stories of abolitionist plotting, though Bennett's was the more sensational. In October 1835 Bennett claimed knowledge of an English plot to flood America with tracts and money to fight for abolition, the ultimate purpose being the destruction of the Union.[30] This, he insisted, was the beginning of a great conspiracy. Ten days later, he claimed to have exposed a plot by a secret group who planned to use this money to purchase the *New York Evening Post* and turn it into an abolitionist propaganda organ. From time to time

**37**

during the next few years, *Herald* editorials were devoted to reviving the fear of this conspiracy. Then in the fall of 1838 as part of a campaign against the Locofocos, an insurgent group in the state's Democratic Party, Bennett claimed that the abolitionists, Locofocos, and English radicals were allies in a plot to destroy America. In one issue Bennett warned:

> This is no fancied picture. We are on the brink of danger. . . . The abolitionists of England are operating here. *We know the fact.* Between now and the election we shall develop a conspiracy that will astonish the whole Union.[31]

Soon after Bennett sailed for England, letters appeared in the *Herald* providing evidence of a great international abolitionist conspiracy. Abolitionists were even accused of fomenting a revolution in Canada against English rule.[32]

Obviously, Bennett hoped to sell newspapers to anti-English readers, and this reporting of an abolitionist plot was the publicity stunt of one single editor. However, such writers as Catherine Beecher, in her *Essay on Slavery,* the editors of the *Boston Transcript,* the *Eastern Argus* of Portland, Maine, and the magazine *North American Review* also put forward the idea of an English abolitionist conspiracy. James Kirke Paulding, who had been so critical of Mrs. Trollope, pointed to an English abolitionist conspiracy in his book *Letters from the South.* Paulding launched into an attack on the British for their interference. He insisted that this was part of a plot of European despots against Americans and their institutions, a plot launched because these despots were in danger of being overthrown: "This hostile feeling toward our national character and institutions had lately assumed a new and more mischievous disguise. It came masked under the semblance of humanity toward the slave." [33]

George Thompson's reception upon his visit to America was perhaps the most convincing evidence of how strongly northerners resented foreign criticism of slavery and foreign activity in the American antislavery movement. When a mob in Boston attacked William Lloyd Garrison in October 1835, the police probably saved his life by shouting, "He's an American, he's an American." Actually, the mob had wanted not Garrison, but the English reformer and abolitionist George Thompson. Thompson, who had been touring the New England states on behalf of the abolitionists, had already faced hostile crowds in New Hampshire and Massachusetts.[34] Almost every newspaper in New England condemned him, and his announced visit to Boston led to warnings that he would meet a crowd ready to use violent means to silence him, were he to attempt to speak there.[35]

In their attacks on Thompson northern newspaper and magazine editors constantly emphasized his nationality. Insisting that an Englishman had no right to interfere in America's internal affairs, they reminded their readers that foreigners like Thompson had called Americans sinners or apologists for sin, and that Englishmen failed to appreciate the complicated nature of the American slavery problem. The editors usually concluded by attributing Thompson's calls for immediate abolition to his ignorance or his desire to see American institutions destroyed. The Philadelphia *United States Gazette* condemned the Boston riot, but called Thompson an interfering foreigner and later reiterated a charge printed in the *New York Commercial Advertiser* that Thompson had urged slaves to cut their masters' throats.[36] Both papers insisted that Thompson had once stolen money. Lynde Walter, editor of the *Boston Transcript,* accused Thompson of being "a wandering insurrectionist" and pointed specifically to what the editor believed to be an attempt to break up Andover Theological Seminary.[37] Soon thereafter, the *Transcript* published the following notice:

### THOMPSON THE ABOLITIONIST

That infamous foreign scoundrel Thompson will hold forth this afternoon at *The Liberator* office no. 46 Washington Street. The present is a fair opportunity for the friends of the Union to smoke Thompson out! It will be a contest of the Union. A purse of $100 has been raised by a number of patriotic citizens to reward the individual who shall first lay violent hands on Thompson so that he may be brought to the tar kettle before dark! Friends of the Union be vigilant! [38]

Editor Walter insisted no American should put up with such action by a foreigner. This was four months before the Boston riot. During these four months Thompson began his tour and riot-inciting anti-Thompson remarks were published by many newspapers, including the Providence *Rhode Island Country Journal,* the *New Bedford Mercury,* the *Boston Transcript,* the *New York Commercial Advertiser,* and others.[39] The editor of the *Eastern Argus* referred to Thompson as a man touring through the "Northern and Middle States at the expense of the good old ladies of Glasgow." [40]

The New Hampshire legislature singled Thompson out in its report on abolition, called him a foreign conspirator, and those American abolitionists who invited him to this country "deceivers of the American people." [41] Thus, the Boston riot was the outgrowth of the frequent intolerant remarks made by respectable sources. This antiforeign reaction obviously reflected a strong American nationalism.

The 1830's are frequently characterized as a period of buoyant optimism based on the great economic and geographic expansion of the time. During this decade, also, many Americans believed that their political institutions might serve as a model to the rest of the world, that this was America's mission. All this optimism and these beliefs were expressed in the form of a vigorous nationalistic spirit. Yet, the defense of those American institutions sometimes took the shape of an antiforeign, anti-abolitionist crusade. The South was, of course, part of America, a region to which northerners looked with pride, and criticism of the South could be construed as an attack on America. Abolitionists who denounced the South, whether foreign or

American touched a sensitive spot; for northern respect and admiration, even pride in that region, were surprisingly great. Northerners in the 1830's thought the object of abolitionist efforts—the Negro—inferior, and the object of abolitionist attacks—the southern planter—superior.

In *Cavalier and Yankee* William Taylor has argued that the northern public, for the most part, was favorably inclined toward the planter. Taylor's findings and my own observations come together to suggest that the North in the 1830's had a romantic image of the South.[42] Northern novelists often glorified the South. It was not the South alone that created the image of the gentleman planter: he was a national myth with a national connotation. To many northerners the planter, by living close to nature and at the same time displaying all the social graces, proved that the freedom of the American frontier was compatible with order and morality: American freedom would not lead to French revolutionary license. The northerner read of planters who, though wealthy, shunned excessive display or pursuit of wealth, but instead selflessly turned to law and politics. In other words, the northerner found the southern planter the ideal citizen of a republic of virtue. Therefore, many northerners refused even to listen to abolitionist denunciations of the slaveholder.

The romance of southern plantation life was given full play in James Kirke Paulding's *Letter from the South,* and in John Pendleton Kennedy's *Swallow Barn* which was one of the most popular novels of the day. Kennedy, a native of the Delaware Valley, described a plantation life that had lost some of its greatness, but that still had much of the old romantic tradition about it. John A. McClung described the idyllic plantation life in his novel *Camden, A Tale of the South,* and the anonymous author of *Rose-Hill* offered a similar picture of southern life. These were only a few of the many novels glorifying the South.

Novelists were not the only northerners sympathetic to the South. A New Hampshire legislative committee concluded by assuring southerners that northerners "are not yet prepared to hear with complacency the intelligent planters, the able politicians, the high-minded men of the South, denounced as traitors to the cause of religion, as harsh and unfeeling masters." [43]

Even though most northerners disliked slavery, they were extremely careful to point out the dangers of ending the institution and to insist that it was a southern matter. This position was developed into an argument as to the constitutionality of ending slavery and the legal and social ramifications of its abolition. We will consider these arguments in the next chapter. Whatever the reasons, many northerners insisted that any attempt by abolitionists outside the South to end slavery constituted meddling by outsiders.

In April 1833 the *New York Evening Post* printed an editorial concerning relations between North and South. The paper noted that "certain nullification journals . . . are trying to excite the prejudice of the South against the

North in relation to the question of slavery." [44] In addition, the editorial continued, a small group in the North was advocating immediate emancipation and opposition to the Colonization Society. This latter group, the editors assured the South, had been trying for several years to win widespread support in the North, but without success. The paper decried the efforts of a few extremists to create North-South tension.

But the slavery question remained after the nullification controversy had ended, and the *Post* made frequent reference to the problem. In June 1833 the paper came out editorially for colonization. In August, *Post* editor William Cullen Bryant attacked the abolitionists. Noting that most Northerners regretted the existence of slavery in America, the editor insisted:

> There is not the slightest disposition to interfere in any improper and offensive manner, except among certain fanatical persons, and those few in number, we regard it to be as well settled as any fact in relation to public opinion ever discussed in the public journals. [45]

A contributor to the New York *Knickerbocker Magazine* warned his readers with regard to abolitionists, "Each man has his hobby, in riding which, it would be well for him not to trample on the rights of his neighbor." [46] The *Eastern Argus* of Portland, Maine, denounced the abolitionists even more vigorously. The *Argus's* editor noted the agreement among almost all northern papers in their

anti-abolitionist stand and called slavery a southern problem. However, he decried anti-abolitionist meetings, insisting that the South wanted a silencing of any discussion of
slavery, whether favorable or unfavorable.[47]

Many northerners insisted that the slavery problem must
be left to southerners to solve. In 1832 the Colonization
Society journal the *African Repository* referring to the new
abolitionists for the first time, expressed its strong disap-
proval of "the crude and fantastic notions of a few *radicals*
or *ultras* . . . who undertake not only to judge what the
South must do, but to do it for them." [48] A writer who
called himself "a Connecticut man" and a former abolitionist proclaimed that any northern interference would only
slow down emanciption and that southerners were best
equipped to handle the problem.[49] The *Boston Transcript*
and the *Knickerbocker Magazine* also made this point.[50]
James Fenimore Cooper insisted, in a chapter on slavery in
his book *The American Democrat,* that for the North slavery was only an abstract question of principle while for the
South it was of the highest practical importance. Thus it
was the South that was best prepared to deal with slavery,
and northern interference in this delicate matter could lead
only to the worst kind of disorder.[51]

Cooper accused the abolitionists of prejudice by which
he meant the tendency of one group to try to force its ideas
on another. In discussing this question the author took the
reformers to task. What right, he asked, had one part of the
country to try to force its customs upon another? [52]

As to the right to petition, Cooper noted that Congress was "not bound to waste its time in listening to and in discussing the matter of petitions, on the merits of which that body has already decided," while states were legally prevented from petitioning. "The danger of the practice is derived from the tendency of creating local feelings, through the agency of local government, and of thus endangering the peace of the union." [53] Once again it was a matter of imposing on the rest of the country the standards of one section, standards that might be set up by a small but vocal minority within that section.

Catherine Beecher warned in her attack on the abolitionists that the North should not interfere in the affairs of the South. Moral suasion, the method used by all reformers, would be effective only when an individual exhorted the community of which he was part; an outsider would only cause resentment. Thus, the abolitionists had no business exhorting the South and indeed were only causing resentment there.[54]

The arguments put forward by northerners against outside interference in a southern problem was in some quarters carried far beyond just insistence on the southerner's right to handle his own affairs. Abolition seemed to endanger all of American society, for its demands to end slavery raised legal questions, fears of a future Negro-white society, and other seemingly dangerous issues of national concern.

# NOTES

1. Samuel May, *Recollections of the Anti-Slavery Conflict* (Cambridge, Mass. 1869), p. 144.
2. Though not all visiting foreign writers despaired at conditions in America, there were enough denunciatory statements to arouse the public. Almost every American newspaper and magazine of the period I have examined (more than 50) attacked one or more hostile foreign critics.
3. The editors of several magazines attacked all Englishmen who denounced Americans for condoning slavery. See the *North American Review* (Boston), XLI (1835), 170–171; *American Quarterly Observer* (Boston), January, 1833, pp. 95–101. See *Atkinson's Saturday Evening Post* (Philadelphia), June 13, 1835, p. 141, for a bitter attack on Gustave de Beaumont and his antislavery novel *Marie*.
4. Frances Trollope, *Domestic Manners of the Americans* (4th ed., London and New York, 1832), p. 56.
5. *Ibid.*, pp. 29–30.
6. Asa Greene, *Travels in America* (New York, 1833). The *New York Mirror,* October 19, 1833, p. 127, praised Greene's book.
7. James K. Paulding, *The Lion of the West* (new ed.; Stanford, Calif., 1954), *passim*.
8. Greene, *op. cit.,* p. 1.
9. Harriet Martineau, *Society in America* (New York, 1837), *passim*.
10. Such attacks appeared in the *North American Review,* XLI (July, 1835), 181; the *Boston Transcript,* February 5, 9, 1839; the *New York Herald,* October 20, 1838; the *New York Review and Quarterly Church Journal,* III, 5, 130–133.
11. Seymour Drescher, "America and French Romanticism during the July Monarchy," *American Quarterly,* XI (Spring 1959), 3–21.
12. Drescher cites Balzac, Chateaubriand, Dumas père, Hugo, Lamartine, and others.
13. *Ibid.,* p. 18.
14. Gustave de Beaumont, *Marie, or Slavery in the United States* (new ed.; Stanford, Calif., 1959), *passim*.

15. *Ibid.,* p. 78.
16. *Ibid.,* pp. 123–124.
17. Calvin Colton, *The Americans* (London, 1833). Colton, a prominent New Yorker and member of the American Colonization Society, denounced the abolitionists in two books: *Colonization and Abolition Contrasted* (Philadelphia, 1835), *passim,* and *Abolition a Sedition* (Philadelphia, 1839), *passim.*
18. Colton, *The Americans,* p. 14.
19. *Ibid.,* p. 156. This argument was frequently used by northerners in their attacks on the British.
20. *Ibid.,* pp. 156–157. Of some 50 newspapers examined, only one, the *New York Herald,* was opposed to the work of the Colonization Society. In their attacks on the abolitionists these papers often mentioned that the work of the antislavery men might endanger the possible success of the colonizing scheme. Thus, Colton was stating a familiar argument.
21. John Quincy Adams, *Diary* (Allan Nevins, ed., New York, 1951), p. 462.
22. Catherine E. Beecher, *An Essay on Slavery and Abolitionism* (Philadelphia, 1837), p. 145.
23. *Boston Transcript,* March 11, 1836.
24. C. Beecher, *op. cit.,* pp. 44–45; *North American Review,* XLI, 1835, 170–171.
25. The *New York Commercial Advertiser,* quoted by the *Liberator* (Boston), October, 1833.
26. Samuel F. B. Morse, *Foreign-Conspiracy against the Liberties of the United States* (6th ed., New York, 1844).
27. See Vernon Stauffer, *New England and the Bavarian Illuminati* (New York, 1918), for the best discussion of the efforts of Jedidiah Morse and other New England Federalists to raise the specter of a Masonic conspiracy.
28. The standard work is Ray Allen Billington, *The Protestant Crusade 1800–1860* (New York, 1938).
29. See David Brion Davis, "Some Themes of Counter-Subversion: An Analysis of Anti-Masonic, Anti-Catholic, and Anti-Mormon Literature," *Mississippi Valley Historical Review* XLVII (September 1960), 205–224, and Lorman Ratner, "Anti-Masonry in New York,

An Aspect of Pre-Civil-War Reform" (unpublished master's essay, Cornell University, 1958), for discussions of the conspiracy theme in the anti-Masonic movement of the 1820's.

30. *New York Herald,* October 17, 19, 1835.
31. *Ibid.,* October 19, 1835.
32. *Ibid.,* October 20, 1838.
33. James K. Paulding, *Slavery in the United States* (New York, 1836), pp. 117–118.
34. See Theodore Lyman, Jr., *Papers Relating to the Garrison Mob* (Cambridge, Mass., 1870), p. 21.
35. Thompson spoke in Concord and Nashua, New Hampshire, Lowell and Lynn, Massachusetts, and many smaller towns on his tour of the northern New England states.
36. *United States Gazette* (Philadelphia), February 5, 1836.
37. *Boston Transcript,* July 21, 1835. On August 8 the *Transcript* reported that a mob had broken up a Thompson meeting in Lynn; in late August a meeting of prominent Bostonians at Faneuil Hall produced a resolution calling for the silencing of Thompson. In October, when rumors circulated that Thompson was in Boston, a notice was posted calling for all citizens to join in tarring him and running him out of town. Then came the Garrison riot, precipitated because the opponents of antislavery believed Thompson would be the main speaker at an abolitionist meeting.
38. See Lyman, *op. cit.,* p. 14.
39. On March 11, 1836, the *Transcript* denounced Thompson, the Irish leader Daniel O'Connell, and the English radical Fanny Wright, for being meddling foreigners, because they spoke in America against slavery. The *New Bedford Mercury* (Mass.), October 30, 1835, denounced Thompson as an English fanatic. The *Newburyport Daily Herald* (Mass.), October 24, 1835, followed the same line; so did the *Eastern Argus* (Portland, Me.), August 7, 1835, and many other New England and New York papers I examined.
40. *Eastern Argus,* August 7, 1835.
41. Samuel May Collection Tract #261 (Cornell University Library, Ithaca, N. Y.).
42. See William R. Taylor, *Cavalier and Yankee* (New York, 1961). Taylor argues convincingly that northerners had a great deal to do

with the creation of the myth of the South and the southern planter. My studies of the literature of the period led me to a similar conclusion before reading Taylor's work.

An interesting discussion related to Taylor's thesis is raised by Perry Miller in "The Romantic Dilemma in American Nationalism and the Concept of Nature," *Harvard Theological Review,* XLVI (October, 1955), 239–254. Miller discusses Americans' fear that romantic nature is gone, and with it those virtues ascribed to nature and so distinctly American. The ideal image of the republic was of a virtuous, often agrarian, people. This virtue would be lost if we became a commercial nation. The similarity of Miller's views with those of Taylor, and most recently Charles Sanford, in *The Quest for Moral Paradise* (Urbana, Ill., 1961), is obvious.

43. Samuel May Collection Tract #261.
44. *New York Evening Post,* April 25, 1833.
45. *Ibid.,* August 7, 1833.
46. *Knickerbocker Magazine,* XI (1837), 321.
47. *Eastern Argus,* August 7, 1835.
48. *African Repository* (Washington, D.C.), VIII, 143.
49. Anon., *An Inquiry into the Condition and Prospects of the African Race in the United States and the Means of Bettering its Fortunes.* (Philadelphia, 1839), p. 149.
50. *Boston Transcript,* December 22, 1832; *Knickerbocker Magazine,* XI (1838), 328.
51. James F. Cooper, *The American Democrat* (new ed.; New York, 1931), p. 170.
52. *Ibid.,* p. 53.
53. *Loc. cit.*
54. C. Beecher, *op. cit.,* pp. 12–14, 35–36.

# 3

---

# *The Union, States' Rights, and Individual Rights*

The first two chapters have concentrated on anti-abolitionism's foundation on racism, its resentment of foreigners interfering in America and of outsiders meddling in southern affairs. This chapter will consider another series of responses to antislavery: the argument that abolition endangered the Union, challenged states' rights, and intruded on the rights of individuals. The abolitionists saw their cause as the freeing of enslaved Negroes, but in working to free the Negroes they unintentionally raised meaningful and complex legal and constitutional problems. The abolitionists could have been rationally challenged on these points; yet, here as elsewhere, anti-abolitionism was usually expressed in slogans and emotional appeals rather than in rational argument. James Kirke Paulding's attitude was typical:

> It [abolition] has become the fruitful theme of calumny, declamation and contention; the stalking horse of political parties and fanatical reformers. It has . . . disturbed the peace of communities and states. It menaces the disruption of our social system, and tends directly to a separation of the Union. . . . The obligations of the truth have been sacrificed to unmitigated reproach, and the laws and Constitution of the country attempted to be trampled underfoot, in the hot pursuit of the rights of humanity. The feeling and good name of millions of our fellow-citizens have been grossly assailed, their rights invaded, their firesides and social institutions disturbed, and their lives endangered without any regard to the dictates of our moral code. . . . In asserting the natural rights of one class of men, the Constitutional rights of another have been denounced as violations of the law of God . . . unbrotherly warfare has been, still is waging against a large portion of the good citizens of the United States, which, if continued, must inevitably separate this prosperous and happy union.[1]

The 1830's have been characterized both as a time when Unionism, personified by Andrew Jackson, grew strong and when states' rights, personified in John Calhoun and the nullification controversy, was also on the upswing. These two ideas were compatible, and indeed both were strongly evident at the same time. The Union was viewed in a mystical sense. It was the compact of states engaged in the task of economic growth and territorial expansion. States' rights, however, was a legalistic concept. The old Jeffersonian localism called for government to operate primarily on the local level. The Union would accomplish the great goals of society while the states would be responsible for its day-to-day operations. Many northerners feared that the abolitionists threatened the existence of the Union by raising an issue that might force a group of states to secede. The abolitionists seemed to threaten the localist equality position by demanding federal action on slavery, which was almost universally viewed as a state matter.

Whatever the actual danger of disunion in the nullification controversy, it raised the specter of disunion just as the new abolitionists appeared. Although the antislavery men made no appeal at this time to expel the South from the Union (on the contrary, the sinners were to be saved), the northern public thought that antislavery efforts would further agitate an already aroused South.

Following a lengthy discussion of nullification, the editor of the *Boston Transcript* warned:

> It cannot be doubted that if the course provided by the editor of *The Liberator,* and his collaborator was generally countenanced by the people of the non-slaveholding states . . . it would tend to the speedy disintegration of the

Union. New England would be disloyal to the federal compact. . . . The fact is that comparatively speaking, few persons sanctioned these measures, who understand their actual bearing on the slaves, the free blacks, or the white citizens of the South.[2]

Two years later, when George Thompson was due to appear in Boston, the *Transcript* carried the text of an anti-Thompson circular mentioned earlier in which the writers made clear that to attack Thompson was to defend the Union.

Northern politicians, partly reflecting their constituents' views and partly fearful of party division should slavery become an issue, objected to abolition as dangerous to the Union. Thus Edward Everett, while serving as governor of Massachusetts in 1837, made a special point of attacking the abolitionists. Everett insisted the Union could have been founded only with the compromise on slavery, and that abolition would divide the Union.[3] State Attorney General James Austin also warned of civil war if abolition prevailed.[4]

Massachusetts Democrats agreed with their political opponents on many of these points. Democratic leader Robert Rantoul, Jr., claimed the abolitionists were looking for an opportunity to destroy the Union.[5] As early as 1831 George Bancroft made it clear that, though unsympathetic to slavery, he was unwilling to attack it. In 1834, Bancroft delivered his only speech on the subject before 1854. The historian-politician noted that slavery had destroyed Rome, but he was careful neither to ask nor to imply that Americans should end the institution at once. Bancroft's most recent biographer, Russel Nye, claims that Bancroft thought a moderate stand on antislavery might win some votes, but instead Bancroft discovered that it cost him support; he then avoided the subject until the 1850's, when popular sentiment had changed.[6] Bancroft was one of a number of prominent Americans whose attitude toward antislavery changed from hostile to friendly.

Martin Van Buren frequently remarked on his dislike of the abolitionists, and his political allies constantly pointed out that he was a Union man strongly opposed to any movement that might encourage secession.[7] The Democratic president of the Pennsylvania State Senate, James Burden, remarked that the Union could never have been formed if the Founding Fathers had not compromised on the slavery question. "Modern abolitionism," Burden insisted, "had upset the spirit of compromise." [8]

Calvin Colton went even further and insisted the abolitionists were conspiring to destroy the Union, and that destruction of the Union was their avowed goal. In a book entitled *Abolition a Sedition* Colton announced that he would prove that abolition was "at war with the genius and letter of the Federal Constitution and of the Constitutions of the States respectively, and with that compact which created the Union." [9] He believed that by proving this "then clearly there will be presented a constitutional basis on which the movement can be opposed, and by which, if it shall become necessary it can be suppressed." [10] Colton began his discussion by stating that the antislavery movement had started as a religious crusade, but those who sought to use it for political ends had perverted it: "These men turned abolition into a political organization independent of any government, usurping the powers of government." He concluded that the Anti-Slavery Society had become an independent power—self-erected, self-governed, independent, and irresponsible—which sought to destroy the union.[11] He quoted from a number of abolitionist letters and tracts to prove that from its origin the Society had intended political action.[12]

The alleged abolitionist threat to the Union was often coupled with the accusation that the antislavery men were calling upon the federal government to infringe on the rights of states. The anti-abolitionists were not necessarily contradicting themselves by supporting the Union while maintaining the right of states to determine slavery policy. As ardent a Unionist as Daniel Webster insisted that slavery was a state matter and that only the states involved could legislate to end the institution within their borders.[13] Webster was willing to defend the abolitionists' right to petition Congress as long as those petitions called for ending slavery in the District of Columbia, the only area in which he thought Congress had such authority. On several occasions Webster called for the end of slavery in the federal district, but he wrote off any other abolitionist plans as illegal.[14] Typically, Webster opposed the abolitionists as well as slavery.

James Fenimore Cooper insisted that slavery was a state matter outside federal government jurisdiction, though he did think that Congress, by constitutional amendment, could put an end to slavery. But, he continued,

> It would be madness for Congress, in the state of the Country, to attempt to propose an amendment of the Constitution, to abolish slavery altogether, as . . . it would infallibly fail, thereby raising an irritating question without an object.[15]

In 1835 Governor William L. Marcy of New York received requests from several southern governors to return alleged fugitive slaves. Marcy agreed to return the slaves and called on the state legislature to approve his decision. In his message the governor called the abolitionists fanatics and defended southern states' rights.[16] The New York *National Trades Union* denied that Congress even had the right to end slavery in the District of Columbia.[17] The New Hampshire state legislature, as part of a lengthy denunciation of abolition, assured the South that they considered slavery purely a state matter.[18] Paulding's fear that abolition could be accomplished only at the price of disunion and the violation of states' rights was thus taken up and echoed by other critics of antislavery.

The abolitionists were vulnerable to attack as a menace

to the Union and to the rights of states; in addition, abolition's apparent threat to the rights of individuals was frequently cited. One of the abolitionists' basic arguments was
that the slave was a human and that his slave condition
deprived him of his rights, the rights of an American. Anti-
abolitionists found a number of grounds on which to challenge this contention. As we saw in Chapter One, northern
racists denied that the Negro was an equal of the white.
Some northerners argued that the inferior Negro should be
deprived of equal status, that he needed to be kept enslaved
for his own good, and that to offer him equal rights would
endanger the right of northern workingmen to jobs, or
deny southern slaveholders their right to a healthy economy or to security from race violence.

James Fenimore Cooper took the stand that the abolitionist insistence on the right of the Negro to equal status,
or even to freedom, raised a theoretical problem about the
meaning of equality. To Cooper equality was a relative
thing; all men were obviously not created equal; the blacks
and whites, for example, were unequal. In America, under
the democratic system, there was more equality than in
other countries, but Americans quite properly rejected
absolute equality. "The very existence of government at all,
inferred inequality." [19]

Slavery, Cooper noted, was an institution as old as
human history and would probably continue just as long as
some men were in a more advanced state of civilization
than others. Slavery was no more sinful "than it is sinful to

wear a whole coat, while another is in tatters, to eat a better meal than a neighbor, or otherwise to enjoy feast and plenty, while our fellow creatures are suffering and in want." [20] This, then, was the kind of inequality that Cooper believed democracy should leave as is. "According to the doctrines of Christ, we are to do as we would be done by, but this law is not applied to slavery more than to any other interest in life. It is quite possible to be an excellent Christian and slaveholder, and the relations of master and slave, may be a means of exhibiting some of the mildest graces of the character." [21] Cooper could see how, in some ways, the slave benefited from his condition, and he cited the argument that the Negro was better off a slave in civilized America than a free man in barbarous Africa.[22]

Like almost all those who wrote on slavery, James Kirke Paulding discussed the question of whether it was a contradiction of the doctrine of equal rights. He argued that equal rights meant that those who could get rights were entitled to them and denied automatic equality of rights for all. In war slaves were taken, and this was not looked on as a violation of equal rights.[23]

Calvin Colton also engaged in the discussion about equality. As for the argument that slavery was a contradiction of American doctrines, Colton made the point that liberty meant not freedom, but willingness to submit to a government of laws. Laws in themselves were a kind of subjection. Equality meant not some romantic notion of natural rights, but simply the destruction of any kind of feudal privilege; that is, the denial of legal privileges to any special group.[24]

Cooper, Paulding, and Colton met the abolitionist claim that Negroes deserved equal rights by challenging the abolitionist interpretation of equality. From many other quarters came arguments that Negroes either were inferior, and so did not deserve equality, or that because of their inferiority legal equality would actually harm the Negro. One writer in the *North American Review* insisted that "abolitionist proposals would lead Negroes to believe they were equal to whites with dire consequences for both."[25] The editor of the *American Quarterly Observer* argued that slavery was best for the Negro; that the Bible did not condemn the institution; that slave owners were neither unjust nor cruel; that other republics had had slavery; that white society profited by having slaves to do menial tasks, for thus white labor could do more respectable and useful work, and this prevented extreme class differences among whites.[26]

Though few northerners defended slavery this vigorously, Lynde Walter of the *Boston Transcript* did insist that the Negro was unfit for citizenship.[27] James Austin noted that abolition would not end the whites' belief in the Negroes' inferiority.[28] Novelist Robert Montgomery Bird, in a section of his book *Sheppard Lee,* insisted slaves wanted to remain in that condition and considered freedom a punishment.[29] In January 1834 the editor of the American Colonization Society's journal the *African Repository* declared, "Let the abolitionist give up his cause as impossible of execution, hateful to the community, ruinous to the cause of the blacks, and founded upon principles wrong in themselves." [30]

It was even argued that, accepting the need to free the slave, the abolitionist movement would delay rather than further that end. Calvin Colton, among others, insisted that the abolitionists had made discussion of slavery with southerners impossible, had forced the South to take a more radical stand on the issue, and so had actually hurt the cause of the Negro.[31] Another New Yorker, Doctor David M. Reese, a prominent physician and an active temperance advocate, said that he favored the kind of antislavery opinion expressed by such national heroes as Franklin, Jefferson, and John Jay.[32] These men, though they worked for ending slavery, tolerated the slaveholder. They recognized that slavery was an evil but felt that holding a slave was not a sin in itself. Reese insisted that these great men were the true abolitionists and true philanthropists.[33]

Robert M. Bird thought that the abolitionists were selfishly motivated. In *Peter Pilgrim,* Bird chided the abolitionists, saying:

I was somewhat of an abolitionist myself, quite desirous to see all the poor blackies as free as blackbirds; but then I saw clear enough, they never could be liberated, without ruining their masters, as well as all the agricultural interests of the South, unless some means could be devised for supplying their loss, by finding substitutes for them.[34]

The substitute was a mechanical "nigger" who would do all the work and prevent all the moral problems. Bird's central character presented his scheme to the abolition society:

> They could not bear that they should lose the honour, and glory, and profit of completing the great work of emancipation that I, who was not actually a professed member of their society or that anybody save themselves, should reap the splendid regard; and, accordingly, they knocked my model to pieces, maltreated myself, and ended by charging me with madness and bringing me to this place in a strait jacket.[35]

The debate as to the true meaning of equality, that the Negro slave should not have equality, or that abolition was not the best way to attain this, all were indeed theoretical arguments. But at least one group of northerners, the spokesmen for the northern workingmen, viewed the question as a practical one.[36] To this group abolition posed two basic problems. First, it deflected attention away from the plight of northern white laborers who, these men insisted, needed more help than the slaves. Second, if abolitionists succeeded in freeing slaves, the freedmen would flood the northern labor market and deprive northern whites of their right to earn a living. Some workingmen's groups were among the most outspoken and vitriolic of all anti-abolitionists.

The leaders of the crusade for the preservation of America as the land of the simple yeoman artisans made it clear that they spoke of white yeoman-artisans. To include the Negro would be to raise a divisive issue that the workingmen's movement wished to avoid.

The *New York Post*'s acting editor William Leggett insisted that, rather than working for the Negro, the abolitionists were actually "aristocrats," and that antislavery was an aristocratic plot to overthrow the Democrats. In February 1835 Leggett branded the abolitionists as tools of those business interests whose only concern was a supply of cheap labor.[37] George H. Evans, Seth Luther, and the editor of the *National Trades Union* all pictured abolitionists as men who sought to use the spirit of philanthropy for their own selfish purposes. Luther and the *National Trades Union* editor stressed that antislavery was a diversion from the true object of reform.

In 1833, in his *Address to the Workingmen of New England on the State of Education,* Luther decried the lowly condition of the northern laborer as even lower than European labor or slave labor in the South. In the same year he wrote: "We have the philanthopists moaning over the fate of the Southern slave when there are *thousands* of children in this State as truly slaves as the blacks in the South." [38] Evans, the editor of *The Workingman's Advocate,* published in New York, told his readers that abolitionists were men "actuated by a species of theological fanaticism, [who] hoped to free the slaves *more* for the purpose of adding them to their religious sect, than for love of liberty and justice." [39]

Other labor reformers joined the attack on the abolitionists. Orestes Brownson, in the October 1838 issue of the *Boston Quarterly Review,* pointed out that the wage system in the North was far worse than chattel slavery.[40] Labor-paper editor A. H. Wood noted that although workers should oppose slavery, they must also face the fact of job competition from free Negroes.[41] In the issue of September 17, 1836, the editor of the *National Laborer* stated that he opposed slavery, yet he urged the white laborer to look after his own condition before worrying about that of the Negro slaves.[42] In 1838 William Leggett wrote to abolitionist leader James Birney that he was powerless to stop the editor of the *New Era,* a labor journal, from attacking the abolitionists.[43]

Though not involved in the workingman's movement, James Paulding claimed that the slave was not completely at the mercy of the master, that there were certain legal restrictions on the master, and that the slave was better off than the northern or English industrial worker.[44]

Since northerners believed abolitionists threatened and might even destroy the legal, constitutional basis of the country, it was logical for those who opposed antislavery to assume that abolition would bring about the destruction of law and the Constitution, and thus general disorder would sweep the land. Northerners often equated abolitionists with violence—even though it was the reformers who were the targets of the violence—and gave the violence cited as a reason why abolitionist appeals must be rejected.

## NOTES

1. James K. Paulding, *Slavery in the United States* (New York, 1836), pp. 5–6.
2. *Boston Transcript,* December 22, 1832.
3. Paul R. Frothingham, *Edward Everett* (Boston and New York, 1925), p. 131.
4. James T. Austin, *Remarks on Dr. Channing's Slavery by a Citizen of Massachusetts* (Boston, 1835), pp. 45–46.
5. Luther Hamilton, ed., *Memoirs, Speeches and Writings of Robert Rantoul Jr.* (Boston, 1854), p. 719.
6. Russel B. Nye, *George Bancroft* (New York, 1944), pp. 104–106.
7. *Albany Argus,* July 23, 1835.
8. J. R. Burden, *Remarks of Dr. J. R. Burden of Philadelphia County in the Senate of Pennsylvania on the Abolition Question, February 18, 1838* (Philadelphia, 1838), p. 6.
9. Calvin Colton, *Abolition a Sedition* (Philadelphia, 1839), p. 2.
10. *Ibid.,* p. 2.
11. *Ibid.,* p. 3.
12. *Ibid.,* p. 6.
13. Claude M. Fuess, "Daniel Webster and the Abolitionists," *Massachusetts Historical Society Proceedings,* LXIV (1930–1932), 28.
14. J. W. McIntyre, ed., *The Writings and Speeches of Daniel Webster* (Boston, 1903), XII, 210.
15. James F. Cooper, *The American Democrat* (New York, 1931), p. 188.
16. Quoted in the *Albany Argus,* December 29, 1835.
17. *National Trades Union,* July 12, 1834.
18. Samuel May Collection Tract #261 (Cornell University Library).
19. Cooper, *op. cit.,* p. 42.
20. *Ibid.,* p. 162.
21. *Ibid.,* pp. 165–166.
22. *Ibid.,* p. 166.
23. Paulding, *op. cit.,* p. 25.
24. Colton, *op. cit.,* p. 122.

25. *North American Review* (Boston), XXXV (1832), 128–142.
26. *American Quarterly Observer* (Boston), I (1833), 95–101.
27. *Boston Transcript,* December 22, 1832.
28. Austin, *op. cit.,* p. 44.
29. Robert M. Bird, *Sheppard Lee* (New York, 1836), I, 23.
30. *African Repository* (Washington, D.C.), IX, 330.
31. Colton, *op. cit.,* p. 122.
32. David Reese, *The Humbugs of New York* (New York, 1838), pp. 143–164. Reese stressed the differences between such abolitionists as Jefferson, Franklin, Jay and those "modern abolitionists," whom he termed "ultra." The ultra abolitionists, he warned, were flooding the country with literature, trying to move into the churches, and were supported by "pseudo-philanthropists."
33. *Ibid.,* pp. 163–164.
34. Robert M. Bird, *Peter Pilgrim* (2 vols., Philadelphia, 1838), I, 106.
35. *Ibid.,* p. 107.
36. Walter Hugins, *Jacksonian Democracy and the Workingman's Party,* New York, 1960, and William Sullivan, "Did Labor Support Andrew Jackson?" *Political Science Quarterly* (New York), LXII (December, 1947), 569–580, note the non-labor character of these parties. Edward Pessen, however, in "The Workingman's Movement of the Jacksonian Era," *Mississippi Valley Historical Review,* XLIII (December, 1956), insists the parties were truly composed of workingmen. In either case, the reform character of those parties seems clear. Whether purely a political body or a labor movement, the workingmen's parties were supporters of a great variety of reforms and dreamed of the good society.

    For more detailed accounts of the relation of labor to slavery see Bernard Mandel, *Labor, Free and Slave* (New York, 1955); William H. Lofton, "Abolition and Labor," *Journal of Negro History,* XXXIII (July, 1948), 249–283, and Joseph Rayback, "The American Workingman and the Anti-Slavery Crusade," *Journal of Economic History,* III (November, 1943), 152–163. All three stress the diversity of attitudes among labor reformers on the abolition question. All agree that labor leaders were generally opposed to abolition.
37. *New York Evening Post,* February 10, 1835.
38. Seth Luther, *Address to the Workingmen of New England on the*

*State of Education,* quoted by Arthur Schlesinger, Jr., *The Age of Jackson* (Boston, 1953), p. 425.

39. *Workingman's Advocate,* New York, November 21, 1835.
40. *Boston Quarterly Review,* October, 1838.
41. See Bernard Mandel, *Labor, op. cit.,* pp. 81–84.
42. See Philip Foner, *History of the Labor Movement in the United States* (New York, 1947), p. 273.
43. See Dwight Dumond, ed., *The Letters of James Gillespie Birney* (Washington, D. C., 1938), I, 477.
44. Paulding, *op. cit.,* p. 123.

# 4

---•---

# *Fears of Radicalism and Violence*

The abolitionists continually faced the traditional northern belief in the inferiority of the Negro, and their efforts intensified rather than weakened it. Those who subscribed to this dogma of the Negro's inferiority frequently objected to abolitionism, claiming it was impractical in a biological sense, as well as politically and morally. Accordingly, abolitionists were described as impractical, as madmen, pseudo-philanthropists, and in other such terms.

The *Norwich Courier,* in Connecticut, defended the right of abolitionists to be heard but referred to their cause as "an insane project—one which no man in full possession and exercise of his faculties can contemplate as being practicable, or at the present desirable." [1] The *Connecticut Observer* and the *Hartford Observer* concurred in referring to abolition as "madness." [2] The *New England Magazine* in Boston, referred to the antislavery advocates as "rhymers, antiquarians, saints militant, and the like." [3] The editor considered these men "insane philanthropists espousing highly dangerous fanatic doctrines." [4] *American Quarterly Observer,* also published in Boston, used similar language and arguments when discussing antislavery.[5] The editor of the *Emporium and True American,* in Trenton, New Jersey, referred to abolitionists as "rum-mad fanatics who have become so infatuated that they will stop at nothing short of the emancipation of the whole slave population." [6]

Logically, since the anti-abolitionists argued that their opponents were impractical and visionary, they might have concluded that abolitionists could well be left to themselves without harmful results. But, as we have seen, there was a real fear of civil disunion and even armed conflict in the North of the 1830's. In addition to their deep apprehension about the Constitution, now increased by South Carolina's nullification efforts, northerners felt an even deeper terror of slave insurrection and race war in all parts of the country. Nat Turner's insurrection in 1832, and the revolt in the British West Indies, provided a plausible foundation for this fear. In 1835, in Baltimore, Maryland, Hezekiah Niles wrote in *Niles's Register*:

> During the last and present week we have cut out . . . more than *five hundred* articles, relating to the various *excitements* now acting on the people of the United States. . . . *Society seems everywhere unhinged. . . !* We have the slave question in many different forms, including the proceedings of *kidnappers* and *manstealers* and others belonging to the *free Negroes* . . . an awful political outcry is about to be raised to rally the poor against the rich. . . . The character of our country seems suddenly changed, and thousands interpret the law in their own way. . . . The Republic seems threatened.[7]

Accordingly, anti-abolitionists frequently seem to have felt that their opponents, although too unrealistic to achieve their goal, were dangerous in the context of the times. Thus they feared abolitionists, in their efforts to free the slaves, might "succeed" in nullifying the federal Union, dislocating northern society, and instigating rebellion and race war in the South.

The intensity of these fears was both a cause and a symptom of the fact that abolitionists were loosely identified with all sorts of radicals and social undesirables. Whig politicians equated the abolitionists with Locofocos, a supposedly radical insurgent group of New York Democrats, Democrats with Federalists. Conservatives believed that the abolitionists were Jacobins, while radicals saw them as agents of a conservative plot to overthrow democracy. James Gordon Bennett, though he too opposed abolition, chided his countrymen for their hysteria that led them to fear Catholics, abolitionists, bankers, gamblers, "or the what-nots." [8] Gordon was correct about the inaccuracy of these accusations; yet, they were effective in focusing sentiment against the abolitionists. They account for and symptomize the fact that the abolitionists were often dissociated from other, more widely-accepted, contemporary reforms, and that they were so consistently charged with endangering the political structure of the Union and the social fabric of America.

The case against the abolitionists was covered extensively by the editor of the *New York Commercial Advertiser*:

> Notwithstanding the strong censure applied by the whole country to the numerous publications from the same mischief-working press . . . the same coterie of pseudo-philanthropists have here put forth a more formidable and still more offensive publication in the face of warnings of North and South. . . . Not content with having distracted the churches, destroyed the peace of families and communities, embarrassed the literary and religious institutions, menaced the property and even the existence of the union, involved the officers of our government in dangerous perils, and created the most appalling apprehensions of a civil and servile war, they are still unmoved. . . .[9]

The writer noted that he had once considered the abolitionists well-meaning but misguided, but their latest publication, coming at this time of *crisis,* proved the antislavery men were determined to resist public opinion and risk the future of the country to attain their ends.[10] The *New York Evening Post* accused abolitionists of using fanatical tactics and the *New York Commercial Advertiser* denounced Garrison as a newspaper man unfit to set type.[11] Connecting Garrison with Nat Turner's revolt in Virginia, a slave uprising in which 57 whites and over 100 Negroes were killed, the editor insisted that "Garrison's rockets, harmless in the North, are torpedoes and infernal engines at the South and patriotism requires that they should be destroyed before they explode." [12]

Governor William L. Marcy of New York, in a statement in 1835, assured southerners that northerners considered abolitionists fanatics:

> Our citizens are generally aware of the mischief these proceedings [Anti-Slavery Convention] are doing among our southern brethren. Large and highly respectable public meetings in all parts of the State have already been assembled and have expressed their sentiments on the subject in the fullest possible terms of reprobation. . . . The feeling of almost the entire population here, is what the South could wish it to be. The powerful energy of public opinion has been brought to bear directly on this subject and has exerted and is now exerting a benign influence in repressing the fanaticism that has arisen in this section of the Union.[13]

Marcy referred to the abolitionists as "sinister, reckless, agitators." [14]

The editor of the *North American Review* in Boston observed that the Colonization Society, in contrast to abolition, "send abroad no influence to disturb the peace, or endanger the security or prosperity of any portion of the country." [15] A reviewer of *Slavery,* a book by the abolitionist Lydia Maria Child, criticized Mrs. Child for adhering to antislavery doctrines and listed his objections to abolition. He claimed abolitionists sought to arouse "public passions." [16]

James Kirke Paulding's anti-abolitionist attacks culminated in his insistence that abolition, like the other "violent reforms" with which it had associated, as a result of its perfectionist doctrines would lead to anarchy, dissension in society and in the churches, and even to destruction of the family. In the final chapter, "On the Fanaticism of the Abolitionists, and Its Hostility to Religion, Morals, Liberty, Patriotism, and Social Virtues," Paulding accused the abolitionists of inciting violence, of undermining the New and Old Testaments, of violating the sanctity of the home, and of defiling the country.[17]

The president of the Pennsylvania State Senate, James Burden, offered the most sweeping condemnation of all. As part of a long denunciation of abolition he stated:

It has held out expectations to the colored people which cannot be realized—it has led their young men to a course which has produced reaction—it has given to the wanton and unthinking excuse for persecution— . . . it has been humane in the abstract, but dreadfully cruel in the reality.[18]

If abolitionists were to continue, Burden warned the State Senate, southerners would be driven to such a state of fear that they would force all free Negroes to migrate to the North. This, he pointed out, in a year of severe economic depression might lead to additional wage competition which would further degrade both the free Negroes and the many whites then out of work. The white female would be forced to face "the dreadful choice of prostitution or starvation. Vice will increase greatly. Working men will be discouraged, families will shrink in size." [19] In other words, Burden described the breakdown of the entire social order, the destruction of everything from the family to the Union—all as a result of abolitionist activities.

Pennsylvania was not the only state in which political leaders branded abolitionists as reckless and fanatic agents of disunion, perpetrators of race war, and agents of a foreign power. Both political parties denied any association with the antislavery men and sought to brand their opponents as abolitionists. Unless these many political leaders completely misread the signs of the time, the northern public must have been generally and strongly anti-abolitionist.

Of all these alleged results of abolitionist radicalism, the most feared was actual violence. As we have seen, northerners in the 1830's had a fear of civil war, made more concrete now by South Carolina's nullification efforts, and strong fears of slave insurrections and race war. As we saw in Chapter Three, over the years there had been a number of incidents of unrest. These incidents together with the

Nat Turner rebellion of 1832 were placed by some at the abolitionists' door and seemed to justify apprehension.

Although abolitionists insisted that emancipation could be accomplished without violence, northern critics sometimes noted that violence had followed emancipation in the British West Indies. The New York *National Trades Union* claimed that emancipation in the West Indies had resulted in race violence and that a full-scale revolution was feared.[20] James Kirke Paulding took special note of the situation in the West Indies; he believed that emancipation there had done great harm to both Negroes and planters and had caused violence and general disorder.[21] Following the Nat Turner rebellion, the *New York Evening Post* carried a lengthy editorial which pointed out that there had been enough slave unrest to "cause the people of the more northern states to be ready, in case of need, to extend to the [southern whites] ample assistance in men and munitions." [22] Though the paper made no mention of abolitionists for a time, it carried reports that whites led the revolt. The Augusta, Maine, *Kennebec Weekly Journal* insisted that "we should give our southern brethren some assurance that while we depreciate the existence of slavery among them . . . we set our faces against all measures calculated to occasion the calamities they apprehended." [23] Another editor associated the American abolitionists with the radical movement responsible for the French Revolution, the demand for greater liberty in England, as well as with the agitation to emancipate American slaves.[24]

In August 1835 the *Boston Transcript* warned that immediate abolition would lead Negroes to insurrection and that the white population of the South was in danger. Though unsympathetic to the South, the *Transcript* wanted to make clear that southerners misjudged the North if they thought that section in any way condoned abolitionist doctrines which the South blamed for inciting servile insurrection, specifically the Nat Turner revolt.[25] The *Transcript* expressed concern over the "brute passions" of Negro slaves. The editor of the Maine *Eastern Argus* accused the abolitionists of fomenting slave revolts and remarked that the attempt of a Boston slave to kill his owner was the "fruit of abolition." [26]

For the *New Jersey Journal* the abolitionists were the cause rather than the victims of violence. The paper predicted servile war and even civil war, should abolition sweep the North.[27] The *Newburyport Daily Herald,* commenting on the anti-abolition riots in New York in October 1833, stated that, though opposed to mob violence, it had "no sympathy with the anti-slavery party." [28] The editor reminded his readers he had always disapproved of abolition schemes. He now warned those schemes would lead both to civil and servile war. The *Daily Herald* reported that the people of Boston "without distinction of parties, are decidedly opposed to the unreasonable designs of the immediate abolitionists." [29] Later in the year, after the Garrison riot, the paper, like many others, objected to the use of force, but referred to Garrison and George

Thompson as "infuriated fanatics." [30] The *Herald* carried similar remarks regarding mob action and abolitionists in issues following the murder of Elijah Lovejoy, an abolitionist newspaper editor killed in Alton, Illinois, in 1837 while defending his press and the burning in 1838 of Pennsylvania Hall built by Philadelphia abolitionists as a place in which they could meet.

In a report of January 1837, a committee of the New Hampshire House of Representatives stated: first, since slavery had existed for a long time, the present generation of southerners should not be held responsible for it; second, it would take a long time before slavery would disappear; third, slaves might easily be aroused by abolitionist efforts and resort to violence which would mean the death of many whites and the destruction of much property. [32] The New Hampshire *Portsmouth Weekly Journal* added its warning that abolition would mean slave insurrection. [33]

This horrifying accusation that slave uprisings would result from abolitionist agitation explains why so many northerners opposed abolition so strongly; yet, there was the even more appalling charge that abolition might lead to general race war. During the summer of 1835 the *Pennsylvanian,* one of the two leading Democratic papers in Philadelphia, noted the excitement then being stirred up concerning abolition. The editor called the abolitionists madmen and accused them of fomenting a servile war in the South. The paper warned that if the antislavery men continued their efforts the southern states, for their own safety, would have to exile all their free Negroes who would then come north. These free Negroes, the editor wrote, would "thus increase a population among us which already has been the cause of repeated tumults and disorders."[34] The *Pennsylvanian* urged its readers to oppose abolition and support colonization.

In 1832 the *North American Review* published a reply to a letter praising the American Colonization Society. The *Review*'s writer, after providing a history of the Society, insisted that most slaveholders wanted free Negroes removed from the country in order to avert race war. Pointing out that the colored man was biologically inferior to the white, the author called on the public and the government to combine and help return these Negroes to Africa.[35]

James Gordon Bennett wrote in his *New York Herald* that the abolitionists "stirred the Negroes up so that they are seeking white mates."[36] The theme of sexual relations between the races made good copy, and Bennett mentioned it often thereafter. In the spring of 1838 the *Herald*'s editor claimed abolitionists were bringing Negroes into the city and arming them in preparation for a race war.[37] The New York *Knickerbocker Magazine,* noting the danger of racial violence, called the abolitionists "amateur philanthropists" and likened them to "an experimental philosopher . . . who was anxious to wager . . . that he could perforate a keg of gun powder . . . without endangering the contents or the lives of the lookers-on."[38] Like most northerners, the *Knickerbocker*'s editor considered the price of abolition more than the product was worth. The editor of the *National Trades Union* also worried about race conflict and referred to the "mad and tantalizing course of the immediate abolitionists." [39]

Warnings of race war were not limited to newspaper editors, who might have exaggerated to attract readers. President Noah Porter of Yale published a letter in which he warned that abolition would lead to race violence.[40] James Fenimore Cooper insisted that despite the relative mildness of American slavery, if the day arrived when slavery was ended and the two races had to live together, there would be a race war resulting in the extermination of either whites or Negroes. Cooper warned that Negro inferiority would make it impossible to ever amalgamate the Negro and consequently he was bound to clash with the white.[41] James Austin of Massachusetts made the same point, as did the staunch anti-abolitionists James Kirke Paulding, Calvin Colton, and Robert Montgomery Bird. All feared what one writer referred to as "the peculiar relation of the black and white races in this country."

Anti-abolitionists saw the antislavery men as the perpetrators of doctrines that would produce anarchy. But, ironically, the most obvious and immediate acts of violence were those committed by anti-abolitionists. Violence was resorted to in order to prevent violence. As Doctor David M. Reese of New York put it, "pseudo-philanthropists" backed the current abolitionist movement. The leaders of this new movement were intemperate when discussing slavery and, as a result, their fanaticism led to more fanaticism.[42] Anti-abolitionists found themselves in the difficult position of either defending the abolitionists' rights or committing mob violence. They often tried to escape the dilemma by rejecting mob violence, but blaming such action on the abolitionists.

After 1835 the abolitionists devoted much of their effort to circulating and then presenting petitions to various legislative bodies. Increasingly, the question of abolition became one of whether these white Americans should be heard. Thus the slavery issue was partially obscured by the struggle for the maintenance of the civil rights of whites. Northern mobs were willing to use violence to silence antislavery men like Garrison and Thompson; but no responsible citizen could condone such actions. The press and the politicians disliked what the abolitionists said but were reluctant to infringe upon their right of free speech. The attempts to solve this dilemma ranged from John Quincy Adams' resolute defense of that right, through evasions of the question, to an insistence that the antislavery men brought violence upon themselves.

In 1835 John Quincy Adams confided to a friend, "With the slave and abolition whirligig I hope to have no concern but upon other questions I cannot be silent and must speak my mind." [43] Adams made it clear that he supported abolition out of a sense of duty to governmental process rather than out of sympathy with antislavery. In addition, the New Englander expressed concern that his defense of principle might cost him re-election since many of his constituents objected to aiding antislavery men for any reason. Like Adams, Caleb Cushing, the only other New England congressman willing to present abolitionist petitions, helped the abolitionists because he believed they had a legal right to be heard, though he disagreed with what they said. Cushing also believed he jeopardized his political future by going against popular sentiment in his state regarding abolition.[44]

Concern for the rights of abolitionists did temper some anti-abolitionist attacks. When the Democrats led the fight to silence Adams in 1837, the *Boston Atlas* criticized the ex-President, but at the same time accused his critics and Democratic political opponents of denying a basic right. The paper accused Democrat James Buchanan of Pennsylvania of betraying the North when he attacked the right of petition.[45] Lynde Walter of the *Boston Transcript* often mentioned that, though he disagreed with abolitionists, he would defend their civil rights. But to carry this out was another matter. The *Transcript* supported Adams in the petition controversy, but later rejected abolitionist claims that the government's halting of abolitionist materials sent through the mails was also a violation of guaranteed rights. In addition, the editor insisted that abolitionists should be prevented from sending their literature through the South.[46]

Free speech was the ultimate concern of men like Adams. But many other northerners, when faced with the problem of abolitionist rights were ambivalent; some infringed on the Constitution which they were so eager to protect, and others embraced the very tactics they deplored when abolitionists used them. Accordingly, the position of the members of the Massachusetts state legislature was more typical than Adams' stand. When the abolitionists tried to submit petitions to that body, the legislaure imposed their own "gag rule" and denied the abolitionists the right of petition.[47] Long-time Massachusetts Federalist leader Harrison Gray Otis, reflecting the legislature's sentiments, demanded an end to antislavery agitation in any form and from any source.[48]

The *Boston Transcript* denounced mob violence but at the same time blamed Garrison and Thompson for inciting to riot. As to freedom of speech, editor Lynde Walter called Thompson a "quack" who had no right to speak. Walter said nothing about Garrison's rights nor did he comment on Lovejoy's rights, but mob violence was difficult to disregard. In November 1837 when Elijah Lovejoy was killed the *Transcript* reprinted a description of the event but offered no editorial comment. When Pennsylvania Hall was burned in 1838, Walter devoted his editorial page to decrying what he believed was the cause of the violence: the mixing of the races. It seems the mob rioted because of reports that white women and Negro men were walking together.[49] Thus Walter saw the Philadelphia incident as a result of abolitionist defiance of accepted customs in race relations. But incidents such as this made the anti-abolitionists uncomfortable.

The *Boston Atlas* also discussed the burning of Pennsylvania Hall. The *Atlas* decried the act, exonerated the abolitionists from blame, and attributed the whole affair to the work of radical Democrats.[50] Shortly before the 1840 election, the paper claimed that the whole abolitionist agitation was part of a plot of "southern aristocrats" and northern radicals to destroy the Union.[51] It seems that the *Atlas* preferred developing this plot to discussing antislavery directly.

Perhaps no northern newspaper editor was more aware of the dilemma posed by violent attacks on abolitionists than the intensely anti-abolitionist James Gordon Bennett, founder and editor of the *New York Herald*. Bennett was as fanatical as anyone in his attacks on abolitionists and yet, despite his claims that the abolitionists were involved with foreign conspirators and that antislavery men were stirring up race war, he refused to condone violence used against them. Shortly after the Lovejoy murder, the *Herald* accused the "Wall Street Press" of having stirred up the public.[52] However, here and elsewhere Bennett made clear his concern that such attacks strengthened the abolitionist position. Before 1837 Bennett had shown considerable uncertainty as to how to handle this problem. Facing the anti-abolitionist riots in October 1835, the *Herald* called on the public to silence the abolitionists by means other than force.[53] In 1836 Bennett warned his readers that the riots had failed to end abolition and that, in fact, the anti-slavery advocates were stronger and more radical than ever.[54]

Clearly, after 1837 Bennett was convinced that violence against abolition was strengthening rather than weakening the movement. His objections to violence were primarily tactical, not constitutional.

The *New York Evening Post* also opposed antislavery, though this paper was more moderate in its anti-abolition than the *Herald*. Through the violence-filled summer of 1835 acting editor William Leggett pressed his attack against antislavery but called for calm, legal action to silence the movement.[55] In 1837, after the Lovejoy killing, the *Post* warned that violence was morally wrong and strengthened the abolitionist cause, making legal suppression of it more difficult.[56] The paper called on the northern press to encourage calm reason rather than mob action, both for moral reasons and as a practical measure to stop the spread of abolition. Like Bennett, the *Post*'s editors Leggett and William Cullen Bryant had changed their attitude on the question of violence. Bryant had commented, after an anti-abolitionist riot in New York in 1833, that mob action was to be expected when men as radical as the abolitionists insisted on making public speeches.[57]

The right to express an unpopular view was fundamental in a free society but many northerners believed that, if it were expressed, society would be destroyed. Some northerners were convinced that abolitionists not only provoked violence but that their doctrines, if carried out, would produce it. Thus newspaper editors, politicians, and others found themselves caught between their defense of legal process and their fear that abolitionists would destroy that process. As the historian Russel Nye has shown, eventually mob action against abolitionists forced many anti-abolitionist northerners to be sympathetic to, if not actually in agreement with, the antislavery position.[58] But in the 1830's the abolitionists still seemed the primary menace to social order.

### NOTES

1. *Norwich Courier*, July 31, 1833.
2. *Connecticut Observer*, quoted by the *Norwich Courier*, July 16, 1834; *Hartford Observer*, quoted by the *Courier*, July 30, 1834.
3. *New England Magazine* (Boston), XI (1833), *passim*.
4. *Ibid.*, pp. 252–253.
5. *American Quarterly Observer* (Boston), I (1833), 95–101.
6. *Emporium and True American* (Trenton, N.J.), May 25, 1838.
7. *Niles's Register* (Baltimore), September 5, 1835.
8. *New York Herald*, September 1, 1835.
9. *New York Commercial Advertiser*, October 12, 1835.
10. *Ibid.*, October 12, 1835.
11. *Ibid.*, April 10, 1832.
12. Quoted by the *Liberator* (Boston), October 1833.
13. *Albany Argus*, August 11, 1835.
14. *Ibid.*, January 7, 1837.
15. *North American Review* (Boston), XXXV (1832), 128–142.
16. *Ibid.*, XLI (1835), *passim*.
17. James K. Paulding, *Slavery in the United States* (New York, 1836), p. 281.
18. J. R. Burden, *Remarks of Dr. J. R. Burden of Philadelphia County in the Senate of Pennsylvania on the Abolition Question, February 18, 1838,* (Philadelphia, 1838), p. 9.
19. *Ibid.*, p. 10.

20. *National Trades Union,* August 16, 1834.
21. Paulding, *op. cit.,* p. 28.
22. *New York Evening Post,* September 20, 1831.
23. *Kennebec Weekly Journal* (Augusta, Me.), August 21, 1835.
24. *Ibid.,* September 30, 1831; October 12, 1832; May 12, 1833; September 11, 1833; and *passim.*
25. *Boston Transcript,* August 21, 1831.
26. *Eastern Argus* (Portland, Me.), August 11, 1835.
27. *New Jersey Journal* (Elizabethtown, N.J.), November 10, 1835.
28. *Newburyport Daily Herald* (Newburyport, Mass.), October 8, 1833.
29. *Ibid.,* October 8, 1833.
30. *Ibid.,* October 24, 1835.
31. *Ibid.,* November 24, 1837; May 22, 1838.
32. Samuel May Collection Tract #261 (Cornell University Library).
33. *Portsmouth Weekly Journal* (Portsmouth, N. H.), August 21, 1835.
34. *Pennsylvanian* (Philadelphia), August 24, 1835.
35. *North American Review,* XXXV (1832), 128–142.
36. *New York Herald,* December 13, 1836.
37. *Ibid.,* May 23, 1838.
38. *Knickerbocker Magazine,* XI (1838), 328.
39. *National Trades Union,* July 12, 1834.
40. *New York Evening Post,* August 7, 1833.
41. James F. Cooper, *The American Democrat,* (new ed.; New York, 1931), pp. 166–167.
42. David M. Reese, *Humbugs of New York* (New York, 1838), pp. 113–114.
43. John Quincy Adams, "Letter to Doctor Benjamin Waterhouse, October 15, 1835," quoted in Samuel F. Bemis, *John Quincy Adams and the Union* (New York, 1956), p. 329.
44. Claude M. Fuess, *The Life of Caleb Cushing* (2 vols., New York, 1923), I, 155.
45. *Boston Atlas,* January 19, 1838.
46. *Boston Transcript,* May 19, 1838.
47. *Liberator* (Boston), March 8, 1836. Garrison wrote a lengthy account of the proceedings. He cited numerous anti-abolitionist remarks made by many members of the Massachusetts legislature.

48. Samuel Eliot Morison, *The Life and Letters of Harrison Gray Otis, Federalist, 1765–1848* (2 vols., Boston, 1913), II, 273.
49. *Boston Transcript,* May 19, 1838. Every newspaper I examined carried the story that white women delegates to the convention were seen walking arm in arm with colored male delegates.
50. *Boston Atlas,* May 22, 1838.
51. *Ibid.,* September 11, 1838.
52. *New York Herald,* January 6, 1837; November 27, 1837.
53. *Ibid.,* October 27, 1835.
54. *Ibid.,* October 21, 1836.
55. *New York Evening Post,* July 8, 1834.
56. *Ibid.,* November 18, 1837.
57. *Ibid.,* April 25, 1833.
58. Russel Nye, *Fettered Freedom* (East Lansing, Michigan, 1949), *passim.*

# 5

———•———

# *The Churches Face the Moral Crusade*

The churches in America had to give more attention to antislavery than did any other group or institution in the country. The churches had to face the issues raised by the antislavery movement, because a number of clergymen and prominent lay leaders were abolitionists. The churches' attempts to find a satisfactory position on the question of abolition, and the specific stands the various religious institutions took, tell a very special story of the place abolition had in the North of the 1830's. As we examine that story, we will also trace the anti-abolitionist response in more detail, and from an institutional rather than a thematic point of view.

The abolitionist movement was, of course, largely based on a religious foundation, and such antislavery leaders as Theodore Weld and Arthur Tappan were also closely associated with many other church-sponsored reforms. Weld, like most abolitionists, viewed antislavery as a moral awakening of the North to the immorality of slavery. Abolitionists regularly spoke before some church congregations, and there were clergymen prominent in the antislavery ranks. But, just as antislavery failed to attract any major support among college presidents, newspaper and magazine editors, prominent writers, or politicians, it also failed to win over many prominent churchmen or to gain support from any of the important religious sects or denominations. Considering the intensity of expressions of anti-abolitionist sentiments, the issues this raised in the North, and the abolitionists' claim that theirs was a moral crusade, it is not surprising that many churchmen rejected antislavery. Their rejection was based not only on the usual reasons of racism and fear of disunion and violence, but also on the fear that antislavery would disrupt their religious institutions. This widespread clerical anti-abolitionism is another indication of the extent of northern anti-abolitionism and of the fears the abolitionists unintentionally had raised.

Historians have described the schism of 1837 in the Presbyterian church as one of the first instances of an American institution dividing over the slavery question.[1] This claim, however, is misleading. The Presbyterian church split over doctrinal questions, questions that had been argued for a long time and that came to a head in 1837 in the midst of a great period of evangelical activity. Antislavery was important only as an element in this doctrinal debate. In order to understand the role of antislavery in this schism, we must consider the controversies within the church that led to the final split.

In 1801 the Presbyterian and Congregational churches, worried about the loss of membership as New Englanders moved West, joined together in a plan of union. Concerned for the salvation of those who were moving beyond the bounds of the established churches into areas where properly trained clergymen were unavailable, the church sent missionaries into the frontier region, and by the mid-1820's a wave of revivalism was sweeping western New York and the Western Reserve of Ohio. The missionaries conducting these revivals began to bring large numbers of people into the two churches, and hence the American Missionary Board, which controlled the funds for these actitivites, assumed an increasingly important place within the church structure.[2]

When Charles Grandison Finney turned to the ministry and, in the 1820's, had great success in conducting revivals, the more orthodox wings of both churches feared that the interdenominational missionary groups, which were closely associated with evangelism, would gain control of the church organization. Thus, they feared, Finney's new theology might subvert orthodox church doctrine. Perhaps the most dangerous part of the new doctrine, as the conservatives saw it, was typified by the preaching of the radical Presbyterian minister Albert Barnes. In a sermon entitled "The Way of Salvation," published in 1829 and violently attacked by both Old-School and more moderate New-School men, Barnes said of salvation, "No man has a right to conclude that he is shut out from salvation, *except by fact,* if he loves sin, and will not repent. . . . If *he* should repent and believe, as he would be saved and be among the elect, and give the glory to God." [3] Presbyterian leaders like Charles Hodge rejected any doctrine in which salvation was so simply attained, and which granted such easy admittance into the ranks of the elect.

As for the growing power of the Home Missionary Society, Hodge's Princeton colleague Samuel Miller spoke for the anti-evangelical Old-School Presbyterians when he wrote, in 1833, in his *Letters to Presbyterians on the Present Crisis in the Presbyterian Church:*

> Yet we all know that they [Board of American Home Missionary Society] have no public standards to which they engage to be conformed. They have no confession of faith; no ecclesiastical responsibility. They may deviate greatly and grievously from the purity of the gospel; and if this should ever occur there will be no other power than the vague and

ever varying power of public sentiment to call them to account or to arrest their wayward career.[4]

Moderates considered that the New-School (pro-evangelical) men, who were associated with interdenominational societies and in a few cases became abolitionists, would destroy the discipline of the church, since these reformers worked in societies outside the control of the Presbyterian General Assembly. Though few New-School men actually participated, abolition was the kind of crusade to which the revivalistic type of New-School theology might lead. Old-School men considered the participation of some New-School men in the abolitionist movement proof of the danger of evangelism.

In 1836 Charles Hodge, editor and chief contributor to the *Biblical Repertory and Theological Review,* a journal of the Theological Seminary at Princeton, stated:

> The assumption that slaveholding is itself a crime, is not only an error, but it is an error fraught with evil consequence. It not merely brings its advocates into conflict with the scriptures, but it does much to retard the progress of freedom: it embitters and divides the members of the community, and distracts the Christian Church.[5]

In 1838 Hodge said, when commenting on West Indian emancipation, that abolitionists were "fighting against scripture" and that "they consider their own light as more sure than the word set down in scripture." [6] Hodge considered this point crucial. The abolitionists, like the revivalists who sought to direct the activities of the church into associations for reform, failed to follow the literal statements of the Bible. Once the ministers were broadly interpreting the Bible, church discipline would break down. What to Hodge and the Old-School Presbyterians was radicalism would become dominant.

Aside from pointing to abolition as the worst consequence of evangelism, the *Biblical Repertory* neglected the subject. From 1831 to 1839 only three articles in the *Repertory* mentioned antislavery: the two already cited, and a note in favor of colonization published in 1833. This hardly seems the kind of coverage the principal organ of the Presbyterian church would give to an issue that threatened to divide the church.

On the question of evangelical activity, the opposition to Hodge and to the Princeton Old-School men came mainly from the evangelist Charles Finney and the group of reformers who had accepted his stand. Finney, though more sympathetic to abolition than the Old-School Presbyterians, refused to join the abolitionist movement.

In 1836, after his revivals had made him famous, Finney became president of Oberlin College, a college then controlled by New-School Presbyterians and a center of reform activity. Several of Oberlin's prominent faculty members had publicly supported antislavery, and the school had offered admittance to the students of Lane Seminary when they left that institution following their antislavery discussions. The Lane students, faculty members such as Beriah

Green and Presbyterian philanthropist and antislavery leader Lewis Tappan, sought to convince Finney to join the antislavery cause, but without success.[7]

Theodore Weld was among those evangelists who played an important role in carrying out the work of the American Anti-Slavery Society. Weld was a former disciple of Finney, and he too attempted to convince Finney to join the antislavery crusade. It was in answer to Weld's appeal that Finney wrote a letter explaining why he rejected abolition:

> Br. Weld is it not true, at least do you not fear it is, that we are in our present course going fast into a civil war? Will not our present movements in abolition result in that: . . . Nothing is more manifest to me than that the present movements will result in this unless your mode of abolitionizing the country be greatly modified. . . . How can we save our country and affect the speedy abolition of slavery? This is my answer. . . .
> The subject is now before the public mind. It is upon the conscience of every man, so that now every new convert will be an abolitionist of course. Now if abolition can be made an appeal of a general revival of religion all is well. I fear no other liberty of the soul of the slave. One alarming fact is that the absorbing abolitionism has drunk up the spirits of some of the most efficient moral men and is fast doing so [to] the rest, . . . This I have been trying to resist from the beginning as I have all along foreseen that should that take place, the church and world, ecclesiastical and state leaders, will become embroiled in one common infernal squabble that will roll a wave of blood over the land. The causes now operating are in my view as certain to lead to

this result as a cause is to produce effect, unless the public mind can be engrossed with the subject of salvation and make abolition an appendage of the revival in Rochester. . . . The fact is D [ear] W [eld] our leading abolitionists are good men, but there are but a few of them *wise* men.[8]

Finney considered reform possible only if men were awakened and made to see the evil around them. The spirit of religion would automatically produce antislavery advocates, but to pursue it as an objective apart from all others would be disastrous. He remained outside the antislavery movement because it differed from his idea of what a reform movement should be. Finney rejected abolition because it sought to destroy slavery by direct attack on that institution and the men who participated in it. For Finney, reform should be a spiritual awakening of the nation, not a crusade to change part of the fundamental social system— at least not as the first step. Though some of his followers did join, many stayed away.

There seems no reason to assume, as some historians have done, that the New-School Presbyterians were abolitionists. Some of them were; some were sympathetic to antislavery but not to abolition; others took no stand. In 1838 the New-School General Assembly met in Philadelphia and when a memorial on slavery was presented, the General Assembly insisted it be withdrawn. Meeting in 1839, the General Assembly declared that the question of slavery was outside its province.[9]

Only after 1850 did the New-School Assembly vote to regard slavery as "intrinsically an unrighteous and oppressive system opposed to the proscriptions of the law of God." [10] In 1839 the *American Biblical Repository,* journal of the New School, discussed the schism. The writer never mentioned antislavery.[11] Even a pro-abolitionist Presbyterian like Joshua Leavitt, editor of the *New York Evangelist,* indicated that his prime concern was that Presbyterians be active in reform; in the *Evangelist,* he devoted more space to other reforms than to antislavery.[12] In August 1837 Leavitt wrote, "We shall not make the abolition question the all absorbing topic, we shall not be men of one idea." [13]

Considering the stand taken by leaders of the Presbyterian church, we can assume that, although there were ministers of this denomination who preached abolitionist doctrines, the Presbyterian laity were, for the most part, not subject to such appeals. In October 1835, in a sermon entitled "A View of the American Slavery Question," the Reverend E. P. Barrows of the First Free Presbyterian Church of New York said, though he favored antislavery in principle, he felt it unfair to condemn slaveholders to the point of barring them from church membership, because the conditions under which emancipation might be accomplished were so difficult.[14]

The Reverend Gilbert McMaster of the Reformed Presbyterian Church in Duanesburgh, New York, published a sermon he had delivered in 1832 in which he said: abolition denied states' rights; slavery was an evil, but no worse than other evils sanctioned by the Constitution; slavery might be wrong but it would take a long time to correct it, and the slaveholders would be the ones to end the institution.[15]

The Dutch Reformed wing of the Presbyterian church adopted an even stronger anti-abolitionist position. The journal of the Dutch Reformed Church of New York, the *Christian Intelligence,* carried notices supporting colonization and the idea that the church's duty was to send missionaries to the Negroes in Africa. The editor made it clear that he felt a sense of duty to the Negro as an object for good works, but that Americans were opposed to incorporating Negroes into white society.[16] As another Dutch Reform journal put it, "Sinful as slavery is it is not more so than a plan of emancipation might be made to be." [17] In Philadelphia Ashabel Green, editor of the Presbyterian *Christian Advocate,* stated his dislike of slavery, his fear of abolition, and his support for colonization.[18]

These are only a few examples of statements by Presbyterian clergymen which indicate that clergy's opposition to abolition. Neither the Presbyterian church organization nor the interdenominational reform societies which Presbyterians and Congregationalists dominated were happy about any movement as potentially decisive as abolition.

The clergymen of the Congregationalist church were a college-trained group, strong in New England and areas where New Englanders had settled. With their closely associated Presbyterian brothers the Congregationalist clergy dominated the boards of directors of the various reform movements of the day. A number of historians have sought to establish that these clergymen "had a definite pattern for America to which they wanted the nation to conform." [19] These "theocrats," who were strongest among the New England Congregationalists, used reform movements to accomplish their ends.

Though the "theocrats" were associated with a variety of reform societies, their solution to the Negro problem was to support the American Colonization Society and to reject the idea that the Negro could be part of the American nation.[20] Ralph Gurley, secretary of the American Colonization Society, Samuel Mills, one of its founders, Robert Finley, another important figure in the founding of the Society, all were "theocrats." [21]

Among the leaders of the Congregational church, the New Englander Lyman Beecher serves as a good example of a "theocrat" who rejected abolition. The "theocrats" considered Andrew Jackson a special menace and had started a concerted drive in 1829 to awaken the country to the danger of oversecularism in government and society.[22] Though personal enemies, Beecher and Finney both believed their goal to be the preparation of Americans for the Second Coming. If this was accomplished, all reforms would follow. Beecher believed that to work for a particular and singled-out reform would only endanger the greater cause.[23]

In 1834 Beecher accepted a call to head the newly formed Lane Theological Seminary in Cincinnati. He went West to fight atheism and popery, forces which posed a threat to a moral America. At Lane, Beecher found himself in the middle of an antislavery controversy. Arthur Tappan, antislavery leader, backed Lane financially. In a letter to Tappan Beecher explained why he prohibited further discussion of abolition. Though the crux of his argument was that he wished to see slavery end, he felt the best means to accomplish this was to make it as easy as possible for slaveholders to manumit—colonization would do just that.[24]

After the Lane project collapsed, Beecher returned to Boston. There, as one of his reform projects, he established the American Union, a group claiming to stand for "moderate abolition." Beecher hoped the American Union would bring together abolitionists and colonizationists. The "theocrats" constantly faced dissension in the ranks and the antislavery debate threatened to create a divisive issue. Thus Beecher sought to close the fissure; but Garrison denounced the American Union as a Colonization Society front, and it failed in its purpose.[25] Beecher wrote to his son William in 1835: "I hope and believe that the abolitionists as a body will become more calm and less denunciatory, with the exception of the few he-goat men, who think they do God service by butting every thing in the line of their march which does not fall in or get out of the way.

They are the offspring of the Oneida denunciatory revivals." [26] But Beecher, who was now embroiled in doctrinal controversies, dropped the antislavery debate.

The "theocrats" continually had to reckon with the potential division that abolition might cause among them. In 1837 Lyman Beecher's daughter Catherine Beecher, who had been with him in Cincinnati, wrote a tract in which she further developed the American Union's arguments against the abolitionists. In *An Essay on Slavery and Abolitionism: Letters Addressed to Angelina Grimké,*[27] Catherine started out by chiding Miss Grimké, a Quaker abolitionist soon to be the wife of Theodore Weld, for taking part in the abolitionist movement. This, she asserted, was not the proper role for a woman.[28]

Miss Beecher addressed herself to the apparently growing success of the movement her father had rejected. She declared that the abolitionists' course could only lead to violence and that "It is not so much by exciting feelings of pity or humanity, and Christian love, towards the oppressed, the elements that made other reforms successful as it is by awakening indignation at the treatment of the abolitionists themselves that their cause has prospered." [29]

She went on to say that though the abolitionists had not done this purposely, it had happened. "The Christian way would have been to respect the opposition's ideas and argue rationally against them." [30] The abolitionists were so engrossed in their single cause, wrote Miss Beecher, that they became irresponsible in their attacks on all those who disagreed with them:

> Abolition tries to coerce rather than persuade public opinion. They claim to preach the truth but don't consider whether they are making the evil better or worse. They say they leave the consequences to God. What they must accept is that the propriety and duty of a given course is to be decided by *probabilities as to its results;* and these probabilities are to be determined by the *known laws of mind and the records of past experience.*
>
> For only one of two positions can be held. Either that it is the duty of all men to remonstrate at all times against all violations of duty, and leave the consequences with God; or else that men are to use their judgement, and take the part of remonstrance only at such time and place, and in such manner, as promise the best results. Slavery will come to an end. What is to be gained or lost by forcing immediatism? [31]

Miss Beecher then repeated that reform must come from within; she told the abolitionists that "reformers must first exempt themselves from fault, to learn humility and meekness. They must be discreet. They are teachers who must have the help of the parent." [32] To the Beechers abolition was a stumbling block in the way of reform, rather than a crusade to accomplish reform.

The opinions of the Beechers and other Congregationalist reformers were expressed in the pages of the *Boston Recorder,* a weekly newspaper. The *Recorder* supported a host of reform associations. On the question of slavery Calvin

Stowe, the paper's editor, reflected the view of most New England Congregationalists that the American Colonization Society provided the best answer.[33] William Lloyd Garrison made it a point to attack the *Recorder*'s stand on the slavery question. In answer, Stowe defended its colonizationalist position on the grounds that it would "save Africa" and that the purpose was more than just getting rid of Negroes. As to the question of whether slaveholders were sinners, the paper's stand was that reform associations should withhold judgment.[34] Shortly after Garrison had published *Thoughts on African Colonization,* in which he attacked the colonization principle, the *Recorder* published rejoinders.

By the mid-1830's the *Recorder* declared that corrupt men were using the antislavery societies, and that most of the members, who doubtless meant well, were being led astray. Following the riots of 1835, the paper noted, though the abolitionists did not intend slave insurrection their doctrines would produce it, and the abolitionists would be helpless to stop such violence just as they were helpless to stop anti-abolitionist riots in the North.[35]

Many Congregationalist clergymen in New England agreed with the *Recorder*'s stand on slavery, abolition, and colonization. We saw that Lyman Beecher, though he rejected abolition, did make an effort to bring about a compromise between colonization and antislavery. Another leading Congregationalist, Horace Bushnell, rejected any such compromise. Bushnell, who by 1839 had become a prominent clergyman in Connecticut, made very clear his opposition to an antislavery movement.[36] In January 1839 Bushnell discussed slavery before the congregation of the North Church in Hartford. He had spoken on the subject before but this was, in his words, a summing up of his views on the course of abolition. Bushnell's first objection to the abolitionists' doctrines was their harshness toward slaveholders. He found the claim that all slaveholders were sinners most disturbing:

> If our countrymen are guilty in this matter of slavery, it is not holding what they know to be truth concerning it—not doing what they are able, as individuals, properly enlightened, to produce a right action in their legislatures—and neglecting, in the meantime, to guard the well-being of their slaves by acts of parental and Christian kindness. That many of them incur great personal guilt in the matter is not to be questioned. But yet, when we speak of them, we ought to remember the fearfulness and difficulty of their state. Which way soever they turn, they meet the view of something dark or frightful.[37]

Bushnell exonerated slaveholders from the guilt of slavery by arguing that the present generation had inherited slavery and not created it. Southerners had been brought up in a society in which slavery was accepted. Slavery was a crime, but "if there was ever a people on earth involved in crime, who yet deserved sympathy and gentleness at the hand of the good, it is the slaveholding portion of our country."[38]

After describing the evils of slavery, evils that stemmed from the fact that slavery destroyed the sanctity of the home and prevented the individual from exercising proper control over his person, Bushnell appealed to the South:

> This institution is your own, not ours. Take your own way of proceeding. . . . Invent any new fashion of society you please. . . . But let me declare to you that, until you have established the family state and made it sacred, till you have given security to the body, till you have acknowledged the immortal mind and manhood of your slave, you do an offense to God and humanity. . . . In this sense, I am ready to go for the abolition of slavery.[39]

Bushnell then turned his attention to the abolitionists. He assured them that the moral position of the entire world was against slavery, that slavery was basically immoral and would be destroyed. But he also insisted that their program was the wrong way to bring reform: "either with you, or without you . . . the river flows inevitably—abolition may only muddy the water." [40] The Congregationalist based his analogy on the belief that the abolitionists, by calling for the acceptance of the Negro as an equal, held a false view of the Negro's capabilities and potentialities:

> The vision of a new created, enlightened race of Christian freemen, which they ever hold up before them [the abolitionists]. . . . I am sorry to feel, has too slender a support in history where an uncultivated and barbarous stock has been elevated in the midst of a cultivated and civilized stock. . . . The Irish for example can't really become

Americans. They become extinct. It is very seldom that their children, born in this country live to a mature age. Intemperance and poor living sweep them away.[41]

The Congregationalist clergy, as well as the members of other religious and secular groups in American society, represented a range of views on the issue of abolition, and most of them objected to it. A few Maine Congregationalist ministers called for support of abolition, but they met with a storm of criticism. Congregationalists there as elsewhere either supported the American Colonization Society, or were apologists for slavery.

For a time William Lloyd Garrison numbered among his supporters a group of Massachusetts Congregationalist ministers. By 1837, however, many of these ministers joined in attacking Garrison because he began associating the movement with women's rights.[42] These clergymen, however, advocated antislavery; but Lyman Beecher, Horace Bushnell, Leonard Bacon, and most of the leaders of the Congregational church stopped short of even nominal support of the abolitionist cause. Since the Congregationalists did not have a general conference, the church never formally debated the issue.

The Methodist church was organized into regional conferences, which were under the jurisdiction of the General Conference. Here the antislavery men had their chance to try to win over at least their regional conferences. The abolitionists were probably more numerous among northern Methodists than in any other denomination.[43] Yet, these

antislavery advocates met strong opposition even in the
New England, New Hampshire, and New York conferences where they were most prominent. The bishops of
these conferences, without exception, exerted their influence and the power invested in them by the church to
block the abolitionists.[44]

In the early 1820's the Methodists, leading the way in
missionary activity both at home and overseas, decided to
send a mission to the American Negro colony in Liberia.
The church had strongly supported the American Colonization Society, and the mission brought even closer cooperation between the two. When, in the 1830's, abolitionists
began a strong attack on the Colonization Society in New
England, Bishops Hedding and Waugh, Professor Whedon
of Wesleyan, and Doctor Fisk, who was the president of
that college, all opposed the organized antislavery movement.

In several histories of the Methodist church, the long
fight between the antislavery forces and the Methodist hierarchy has been discussed at length.[45] We shall consider
here the nature of the anti-abolitionist sentiment that was
so strong in the North.

The Methodist General Conference of 1836 met in
Cincinnati, just across the Ohio River from the slave-state
Kentucky. Cincinnati had a strong anti-abolitionist history
dating from the violent opposition to the "Lane Rebels"
who had sought to educate the city's free Negroes. And

James G. Birney, the future antislavery leader, faced mob action against his press and himself in 1836, soon after he began editing an antislavery journal.[46] Obviously, Cincinnati was an unfavorable location for those Methodist delegates from New England who came to the conference hoping to see an antislavery memorial read and some action taken.[47]

Several days before the conference opened, two of these delegates addressed a meeting of the local antislavery society. Once the conference sessions began, their activities were noted and a debate ensued on the question of censuring them. The debate resulted in a resolution disapproving of "the most unqualified members of the General Conference who are reported to have lectured in this city recently upon, and in favor, of modern abolitionism."

It was traditional for the assembly to open with an address from a representative of the Methodist Church of England. This English representative now joined with the antislavery delegates. In his address he called on the Americans to oppose slavery. The assembly opposed this invitation and declared they were "decidedly opposed to modern abolitionism, and wholly disclaim any right, wish, or intention, to interfere in the civil and political relation between master and slave as it exists in the slaveholding states of the Union." [48] One speaker then pointed out, for the benefit of the English delegate, that there were important differences between the problems of abolishing slavery in England and abolishing it in the United States. Other speakers condemned abolition and called it almost as dangerous a conspiracy as Catholicism.[49]

Though the Methodist antislavery men got nowhere in Cincinnati, they had at least forced debate on the slavery question and had put the official church bodies on the defensive there, as they had already succeeded in doing in the New England Conference.

Orange Scott and La Roy Sunderland, who led the New England Methodist antislavery group, found that opposi-Conference would make it impossible for the antislavery wing to express its views in the Methodist press. Therefore, tion by the bishops and other prominent churchmen of the Sunderland established his own paper in New York, the *Zion's Watchman*. In this paper Methodist antislavery men now expressed their views. When, in 1835, the paper published an appeal to all Methodist clergymen to join the cause of antislavery, Wesleyan's Professor Whedon wrote a "Counter-Appeal," which was signed by President Fisk of that college, and by Edward Taylor, Abel Stevens, and five other leaders of the New England conference.[50]

A "Pastoral Letter" addressed to "The Ministers and Preachers of the New England and New Hampshire Conferences" and signed by Bishops Hedding and Emory followed the "Counter-Appeal." In the letter the bishops declared: "Nothing has ever occurred so seriously tending to obstruct and retard, if not absolutely to defeat, the cause of emancipation as the modern agitation on this subject." [51]

They called upon all presiding elders, preachers, trustees, and members to manifest their disapprobation and to refuse the abolitionists the use of their pulpits. When approached to sign a petition against slavery in the District of Columbia, Fisk, president of Wesleyan, refused.[52] In Methodist regional conferences, Hedding, Fisk, and Waugh of New York all exerted their full prerogative to cut off abolitionist petitions and to prevent antislavery debate. In 1838, in the Maine and New York conferences, it was voted to end all discussion of the slavery question.[53] Luther Lee, an abolitionist leader in the Methodist church, was refused the right to speak from a Methodist pulpit in Auburn, New York.[54] Clearly, the Methodist leadership had little sympathy for the abolitionist cause.

Though there were some abolitionists in the northern conferences, most Methodists were anti-abolitionist. The anti-abolitionists were in complete control in all but two conferences, those of New Hampshire and New England, and in all northern conferences the leading figures, bishops, and ministers, stood opposed to antislavery. The revolt of antislavery Methodists resulted from their failure to win over their church.

The Baptists, like the Methodists, had to contend with an English church group that was pressuring them to take an antislavery stand. And like the Methodists, the Baptists' answer showed conclusively that even in the northern churches abolitionism was unpopular.

Baptists sympathetic to antislavery claimed the sect had

a tradition of antislavery that extended all the way back to Roger Williams. Williams had spoken out against the slave trade and had freed Indian slaves in Rhode Island. In the late eighteenth century the church had come out in favor of gradual abolition of slavery, and in the early nineteenth century a group known as the Friends of Humanity, most of whom lived west of the Alleghenies, had taken up antislavery as one of their causes.[55] During the 1830's, however, few Baptists were actually willing to support antislavery.

The English Baptists had been among the leaders in securing freedom of all slaves held in the Empire. Once this was accomplished, they turned their attention to the American scene. In December of 1833 church leaders wrote a letter to their American brethren urging them to take an antislavery stand. After waiting some time (abolitionists claimed the delay was actually an attempt to keep the letter a secret), the American Baptist Convention answered their English critics.[56] The spokesmen for the Convention began by insisting abolition was far more difficult in America than in England. First, the Convention's spokesman pointed out the difference in political structure between the United States and Great Britain, a difference which made it possible for Parliament to legislate for the whole Empire on the subject of slavery, while in the United States the federal system made it necessary for each state to handle the problem. One state could not interfere with another. This was what the Constitution provided, and the Union could be preserved only if Americans followed the dictates of the Constitution. Thus, the Convention spokesman pointed out, slavery existed before the Revolution and had in fact been introduced to Americans by the British.[57]

Next, the American Baptist noted that the large number of slaves in America made immediate emancipation impossible. "It is not believed by many of the sincere friends of the slaves, that their immediate emancipation would be conducive to their own real welfare, or consistent with the safety of the whites. . . . Slaves who have regarded labour as an irksome task can have little idea of liberty, except as an exemption from toil."[58] The Baptist spokesman emphasized that he opposed the immediate emancipation of slaves but that he was willing to defend the American Colonization Society. Baptist missionary groups were especially strong supporters of colonization.

Third, the spokesman for the American Baptist Convention, writing in Boston, pointed out the dangers to Baptist church unity if the Convention took a strong antislavery stand. The Baptists, like the Methodists, had a large southern membership. The writer made clear to his English associates the importance of maintaining friendly relations:

> There is now a pleasing degree of union among . . . Baptists throughout the land. . . . Southern Baptists were liberal and zealous in promoting holy enterprises. Most are slaveholders but because the institution had firm root before they were born.[59]

Some months after this letter was written, a two-man delegation from the English church arrived in America. The delegates, Reverend F. A. Cox and Reverend J. Hoby, were antislavery advocates. Cox and Hoby addressed the Baptist Triennial Convention and toured the West and South. After returning to England, they wrote about their trip and provided a survey of the church in America.[60]

The two ministers began by telling their English audience that though they were abolitionists, they had kept quiet on the subject because "Americans are jealous of foreign interference; of all foreigners who intermeddle in their internal policy, they are most jealous of the English." [61] On no subject was this feeling so strong as on antislavery. The antislavery elements in the Baptist church tried to induce the two men at least to attend their meetings, but Cox and Hoby refused. Antislavery sympathizers in America claimed their refusal resulted from pressure from the executive board of the Triennial Convention. This the Englishmen denied, saying that they disagreed with some of the doctrines set forth by American abolitionists and felt their presence at a meeting would make it seem as though they sanctioned all antislavery ideas.[62] Whichever was the case, it seemed most expedient to these English observers to avoid taking a strong antislavery stand, even in the North.

The Baptist leaders in the North, like those of the other major denominations, expressed a dislike for slavery, but also a fear that abolition meant immediate freedom for the slave who, they believed, was unprepared for it. Many of these clergymen asserted their belief that it was impossible to mix Negroes and whites peacefully, and hence they supported colonization.

Francis Wayland, president of Brown University, was among the American Baptist leaders who expressed their views on the responsibility of the church with regard to the slavery question. In 1838 Wayland published a book entitled *The Limitations of Human Responsibility* in which he attacked the abolitionists and questioned the whole tendency toward what he called associationalism. First, Wayland remarked that true reform resulted from conscience directed by moral impulse. But one had to be very careful to distinguish what was true moral impulse. He warned that men who joined reform movements were often guided by the impulse of others, and this impulse might be false.[63] "Men plead the authority of God whilst they violate law; whilst they infringe the rights of their neighbor against infringement; whilst the individual takes the power of society into his own hands, and whilst society punishes him for transgression." [64] Wayland told his audience that they must not assume responsibility for all things. He then illustrated his point by describing the dangers inherent in a variety of associational forms, among which was antislavery.[65]

Agreeing that slavery was a moral wrong, Wayland asked what the Baptists' duty was with respect to it. How were American Baptists limited in their actions with regard to slavery? He gave his answer in two parts. As citizens of the United States, he said, American Baptists had certain limitations as to action, and as human beings under God's law they were also limited. In discussing the former, he emphasized that the Constitution, by recognizing slavery, was actually a legal restraint. As to the Baptists' limitations as human beings, Wayland made the point that they must respect the rights of fellow human beings in the South. To support abolition would be to support those who would start a servile war. The Baptist leader claimed that the abolitionists had fallen prey to the weakness of many another association, for they had allowed their movement to be taken over by a few "third-rate politicians." He accused the abolitionists of fanaticism for no good purpose and stated that they had actually riveted the slaves' bonds tighter.[66] Wayland's final advice to his readers was individually to speak the truth and hope that men's consciences would lead them to accept it.[67] As an important figure in the Baptist church as well as a recognized scholar and writer, Wayland carried much weight among Baptists.

Other Northern Baptist leaders agreed with Wayland. In 1834 A. A. Phelps, a Congregationalist minister and for a time editor of the American Anti-Slavery Society newspaper the *Emancipator,* formulated a declaration urging immediate emancipation; only 11 Baptist ministers in New England and New York signed it.[68] The leaders of the Baptist church, like those of the Methodists, avoided association with the antislavery movement, while some of these leaders attacked the abolitionists.

The Episcopal church, like so many other denominations, was faced with the problem of taking a stand on the question of engagement in evangelist activities. In upstate New York the church undoubtedly felt the impact of Charles Finney's evangelist efforts. Throughout the late 1820's and into the 1830's Bishop Hobart of New York was engaged in a fight with other Episcopalian church leaders over the issue of evangelism, and the use of evangelist methods by Episcopal ministers. In the Episcopal church, however, even those who held evangelist doctrines rejected the anti-slavery movement. The church either avoided the subject or attacked antislavery. Calvin Colton, who left newspaper work to become an Episcopal clergyman and then gave up the Church for politics, was an outspoken critic of the abolitionist. In a tract written in 1836 Colton attacked all reform associations for giving too much power, through their centralized organization, to the men who led them. Such groups, Colton warned, were bound to get involved in politics, which was not the proper realm of action for churchmen. Colton attacked the whole revivalist trend that was then so strong in many denominations.[69]

In 1839, in his book entitled *Abolition a Sedition* Colton pointed out how abolition was associated with "violent reforms that threatened good social order."[70] As he had warned in 1836, abolitionists had gone into politics. Now he accused them of being an independent (thus uncontrolled) group that both threatened the Union and sought the overthrow of the government. Here was a religious group seeking to subvert the state. He concluded his remarks with the usual anti-abolitionist advice to the British, telling them to mind their own business.[71]

Colton's skepticism about reform was shared by other Episcopal leaders. In 1837 the Episcopal diocese of New York began the publication of a magazine entitled the *New York Review and Quarterly Church Journal.* In July 1838 the *Review,* spurred by the publication of Harriet Martineau's *Society in America,* expressed its views on the slavery question and on the whole subject of reform. The editor, though he accepted the idea of man's potential perfectibility, asked his readers to remember that there is in man a radically corrupt tendency that must be restrained. This, he continued, the perfectionists forgot when they called for even more freedom for the individual. For example, a person might believe the end of slavery desirable but not realize that the problem lies in finding some way to end it. As Miss Martineau wrote of race hatred in America, the editor felt prompted to ask how, if the races hated each other one could expect them to live together in peace, without slavery to govern their relations? [72]

In the next issue, in a review of Francis Wayland's *Limitations of Human Responsibility,* the editor pursued the same theme. The Episcopal journal quoted Wayland at length, taking special note of his views on abolition in such statements as the following:

They [the abolitionists] have raised a violent agitation, without presenting any definite means of constitutionally accomplishing their objective. In the meantime, as combination on the one side always produces combinations on the other, they have embittered the feelings of the South. They have for the present, at least, rendered any open and calm discussion of the subject in the slaveholding states, utterly impossible. They have riveted indefinitely, the bond of the slave. . . . I must come to the conclusion that their efforts must be unwisely directed or else, they would have led to a more salutatory result.[73]

The reviewer praised Wayland's book and indicated that he agreed completely with his views.[74]

The Lutheran church, like the Episcopal church, had to deal with an evangelical wing interested in reform movements. The Lutheran reformers were centered in upstate New York. There were a few, but very few, antislavery men among these Lutherans. In 1836 the Hartwick Synod in New York State split over the question of whether the church should engage in evangelical activities. The Franckean Synod was formed by a handful of Lutheran ministers who sought to bring the church into reform movements. Though they supported abolition, they broke with the church for reasons other than their stand on slavery; antislavery was just one of many reforms they supported. But the great majority of Lutherans thought it improper for an ecclesiastical body to discuss the abolition of slavery or other reforms, or to participate in such activities.[75]

The Unitarian church took the position that slavery in the abstract was an evil, but that immediate abolition would be a grave error. The Unitarian *Christian Examiner and General Review* supported the Colonization Society.[76] The editor, pointing out how Africans in America were degraded, remarked that blacks should be allowed to stay if they wished, though their going to Africa would be best for both races. The *Examiner* called for the gradual extinction of slavery and warned that Garrison's plans would produce too rapid a social change: the French Revolution provided evidence of the danger of such change.[77]

William Ellery Channing was a reformer who rejected reform movements. Channing was convinced that all men were equal in that all had the same opportunity of infinite improvement of themselves; he considered such improvement a matter of personal concern and not the object of group crusade.[78] It is not surprising that this New England Unitarian would reject the appeals for his membership in the New England Anti-Slavery Society. But Channing chose to say a good deal more about his reasons for refusing to join an antislavery society. His pronouncements on abolition provide interesting insights into the reasons why many humanitarian-minded northerners rejected what seems on the surface the most humanitarian of causes.

Channing considered the abolitionists living proof of why reform must be achieved through the working of personal conscience rather than through outside group pressuring. In 1837, following the murder of abolitionist editor Elijah Lovejoy, Channing wrote that when "an enterprise of Christian Philanthropy" leads to and is involved in the use of force it is time to stop. Abolitionists must not pursue their objective if it means "wading through blood." [79] In the same letter Channing reprimanded the abolitionists for claiming that slaveholders disqualified themselves from church membership. The Unitarian leader considered such attacks on slaveholders as entirely apart from the true spirit of reform and lacking in compassion for the sinner who in time can be saved.

Guided by his definition of reform, Channing had supported the idea that abolition of slavery was a state matter. If the abolitionists had their way, he argued, race war would result. While abolitionists and reformers had succeeded in making the public aware of the "horrors of slavery," Channing wrote, they had also opened discussions of the dangers of immediate emancipation. And the result of antislavery efforts was that the public now sought to avoid discussing the question. Thus, Channing argued, abolitionists had done more to delay emancipation than to speed it up. [80] The antislavery leader Samuel May had good reason to complain:

> All the objections, Doctor Channing alleged against us . . . were the common current objections of that day, hurled at us in less seemly phrases from the press, the platform and the pulpit. . . . It was sad that a man of such a mind and heart as Doctor Channing's could have thought them of sufficient importance to press them upon us as he did. [81]

Despite his objections to the abolitionists, by the end of the decade Channing assumed a position very close to theirs. In 1838 he declared it the moral duty of the North to do something about slavery: a virtual about-face from his earlier stand when he had insisted that it was the duty of the South alone to act. Channing joined the abolitionists in denouncing the annexation of Texas on the grounds that it was a southern move to perpetuate slavery, and he spoke often now of the need to protect the abolitionists' civil rights, attacked colonization, and denied that the abolitionist plan meant amalgamation of the races.[82] However, Channing still refused to join the movement or to support it publicly.

Among the leaders of the Catholic church the dominant view was that slavery as an institution should be let alone, though interest was expressed in bringing religion to the slaves. Bishop Kendrick of Philadelphia asserted that slavery was an old and necessary institution, and that the proper concern of the church was with souls and not with the changing or even challenging of institutions.[83] Faced as they were with widespread anti-Catholic sentiment, it seems likely that church leaders would have avoided an unpopular stand even had they been inclined to oppose slavery.

To this point I have neglected to mention the denomination most often cited as a staunch exponent of antislavery doctrines—the Quakers, with their long tradition of humanitarian activities. They have been left until last in order to bring out clearly the great weight of anti-abolitionist sentiment in the North.

As the Quakers were always prominent among the leaders of the American antislavery movement, most historians have overlooked that many Quakers held slaves. Though many Quaker meetings discussed slavery during the seventeenth and early eighteenth centuries, that institution was neither formally rejected, nor were Quaker slaveholders forced to dispose of their slaves.[84] From the early to the mid-eighteenth century the Quakers, after years of persecution and schism, were seeking unity and were reluctant to risk a split on the slavery issue. They disowned two antislavery radicals, William Southeby and John Farmer, and when Ralph Sandiford and Benjamin Lay sought to revive the crusade in the 1730's, the Philadelphia Quakers took steps to silence them. However, by the late eighteenth century the Society of Friends was turning more markedly toward antislavery.[85]

In the 1730's Quakers began freeing their slaves, and by 1808 the process was complete. During the same period they also were working for the abolition of slavery as a whole. After 1800, with the measure outlawing the slave trade passed and the early leaders gone, the Quakers turned to testimony against slavery and little more.[86] We have already seen how the Pennsylvania Abolition Society, which was dominated by Quakers, ceased its yearly meeting and decreased its activities markedly.

The Quakers, like other religious groups, were divided

over the question of evangelism. A few of the "Orthodox" and some "Hicksites," as the competing groups were called, expressed antislavery views, but neither group was predominantly in favor of abolition.[87] Some "Hicksites" did propose that slavery be attacked by refusing to use slave-made goods. The free-produce movement was inspired by a Quaker drive to boycott goods made by warring nations.[88] However, the Quakers never officially sanctioned such action. There were free-produce stores in Philadelphia, New York, and Boston advertising their wares in the *Liberator* but the movement never became widespread.

Although the Quakers reached the point of refusing to take any slaveholder into membership and provided the antislavery movement with leadership, it would still be inaccurate to say that, by the 1830's, the Quakers were strongly pro-abolitionist. In fact, as we shall see, they were quite strongly opposed to "modern abolition."

The Quakers had allowed some Negroes into membership, but Negroes had to sit on special benches when they attended the meeting. Quaker leader Anthony Benezet favored some scheme of colonization. In 1816, when the American Colonization Society was founded, it received support from many Friends. Benjamin Lundy, who for years led the antislavery movement and who introduced Garrison to the cause, never favored immediate emancipation and sought for a long time to improve colonization schemes. By the late 1820's Quakers, preoccupied with the "Hicksite" controversy and disturbed by the "radicalism" of those abolitionists who called for immediatism, began to withdraw from the antislavery movement. The Baltimore Friends Anti-Slavery Society was disbanded in 1829; in Philadelphia the Free Produce Movement was dropped. As Thomas Drake put it in *Quakers and Slavery in America:*

> The real problem for the Friends . . . lay in the fact that the line between slavery and antislavery which the new doctrine of immediatism drew left no ground on which Quakers could comfortably stand. They had led the country to the point where gradual measures had become suspect in the South and had ceased to satisfy many conscience reformers in the North. They had converted a new generation to antislavery but a generation impatient with the mildness and slowness of the Quaker way. Friends faced the alternative of recasting their anti-slavery testimony and technique, or withdrawing from the vanguard of the anti-slavery ranks.[89]

The Quakers, for the most part, preferred to avoid antislavery.

Radicals like Arnold Buffum and poet John Greenleaf Whittier joined Garrison in the New England Anti-Slavery Society, but they were a distinct minority in the Quaker group. In 1839 William Bassett, a Quaker of Lynn, Massachusetts, wrote a pamphlet in which he took a strong antislavery stand. For this, Bassett was ostracized from the Lynn meeting house and from the Society of Friends.[90] By 1833 Philadelphia Quakers were stating that participation in radical activities that would lead to excitement and violence would cause damage to their faith. Gradually, north-

ern meetings broke off association with antislavery societies. Northern Quakers refused to allow meeting houses to
be used for outside lectures. This injunction was partly responsible for the abolitionists' decision to build Pennsylvania Hall in Philadelphia; many Quakers saw in the burning
of the Hall proof of what might result from association
with the antislavery societies.[91]

Presbyterians, Congregationalists, Baptists, Methodists,
Episcopalians, Lutherans, Unitarians, Catholics, and Quakers—all took stands that placed the majority of their clerical leaders in opposition to the antislavery movement. The
northern public heard few antislavery sermons. They read
or at least were aware that their church leaders countered
the arguments when antislavery men within their
denominations did write or speak.

Once again, we must keep in mind that this does not
mean that the churches in question were dominated by pro-
slavery elements. While there certainly were clergymen
who felt religious groups should avoid the question, there
were others who attacked slavery but rejected abolition.
Northern churchmen expressed all these views.

## NOTES

1. See C. Bruce Staiger, "Abolitionism and the Presbyterian Schism of
1837–8," *Mississippi Valley Historical Review*, XXXVI (December
1949), 391–414. Staiger shows how the question of whether the
Church should engage in evangelistic activity was a divisive issue

long before slavery became an issue. However, he believes that it was the slavery issue that caused the final schism. It is my belief that too few of the important Presbyterian clergymen were sympathetic to antislavery, for this issue to have led to any major schism.

2. Presbyterian or Congregational clergymen dominated such interdenominational associations as the American Home Missionary Society, the American Tract Society, and the Sunday School Union, as well as many societies with more secular aims. For an interesting discussion of the relation of these clergymen to such societies, see Clifford L. Griffin, "Religious Benevolence as Social Control 1815–1860," *Mississippi Valley Historical Review,* LIV (December 1957), 423–444.

3. Quoted by M. W. Armstrong, Lefferts A. Loetscher, and C. A. Anderson, eds., *The Presbyterian Enterprise: Sources of American Presbyterian History* (Philadelphia, 1956), pp. 147–148.

4. Quoted by Clifford M. Drury, *Presbyterian Panorama* (Philadelphia, 1952), pp. 147–148.

5. *Biblical Repertory and Theological Review,* VIII (1836), 298.

6. *Ibid.,* X (1838), *passim.*

7. Lewis Tappan, Beriah Green, and a number of the Lane students wrote to Weld criticizing Finney. See Gilbert Barnes and Dwight Dumond, eds., *Letters of Theodore Dwight Weld, Angelina Grimké Weld and Sarah Grimké* (New York, 1934), I, *passim.*

8. *Ibid.,* I, 320–323.

9. *Presbyterian Enterprise,* p. 164.

10. *Ibid.,* p. 165.

11. *Ibid.,* p. 148.

12. *New York Evangelist.* I read all issues published from 1835 to 1837.

13. *Ibid.,* VIII (August 5), 1837.

14. E. P. Barrows, *A View of the American Slavery Question* (New York, 1836), *passim.*

15. Gilbert McMaster, *The Moral Character of Civil Institutions of the United States* (Duanesburgh, N. Y., 1832), *passim.*

16. *Christian Intelligencer* (New York), April 8, 1837. Americans' conviction, that they, as a superior people, were obliged to help inferior people, constituted an important element in the missionary impulse. Supporters of missionary work viewed their cause as national as well as theological.

17. *Religious Monitor and Evangelical Repository* (Albany), VII (1830–1831), 35.

18. *Christian Advocate* (Philadelphia), XI (1834), 568.

19. John R. Bodo, *The Protestant Clergy and Public Issues 1812–1848* (Princeton, N. J., 1954), preface, viii. See also Griffin, "Religious Benevolence," and Richard L. Power, "A Crusade to Extend Yankee Culture," *The New England Quarterly,* XII (December 1940), for discussions of theocracy.

20. See Charles Cole, *The Social Ideas of the Northern Evangelists* (New York, 1954), p. 162.

21. Bodo, *op. cit.,* pp. 123–124.

22. Charles I. Foster, *An Errand of Mercy: The Evangelical United Front, 1790–1837* (Chapel Hill, N. C., 1960), p. 179.

23. Constance M. Rourke, *Trumpets of Jubilee* (New York, 1927), p. 73.

24. Lynian Beecher, *Autobiography and Correspondence* Charles Beecher, ed.(2 vols., New York, 1865), II, 323.

25. Garrison devoted several editorials to denouncing the American Union as a front for the Colonization Society.

26. L. Beecher, *op. cit.,* 345.

27. Catherine Beecher, *An Essay on Slavery and Abolitionism* (Philadelphia, 1837).

28. Initially the Grimké sisters were hesitant to make public appearances. When they did begin lecturing in support of antislavery, they added feminism as another cause to support. Feminism was classed with abolition as a radical reform, a dangerous movement aimed at upsetting society. Garrison also supported feminism and so further cemented the relation, in the public mind, between these two reforms.

29. *Ibid.,* pp. 12–14, 35–36.

30. *Ibid.,* p. 38.

31. *Ibid.,* pp. 44–45.

32. *Ibid.,* p. 145.

33. The Congregational church journal *Quarterly Register of the American Education Society* (Boston) noted that "all the important Ecclesiastical Bodies in the country . . . have expressed a decided friendship for its plans." III (1831), 61.

34. *Boston Recorder,* August 31, 1831; January 30, 1833.

35. *Ibid.*, August 7, 1835.
36. In 1841 Bushnell was offered the presidency of Congregationalist Middlebury College.
37. Horace Bushnell, *A Discourse on the Slavery Question Delivered in the North Church, Hartford, Connecticut, January 10, 1839* (Hartford, 1839), pp. 5–6.
38. *Ibid.*, p. 6.
39. *Ibid.*, p. 8.
40. *Ibid.*, p. 11.
41. *Ibid.*, p. 11.
42. In "the Clerical Appeal" a group of Congregationalists, who belonged to the New England Anti-Slavery Society, attacked Garrison's methods and his associating abolition with women's rights.
43. More Methodist ministers, Garrison claimed, supported antislavery than clergymen of any other denomination.
44. Crawford Barclay, *Early American Methodism* (New York, 1949), II, 83–84.
45. See Charles B. Swaney, *Episcopal Methodism and Slavery* (Boston, 1926); John N. Norwood, *The Schism in the Methodist Episcopal Church* (Alfred, N. Y., 1923); Barclay, *Early American Methodism.*
46. Upon leaving the American Colonization Society to join the American Anti-Slavery Society, Birney moved to Cincinnati and began publishing an antislavery journal. An anti-abolitionist mob forced him to leave the city for a time. See Betty Fladeland, *James Birney: Slaveholder and Abolitionist* (Ithaca, N.Y., 1955), *passim.*
47. Norwood, *op. cit.,* p. 30.
48. *Debate on Modern Abolitionism in the General Conference of the Methodist Episcopal Church* (Cincinnati, 1836), *passim.*
49. *Loc. cit.*
50. Barclay, *op. cit.,* 104.
51. *Ibid.,* 105.
52. Swaney, *op. cit.,* p. 48.
53. *Ibid.,* p. 73.
54. *Ibid.,* p. 106.
55. For an account of the activities of the Friends of Humanity see Joseph M. Shea, "The Baptists and Slavery, 1840–1845" (unpublished Master's dissertation, Clark University, 1933).
56. *Baptist Magazine* (London), January 1835, p. 8.

57. *Loc. cit.*

58. *Loc. cit.* Cox was a member of the British Anti-Slavery Society. He failed to attend the American Society meeting because American Baptist leaders convinced him that it would be best if he avoided any contact with American abolitionists. In England George Thompson denounced Cox, calling him a coward for yielding to pressure and being frightened away from the abolitionists because they were unpopular.

59. *Loc. cit.*

60. F. A. Cox and J. Hoby, *The Baptist in America* (New York, 1836), *passim.*

61. *Ibid.*, p. 101.

62. *Ibid.*, pp. 101–102.

63. Francis Wayland, *Limitations of Human Responsibility* (Boston, 1838), p. 4.

64. *Ibid.*, p. 10.

65. *Ibid.*, p. 13.

66. *Ibid.*, pp. 162, 173.

67. *Ibid.*, p. 170.

68. A. A. Phelps, *Lectures on Slavery and Its Remedy,* quoted by Barclay, *op. cit.,* II, 102.

69. Calvin Colton, *Thoughts on the Religious State of the Country with Reasons for Prefering the Episcopacy* (New York, 1836), p. 95.

70. Calvin Colton, *Abolition a Sedition* (Philadelphia, 1839), pref.

71. *Ibid.*, p. 106.

72. *New York Review and Quarterly Church Journal,* III (1838), 130–132.

73. *Ibid.*, 394.

74. *Loc. cit.*

75. The Lutheran church was split by a conflict between those who wished to Americanize the church and those who wished to retain the old-world forms and doctrines. The Hartwick Synod encompassed much of upstate New York and some of western New England. This synod favored Americanizing, which meant, among other things, turning to evangelist activities; this led to debate within the church and the synod. See Harry J. Kreider, *History of the United Lutheran Synod of New York and New England* (Philadelphia, 1954), I, 92–102; Robert Fortenbaugh, "American

Lutheran Synods and Slavery, 1830–1860," *Journal of Religion,* vol. XIII (January 1933).

76. *Christian Examiner and General Review* (Boston), XIII (1833), 108.

77. *Ibid.,* (1833), 308; XXVI (1839), 304–307.

78. For the best expositions of Channing's views see David P. Edgell, *William Ellery Channing: An Intellectual Portrait* (Boston, 1955); and Madeline Rice, *Federal Street Pastor* (New York, 1962).

79. William Ellery Channing, *A Letter to the Abolitionists* (Boston, 1837), p. 5.

80. William Ellery Channing, *Slavery* (Boston, 1835), p. 118.

81. Samuel May, *Recollections of the Anti-Slavery Conflict* (Cambridge, Mass., 1869), p. 185.

82. In a letter to Jonathan Phillips, published in Boston in 1839, Channing continued to defend the abolitionists' civil rights, but he insisted he was not sympathetic to their cause.

83. Joseph D. Brokhage, *Francis Patrick Kendrick's Opinions on Slavery,* (Washington, D. C., 1955), p. 237.

84. Thomas E. Drake, *Quakers and Slavery in America* (New Haven, 1950), pp. 22, 32.

85. *Ibid.,* pp. 39–48.

86. *Ibid.,* p. 112.

87. *Ibid., passim.* The discussion of Quaker doctrinal controversies was drawn from this work.

88. The *Liberator* carried advertisements for goods sold in free produce stores, and Garrison occasionally urged subscribers to patronize these stores.

89. Drake, *op. cit.,* p. 132.

90. *Letter from William Bassett, Lynn, Massachusetts, 1839;* reprinted as an antislavery tract by the American Anti-Slavery Society.

91. I found evidence that antislavery societies were unpopular in Philadelphia as early as 1823. In that year Governor Coles of Illinois, fearing that his state might fall under pro-slavery influence, wrote to his friend Nicholas Biddle asking for aid. Biddle referred Coles to a wealthy Quaker merchant and philanthropist, Roberts Vaux. Biddle told Coles not to mention that he got help from Vaux, because Vaux did not wish to be associated with the antislavery movement. Biddle wrote: "The abolition Society of this city had been the subject, whether justly or not I am unable to determine, of

much hostility at a distance, and would be rather injurious than beneficial to have it supposed that the society was active in the cause which you are supporting." See "Cole Letters," *Journal of Negro History*, III (April 1918), 158–195.

92. Drake, *op. cit.*, pp. 157–158.

# 6

---•---

# *Abolition and the Anxieties of an Age*

Anti-abolitionism was widespread and intense in the North of the 1830's. It was founded on the prejudice of racism and the belief that the antislavery movement encouraged foreign criticism of America and even outright foreign interference. The grave charge made by opponents of abolition was that the movement threatened the Union, the Constitution, the right of states to govern their own affairs, and that it could lead to violence and race war. Quite unintentionally, the abolitionists had raised and aggravated a whole series of basic and complex issues. The fears and passions which these issues aroused dominated anti-abolitionism; consequently, the northern objections to antislavery were not only far-reaching—extending to every geographical area and segment of society—but also often more emotional than rational. This concluding chapter will be an attempt to explain these issues and their significance for the anti-abolitionist response.

The twentieth century has been called an age of anxiety. Critics of this view have often noted that all ages are times of anxiety. Certainly, men have always experienced concern but anxiety seems to diminish at some times and grow at others, and its impact on the course of events seems greater at one time than another. It is important, however, to remember that both confidence and anxiety may become more intense in the same society and at the same time, for optimism about the future may be coupled with deep fears.

This combination of confidence and anxiety showed itself in the 1830's, in a confidence in America's ability to absorb immigrants as long as they were white Protestants —and in a fear that Catholics neither could nor wished to be absorbed, and in an anxious conviction that Negroes were incapable of becoming part of American society. Americans, in the 1830's, felt an intense nationalism, yet a concern about the increased power of the national government; a confidence in the future of the Union, but concern for its future should major problems be raised; a confidence in the strength and superiority of America in relation to Europe, but a constant fear of foreign conspiracy; a recognition of the great economic development of the country, combined with a fear of rapid economic change. Americans believed social evils could be eradicated, but they feared that God intended for men always to face evil in their world.[1]

The abolitionists raised or aggravated problems which in one way or another touched upon all these sources of fear and confidence. To begin with, there was a racial problem in the North; even though slavery had ended, there existed profound and obvious inequalities and antagonisms between the races. A few anti-abolitionists considered racism in America to be a reason for rejecting antislavery, but most anti-abolitionists were racists who took Negro inferiority for granted and so rejected (as totally impractical) any antislavery proposal that did not include colonization. Charles Finney and William Ellery Channing objected to abolition not because they were racists but because so many other northerners were. They feared that adding freed slaves to the northern Negro population would intensify already existing problems. This was a rational perception of a real difficulty. But it is evident that anti-abolitionism also drew much strength from a less rational source—the racism of many anti-abolitionists themselves. Politicians, newspaper editors, and even reformers like Lyman Beecher and Horace Bushnell opposed any movement that would place the Negroes on equal terms with whites. Many anti-abolitionists simply accepted Negro inferiority as a fact and launched highly emotional, irrational attacks on the abolitionists' "desires" for a multiracial America.

In the 1830's Americans were already debating two basic political issues: the respective powers of the federal government and the states, and the possible dangers resulting from an increased electorate. Abolitionists raised the question of local versus national authority and so ran head on into an already sensitive problem. Though abolitionists did not ask for the Negro vote, they were thought to be seeking full rights for Negroes. Anti-abolitionists accused the antislavery men of being unconcerned about the political consequences of their demands, or even of intentionally fomenting discontent and problems in order to destroy the Republic. Abolitionists were also accused of using their cause as a front in order to gain power.

When anti-abolitionists argued that abolition threatened the right of states to govern their own affairs and even the continuation of the Union, they were pointing to real dangers. Abolition had been accomplished in the North on a state-by-state basis, but the new abolitionists called for national action. Furthermore, the South Carolina nullification controversy had focused attention on the possibility of disunion, and northerners were busy closing the ranks of the Union, ranks which abolition threatened to tear apart. Abolitionists challenged local authority and so threatened the

Union; they also promoted highly unpopular doctrines that might be so repugnant to southerners as to cause them to leave the Union in protest. Thus, northerners rejected antislavery not only because they feared the southern response, but also because of concern about the fate of the North, should antislavery men win their objectives. Men like James Paulding, James Austin, and the anonymous author of *A Sojourn into the City of Amalgamation* insisted that if antislavery succeeded, not only would the South secede, but those who remained in the Union would be dominated by the Negro.

The right of states to determine the fate of slavery was often linked to the argument that the slavery question was really the Negro question, and that both North and South felt this was a peculiar, inferior, race. If the Negro was inferior, what would happen to a political system in which inferior men were given equal rights? James Fenimore Cooper, Calvin Colton, Francis Wayland, and others warned about taking equality too literally. All men, they argued, were not equal in an absolute sense. If Americans came to accept Negro equality, they would believe all men were equal, and politics would simply become a contest of demagogues, each seeking to convince the people that he was going to carry equality further than his opponents. The confidence that America could absorb alien groups, weak when applied to Catholics, was almost nonexistent with regard to Negroes. The political system would be in grave danger should such groups participate in it; Negroes could easily be used by men whose sole interest was their own acquisition of power.

The problem arose as to whether men who preached subversive, potentially dangerous doctrines should be allowed to speak. Only Calvin Colton tried to focus attention on the question of whether abolition was actually seditious and so could be ended by legal means. Most of the other anti-abolitionists were not willing to consider the question at this level. Though anti-abolitionists refused, at least publicly, to condone the work of mobs, they explained mob violence as the natural outcome of the preaching of racial equality. Northerners feared that the political system would be unable to withstand such shocks.

The 1830's were a time of rapid economic change and uncertainty. To those concerned with the condition of factory workers or artisans who were hurt by competition with factory-produced goods, the abolitionist call for America to awaken to the plight of the Negro seemed to be a diversion from this major concern. More broadly, the abolitionists raised the problem of how to assure economic success for all Americans. Could the economy absorb millions of slaves once they were freed? Could the southern economy stand the loss of slave labor? Would the end of slavery mean that white men would be forced to do degrading work once done by slaves? It was entirely reasonable for labor spokesmen like Seth Luther, George Henry Evans, and the editors of the *National Trades Union* to warn of the problems of labor competition; but they became irrational when they insisted that abolitionists were agents of a wealthy class that wished to use antislavery in order to reduce wages. The fear that southerners would suffer from the loss of slave labor was also never discussed rationally. Would slaves remain on and continue to work plantation land? Was slavery more profitable than the use of free labor? Anti-abolition-ists failed to ask such questions, but instead took the posi-tion that ending slavery and destroying southern economic life were synonymous. Thus the abolitionists ran afoul of northern confidence in the existing economic system, and of northern anxiety as to the future of that system. Anti-abolition took the form of emotional attack rather than reasonable debate.

The combination of confidence and anxiety, evident in northern attitudes toward political and economic develop-ment, was also apparent in a more general attitude toward the future of American society. This was an age of reform, but abolitionist insistence on complete eradication of the evil—slavery—was not consistent with contemporary reform thinking.

A common belief of the 1830's was that God had chosen America to be the place where man would succeed in establishing an ideal society. The old Puritan vision of the City on a Hill had never died. Benjamin Franklin, George Washington, and in this era Andrew Jackson epit-omized the American belief that the country had combined the best of nature and civilization. But this optimism, so often expressed in an extreme chauvinism, rested partly on the feeling that anything so good must constantly be on guard lest it fall from grace. Americans of this period read their Bible and took it literally; the conflict of good and evil was very real to them. The abolitionists pointed out a basic flaw in American life. But anti-abolitionists insisted that the flaw was a carry-over from pre-Revolutionary days, an English institution; or they denied it was a flaw at all and developed defenses of slavery, calling it a humane way to treat an inferior people. Those who recognized slavery as an evil were quick to point out that the only proper way to end it was to remove the Negro from American society; accordingly, they supported colonization. In fact, most pre-Civil War reform movements did not demand the complete elimination of the evil they worked against. Thus, temperance men accepted that some men would always drink and simply called on the rest of society to insulate themselves from the evildoers. Abolitionists demanded an end to the evil and were intolerant of the slaveholder; but this was both too great an admission of an American failure and too unreasonable a demand on man and God for northerners to accept. Thus, even many of the clergy evaded the issue by denying that slavery was a moral problem or arguing that, even if it was a moral issue, abolition was not the moral way to resolve it.

In sum, the abolitionists offered the North a set of views and recommendations for action that could well be characterized as unreasonable, radical, dangerous, and unlawful.

Yet, the anti-abolitionists were not content to point out the flaws in antislavery logic, the legal and perhaps even moral grounds for rejecting the abolitionists' views and programs. Escapism as well as irrationality were evident in the anti-abolitionist arguments. This escapism and irrationalism resulted as much from exaggerated confidence and anxiety as from the real issues involved.

Between 1840 and 1860 the relation between abolitionists and the northern public underwent significant change. As late as 1860 or even 1863, the date of the New York anti-Negro "draft riots," northerners were still prejudiced against Negroes. However, that prejudice no longer was manifested in violence against abolitionists. The Texas question, the Mexican War, the struggle over slavery in Kansas, etc., all point to increasing rather than decreasing problems; yet, abolitionists now had found a place in the North as legitimate critics of an aspect of American life. Nationalism was growing stronger—as evidenced in the Know-Nothing movement, the strength of the Constitutional Union party, and the nationalist pose now assumed by both the North and South. But nationalism no longer claimed antislavery as its enemy. In 1837 John Quincy Adams stood almost alone among respectable New Englanders willing to allow abolitionists free speech. In 1856 moderate antislavery supporters like Charles Sumner represented the Bay State in Congress, and Theodore Parker and others were willing to break the law in fighting the Fugitive Slave Act. Garrison, who was mobbed in the

1830's, found a large and interested audience in the 1850's. Antislavery still had not captured the North, but it was now an acceptable reform movement, a respectable cause, since it sought to assure the secular and theological future of the country in the face of its enemies, the slaveholders.

In the 1830's anti-abolitionists rejected antislavery out of both their optimism and pessimism about the condition of America. However, in the 1850's the "slave power" became the accepted cause of tension. We are familiar with the reaction of northerners to the events of the 1850's. Southern acts of violence and accusations against the North combined to convince northerners that the South threatened the security of the nation. The abolitionists, as Russel Nye points out, encouraged that belief.[2]

The sources of public opinion we have here surveyed reflected and shaped the new abolitionist image. Politicians like William Seward, who in the 1830's had rejected the antislavery cause, in the 1850's found it convenient and politically valuable to support abolition. Reformers such as the Beechers and Charles G. Finney, who in the 1830's had rejected antislavery, now found abolition a deserving cause —while the press, which in the thirties had branded abolitionists as conspirators perpetrating acts of violence, leveled the same charges against the South. Romantic novels about the South, so popular in the North during the 1830's, were disappearing in the 1850's. Instead northerners now read Harriet Beecher Stowe's sentimental novel of family disruption and the evils of slavery and were critical of the slave system and of at least some of those who were involved in it. Thus, though they failed to change northern attitudes toward the Negro and still were unable to convince most northerners that they had the remedy to the slavery problem, the abolitionists of the 1840's and 1850's found they were no longer the enemies of the people. The southern slaveholder, rather than the abolitionist, was the target of attack; for now the slaveholder personified the threat to American confidence and provided the basis for American anxieties.

## NOTES

1. This combination of confidence and anxiety has been noted or can be observed in a number of recent studies of the period. It is pointed out by Marvin Meyers, *The Jacksonian Persuasion* (Vintage ed., New York, 1957), and by William Taylor, *Cavalier and Yankee* (New York, 1961). Paul Nagle, *One Nation Indivisible* (New York, 1964), and George Dangerfield, *The Awakening of American Nationalism* (New York, 1965), provide evidence of the tension between nationalism and localism. R. W. B. Lewis, *American Adam* (Chicago, 1955), and Leo Marx, *The Machine in the Garden* (New York, 1964), study the theme as found in the literature of the time. The problem of fear of foreign conspiracy is most interestingly handled by Ray Billington, *The Protestant Crusade* (New York, 1938), and recently by David Davis, "Some Themes of Counter-Subversion." *Mississippi Valley Historical Review*, XLVII (September, 1960), 205–224. Meyers, *op. cit.,* Bray Hammond, *Banks and Politics in America from the Revolution to the Civil War* (Princeton, 1957), and Arthur Schlesinger, Jr., *The Age of Jackson* (Boston, 1953), all provide evidence of both economic disruption and success in the 1830's. The view of pre-Civil War reform as a move-

ment more concerned with isolating than with eradicating evil is presented by Timothy Smith, *Revivalism and Social Reform in Mid-Nineteenth Century America* (Nashville, 1957), by Clifford Griffin, *Their Brothers' Keepers* (New Brunswick, 1960), and others.

2. See Russel Nye, *Fettered Freedom* (East Lansing, Mich., 1949).

# *Bibliography*

## I. INTRODUCTION

I have organized the following bibliography to suggest the techniques used in preparing this volume. In each category selection has been made from a much larger body of material. Only some of the sources consulted are included in the bibliography.

To develop my topic it was necessary to become familiar with a variety of literature. I read both historical and sociological literature dealing with the Negro in the North. In order to become familiar with abolitionist activities and programs I consulted general studies of the antislavery movement, biographies of antislavery leaders, and primary source material. I also sought information as to the general tone of northern life in the 1830's.

The next step was to discover reactions to what abolitionists proposed, what people thought they proposed, and what they thought these reformers might propose. I

*Bibliography*

searched newspapers, magazines, general literature, reports of religious and political organizations, and published statements of religious and political leaders. Although I had to exercise selection in my choice of materials to survey, I sought representative elements in each category. Finally I looked for specific reactions to abolition and not just evidences of anti-abolition.

## II. THE NEGRO IN AMERICA BEFORE 1840

Allport, Gordon. *The Nature of Prejudice.* Abr. ed., New York, 1958.

Andrews, Charles C. *The History of the New York African Free Schools.* New York, 1830.

Anon. *An Inquiry Into the Condition and Prospects of the African Race in the United States and the Means of Bettering Its Fortunes.* Philadelphia, 1839.

Aptheker, Herbert. *A Documentary History of the Negro People in the United States.* New York, 1951.

Aptheker, Herbert. *The Negro in the Abolitionist Movement.* New York, 1941. (Pamphlet.)

Aptheker, Herbert. *Slave Insurrections in the United States, 1800–1860.* Boston, 1938.

Aptheker, Herbert. *To Be Free.* New York, 1948.

Brawley, Benjamin. *A Short History of the American Negro.* New York, 1913.

Brawley, Benjamin. *A Social History of the American Negro.* New York, 1921.

Brown, Sterling. *The Negro in American Fiction.* Washington, D.C., 1937. (Pamphlet.)

Butcher, Margaret J. *The Negro in American Culture.* New York, 1957.

Carroll, Joseph C. *Slave Insurrections in the United States, 1800–1865.* Boston, 1938.

Catterall, Helen T. *Judicial Cases Concerning American Slavery and the Negro.* 4 vols. Washington, D.C., 1936.

Dubois, William E. B. *The Philadelphia Negro, A Social Study.* Philadelphia, 1899.

Dubois, William E. B. *The Suppression of the African Slave-Trade to the United States of America, 1638–1870.* Rev. ed. New York, 1954.

Dykes, Eva B. *The Negro in English Romantic Thought.* Washington, D.C., 1942.

Freeman, F. Yardee. *A Plea for Africa.* Philadelphia, 1836.

Frazier, E. Franklin. *The Negro in the United States.* Rev. ed., New York, 1957.

Greene, Lorenzo J. *The Negro in Colonial New England.* New York, 1942.

Hartgrove, William B. "The Negro Soldier in the American Revolution," *Journal of Negro History,* I (April, 1916), 110–131.

Haynes, Leonard L., Jr. *The Negro Community within American Protestantism, 1619–1844.* Boston, 1953.

Herskovits, Melville J. *The Myth of the Negro Past.* New York, 1941.

Hirsch, Leo H. "The Negro in New York, 1783 to 1865," *Journal of Negro History,* XVI (October, 1931), 382–473.

Johnson, James W. *Black Manhattan.* New York, 1940.

Kallen, Horace M. *Cultural Pluralism and the American Idea.* Philadelphia, 1956.

Litwack, Leon. *North of Slavery.* Chicago, Ill., 1961.

Mehlinger, Louis R. "The Attitude of the Free Negro toward African Colonization," *Journal of Negro History,* I (July, 1916), 276–301.

Myrdal, Gunnar. *An American Dilemma.* New York, 1944.

Odum, Howard. *Race and Rumors of Race.* Chapel Hill, N. C., 1943.

## Bibliography

Penn, I. Garland. *The Afro-American Press and Its Editors.* Springfield, Mass., 1891.

Quarles, Benjamin. "The Colonial Militia and Negro Manpower," *Mississippi Valley Historical Review,* XIV (March, 1959), 643–652.

Ruchames, Louis. "Jim Crow Railroads in Massachusetts," *American Quarterly,* VIII, (Spring, 1956), 61–75.

Ruchames, Louis. "Race, Marriage, Abolition in Massachusetts," *Journal of Negro History,* XL (July, 1955), 250–273.

Samuelson, Babette. "The Patterning of Attitudes and Beliefs Regarding the American Negro: An Analysis of Public Opinion." Unpublished Ph.D. dissertation, Radcliffe, 1945, Boston.

Simpson, George E. and Yinger, J. Milton. *Racial and Cultural Minorities.* New York, 1953.

Tannenbaum, Frank. *Slave and Citizen: The Negro in the Americas.* New York, 1947.

Turner, Edward R. *The Negro in Pennsylvania, Slavery-Servitude-Freedom, 1639–1861.* Washington, D.C., 1911.

Wagley, Charles and Harris, Marvin. *Minorities in the New World.* New York, 1958.

Warner, Robert A. *New Haven Negroes: A Social History.* New Haven, 1940.

Weatherford, W. D. *American Churches and the Negro.* Boston, 1957.

Wesley, Charles H. *Negro Labor in the United States.* New York, 1927.

Williams, George W. *History of the Negro Race in America, 1619–1880.* 2 vols. New York, 1883.

Williams, Robin. *The Reduction of Intergroup Tensions: A Survey of Research on Problems of Ethnic, Racial, and Religious Group Relations.* (S.S.R.C. Bulletin 57.) New York, 1947.

Wish, Harvey. "Slave Insurrections before 1860," *Journal of Southern History,* III (July, 1937), 299–320.

Wright, Marion T. "Negro Suffrage in New Jersey, 1776–1875,"

*Journal of Negro History,* XXXIII (April, 1948), 168–224.

Woodson, Carter. *The History of the Negro Church.* 2nd ed. Washington, D.C., 1921.

Woodson, Carter, ed. *The Mind of the Negro as Reflected in Letters Written During the Crisis, 1800–1860.* Washington, D.C., 1926.

Woodson, Carter. *Negro Orators and Their Orations.* Washington, D.C., 1925.

Woodson, Carter. *The Education of the Negro Prior to 1861: A History of the Colored People of the United States from the Beginning of Slavery to the Civil War.* New York, 1915.

III. ATTITUDES AND VALUES IN THE 1830's

Bendix, Reinhard. *Work and Authority in Industry.* New York, 1956.

Blau, Joseph, ed. *Social Theories of Jacksonian Democracy.* New York, 1954.

Billington, Ray. *The Protestant Crusade, 1800–1860.* New York, 1938.

Burns, Edward M. *The American Idea of Mission.* New Brunswick, N. J., 1957.

Craven, Avery. *Civil War in the Making.* Baton Rouge, La., 1959.

Craven, Avery. *The Coming of the Civil War.* 2nd ed. Chicago, 1957.

Cross, Whitney. *The Burned-Over District.* Ithaca, N. Y., 1952.

Curti, Merle. *The Roots of American Loyalty.* New York, 1946.

Davis, David B. *Homicide in American Fiction, 1789–1860.* Ithaca, N. Y., 1957.

Farnam, Henry W. *Chapters in the History of Social Legislation in the United States to 1860.* Washington, D.C., 1938.

Floan, Howard R. *The South in Northern Eyes.* Austin, Texas, 1958.

Foner, Philip. *The History of the Labor Movement in the United States.* New York, 1947.

Miller, Perry. "The Romantic Dilemma in American Nationalism and the Concept of Nature," *Harvard Theological Review,* XLVI (October, 1955), 239–254.

Myers, Marvin. *The Jacksonian Persuasion.* Stanford, Calif., 1957.

Nevins, Allan. *Ordeal of the Union.* 2 vols. New York, 1947.

Osterweis, Roland. *Romanticism and Nationalism in the Old South.* New Haven, 1949.

Paul, Sherman. *The Shores of America.* Urbana, Ill., 1958.

Riegel, Robert E. *Young America.* Norman, Okla., 1949.

Rourke, Constance M. *Trumpets of Jubilee.* New York, 1927.

Schlesinger, Arthur, Jr. *The Age of Jackson.* Boston, 1953.

Smith, Timothy L. *Revivalism and Social Reform in Mid-Nineteenth-Century America.* Nashville, Tenn., 1957.

Taylor, William R. *Cavalier and Yankee.* New York, 1961.

Van Deusen, Glyndon. *The Jacksonian Era, 1828–1848.* New York, 1959.

Ward, John W. *Jackson: Symbol of an Age.* New York, 1955.

Weinberg, Albert K. *Manifest Destiny: A Study of Nationalist Expansionism in American History.* Baltimore, 1935.

## IV. THE ANTISLAVERY MOVEMENTS

Abel, Annie H. and Klingburg, Frank J. *A Side-Light on Anglo-American Relations, 1839–1858.* Lancaster, Pa., 1927.

Adams, Alice D. *The Neglected Period of Anti-Slavery in America, 1808–1831.* Boston and London, 1908.

*American Anti-Slavery Society Annual Reports.* New York, N. Y., 1834–1840.

Barnes, Gilbert H. *The Anti-Slavery Impulse, 1830–1844.* New York and London, 1933.

Barnes, Gilbert H. and Dumond, Dwight L., eds. *Letters of Theodore Dwight Weld, Angelina Grimké Weld and Sarah Grimké.* 2 vols. New York, 1934.

Barrows, E. P. "A View of the American Slavery Question." New York, 1836.

Bassett, William. *Letter from William Bassett* (American Anti-Slavery Society Tract). Lynn, Mass., 1839.

Beecher, Catherine E. *An Essay on Slavery and Abolitionism.* Philadelphia, 1837.

Beecher, Edward. *Narrative of Riots at Alton in Connection with the Death of Rev. Elijah P. Lovejoy.* Alton, Ill., 1838.

Birney, James G. *The Letters of James Gillespie Birney.* Dumond, Dwight L., ed. 2 vols. New York, 1938.

Birney, William. *James G. Birney and His Times.* New York, 1890.

Brown, Arthur W. *Always Young for Liberty.* Syracuse, N. Y., 1956.

Channing, William E. *A Letter to the Abolitionists.* Boston, 1837.

Channing, William E. *A Letter to the Hon. Henry Clay on the Annexation of Texas to the United States.* Boston, 1837.

Channing, William E. *Slavery.* Boston, 1835.

Channing, William E. *Works.* 19th ed., 6 vols. Boston, 1869.

Child, Lydia M. *The Oasis.* Boston, 1834.

Commager, Henry S. *Theodore Parker.* Boston, 1936.

Curti, Merle. "Reformers Consider the Constitution," *American Journal of Sociology,* XLIII (May, 1938), 878–893.

Dillon, Merton, "The Failure of the Abolitionists," *Journal of Southern History,* XXV (May, 1959), 159–177.

Donald, David. *Lincoln Reconsidered: Essays on the Civil War Era.* New York, 1956.

Dumond, Dwight L. *Anti-Slavery Origins of the Civil War.* Ann Arbor, Michigan, 1959.

Dumond, Dwight L. "Race Prejudice and Abolition," *Michigan Alumnus Quarterly Review,* XLI (April, 1935), 377–385.

*Bibliography*

Dyson, Zita. "Gerritt Smith and the Negro," *Journal of Negro History,* III (October, 1918), 354–359.

Earle, Thomas. *The Life, Travels, and Opinions of Benjamin Lundy.* Philadelphia, 1847.

Edgell, David P. *William Ellery Channing: An Intellectual Portrait.* Boston, 1955.

Elkins, Stanley M. *Slavery: A Problem in American Institutional and Intellectual Life.* Chicago, 1959.

Fladeland, Betty. *James Birney; Slaveholder and Abolitionist.* Ithaca, N. Y., 1955.

Foner, Philip. *Business and Slavery: The New York Merchants and the Irrepressible Conflict.* Chapel Hill, N. C., 1941.

Fox, Early L. *The American Colonization Society, 1817–1840.* Baltimore, 1919.

Garrison, F. P. and Garrison, W. P. *William Lloyd Garrison, 1805–1879.* 4 vols. New York, 1885–1889.

Garrison, William L. *Selections from the Speeches and Writings of William Lloyd Garrison.* Boston, 1852.

Garrison, William L. *Thoughts on African Colonization.* Boston, 1832.

Goodell, William. *Slavery and Anti-Slavery, History of the Great Struggle in both Hemispheres; with a View to the Slavery Question in the United States.* New York, 1852.

Gill, John. *Tide Without Turning: Elijah P. Lovejoy and Freedom of the Press.* Boston, 1958.

Harlow, Ralph V. *Gerrit Smith, Philanthropist and Reformer.* New York, 1939.

Hart, Albert B. *Slavery and Abolition.* New York, 1906.

Jenkins, William S. *Pro-Slavery Thought in the South.* Chapel Hill, N. C., 1935.

Johnson, Oliver. *William Lloyd Garrison.* Boston and New York, 1880.

Korngold, Ralph. *Two Friends of Man: William Lloyd Garrison and Wendell Phillips.* Boston, 1950.

Levy, Leonard W. "The Abolition Riot: Boston's First Slave

Rescue," *New England Quarterly,* XXV (March, 1952), 85–92.

Lloyd, Arthur Y. *The Slavery Controversy 1831–1860.* Chapel Hill, N. C., 1939.

Lowell, James Russell. *Anti-Slavery Papers.* W. B. Parker, ed. 2 vols. New York, 1902.

Lyman, Theodore. *Papers Relating to the Garrison Mob.* Cambridge, 1870.

May, Samuel. *Recollections of the Anti-Slavery Conflict.* Cambridge, Mass., 1869.

Mellon, Mathew T. *Early American Views on Negro Slavery.* Boston, 1934.

Moore, George H. *Notes on the History of Slavery in Massachusetts.* New York, 1866.

Needles, Edward. *An Historical Memoir of the Pennsylvania Society for Promoting the Abolition of Slavery.* Philadelphia, 1848.

Nye, Russel. *Fettered Freedom.* East Lansing, Michigan, 1949.

Nye, Russel. "The Slave Power Conspiracy 1830–1860," *Science and Society,* X (Summer, 1946), 262–274.

Nye, Russel. *William Lloyd Garrison and the Humanitarian Reformers.* Boston, 1955.

Parker, Theodore. *Sermons on Slavery.* Boston, 1848–1858.

Phillips, Wendell. *Speeches, Letters and Lectures.* Boston, 1863.

Power, Richard L. "A Crusade to Extend Yankee Culture," *New England Quarterly,* XIII (December, 1940), 638–653.

Rush, Benjamin. *An Address to the Inhabitants of the British Colonies in America Upon Slavekeeping.* Norwich, England, 1775.

Sewall, Samuel E. *Remarks on Slavery in the United States.* Boston, 1827.

Sherwin, Oscar. *Prophet of Liberty: The Life and Times of Wendell Phillips.* New York, 1958.

Siebert, William H. *The Underground Railroad: from Slavery to Freedom.* New York, 1898.

Skotheim, Robert. "A Note on Historical Method: David Donald's 'Toward a Reconsideration of Abolitionists,'" *Journal of Southern History,* XXV (August, 1959), 356–365.

Small, E. W. and Small, M. R. "Prudence Crandall," *New England Quarterly,* XVII (December, 1944), 506–529.

Stampp, Kenneth. "The Fate of Southern Anti-Slavery," *Journal of Negro History,* XXVIII (January, 1943), 10–22.

Stanton, Henry B. *Remarks in the Representatives Hall on the 23rd and 24th of February, before the Committee of the House of Representatives of Massachusetts. . . .* Boston, 1837.

Stanton, Henry B. *Random Recollections.* New York, 1887.

Swift, Lindsay. *William Lloyd Garrison.* Philadelphia, 1911.

Tappan, Arthur. "Correspondence," *Journal of Negro History,* XII (April, 1927), 179–329.

Tappan, Lewis. *Arthur Tappan.* New York, 1870.

Thistlethwaite, Frank. *The Anglo-American Connection in the Early Nineteenth Century.* Philadelphia, 1959.

Thomas, Benjamin P. *Theodore Weld.* New Brunswick, N. J., 1950.

Weld, Theodore. *Bible against Slavery.* New York, 1838.

Whitfield, Theodore M. *Slavery Agitation in Virginia, 1829–1832.* Baltimore, 1930.

Wolf, Hazel C. *On Freedom's Altar: The Martyr Complex in the Abolition Movement.* Madison, Wisconsin, 1952.

### V. NEWSPAPERS AND MAGAZINES

*Advocate* (changed in 1838 to the *Colored American.* New York and Philadelphia), 1837–1839.

*African Repository* (Washington, D.C.), 1831–1840.

*Albany Argus,* 1835–1837.

*American Quarterly Observer* (Boston), 1831–1840.

*American Quarterly Review* (Philadelphia), 1831–1840.

*Atkinson's Saturday Evening Post* (Philadelphia), 1833–1839.
*Baptist Magazine* (London, England), 1833–1839.
*Bay State Democrat* (Boston), 1838–1839.
*Bentley's Miscellany* (London, England), 1831–1840.
*Biblical Repertory and Theological Review* (Philadelphia), 1831–1840.
*Blackwood's Magazine* (London, England), 1832–1840.
*Boston Atlas*, 1838–1839.
*Boston Quarterly Review*, 1838–1839.
*Boston Recorder*, 1831–1840.
*Boston Transcript*, 1831–1840.
Chamberlin, Joseph E. *The Boston Transcript*. Cambridge, Mass., 1930.
*Christian Advocate* (Philadelphia), 1834.
*Christian Examiner and General Review* (Boston), 1831–1839.
*Christian Intelligencer* (New York), 1832–1838.
*Eastern Argus* (Portland, Me.), 1835–1837.
*Edinburgh Review* (Edinburgh, Scotland), 1831–1840.
*Emancipator* (New York), 1835.
*Emporium and True American* (Trenton, N. J.), 1837–1839.
*Godey's Ladies Book* (Philadelphia), 1831–1839.
*Ithaca Chronicle* (Ithaca, N. Y.), 1835–1839.
*Ithaca Journal* (Ithaca, N. Y.), 1836–1839.
*Jesuit or Catholic Sentinel* (changed to *The Pilot*) (Boston), 1831–1838.
*Kennebec Weekly Journal* (Augusta, Me.), 1831–1838.
*Knickerbocker Magazine* (New York), 1835–1840.
*Liberator* (Boston), 1831–1840.
*Massachusetts Abolitionist* (Boston), 1839.
*Mechanics Magazine* (New York), 1833–1837.
*National Trades Union* (New York), 1834–1837.
Nevins, Allan. *American Press Opinion: Washington to Coolidge.* New York, 1928.
*New Bedford Daily Gazette* (New Bedford, Mass.), 1833–1835.
*New Bedford Mercury* (New Bedford, Mass.), 1833–1839.

*Newburyport Daily Herald* (Newburyport, Mass.), 1832–1839.
*New England Farmer and Horticultural Journal* (Boston), 1833–1839.
*New England Magazine* (Boston), 1832–1839.
*New Jersey Journal* (Elizabethtown, N. J.), 1835–1839.
*New York Commercial Advertiser,* 1832–1837.
*New York Evangelist,* 1835–1837.
*New York Evening Post,* 1831–1837.
*New York Herald,* 1835–1839.
*New York Journal of Commerce,* 1831–1839.
*New York Review and Quarterly Church Journal,* 1837–1839.
*Niles's Register* (Baltimore), 1820–1840.
*North American Review* (Boston), 1831–1839.
*Norwich Courier* (Norwich, Conn.), 1831–1837.
*Pennsylvanian* (Philadelphia), 1831–1839.
*Princeton Whig,* 1835–1839.
*Quarterly Christian Spectator* (New Haven), 1832–1837.
*Quarterly Register of the American Educational Society* (Boston), 1831–1835.
*Reformed Presbyterian* (Newburgh, N. Y.), 1838–1839.
*Religious Monitor and Evangelical Repository* (Albany, N. Y.), 1831–1839.
*Rhode Island Country Journal* (Providence), 1833–1837.
*United States Gazette* (Philadelphia), 1831–1839.
*United States Magazine and Democratic Review* (New York), 1838–1840.
*Zion's Watchman* (New York), 1836.

VI. NOVELS, PLAYS, TRAVEL BOOKS, AND
SOCIAL COMMENTARY

Anon. *The Reign of Reform or Yankee Doodle Court.* Baltimore, 1830.

Beaumont, Gustave de. *Marie, or Slavery in the United States.* New ed. Stanford, Calif., 1959.

Bickley, Lloyd. *The Aristocrat: An American Tale.* 2 vols. Philadelphia, 1833.

Bird, Robert M. *The City Looking Glass: A Philadelphia Comedy.* New York, 1933.

Bird, Robert M. *Nick of the Woods.* Rev. ed. New York, 1939.

Bird, Robert M. *Peter Pilgrim.* 2 vols. Philadelphia, 1838.

Bird, Robert M. *Sheppard Lee.* 2 vols. New York, 1836.

Bolokitten, Oliver (pseud.) *A Sojourn in the City of Amalgamation in the Year of Our Lord 19—.* New York, 1835.

Brothers, Thomas. *The United States of North America As They Are; Not As They Are Generally Described: Being a Cure for Radicalism.* London, England, 1840.

Carruthers, William A. *The Cavaliers of Virginia; or the Recluse of Jamestown.* 2 vols. New York, 1834–1835.

Carruthers, William A. *The Kentuckian in New York or the Adventures of Three Southerners.* 2 vols. New York, 1834.

Cooper, James F. *The American Democrat.* New ed. New York, 1931.

Cooper, James F. *Correspondence of James Fenimore Cooper,* James F. Cooper, ed. 4 vols. New Haven, Conn., 1922.

Cooper, James F. *Home as Found.* Leatherstocking ed. New York, 1896.

Cooper, James F. *Homeward Bound.* Leatherstocking ed. New York, 1896.

Cooper, James F. *The Last of the Mohicans.* Leatherstocking ed. New York, 1896.

# Bibliography

Emerson, Ralph W. *Journals.* Edward W. Emerson and Waldo C. Forbes, eds. 10 vols. Boston, 1909.

Foust, Clement E. *Robert Montgomery Bird: Life and Dramatic Works.* New York, 1919.

Gilman, Caroline. *Recollections of a New England Bride and a Southern Matron.* New York, 1838.

Greene, Asa. *Travels in America.* New York, 1833.

Grossman, James. *James Fenimore Cooper.* New York, 1949.

Hall, Captain Basil. *Travels in North America in the Years 1827–1828.* 2nd ed. 3 vols. Edinburgh, 1830.

Herold, Amos L. *James Kirke Paulding: Versatile American.* New York, 1926.

Kennedy, John P. *Swallow Barn or a Sojourn in the Old Dominion.* Philadelphia, 1832.

McClung, John A. *Camden, A Tale of the South.* 2 vols. Philadelphia, 1830.

Martineau, Harriet. *Society in America.* 2 vols. New York, 1837.

Martineau, Harriet. *Retrospect of Western Travel.* 3 vols. London, England, 1838.

Mesick, Jane L. *The English Traveler in America 1785–1835.* New York, 1922.

Murray, Charles A. *Travels in North America.* 2 vols. New York, 1839.

Paulding, James K. *Letters from the South by a Northern Man.* New York, 1835.

Paulding, James K. *The Lion of the West.* New ed. Stanford, California, 1954.

Paulding, James K. *Slavery in the United States.* New York, 1836.

Pierson, George W. *Beaumont and Tocqueville in America.* New York, 1938.

Quinn, A. H. *A History of the American Drama.* Rev. ed. New York, 1943.

Spiller, Robert E.; Thorpe, Willard; Johnson, Thomas; Canby, Henry S., eds. *Literary History of the United States.* Rev. ed. New York, 1955.

**156**

Tocqueville, Alexis de. *Democracy in America.* New ed. 2 vols. New York, 1945.

Trollope, Frances. *Domestic Manners of the Americans.* 4th ed. London and New York, 1832.

Turner, Lorenzo D. "Anti-Slavery Sentiment in American Literature," *Journal of Negro History, XIV* (October, 1929), 371–492.

A Virginian (pseud.). *Rose-Hill.* Philadelphia, 1835.


VII. THE CHURCHES AND ABOLITION


Andrews, Rena M. "Slavery Views of a Northern Prelate," *Church History,* III (March, 1934), 60–78.

Armstrong, Maurice W., Loetscher, Lefferts A., Anderson, Charles A., eds. *The Presbyterian Enterprise, Sources of American Presbyterian History.* Philadelphia, 1956.

Bacon, Theodore D. *Leonard Bacon.* New Haven, 1931.

Barclay, Crawford. *Early American Methodism.* 2 vols. New York, 1949.

Barnes, Albert, *The Church and Slavery.* Philadelphia, 1857.

Beecher, Lyman. *Autobiography and Correspondence of Lyman Beecher.* Charles Beecher, ed. 2 vols. New York, 1865.

Bodo, John R. *The Protestant Clergy and Public Issues, 1812–1848.* Princeton, N. J., 1954.

Brokhage, Rev. Joseph D. *Francis Patrick Kenricks' Opinion on Slavery.* Washington, D.C., 1955.

Brookes, George S. *Friend Anthony Benezet.* Philadelphia, 1937.

Bushnell, Horace. *A Discourse on the Slavery Question. Delivered in the North Church, Hartford, Connecticut, January 10, 1839.*

Clark, Calvin M. *American Slavery and Maine Congregationalists.* Bangor, Maine, 1940.

Cole, Charles C., Jr. "Horace Bushnell and the Slavery Question," *New England Quarterly,* XXIII (March, 1950), 19–30.

## Bibliography

Cole, Charles C. *The Social Ideas of Northern Evangelists.* New York, 1954.

Colton, Calvin. *The Genius and Mission of the Protestant Episcopal Church in the United States.* New York, 1853.

Cooke, George Willis. *Unitarianism in America.* Boston, 1902.

Cox, Rev. F. A. and Hoby, Rev. J. *The Baptists in America.* New York, 1836.

*Debate on Modern Abolitionism in the General Conference of the Methodist Episcopal Church.* Cincinnati, 1836.

*Discussion on American Slavery between George Thompson and Rev. Robert J. Breckenridge.* Boston, 1836.

Drake, Thomas E. *Quakers and Slavery in America.* New Haven, 1950.

Drury, Clifford M. *Presbyterian Panorama.* Philadelphia, 1952.

Fortenbaugh, Robert. "American Lutheran Synods and Slavery, 1830–1860," *Journal of Religion,* XIII (January, 1933), 72–92.

Foss, A. T. and Mathews, E. *Facts for Baptist Churches.* Utica, N. Y., 1850.

Griffin, Clifford S. "The Abolitionists and the Benevolent Societies, 1831–1861," *Journal of Negro History,* XLIV (July, 1959), 195–216.

Griffin, Clifford S. "Religious Benevolence as Social Control, 1815–1860," *Mississippi Valley Historical Review,* XLIV (December, 1957), 423–444.

Kreider, Harry J. *History of the United Lutheran Synod of New York and New England.* 2 vols. Philadelphia, 1954.

Kull, Irving. "Presbyterian Attitudes Toward Slavery," *Church History,* VII (June, 1938), 101–114.

Lyons, Adelaide A. *Religious Defense of Slavery in the North.* (Historical Papers Published by the Trinity College Historical Society, Series XIII.) Durham, N. C., 1919.

McLouglin, William G. *Modern Revivalism.* New York, 1959.

McMaster, Gilbert. *The Moral Character of Civil Government*

*Considered with Reference to the Political Institutions of the United States.* Duanesburgh, N. Y., 1832.

Manross, William W. *The Episcopal Church in the United States, 1800–1840.* New York, 1938.

Moore, Edmund A. "Robert J. Breckenridge and the Slavery Aspect of the Presbyterian Schism of 1837," *Church History,* IV (December, 1935), 282–294.

Norwood, John N. *The Schism in the Methodist Episcopal Church, 1844.* Alfred, N. Y., 1923.

Nueremberger, Ruth A. *The Free Produce Movement: A Quaker Protest against Slavery.* Durham, N. C., 1942.

Pennington, Edgar L. "Thomas Bray's Associates and Their Work among the Negroes," *Proceedings of the American Antiquarian Society* (October, 1938), pp. 311–403.

Rice, Madeline H. *American Catholic Opinion in the Slavery Controversy.* New York, 1944.

Shea, Joseph M. "The Baptists and Slavery, 1840–1845." (Unpublished M.A. dissertation. Clark University, 1933.)

Staiger, C. Bruce. "Abolitionism and the Presbyterian Schism of 1837–1838," *Mississippi Valley Historical Review,* XXXVI (December, 1949), 391–414.

Swaney, Charles B. *Episcopal Methodism and Slavery.* Boston, 1926.

Wayland, Francis. *The Limitations of Human Responsibility.* Boston, 1838.

Weisburger, Bernard A. *They Gathered at the River.* Boston, 1958.

Whedon, Daniel D. *Essays, Reviews and Discourses.* J. S. Whedon and D. A. Whedon, eds. New York, 1887.

Whipple, Charles K. *Relation of the American Board of Commissioners for Foreign Missions to Slavery.* Boston, 1861.

Woodson, Carter, "Anthony Benezet," *Journal of Negro History,* II (January, 1917). 37–50.

Woolman, John. *Extracts on the Subject of Slavery from the Journal and Writings of John Woolman.* New York, 1840.

## VIII. NORTHERN POLITICIANS AND ABOLITION

Adams, John. *Works.* Charles F. Adams, ed. 10 vols. Boston, 1856.

Adams, John Quincy. *The Diary of John Quincy Adams, 1794–1845.* Allan Nevins, ed. New York, 1928.

Austin, James T. *Remarks on Dr. Channing's Slavery by a Citizen of Massachusetts.* Boston, 1835.

Bancroft, Frederick. *Life of William H. Seward.* 2 vols. New York, 1900.

Bemis, Samuel F. *John Quincy Adams and the Union.* New York, 1956.

Brodie, Fawn. *Thaddeus Stevens.* New York, 1959.

Burden, J. R. *Remarks of J. R. Burden of Philadelphia County in the Senate of Pennsylvania on the Abolition Question.* Philadelphia, 1838.

Byrdsall, F. *The History of the Loco-Foco or Equal Rights Party.* New York, 1842.

Coles, Edward. "Letters of Gov. Coles of Illinois." *Journal of Negro History,* II (April, 1918).

Colton, Calvin. *Abolition a Sedition.* Philadelphia, 1839.

Colton, Calvin. *The Americans.* London, England, 1833.

Colton, Calvin. *Colonization and Abolition Contrasted.* Philadelphia, 1839.

Current, Richard N. *Old Thad Stevens.* Madison, Wisc., 1942.

Darling, Arthur B. *Political Changes in Massachusetts.* New Haven, 1925.

Detweiler, Phillip F. "Congressional Debate on Slavery and the Declaration of Independence, 1819–1821," *American Historical Review,* LXIII (April, 1958), 598–616.

Frothingham, Paul R. *Edward Everett.* Boston and New York, 1925.

Fuess, Claude M. *The Life of Caleb Cushing.* 2 vols. New York, 1923.

Fuess, Claude M. "Daniel Webster and the Abolitionists," *Massachusetts Historical Society Proceedings,* LXIV (November, 1930), 28–49.

Greeley, Horace. *Recollections of a Busy Life.* New York, 1868.

Howe, Mark D. W. *The Life and Letters of George Bancroft.* 2 vols. New York, 1908.

Moore, Glover. *The Missouri Controversy, 1819–1821.* Lexington, Ky., 1953.

Morison, Samuel Eliot. *The Life and Letters of Harrison Gray Otis, Federalist, 1765–1848.* 2 vols. Boston, 1913.

Parton, James. *Famous Americans of Recent Times.* Boston, 1867.

Rantoul, Robert, Jr. *Memoirs, Speeches and Writings of Robert Rantoul, Jr.* Luther Hamilton, ed. Boston, 1854.

*Report of the Committee Appointed to Draft Resolutions Relative to the Proceedings of the Advocates of Immediate Abolition of Slavery in the Southern States. Presented to the New Hampshire House of Representatives, January 11, 1837.*

Sellers, Charles G. *James Polk, Jacksonian, 1795–1843.* Princeton, N. J., 1957.

Snyder, Charles M. *The Jacksonian Heritage: Pennsylvania Politics 1833–1848.* Harrisburg, 1958.

Stearns, Frank P. *The Life and Public Services of George Luther Stearns.* Philadelphia, 1907.

Story, William W. *The Life and Letters of Joseph Story.* 2 vols. Boston, 1851.

Tiffany, Nina M. *Samuel E. Sewall, A Memoir.* Boston and New York, 1898.

Trimble, William. "New York Democracy and the Locofocos," *American Historical Review,* XXIV (April, 1919), 396–421.

Tuckerman, Bayard. *William Jay and the Constitutional Movement for the Abolition of Slavery.* New York, 1893.

Van Deusen, Glyndon. *Horace Greeley.* Philadelphia, 1953.

Webster, Daniel. *Speeches and Writings.* J. W. McIntyre, ed. 18 vols. Boston, 1903.

Zahler, Helene S. *Eastern Workingmen and National Land Policy,
1829–1862.* New York, 1941.

### IX. OTHER REACTIONS TO ABOLITION

Brown, Sterling. "Negro Character as Seen by White Authors,"
*Journal of Negro Education,* II (April, 1933), 179–203.

Commons, John R., *et al.,* eds. *Documentary History of American
Industrial Society.* 10 vols. Cleveland, Ohio, 1910–1911.

Commons, John R., *et al. History of Labour in the United States.*
4 vols. New York, 1918–1935.

Ernst, Robert. *Immigrant Life in New York City, 1825–1863,*
New York, 1949.

Gibson, Florence E. *The Attitudes of the New York Irish toward
State and National Affairs.* New York, 1951.

Hartz, Lewis. "Seth Luther, Working-Class Rebel," *New England
Quarterly,* XIII (September, 1940), 401–418.

Jefferson, Thomas. "Thomas Jefferson's Thoughts on the Negro."
*Journal of Negro History,* III (Jan. 1918). Edited writings.

Jefferson, Thomas. *The Works of Thomas Jefferson.* Paul L. Ford,
ed. 12 vols. New York, 1904–1905.

Madison, James. "James Madison's Attitudes toward the Negro."
*Journal of Negro History,* VI (Jan. 1921), 74–112. Edited
writings.

Madison, James. *The Writings of James Madison.* Gaillard Hunt,
ed. 9 vols. New York, 1900.

Lofton, William H. "Abolition and Labor," *Journal of Negro
History,* XXXIII (July, 1948), 249–283.

Mandel, Bernard. *Labor, Free and Slave.* New York, 1955.

Morse, Samuel F. B. *Foreign Conspiracy against the Liberties of
the United States.* 6th ed. New York, 1844.

Morse, Samuel F. B. *Samuel F. B. Morse, Letters and Journals.*
Edward L. Morse, ed. 2 vols. Boston, 1914.

Rayback, Joseph. "The American Workingman and the Anti-

Slavery Crusade," *Journal of Economic History,* III (November, 1943), 152–163.

Reese, Dr. David M. *A Brief Review of the First Annual Report of the American Anti-Slavery Society.* . . . New York, 1834.

Reese, Dr. David M. *Humbugs of New York.* New York, 1838.

Smith, Samuel S. *An Essay on the Causes of the Variety of Complexion and Figure in the Human Species.* 2nd ed. New Brunswick, N. J., 1810.

Stanton, William L. *The Leopard's Spots: Scientific Attitudes toward Race in America, 1815–1859.* Chicago, 1960.

Washington, George. *The Writings of George Washington.* John C. Fitzpatrick, ed. 39 vols. Washington, D.C., 1931.

Wittke, Carl. *Tambo and Bones.* Durham, N. C., 1930.

# Index

# Index

# Index

## DATE DUE

| | | | |
|---|---|---|---|
| | | | |
| | | | |
| | | | |
| | | | |
| | | | |
| | | | |
| | | | |
| | | | |
| | | | |
| | | | |
| | | | |
| | | | |
| | | | |
| | | | |
| | | | |
| | | | |
| | | | |
| | | | |